CALIFORNIA
BREWERIES NORTH
JAY R. BROOKS

STACKPOLE
BOOKS

For my family—Sarah, Porter, and Alice
For their unceasing love, support, and understanding

Published by
STACKPOLE BOOKS
5067 Ritter Road
Mechanicsburg, PA 17055
www.stackpolebooks.com

The authors and the publisher encourage readers to visit the breweries and sample their beers, and recommend that those who consume alcoholic bever-ages travel with a designated nondrinking driver.

Printed in the United States of America

10 9 8 7 6 5 4 3 2 1

FIRST EDITION

Cover design by Tessa J. Sweigert
Labels and logos used with the permission of the breweries

Library of Congress Cataloging-in-Publication Data

Brooks, Jay R.
    California breweries north / Jay R. Brooks. — First edition.
       pages   cm
    Includes index.
    ISBN 978-0-8117-1158-6 (paperback)
    1. Breweries—California, Northern—Directories.   2. Beer—California,
Northern—Directories.   I. Title.
TP572.B86   2013
663'.42097941—dc23
                                                                                2013021832

Contents

The South Bay 123

The East Bay 180

Foreword

Northern California is not only a great place to make craft beer, but also the perfect place to drink it and to read and learn about its history in America. We were honored when our friend and local beer writer Jay Brooks asked us to write the foreword for his new book. This is a first for a couple of small brewery owners who spend our days trying to figure out how to make more Pliny the Elder for an increasingly thirsty country, or managing huge crowds at our little brewpub in Santa Rosa every February when we release Pliny the Younger.

This country has such an interesting history with beer and alcohol in general. In 2012, we finally have more breweries in the United States than we did pre-Prohibition. It took a long time to get here and several brewing pioneers to pave the way. And it has been anything but easy. Only recently has the craft beer revolution really taken off in this country. Northern California has a rich history of brewing pioneers to thank for it, too. In 1965, Fritz Maytag purchased the struggling Anchor Brewing Company in San Francisco. His early years were beyond challenging, but he persevered and now Anchor Steam is pretty much San Francisco's Golden Child of Craft Beer. There is nothing better than a bowl of clam chowder, some sourdough, and a cold glass of Anchor Steam!

In 1976, Jack McAuliffe, America's first nanobrewer, opened New Albion Brewing Company in Sonoma, a small town known more for its world-class wine than its craft-brewing heritage. Jack started his brewery, like many of us, with a roll of duct tape, some bailing wire, a couple bucks, and a heart full of passion. Sadly, Jack was too far ahead of his time, and New Albion lasted only a few years. But his inspiration lives on for so many of us following in his footsteps.

A young engineering student at the Chico campus of California State University was inspired by Jack and his low-budget, hand-built, no-frills brewery and business model. Ken Grossman had a homebrew shop turned microbrewery in 1980 in Chico. He also struggled in the early years while growing his business and his family. Now Sierra Nevada Brewing Company is one of the largest craft breweries in the

United States and one of Northern California's greatest craft beer success stories.

This book is not only an homage to the rich history of craft brewing in Northern California, but an essential guidebook to our local craft breweries written by a guy who really knows his beer. Jay has done an outstanding job of presenting the most relevant information in this well-written guide to Northern California's craft breweries. Thank you, Jay, for giving us the honor and privilege of contributing to your book.

Cheers!
Vinnie and Natalie Cilurzo
Co-owners, Russian River Brewing Company

Acknowledgments

No beer writer drinks and writes in a vacuum. It takes friends, family, colleagues, brewers, and countless others to make the journey both worthwhile and enjoyable. So there are many people to acknowledge and thank for helping me with the journey that made this book possible, and made it a labor of love, too.

First, the fact that I'm writing these words in this book is thanks to the support and friendship of two colleagues, John Holl and Lew Bryson. Over two years ago, John and I were sharing a pint at some now-forgotten beer event, and he casually mentioned that he was working on a book on Indiana breweries for Stackpole Books. I was already familiar with the publisher because my good friend Lew Bryson had written several books for Stackpole. John suggested I should contact them about doing a book on California breweries, and I confessed that I had been thinking about doing just such a project. Lew, whom I often think of as the brother I never had, was kind enough to put in a good word for me, and between the two of them, they made the process of getting a contract painless. It's good to have drinking buddies with connections.

Then there's my editor, Kyle Weaver, who showed infinite patience and understanding as I breezed past one deadline after another, trying to get the book—in the parlance of Goldilocks—just right. After publishing the first two editions of Lew Bryson's *Pennsylvania Breweries*, Kyle was the one who turned it into a series and even now is in the process of lining up authors to fill in the best beer states with his "breweries series" of books. Thanks for everything, Kyle.

I also thank Tom Dalldorf, the publisher of the *Celebrator Beer News*, who brought me on board as the general manager of his brewspaper more than ten years ago, setting the course for my second decade of writing and working in the beer world. His support and encouragement continue to be invaluable.

Because drinking beer, regardless of the setting, is at its heart a shared experience, I want to acknowledge the many thousands of people I've shared a pint with over the years. From Pennsylvania, where I first tasted beer, through the many places since then, from New York

City to San Francisco, and from London to Brussels to Munich and Buenos Aires with many points in between, I've enjoyed countless beers, engaged in untold conversations, and met more people than I ever thought possible, thanks to this liquid gold we call beer.

Then there are the brewers, without whom I'd have nothing at all to write about. It's a symbiotic relationship. I need beer to drink—and write about—and they need someone to tell their stories. So many of the encounters I've had with brewers have turned into lifelong friendships, so much so that I feel truly blessed to work in the best community and industry that exists anywhere.

Last, and most important, I am grateful to Sarah, a beautiful woman I met almost twenty years ago, who agreed to go to a brewpub with me one day after work. I sat her down, ordered a taster for her, and went through the range of beers with her to see if she would like them. Happily, she passed the test, and I asked her out on the spot, which eventually became the location of our wedding reception. Seventeen years later, we have two beautiful children, Porter and Alice, and Sarah still loves good beer almost as much as I do. She's the reason I get up every morning to drink and write and love life.

Introduction

It's a great time to be a beer lover. It may, in fact, be the best time in history to enjoy and appreciate beer. Never before have American craft brewers brought to the market the quality and diversity of products that they are offering today. There have never been more choices of different beers, more original beers, and more places to buy them. And a lot of them, including many of the best, are made in California.

Northern California is the birthplace of the modern craft beer industry. Between Anchor Brewing, the New Albion Brewery, and a few of the earliest brewpubs in the nation, the California Bay Area got a jump on the rest of the country in its passion for better beer.

In the nearly fifty years since Fritz Maytag bought the failing Anchor Brewery to keep his favorite beer from disappearing, and in the thirty-five years since Jack McAuliffe built the first modern microbrewery from scratch out of discarded dairy tanks and other scraps, a lot has happened to the world of beer. Whole new generations are coming of age in a world where they've never known a time when good beer was not available. Even for those of us who witnessed the near death of beer in the United States, only to see it rise from the ashes, it's getting harder and harder to remember a time when, upon entering the average bar, we had no guarantee that something worth drinking would be on tap.

It took the blink of an eye in geological time, but moved at a more glacial pace for those of us who longed to have great-tasting beer more readily available. Over the last three or so decades, a lot of good people opened breweries. Many succeeded, but others failed. New bars and pubs opened that were dedicated to good beer in ways that no one had ever seen before. A few retail stores began dedicating more shelf space to craft beer, and a handful carried only beer, something that would have been unthinkable when only eighty breweries existed in the whole United States, and most of those made beer that tasted the same. These bars and stores represented the front lines where consumers could discover and enjoy these beers.

Despite all the hurdles that craft brewers have overcome and the meteoric growth of beer sales, especially in recent years, the amount of craft beer remains well under 10 percent of all beer sold in the United

States. But the silver lining is that tremendous opportunities remain for craft brewers to find new customers. Over 90 percent of drinking adults—look around you; that means nine out of every ten people—still drink beer made by one of the large international beer companies or importers. And while most of those beers are technically very well made, they leave a lot of flavor on the table. Driven by marketing concerns, economies of large scales, and a need to satisfy shareholders, the large beer companies have to sell a lot of beer to make a profit. A lot. As a result, smaller breweries have one distinct advantage: Their size allows them to experiment, to make smaller batches of beer so that if it's not a hit, there isn't too much of it. It won't hurt their bottom line as much. They can also introduce new beers more quickly, respond faster to consumer demands, and make special releases throughout the year.

This can also be a disadvantage. With the big beer companies, like any national chains, you know exactly what you're getting when you plunk down your money for a six-pack. Smaller breweries have to continually earn their reputations one beer at a time. Fans may forgive one bad beer, but not two or three, which will cause a brewery to lose loyal customers and fans. Distribution is perhaps the biggest hurdle that smaller craft breweries still face. And as more and more breweries are opening, the fight for limited shelf space and tap handles can mean the difference between a successful brewery and one that goes out of business.

Even so, it's important, I believe, to bear in mind that today we have it good. Really good. Better, perhaps, than at any time in history. Never have we had so many different and wonderful beers to enjoy. Never have so many known so much about beer that their breadth and quality can be fully appreciated. Never have there been so many great places—breweries, brewpubs, beer bars, pubs, taverns, restaurants, hotels, and festivals—where craft beers can be found and enjoyed.

To know where we are, we have to understand where we've been and how we got here. So knowing just a little bit of the history of beer and brewing is essential to understand and appreciate the beer you're drinking. It won't make the beer taste any better, but appreciating it more will help increase your enjoyment of the beer in your glass.

Beer and Civilization

The story of beer isn't just part of our history; in many ways it is the story of civilization. Anthropologists are increasingly being won over to the idea that when our hunter-gatherer early human ancestors settled down, it was to brew beer, rather than bake bread, as had previously been thought. Since the 1950s, when the theory was first proposed by Brian Hayden at Canada's Simon Fraser University, more and more evidence has been found that supports the theory that it was brewing beer that sparked our civilization. The earliest evidence we have of humans practicing agriculture dates to about 11,500 years ago, during the Neolithic Period of the Stone Age. When our nomadic ancestors began settling down to take up farming, they had to establish more complex social customs as they interacted with one another more often, and this led to the foundations of bigger, more complex and intricate communities, the precursors of our modern civilization.

It wasn't that brewing beer itself was what may have sparked civilization, but that one of the common facets of these burgeoning societies was feasts, which in fact became an essential part of cultures around the world. The three parts of virtually all traditional feasts are meat, a cereal grain, and alcohol. Another universal aspect of feasts is their reciprocal nature: They created obligations on the part of attendees, which led to escalating customs, and these in turn led to the creation of bonds between people, which gave rise to such things as political power, debts, factions, support networks, and other basic elements of complex societies. It was this natural progression of increasing complexity that led from brewing beer to civilization and eventually to us.

Thus it was alcohol, as an essential and universal part of feasts, that most likely led to the creation of our civilization. But how did we figure out how to brew beer in the first place? An archaeologist at the University of Pennsylvania, Patrick McGovern, believes he has the answer. He thinks that most likely some early man or woman picked up and ate a piece of fruit that had dropped on the ground and had naturally begun to ferment. After the initial bittersweet flavor, something else would have registered as the alcohol entered the bloodstream and began sending new signals to the brain. The euphoria that this caused must have been quite unlike any sensation the person had ever experienced. And McGovern believes that the desire to reproduce the feeling that alcohol brings would have been enough incentive to cause early humans to settle down and grow the necessary crops. You can read all about this notion in McGovern's wonderful book *Uncorking the Past*.

A curious aspect of early alcohol was that it was safer to drink than most of the water at that time. As a result, many scientists now believe that survival often depended on how a person's body reacted to and could tolerate beer. Over time, only people who were genetically predisposed to be able to drink large quantities of beer survived, passing that trait down to their children. Perhaps today most of us have such an ancestor, as evidenced simply by the fact that we're here. Steven Johnson wrote in *The Ghost Map*, "Most of the world's population today is made up of descendants of those early beer drinkers, and we have largely inherited their genetic tolerance for alcohol."

Both beer and wine became hugely popular and were very important to these early societies. The rituals that were significant to them universally included the local alcohol. Over time, which crop was easiest to grow dictated whether a society developed a beer-drinking culture or a wine culture.

The earliest beers did not in any way resemble the beer we drink today. The early Sumerian, Egyptian, and other cultures that made beer brewed unfiltered, cloudy stuff that was consumed communally, with the beer served in tall earthenware jars. People sat around the jars and drank the beer together through long reed straws.

For thousands of years, beers contained no hops. Hops did not become a common ingredient until the late Middle Ages. If the beer was flavored at all, its makers used a variety of different, usually local, ingredients to add a bewildering array of different tastes. Hops were first mentioned as being used in brewing around 822 CE, but they didn't catch on worldwide until roughly the 1400s and were originally added more as a preservative than a flavoring agent.

In 1516, Bavarian brewers created one of the first quality control or food safety laws in history when the Reinheitsgebot, also known as the beer purity law, was enacted. The reasons for this were not entirely noble, as it was at least in part to protect wheat and rye for breadmaking. The Reinheitsgebot stipulated that only three ingredients could be used in brewing: barley, hops, and water. Only German royalty was permitted to brew wheat beers.

You may have noticed that although the Reinheitsgebot allowed for only three ingredients, modern beer is generally made from four constituent parts. That's because in the sixteenth century, people didn't know about yeast. It would be another three hundred years before yeast was understood. The Dutch scientist Antonie van Leeuwenhoek first discovered yeast cells in 1719. But it was Louis Pasteur—better known for the pasteurization of milk—who initially proved that it was yeast that caused the fermentation of beer and wine in his landmark book *Études sur la bière* ("Studies Concerning Beer"). His insights made possible the modern industrial brewery and the ability to make consistent beer that tastes the same from batch to batch.

The Story of American Beer

Like the story of civilization itself, beer is at the very beginning of America's story too. The diary of William Bradford, on board the *Mayflower*, includes the oft-repeated entry that the Pilgrims "could not take time for further search or consideration; our victuals being much spent, especially our beer." It's not quite the barnburner it's often made out to be, but it still shows the importance of beer to the earliest immigrant Americans. That diary entry was written almost a month after the *Mayflower* dropped anchor, as the crew and colonists were searching for a suitable spot to build their settlement.

There was still beer on the ship, but it belonged to the crew. And they weren't going to give it to the colonists, no matter how thirsty Bradford and his companions were, because the crew members needed it for the return trip back to England. After all, they were just dropping off the colonists. Food and other supplies were starting to run low, and the search for a place to build a settlement had turned up two possibilities. With passengers dying from the cold and disease, it made sense to just pick one and start building the new colony.

As more and more Europeans came to our shores, creating more colonies up and down the Atlantic Seaboard, they continued to drink alcohol, in part for the same reasons that their ancestors did—it was still safer than drinking the water. But for a long time, most of the beer consumed was imported from England and the rest of Europe. That was true even as the United States became an independent nation.

Our first president, George Washington, was a beer lover. His favorite style was porter. He even had a favorite porter maker, Philadelphia brewer Robert Hare. In a letter to Hare, Washington's aide Tobias Lear asked him to send porter to Washington: "Will you be so good as to desire Mr. Hare to have if he continues to make the best Porter in Philadelphia 3 gross of his best put up for Mount Vernon? As the President means to visit that place in the recess of Congress and it is probable there will be a large demand for Porter at that time." In 1737, Washington made a diary entry explaining in detail how to make small beer, prompting some historians to believe he was a homebrewer as well.

Washington seems to have presaged modern notions of buying local when he wrote the following to Lafayette in 1789: "We have already been too long subject to British Prejudices. I use no porter or cheese in my family, but that which is made in America."

Our third president and the man who wrote the Declaration of Independence, Thomas Jefferson, also took to homebrewing on his estate, Monticello, after he retired from political life. Before that, his wife, Martha, brewed 15-gallon batches every two weeks on their Virginia estate. In his seventies, Jefferson hired English brewer Joseph Miller, and the pair built a dedicated brewing room and beer cellar at Monticello, where he malted his own grain and grew hops. Jefferson bottled most of his beer and sealed the bottles with corks.

During his term of office, James Madison, our fourth president and the man most responsible for the U.S. Constitution, tried to get a government-run national brewery started and proposed a new cabinet post, secretary of beer, to promote a domestic beer industry. Madison also enacted the Tariff Act of 1789, which he hoped would give the advantage to American brewers, encouraging "the manufacture of beer in every State in the Union."

Up until the mid-nineteenth century, cider was the most popular alcoholic drink in the United States, but beginning in the 1840s, that finally began to change. In Europe, the first pilsners had taken the continent by storm, and in no time they made their way to our shores. A wave of German and central European immigration brought with it brewers seeing an opportunity in the promise of a better life that people saw in American idealism.

In Philadelphia, a brewer named John Wagner became the first to brew German-style lagers in the States during this time. But this type of beer spread not just in Europe and the rest of the world, but throughout virtually every town in America too. Pilsners, and newer styles based on them, are still the most popular kinds of beer made the world over.

When the Civil War began, the North needed money to fight the Southern states. Up until that time, there had been no federal income tax in the United States, and for the first time people had to start paying taxes to fund the war. But it proved not to be enough, and six months into the war, Congress began levying excise taxes on a number of goods, including beer, distilled spirits, cotton, tobacco, carriages (the automobiles of the day), yachts, pool tables, and even playing cards. Lincoln signed the new taxes into law July 1, 1862, and they took effect that September.

Lincoln is also responsible for one my favorite quotes by a politician. "I am a firm believer in the people," he said. "If given the truth, they can be depended upon to meet any national crisis. The great point is to bring them the real facts, and beer." After the Civil War ended, most of the wartime taxes were rescinded, but the rising temperance movement helped keep the taxes on alcohol and tobacco in place.

This was also the golden age of brewing in America. The industrial revolution saw new brewing technologies that made it easier, and cheaper, to make beer in larger quantities, and nearly every town had at least one brewery. At its peak, around 1873, there were 4,131 breweries dotting the American landscape. As a result of a number of factors, however, the number of breweries began to decrease. Some merged, while others were bought by bigger, more successful rivals.

Just forty-five years later, only about one-quarter the number of breweries remained. A year after the ratification of the 18th Amendment in 1919, all brewing came to a sudden halt when the national experiment known as Prohibition began on January 17, 1920. For the next thirteen years, America went dry.

Well, not exactly. Even though Prohibition made beer illegal, many wealthy Americans stockpiled alcohol before it took effect, and that included several presidents. Woodrow Wilson took his private stash of alcohol with him when he left office, and the next president, Warren G. Harding, moved his own collection of booze with him to the White House when he moved in. While Harding, who was known for all-night poker games, continued to drink in the White House along with his political allies, he was responsible for laws making it tougher for the average citizen to have a beer.

As time wore on, Prohibition proved increasingly unpopular, especially in big cities, and the violence that accompanied it, along with the Great Depression, which began in 1929, made it a failed social experiment. When Franklin Delano Roosevelt ran for president in 1932, he campaigned on a promise to end Prohibition, using "Happy Days Are Here Again" as his campaign song. He kept that promise, signing the Cullen-Harrison Act in March 1933, amending the Volstead Act and allowing 3.2% ABW/4% ABV beer to be brewed and served beginning on April 7, 1933, nine months before the 21st Amendment finally repealed it. When he signed the act, he is reported to have said, "I think this would be a good time for a beer." And the very next day he got his wish, when Anheuser-Busch sent a team of Clydesdales to deliver a case of Budweiser to FDR at the White House.

Only a fraction of the breweries that were operating before Prohibition, less than 800, reopened when it was repealed in 1933. Of those that successfully started brewing again, only a relatively small percentage managed to remain open for very long. As a result, by 1950 there were just over 400 left, and that number continued to plummet. Postwar America also saw changes to the way businesses operated, as local ones were overshadowed by national companies able to advertise on the newfangled television networks that brought their messages into millions of homes across the country. Coupled with the newly built interstate highway, which allowed efficient shipping of goods to all points on the map, the bigger national breweries continued swallowing up their smaller regional rivals. By 1960 the number of breweries had dropped to around 230, and in 1983 the brewing industry reached its nadir, with a mere 80 breweries still open, owned by just 51 independent companies.

After Prohibition, making wine at home became legal again but homebrewing remained illegal, supposedly due to an inadvertent omission. But it took another forty-five years to correct that "typo." And it was in part thanks to our thirty-ninth president, Jimmy Carter. In late 1978, he signed HR 1337 into law, which included an amendment by California senator Alan Cranston authorizing adults to legally brew in the home. Legalizing homebrewing had a profound effect on brewing, because so many homebrewers went on to become commercial brewers, starting hundreds, if not thousands, of craft breweries—enough that we can even forgive President Carter's brother for Billy Beer.

California's Beer Legacy

In California, the local Native Americans who lived here before European settlers arrived had their own long tradition of fermented beverages, notably using maize (corn) and other local ingredients. But these early unhopped beers had more in common with the ancient Sumerian beers than the modern beers we're familiar with.

The modern history of California beer starts with the gold rush, which really jump-started brewing on the West Coast, most notably in San Francisco. After the gold rush began at Sutter's Mill back in 1849, San Francisco's population soared as thousands poured into the city, most of them thirsty. As a result, dozens of breweries sprang up in the years that followed.

The earliest breweries in California were ale brewers. The first is believed to have been the A. Schuppert Brewery, opened in 1849 at the corner of Jackson and Stockton Streets in San Francisco. The second was most likely Hartmann & Scherrer, founded in 1851 by John Joseph Hartmann. Located in San Jose, it was a very small brewery and is reported to have brewed just 14 barrels of Steam beer in their first year, though by around 1880 that had increased to a yearly output of 14,000 barrels. By September 14, 1874, there were enough California brewers that they banded together and formed the Brewers Protective Association in San Francisco.

The first malting house was opened in 1853 by Thomas Lee, who emigrated from England. It was located in San Francisco, where shortly thereafter the same year, a second malthouse was opened by Thomas Andrew. A few years later, in 1857, Herman Zwieg opened a third malthouse on Rich Street, near South Park, eventually buying out Lee's business.

The first lager brewed in California was not made in San Francisco, but far from there, in the Sierra Nevada. The town of Boca was located in northeast California, roughly six and a half miles from Truckee. In

1880, it had a population of around two hundred people, though today it's a ghost town. The Boca Brewery was founded in 1875 and closed in 1892, four years before the Anchor Brewery opened. Boca was the only lager brewery in California until 1882, when Fredericksburg Brewery, in San Jose, added a lager brewing facility. Around this same time, the first lager brewery in San Francisco, the Wieland Brewery, also opened.

The modern era of brewing in California, and craft brewing generally, began on September 24, 1965. On that day, Fritz Maytag bought 51 percent of the Anchor Brewery in San Francisco and forever changed the course of beer in America. For a full account of Anchor's legacy, see "A word about . . . Anchor Brewing, America's Original Craft Brewer," on page 57.

By the 1970s, just a small number of breweries were left in the United States, and except for Anchor and a few others, almost all of them were making very similar light industrial lagers. Most American beer tasted the same, no matter where you bought it or what brewery had brewed it. Brewers were competing on brand image, not taste or flavor. As a result, there was little diversity in the beers offered by the remaining breweries. The rest of California, and indeed most of the country, was a barren beer wasteland.

But then something happened.

What happened next, or why, is a subject that will undoubtedly vex historians for years to come. Many theories abound. Some say that as air travel became cheaper, many more Americans traveled abroad, discovering that not all beer tasted the same. They returned with a desire to drink these exotic, flavorful beers but were hard-pressed to find them at home. Similarly, many people serving in the military around the globe found the same thing, as they sampled the local beers wherever their duty stations were located. Still others point to the rise of "California cuisine" and the importance it placed on local, fresh ingredients in food. It was a small step from such artisanal food to craft beer, as it laid the foundation for changing tastes.

Homebrewing was finally legalized in 1978, although the hobby had been growing underground for many years. It was the most passionate homebrewing hobbyists who worked behind the scenes to legitimize their brewing passions and make it legal again to brew beer at home. Not surprisingly, homebrewers wanted to make beers that were different from what they could buy at the local store or bar.

Whatever the reason, the time was almost right, as the next big event in craft-brewing history took place in the town of Sonoma, right in the heart of wine country, in 1976. That was the year naval veteran Jack McAuliffe, an engineer by trade, incorporated the New Albion Brewery,

America's first modern microbrewery, built from scratch in a small corrugated tin building. The following year, New Albion was selling three different kinds of ale. For the full story of New Albion Brewery, see "A word about . . . New Albion, America's First Modern Microbrewery," on page 120. Sadly, New Albion was ahead of its time, and McAuliffe was unable to persuade any bank to fund his growth so he could take the brewery to the next level. He simply couldn't get any lenders to understand what he was trying to do, so by 1983 he was out of business.

Inspired by what both Anchor and New Albion had done, however, brewers began to open small breweries at an increasingly rapid pace in the 1980s, and people began to take notice. The press started writing about the novelty of small and local breweries, as if it were the strangest thing they'd ever encountered. Thanks to these pioneers, the nascent craft beer industry began to gather steam (beer).

Out of the ashes of New Albion rose what is today one of California's largest craft breweries. Jack McAuliffe's assistant brewer Don Barkley bought the equipment and cofounded Mendocino Brewing Company. When it opened, it was the second brewpub in America, a new type of brewery restaurant that had debuted the previous year in Washington State. Over the next few years, two more California brewpubs opened their doors: Buffalo Bill's in Hayward opened in September 1984, and Berkley's Triple Rock Brewery & Alehouse began brewing in 1985, opening early the following year. Thus of the first five brewpubs in the United States, three of them were in California.

A little farther north, Chico homebrew shop owner Ken Grossman also dreamed of opening his own small brewery. Inspired by both Anchor and New Albion, Grossman took welding lessons at the local community college so he could build his own brewery. He opened Sierra Nevada Brewing Company in 1980, and his Sierra Nevada Pale Ale created a brand new beer style, American-style pale ale, breaking from the English pale ale it was based on. It became one of the microbrewery revolution's early success stories, and today Sierra Nevada is one of the largest craft breweries not only in California, but in the entire country.

From those humble beginnings, small California breweries continued to open, first concentrated in the north but spreading throughout the state. As of the end of 2012, at least 350 breweries were making beer in California, with another 100 or more in various stages of planning, meaning that there will almost certainly be 400 California breweries very soon and possibly as many as 500 or 600 in a few short years.

Of the 50 largest craft breweries in the United States, 12 are located in California, meaning that 24 percent, or nearly a quarter, of the country's largest craft breweries are California businesses. Sierra Nevada is the second-largest craft brewery in the nation, followed by Lagunitas (9), Stone (11), Anchor (22), Firestone Walker (23), BJs Restaurant & Brewery brewpub chain (33), Bear Republic (35), Lost Coast Brewery (36), North Coast (38), Gordon Biersch production brewery (40), Karl Strauss Breweries (44), and Anderson Valley (50). Eight of these are in Northern California.

Nationwide, craft beer represents around 6.5 percent of the total beer market, but in California, its share is nearly 13 percent, twice the national average. And it's not just a matter of quantity, but quality too. Each year, California brings home more medals from the Great American Beer Festival than any other state. At the biennial World Beer Cup in 2012, fifty-four countries entered almost four thousand beers in ninety-five separate categories. In that competition, California breweries won fifty-five medals, more than any other state—and any other nation.

California may be the Golden State, founded upon gold deposits discovered in 1849, but today liquid gold—copper-colored ales and golden-hued lagers—may be its most important treasure. California gave birth to American craft beer, an entire new industry that has made the United States the envy of the brewing world.

Breweries vs. Brewpubs

Though there are shades of gray, understanding the difference between breweries and brewpubs is fairly simple. Breweries, often called production breweries, are places that brew all, or at least the majority, of their beer to sell somewhere else. They package it, in kegs, bottles, or cans, and most often sell it through a distributor that sells it to a retailer—a bar, restaurant, or store—so that you, the consumer, can buy it.

Brewpubs, on the other hand, make their beer to be sold right where they brew it. They almost always have a restaurant too, so that you can get a meal and have their beer with the food they serve. They also sometimes sell some of the beer to go, either in growlers or occasionally in conventional packages like bottles or cans. If they start selling more than a certain amount of packaged beer to go, then their status usually changes and they'll be considered a production brewery.

While most brewpubs are the same or similar, there are different kinds of production breweries. They may differ in size, how the business is organized, or where they do the actual brewing. All you really need to know is the two basic types, but to learn more about the numerous kinds of breweries, see "Brewery Types" in the Glossary at the back of this book.

My Love Affair with Beer

I grew up in what I nostalgically refer to as "Dutch Wonderland," an area in rural eastern Pennsylvania settled by German-speaking immigrants and known for its Pennsylvania Dutch heritage (the "Dutch" is an anglicized corruption of *Deutsch*, meaning German). That German heritage brought with it a thirst for lagers, and when I was a child, the area was dotted with numerous regional breweries.

My hometown brewery made Reading Premium Ale, "the friendly beer for modern people," but closed in 1976, when I was a junior in high school, as eventually did most of the beer brands of my childhood, although nearby Yuengling Brewery, which opened in 1829, remains the oldest brewery in America. The one thing they all had in common was that they made very similar-tasting beers.

But after high school, I joined the U.S. Army and was stationed in New York City, playing sax and clarinet in a military band. It was there that I also discovered that not all beer was the same, as New York in the late seventies was home to a burgeoning market for imported beers.

It was thirty-five years ago that I parted the velvet curtain, designed to keep out sunlight and sound, and walked into a dark jazz club in New York City's Greenwich Village. As we listened to some smoldering live music, my friends and I ordered the cheese plate and looked over the beer menu. None of the usual lagers I'd grown up on were listed, only then-unknown imported beers like Bass Ale, Guinness, and Pilsner Urquell. I took my first sip of Bass and my life has never been the same. I was hooked.

From that moment until today, I've been on a journey of discovery that I suspect will never end. There will always be another brewery to explore or festival to attend, where I'll find a new beer to enjoy and a meal to pair it with. As my knowledge and appreciation of beer have grown, I've found that beer is best when it's shared, and happily, I'll be sharing some beer and breweries with you in the pages of this book.

I left the East Coast for California just before the microbreweries took root there, and just as things were getting interesting in the West, arriving in the Bay Area in 1985. So in 1987, when my grandfather's nephew's wife, Carol Stoudt, opened the first microbrewery in Pennsylvania, I'd already been living in the Bay Area for two years, watching the craft beer scene grow from the seedlings sown by Anchor Brewery and New Albion into the vibrant community it is today.

I began homebrewing and hosting tasting parties in my home to educate myself and my friends about craft beer. In the summer of 1991, I visited more than five hundred bars in the South Bay, which resulted in my first book, *The Bars of Santa Clara County: A Beer Drinker's Guide to Silicon Valley.* A few years later I became the beer buyer for the local chain Beverages & More. I left BevMo in 2001, when my son Porter was born, to be the general manager of the *Celebrator Beer News,* the local brewpaper published in Northern California for the past twenty-five years by Tom Dalldorf. But within a few years, Porter was diagnosed as autistic, and I quit my full-time job to stay home with him and began working as a freelance beer writer and publishing my beer blog, the Brookston Beer Bulletin.

Since then I've taken brewing classes at the University of California's Davis campus and attended Hop School in Yakima, Washington, where 70 percent of all American hops are grown. I've been a beer judge at small and large events on three continents, including the Toronado Barleywine Festival, the Great American Beer Festival, the Great British Beer Festival, the World Beer Cup, and the World Beer Awards. I've published features and columns in almost any beer magazine you can name, and I've been interviewed about beer on radio, podcast, television, and film. I've contributed to such beer books as *1001 Beers You Must Try before You Die* and *The Oxford Companion to Beer.* I also helped cofound and organize SF Beer Week, during which hundreds of beer events take place over ten days every February.

But despite my two-plus decades writing about beer and working in the beer community, one my favorite things to do has remained unchanged: I love the simple pleasure of visiting a brewery and drinking its beer, listening to the brewer talking reverently about how and why he made each beer. There's nothing quite like sampling beer at the source, seeing the gleaming copper and stainless steel brewing equipment. I take hundreds of photos at breweries and generally refer to the resulting pictures as "brewery porn." My goal with this book was to capture my passion for beer and brewing and provide the tools for you to make your own pilgrimages.

How to Use This Book

With so many breweries to visit, I tried to provide the information you'll need while at the same time using the space as economically as possible, preferring it to be information-rich with Spartan design.

For each brewery, you'll find the most important information at the top: the name, address, phone number, and website, along with the Twitter and Facebook names, if it has them. Following that is my take on the brewery, impressions of the place, the experience you're likely to have there. Some descriptions include an overview of the brewery's history, while others are so new they're just starting to write their stories. But each essay provides a different take on each brewery, since each brewery is different, with a goal of trying to entertain as well as inform.

Lastly, for each brewery there's a long list of general information that includes the following:

Opening: When it opened, in case you want to celebrate the anniversary.

Type: Is it a brewpub or a production brewery or something else? One thing to keep in mind, though, is that for the several brewing companies that have their beer contracted or make it at another brewery that they either share or rent, the information about the brewery will refer you to the listing for the host brewery.

Owners: Who's responsible for the company.

Brewer: Who actually makes the beer. Sometimes the owner and brewer are the same person, but sometimes they're not.

Guild membership: Guilds are trade association of breweries that are created to support one another, promote beer in their area, and also lobby for favorable treatment and reasonable laws governing their industry. In addition to the Brewers Association and other national trade associations, most states have their own guilds, and California is no exception. Because California is so large, at least six guilds operate in the state, of which four cover the region of Northern California. The California Craft Brewers Association (CCBA) includes craft breweries throughout the entire state; the San Francisco Brewers Guild (SFBG) includes breweries in the city and county of San Francisco; the Bay Brewers Guild (BBG) includes breweries in the South Bay, from Santa Clara to Monterey County; and the Northern California Brewers Guild (NCBG) is for breweries that are generally in the northern part of the state, starting in the Bay Area. In addition, many breweries are members of the Brewers Association (BA), which is a national trade organization headquartered in Boulder, Colorado. The BA is also the organization that hosts the Great American Beer Festival (GABF) and the World Beer Cup.

System: For true beer geeks and "brewery porn" (my term for photos of brewing equipment) fans, this is the size and type of brewing equipment, as well as who manufactured it, followed by the brewery's annual capacity, which is the maximum amount of beer it could brew in one year.

Annual production: This is how much beer the brewery makes each year, expressed in barrels (1 barrel = 31 gallons). It's usually the previous year's production, however, and most breweries make more beer year after year.

Tours: If and when the brewery offers tours, and information about reservations so you can plan your visit in advance.

Hours: When is the brewery open? This is to ensure that you don't find yourself staring at a locked door with no beer in sight.

Food: Many breweries also offer food to go with their beer, from simple snacks to full menus. This gives you some insight into the type and quantity of food the brewery offers and often includes how good the french fries are, simply because I'm obsessed with potatoes.

Extras: Many breweries have special events or other unusual features. If they do, this is where you'll find out about them. This is essentially a catchall of any other information that may make your visit more pleasurable. Are kids allowed? Does the brewery allow cigar smoking? Is there an outdoor patio? Questions of this nature will be answered here before you even thought to ask them.

Gift shop: Does the brewery sell merchandise with its logo on it or beer to go or other tchotchkes?

Around the edges and in sidebars, you'll also be able to find the following:

Beers brewed: These are the beers that the brewery makes year-round, along with the regular seasonal beers it produces at special times throughout the year.

The Pick: With so many beers, it's often difficult to know where to start or what to drink. The Pick is my suggestion for you. It's usually my favorite beer the brewery makes.

How This Book Is Divided Geographically

California is a big state; really big. Only Alaska and Texas are bigger, but in terms of the number of breweries, the Golden State is unrivaled. As this book was going to press, over 325 California breweries were pumping out beer, more than any other state by a wide margin, with the next closest state having only approximately half our number. Because of the large number of breweries, for the purposes of this series, the state has been split into two roughly equal halves, at least in terms of breweries. The dividing line goes across the middle of the state, from the Monterey Bay to the Nevada border. This book on Northern California covers the region from Santa Cruz to the northern border with Oregon.

Even with the state divided roughly in half, Northern California is pretty big. The whole area covered in this book is slightly larger than the entire state of Washington, with around the same number of people as Pennsylvania. California contains fifty-eight counties, but these are not of equal size by any stretch of the imagination. Therefore, as defined for the purposes of this book, Northern California contains forty-one counties, with the remaining seventeen in the south, including the largest counties in the southeastern part of the state.

Within each chapter, breweries are further grouped into nine distinct areas in such a way as to benefit the traveler, encompassing regions like the High Sierras and the Central Valley North. By far, most of Northern California's breweries are clustered in and around the San Francisco Bay Area, but other pockets of breweries can be found in cities like the state capital, Sacramento. In more remote and mountainous areas, the breweries are as spread out as the landscape, and I've endeavored to group them in a way that makes the most sense.

BREWERY LOCATIONS

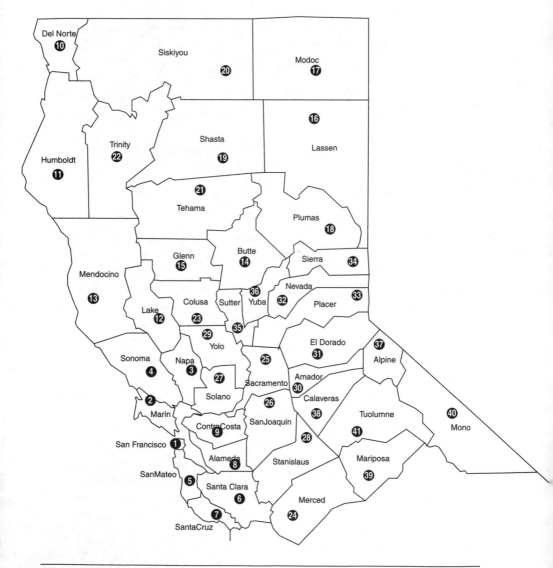

㉝ Loomis Basin Brewing Company
❻ Los Gatos Brewing Company
⓫ Lost Coast Brewery & Café
❷ Lucky Hand

⓫ Mad River Brewing Company
❶ Magnolia Gastropub & Brewery
㊵ Mammoth Brewing Company
❷ Marin Brewing Company
❺ Mavericks Beer Company
⓭ Mendocino Brewing Company
❷ Mill Valley Beerworks
❹ Moonlight Brewing Company
⓴ Mt. Shasta Brewing Company
❷ Moylan's Brewery and Restaurant

❸ Napa Smith Brewery
㉕ New Helvetia Brewing Company
⓭ North Coast Brewing Company

❽ Oakland Brewing Company
㉜ Ol' Republic Brewery
㉛ Old Hangtown Beer Works
❹ Old Redwood Brewing Company
❹ 101 North Brewing Company

❶ Pacific Brewing Laboratory
❽ Pacific Coast Brewing Company
❻ Palo Alto Brewing Company
❹ Petaluma Hills Brewing Company
❶ Pine Street Brewery
❷ Pizza Orgasmica & Brewing Company
㉛ Placerville Brewing Company
❽ Pleasanton Main Street Brewery
㊴ Prospectors Brewing Company
❽ Pyramid Alehouse, Brewery & Restaurant

❽ The Rare Barrel
❻ Red Branch Brewing Company
   (Rabbit's Foot Meadery)
⓫ Redwood Curtain Brewing Company
㉕ River City Brewing Company
❻ Rock Bottom Restaurant & Brewery
㉝ Roseville Brewing Company
㉕ Rubicon Brewing Company
㉕ Ruhstaller Beer

❹ Russian River Brewing Company
❹ Ruth McGowan's Brewpub

❼ Santa Cruz Ale Works
❼ Santa Cruz Mountain Brewing
❼ Sante Adairius Rustic Ales
❾ Schooner's Grille and Brewery
❾ Schubros Brewery
❼ Seabright Brewery
❶ Shmaltz Brewing Company
⓮ Sierra Nevada Brewing Company
⓫ Six Rivers Brewery
㊳ Snowshoe Brewing Company
❶ Social Kitchen & Brewery
❹ Sonoma Springs Brewing Company
❶ Southern Pacific Brewing
❶ Southpaw BBQ & Southern Cooking
❶ Speakeasy Ales & Lagers
❺ Steelhead Brewing Company
❹ St. Florian's Brewery
㉘ St. Stan's Brewing Company
㉛ Stateline Brewery & Restaurant
❻ Strike Brewing Company
❹ Stumptown Brewery
㉙ Sudwerk Privatbrauerei Hübsch
㉟ Sutter Buttes Brewing

㉝㉜ Tahoe Mountain Brewing Company
❹ Third Street Aleworks
❶ Thirsty Bear Brewing Company
❻ Tied House Brewery & Café
㉕ Track 7 Brewing Company
❽ Triple Rock Brewery & Alehouse
❶ Triple Voodoo Brewing
❽ Trumer Brauerei
㉕ Twelve Rounds Brewing Company
❶ 21st Amendment Brewery & Restaurant

⓭ Ukiah Brewing Company & Restaurant
❼ Uncommon Brewers

❹ Warped Brewing Company
⓮ Western Pacific Brewing & Dining
⓳ Wildcard Brewing Company
❽ Working Man Brewing Company

San Francisco

San Francisco is unique in that it is both a city and a county. Also known as the City by the Bay, it was built on forty-three hills surrounding the world's largest landlocked harbor. It was founded in 1776 and its original name, Yerba Buena, means "good herb" or "good grass." The city was incorporated in 1850, the year after the California gold rush that gave the local football team its name—the 49ers. The other effect of the gold rush, besides the rapid growth of breweries, was that the city rapidly emerged as the West Coast's largest city at that time.

The gold rush made San Francisco a gateway city, and the population exploded, bringing with it a desire for another type of gold, liquid gold—beer. Thirsty prospectors and newly mined riches created a demand for beer, and a number of breweries were built in the city. By 1896, San Francisco had more than two dozen breweries, one of which was Anchor Brewery. Between the gold rush and the 1906 earthquake, nearly seventy breweries opened and closed. The physical devastation of the earthquake followed by the financial devastation of Prohibition took its toll, and after 1933, only thirteen breweries operated in San Francisco. Of these, only Anchor survives to the present.

Because the city's physical size is fixed, growth is confined to building up or finding creative uses for what land there is available. The city is only about 70 percent of the size of Washington, D.C. There are, however, almost as many people packed into that space as in the entire state of South Dakota.

San Francisco is undoubtedly the most famous city in Northern California and a worldwide tourist destination. It's the thirty-fifth most visited city in the world, and the sixth in the United States. There are countless things to do and see in the city, from visiting its many unique neighborhoods to its famous tourist attractions, including Alcatraz, Fisherman's Wharf, Coit Tower, the Transamerica Building, Golden Gate Bridge, and Lombard Street, billed as "the world's crookedest street." There's a lot to see and do in Golden Gate Park, from playing Frisbee golf to watching the buffalo roam, and the city has several world-class art museums, as well as numerous history, heritage, and cultural museums.

San Francisco's liberal reputation is well deserved, and you should keep an open mind when visiting. You won't be in Kansas, or wherever you came from, anymore. Luckily, unlike most of the rest of the state, the city is easy to get around in without a car. In addition to buses, you'll also find Muni Trains and BART, the Bay Area Rapid Transit, which can get you to many places within the city and beyond, taking passengers to many destinations in the East Bay and parts of the South Bay along the peninsula. You can also ride a cable car if you don't mind waiting in long lines.

Despite its space limitations, the city also boasts a large and growing concentration of breweries, beer bars, and restaurants. There is nightlife to spare. San Francisco is simply one of the best places in the nation to eat, drink, and play.

Almanac Beer Company

2325 Third Street, Suite 202, San Francisco, CA 94107
415-992-3438 • www.almanacbeer.com
Twitter @almanacbeer • Facebook.com/almanacbeer

When I first met Jesse Friedman, he was a blogger and homebrewer. His blog, Beer & Nosh, focused on food and beer equally and included beautiful photography and write-ups of his experiences. At the same time, he was continuing to brew at home and was hatching a plan that eventually became the Almanac Beer Company, founded with Damian Fagan, who manages the nonbrewing part of the business, including the graphic design and day-to-day business operations.

It's a high-concept idea, but one that nestles beautifully in the food-centric, organic, locavore world of San Francisco cuisine. With their great slogans like "Farm to Barrel" and "Beer Is Agriculture," you immediately know what the plan is. Jesse and Damian strive to use as many local ingredients as possible and to bring back seasonality in their beers. Before technology and refrigeration, all food was dependent on the growing season. It seems almost quaint now, but it wasn't long ago that you couldn't get certain fruits or vegetables when they were out of season.

Back then, you consulted your almanac to know when to plant and when to harvest. Almanac Beer is using the same approach to make seasonal beers that reflect and use ingredients from each season. Since each is different, I can only tell you some of the beers they've made so far. Their first release used four different types of blackberries from the Sebastopol Berry Farm in Sonoma County and was aged in oak red wine barrels for nearly a year. The base beer was a Belgian-style golden ale brewed with Citra hops and refermented in the bottle. A second offering, the Winter Wit, used fresh local oranges from Hamada Farms in Kingsburg and, as with all of their beers, involved the farmer in the process of selection. They chose three types—navel, cara cara, and blood oranges—and also used ginger root from a Morgan Hill nursery. Each beer is then aged in wooden barrels and bottle-conditioned.

Beers brewed: Year-round: Honey Saison (brewed with honey, ginger, and French oak) and Extra Pale Ale (brewed with mandarins and American oak). Seasonals: The seasonal releases change with each season and harvest. Some of the past special releases included Winter Wit (brewed with oranges and ginger), Farmhouse Pale (dry-hopped saison with plums), and Biere de Mars (brewed with organic fennel).

So no matter what season it is, Almanac Beer will have at least one beer available that was designed specifically for that time of year, though if you're lucky there may also be some older vintages still left over from previous seasons. But since no two will be alike, there's always something new to try, season after season. It's a small-batch concept that works, in part at least, because they can keep costs down by renting a brewery to make their beer. Beer that's aged is generally more expensive to make because of the time that it sits, maturing and fermenting into its full potential. It's the reason hundred-year-old whiskey costs more than the ten-year-old stuff. So while many may balk at a purchasing a single bottle of beer for $15 to $20, the time and effort put into most barrel-aged beers actually makes them a good value. The harder part for Jesse and Damian will be growing larger and building their own brewery, which is on their list of long-range goals. But with just a couple seasons under their belt, their future looks bright.

Because of their background with food, they place a special emphasis on how each release will work with a variety of local foods. By borrowing the concept of vintages from the Bay Area's boutique wine scene, Almanac Beer is a marriage of the best of both worlds. Almanac makes interesting beers season after season that you can taste just once—or at least as many times as you buy a bottle—and then effectively never again. Mark your almanac to remind you when each new release is available.

Almanac Beer Company

Opened: June 2011.

Type: Gypsy brewery.

Owners: Jesse Friedman and Damian Fagan.

Brewer: Jesse Friedman.

Guild membership: SFBG.

Packages available: 750-milliliter and draft special releases seasonally; 12-ounce four-packs and kegs year-round.

Hours: Not open to the public.

Gift shop: Merchandise is available on the website.

Anchor Brewing Company

1705 Mariposa Street, San Francisco, CA 94107
415-863-8350 • www.anchorbrewing.com
Twitter @anchorbrewing
Facebook.com/anchorbrewing

Anchor is history itself. It's San Francisco's only surviving pre-Prohibition brewery and also has the distinction of being America's first craft brewery. It was craft before craft was cool. If you can only visit one brewery while visiting the Bay Area, this is the one to see. You'll need to plan ahead, but it will be worth it. The whole brewery has the feel of a working museum.

Originally opened in 1896, Anchor's roots go even deeper, back to the beginning of the gold rush in 1849, when German brewer Gottlieb Brekle first arrived in San Francisco with his family in tow. Twenty-two years later, he bought a billiard parlor saloon on Pacific Street that he turned into a brewery in 1871. In 1896, Brekle sold the brewery to Ernst F. Baruth and his son-in-law Otto Schinkel Jr., who renamed it Anchor Brewery. From then until Prohibition closed the brewery in 1920, a series of owners came and went, all making Anchor Steam Beer, one of America's few original styles of beer. For a full account of this type of beer, see "A word about . . . Steam Beer" on page 257.

After Prohibition, like many breweries, Anchor struggled under different owners. It was teetering on the brink of bankruptcy when, in 1965, recent Stanford graduate Fritz Maytag stepped in and rescued the brewery, initially buying 51 percent of the business. To say that Maytag turned around the brewery's fortunes would be an understatement. To say that he changed the course of brewing in America would not be going too far. For the first six years, Maytag exhaustively researched the history of brewing and steam beer, traveling to England and elsewhere to observe traditional brewing practices firsthand. By 1971, he was ready, and his brewery introduced Anchor Steam Beer in bottles for the first time since before Prohibition. Building on that success, they followed with more beer "firsts" throughout the 1970s. To see more about Anchor's legacy, see "A word about . . . Anchor Brewing, America's Original Craft Brewer" on page 57.

By the late 1970s, success necessitated a bigger brewery. In 1979, the brewery moved to its present location on Potrero Hill, installing the fifties-built copper Ziemann brewhouse that has become the centerpiece of the brewing operations. The 1937 four-story building had originally been a coffee roastery. It's a gorgeous old building, both inside and out. Sitting on the corner of Mariposa and De Haro Streets, it's a majestic sight, with the corner tower reaching to the sky, flagpole on top. Inside, it's like stepping back in time.

From the main entrance, you take a flight of stairs to the main brewery floor, where there's a reception area, a few offices, the taproom bar and museum, and those iconic copper kettles. The open fermenters and the hops room are also on that floor, while the bottling line and fermenters are down one floor. But it's the taproom where you'll spend the most time. That's where you start and end a tour, and where the brewery entertains and hosts events. Inside the taproom, you'll find breweriana and historic memorabilia on the walls, in display cases, and behind the bar. It's like a museum where you can have a pint of beer.

Maytag was also a pioneer in microdistilling, having started making Anchor's Old Potrero Rye Whiskey, a pot-distilled whiskey using 100 percent rye malt, in 1993. The distillery today makes three different whiskeys: Old Potrero Single Malt 18th Century Style Whiskey, aged in uncharred oak barrels for a minimum of two and a half years; Old Potrero Single Malt 19th Century Style Straight Rye Whiskey, aged in new charred oak barrels for over four and a half years; and Old Potrero Hotalings Single Malt Whiskey, a now seventeen-year-old single-barrel-per-year release. It also makes two gins: Junipero Gin and Genevieve Gin. The distillery is located in the basement of the brewery

Curiously, because of the real estate market's ups and downs, along with the dot-com boom and bust, many companies fled the city over the past few decades, leaving the Anchor Brewery today as the largest manufacturer of any product in San Francisco.

Beers brewed: Year-round: Anchor Steam Beer, Liberty Ale, Anchor Porter, Old Foghorn Barleywine Style Ale, Anchor Small Beer, and Brekle's Brown. Seasonals: Anchor Bock Beer (January–April), Anchor Summer Beer (April–September), Humming Ale (July–November), and Anchor Christmas Ale, a.k.a. Our Special Ale (November–January). In addition, Anchor also produces quarterly specialty beers under the Zymaster Series name. From time to time, the brewery releases Our Barrel Ale, a blend of three of its beers in 1.5-liter magnums.

The Pick: While it's tempting to pick Anchor's flagship Steam beer, the first beer I order every time I visit the brewery is Liberty Ale. It's the first beer I know of to really showcase Cascade hops, and it was also one of the first single-hop beers. It effectively presaged the IPA craze, and I can only imagine how it must have been received in 1974 when it was first released. It has great citrus aromas and flavors, crisp and clean, and great balance throughout. Almost forty years later, it still tastes fresh and delicious.

In 2010, the new era of Anchor began, when Fritz Maytag sold the business to the Griffin Group, a partnership between drinks business veterans Keith Greggor and Tony Foglio. The pair met in the early 1980s while working for International Distillers and Vintners, which later became Diageo, the spirits giant and owner of Guinness. They left Diageo in 1998 to take over Skyy Vodka, building it into a powerhouse brand before selling it to the Campari Group in 2007. Since creating the Griffin Group, they've also purchased a minority interest in Scotland's notorious BrewDog and bought Preiss Imports, a company carrying a dizzying array of spirits along with the distribution rights to two imported beer brands, Cooper's of Australia and BrewDog.

Apart from changing the official name to Anchor Brewers & Distillers, the new owners made few changes, especially not to the iconic beer or spirits brands that Anchor has built, although they've slowly begun making additions to the lineup. For example, they launched Brekle's Brown and added the one-off Humming Ale to their seasonal offerings. They also started the Zymaster Series, quarterly draft-only releases created by longtime brewmaster Mark Carpenter. So far, they've released two in the series: California Lager, based on the first lager brewed in California, and Mark's Mild, one of my favorite styles of beer and one of the most underappreciated.

Brewery president John Dannerbeck, Fritz Maytag's nephew, has continued in his role, reporting to Greggor, who often works from his home in Marin. Foglio became chairman, while Maytag has continued his involvement as chairman emeritus. Most changes have been on the marketing side, with Anchor adding to the existing sales and marketing force. Anchor has been operating at near capacity for a number of years, so the new owners are also looking for ways to increase their annual output. They installed a new bottling line last year, and other modifications are under way to fit more fermenters in the building so they can brew more beer.

One thing that's abundantly clear about the new owners, and especially Keith Greggor since they took over, is that they're nearly as passionate as Maytag when it comes to the respect they have for the Anchor brand. They're genuinely excited and humbled at both the prospect and the responsibility of carrying on the legacy of Anchor Brewery. Both Greggor and Foglio have spent their entire careers building brands, so they understand what they have. The future of Anchor Brewery is in good hands, and it will continue to be an exciting brewery to watch.

Anchor Brewing Company

Opened: 1896.

Type: Production brewery.

Owners: Keith Greggor and Tony Foglio.

Brewer: Mark Carpenter.

Guild membership: BA, CCA, SFBG.

System: 125-barrel Ziemann brewhouse built in the 1950s, bought by Anchor in 1977; 120,000 barrels annual capacity, with plans to increase that number currently being implemented.

Annual production: 103,616 barrels (2011).

Packages available: 12-ounce six-packs, 22-ounce bottles, 1.5-liter magnums, and 5.16- and 13.2-gallon kegs.

Tours: Monday through Friday, 10 a.m. and 1 p.m. Reservations are required and can be made by telephone only, though they can be made up to six months in advance.

Hours: Monday through Friday, 9 a.m. to 5 p.m.

Extras: For those visiting the brewery for tours, the taproom provides a warm, comfortable place steeped in brewing history to learn about the Anchor Brewery and to sample the beers.

Gift shop: Anchor merchandise and souvenirs are sold at the brewery, and additional merchandise is available on steamgear.com.

Barrel Head Brewhouse

1705 Fulton Street, San Francisco, CA 94117
415-745-1570 • www.barrelheadsf.com
Facebook.com/BarrelHeadBrewhouse

The Barrel Head Brewhouse will be located in the NOPA, or North of the Panhandle, neighborhood of San Francisco. The building is on Fulton by the corner of Masonic, only three blocks from the Golden Gate Park Panhandle. The historic building features huge windows and wooden timbers, which the website describes as "providing the skeleton for a dynamic space that will be enhanced by warming touches such as a hand-crafted wooden stave bar, weathered tables, gas lanterns and a fireplace."

They plan to brew handcrafted beers on-site and offer a menu described as "both sophisticated and fun, with a focus on sustainability and ingredients exclusively from local farms." Ivan Hopkinson was a brewer with Beach Chalet and also operates the BrewTruc, a forty-foot brewery on wheels.

Barrel Head Brewhouse

Opened: September 2013.

Type: Brewpub.

Owners: Ivan Hopkinson, Natasha Gatto, and Tim Tattan.

Brewer: Ivan Hopkinson.

Guild membership: SFBG.

System: 7-barrel brewhouse, 1,000 barrels annual capacity.

Tours: By appointment only.

Hours: To be determined; check the Facebook page or website for updates.

Food: The Brewhouse menu is planned to include a variety of food, from "nibbles" to soup to entrées.

Gift shop: The brewpub plans to offer T-shirts, sweatshirts, jackets, and glassware.

The Beach Chalet Brewery & Restaurant

1000 Great Highway, San Francisco, CA 94121
415-386-8439 (415-FUN-VIEW)
www.beachchalet.com
Twitter @parkchalet • Facebook.com/pages/Beach-
  Chalet-Brewery-Restaurant/168600289861491

While there are many reasons to go to the Beach Chalet, first and foremost is location. The Beach Chalet overlooks the Pacific Ocean along the Great Highway on the western edge of Golden Gate Park. It's located right next to the Dutch Windmill, built in 1902, and Queen Wilhelmina's Tulip Garden. If you can choose when to visit the Beach Chalet, go in March or April, when thousands of tulips and Icelandic poppies are in flower.

The Golden Gate Park Visitors Center, a Spanish Revival building constructed in 1925, had been empty and falling into ruin for seventeen years before Gar and Lara Truppelli took over the space, completely renovating it in 1996. Downstairs, it was restored to its former glory, including more than 2,000 square feet of murals created by Lucien Labaudt in the mid-1930s. Labaudt was a French artist who relocated to San Francisco in 1906 and founded the California School of Design. During the Great Depression, FDR's administration funded a number of large-scale art projects in an effort to stimulate the economy through the Works Progress Administration (WPA). The Beach Chalet murals were the last of the great WPA projects. Come to the Beach Chalet for the history, and stay for the beer and food.

Take the stairs to the second floor and you'll find the brewpub, with spectacular views of the ocean across the street. The extensive menu consists of American fare and includes a wide selection of appetizers, making it a great place to just sit, drink, and nibble.

Brewer Aron Deorsey makes a wide selection of beers right behind the bar. He always has a few beers available year-round that you can count on, but brews a dizzying number of seasonals and one-offs, just because he can. You never know what exciting discovery you might find whenever

Beers brewed: Year-round: VFW (Veterans of Foreign Wars) Light, Presidio IPA, California Kind, Riptide Red. Seasonals: Saison du Chalet de la Plage (spring), Smokey the Beer (summer), Fogtown Brown (fall), and Ocean Beach Oktoberfest (fall). Rotating: Wheat Series, Pale Ale Series, and Dark Side Series.

The Pick: I personally like Aron's Riptide Red Ale, a malty amber ale with nice toffee and caramel sweetness. It's an easy-drinking beer perfect for watching the Pacific Ocean outside the window.

you stop by for a beer. He's been the Beach Chalet's brewer for years and knows that system like the back of his hand.

Deorsey also makes the beer exclusively for several other restaurants owned by the Truppellis. Right next door, or technically behind the Beach Chalet, sits the Park Chalet. Surrounded by the park, it features an open-air dining area, an outdoor patio, and lawn seating, with a smaller menu that includes lots of small-plate dishes and pizza. You can find all of the Beach Chalet beers here, too, along with a few that Deorsey brews just for the Park Chalet.

Across the Bay in Oakland, the Truppellis opened the Lake Chalet in 2009. This seafood bar and grill is located on Lake Merritt, Oakland's recreational lake, in a former pumping station building originally constructed in 1909. For the Oakland restaurant, Deorsey has created several house beers, such as Lake Merritt IPA, Regatta Red, and Lady of the Lake, which he describes as a "crisp domestic style ale with just a hint of hops sneaking in at the end." Also in the East Bay, Deorsey brews beer for the Honor Kitchen and Cocktails on Powell Street in Emeryville. So to try all of the Beach Chalet beers, you'll actually need to go to four different places. Happily, they're all good restaurants with their own unique beers, making the quest a worthwhile one.

Beach Chalet Brewery & Restaurant

Opened: December 31, 1996.

Type: Brewpub.

Owners: Gar and Lara Truppelli.

Brewer: Aron Joseph Deorsey.

Guild membership: CCBA, SFBG, NCBG.

System: 15-barrel Specific Mechanical, with four 15-barrel fermenters and seven 15-barrel bright tanks, 1,700 barrels annual capacity.

Annual production: 1,560 barrels.

Packages available: 22-ounce bottles, 2-liter growlers, and 5- and 15.5-gallon kegs.

Tours: Walk-in tours generally available Monday through Friday, 9 a.m. to 6 p.m. Weekend tours by appointment only.

Hours: Monday through Thursday, 9 a.m. to 10 p.m.; Friday, 9 a.m. to 11 p.m.; Saturday 8 a.m. to 11 p.m.; Sunday 8 a.m. to 10 p.m.

Food: Sandwiches and entrées, with an emphasis on steak and fresh fish, and pasta, soups, and salads. There are also separate happy hour, breakfast, and Sunday brunch menus.

Extras: Live music is performed both during the week and on the weekends.

Gift shop: You can buy Beach Chalet beer, T-shirts, sweatshirts, logo glasses, and other San Francisco souvenirs.

Cellarmaker Brewing Company

1150 Howard Street, San Francisco, CA 94103
www.cellarmakerbrewing.com
Twitter @CellarmakerBeer
Facebook.com/CellarmakerBrewing

Cellarmaker is one of San Francisco's newest breweries and is in the SOMA (South of Market) district of the city, on Howard, between Seventh and Eighth Streets. Founder Connor Casey is a veteran of both the wine and beer industries, having worked for the Fritz Winery, City Beer Store, and Marin Brewing Company.

His brewery is a new concept of sorts. Although he offers some fresh, hoppy beers that are ready to drink now, many if not most of his beers are designed to be cellared and aged. Many of the sour or dark beers should age gracefully and will likely develop new flavors over the years. The brewery is encouraging customers to experiment with aging them different lengths of time to experience new flavors each time they try them. Cellarmaker will rarely make the same beer more than twice a year, and its lineup will constantly be rotating, changing with the seasons, depending on what fresh fruits are available and what wine and bourbon barrels can be found.

The red brick brewery building boasts twenty-five-foot-high ceilings and skylights. The overall vibe of the place is an urban industrial garage. Inside, brushed-metal stools and chairs mingle with multicolored wood tables, bar top, and backbar. Modern lighting hangs from the wall, and a roll-up door can be raised when the weather turns warmer. The tasting room is planned to have a dozen tap handles, which will dispense small pours, pints, and 1-liter swing-top growlers to go.

Brewer Tim Sciascia was the assistant brewer at Marin Brewing for the last several years and also brewed at Samuel Adams in Boston, his hometown. In addition to hoppy beers, he'll focus on Belgian-style saisons and darker beers as well. He's sourcing the most unusual hops he can find, from places like New Zealand and experimental varieties from the Pacific Northwest. Other plans include brewing funky and sour beers aged in red and white wine barrels, sometimes aged on favorite fresh fruits from local farms, such as a sour blonde

Beers brewed: Year-round: None. Seasonals: The focus is on an ever-changing lineup of beers, both those brewed to be consumed fresh and many others aged or meant to be aged.

ale with pluots aged in chardonnay barrels, a saison with some Brettanomyces aged on freshly sliced peaches in a sauvignon blanc barrel, and a sour brown aged in pinot noir barrels with blackberries. On the other end of the barrel spectrum, expect big, chewy stouts aged in bourbon. The driving force is a desire to experiment and discover new possibilities in beer flavors as they go. It should be fun to play along, especially since you'll never know what you can expect from one visit to the next.

Cellarmaker Brewing Company

Opened: Late summer 2013.

Type: Production brewery, with tasting room.

Owner: Connor Casey.

Brewer: Tim Sciascia.

Guild membership: SFBG.

System: 10-barrel Premier Stainless, 1,000 barrels annual capacity.

Packages available: Growlers, 22-ounce bottles, and 750-milliliter bottles.

Tours: Available by appointment, or feel free to ask during a visit. If someone has some free time, he or she will be happy to show you around the brewery.

Hours: Tuesday and Wednesday, 3 to 11 p.m.; Thursday through Saturday, noon to midnight; Sunday, noon to 6 p.m.

Food: No food is available, but visitors are welcome to bring their own food to the brewery. There is also a rotating selection of food trucks stationed outside.

Extras: Live music whenever possible. When the weather is nice, the staff will lift the garage door to enjoy the San Francisco sunshine.

Gift shop: A small selection of brewery merchandise is available in the tasting room.

Cervecería de MateVeza

MateVeza

3801 18th Street, San Francisco, CA 94114
415-273-9295 • www.cerveceriasf.com /
www.mateveza.com
Twitter @cerveceriasf / @MateVeza
Facebook.com/cerveceriasf /
Facebook.com/MateVeza

If you've ever been to Argentina, you know what a big deal Yerba mate tea is there. Part social ritual and part teatime, it's everywhere, no matter where you are. In South America, the approach to tea is the opposite of what we're used to. While we put the tea in a bag or strain it out of the cup we drink from, Yerba mate is brewed in a gourd—also known as a *guampa* or *porongo*—with hot (not boiling) water and sipped through a metal straw that has a filter at the bottom so you don't drink the leaves. The gourd is passed between friends in a kind of ritual.

While in college, MateVeza founder Jim Woods had his first taste of mate and was immediately hooked, later traveling through South America to visit its origins and sample the local tea. A few years later, he was drinking a pale ale when he noticed that it was similarly bitter and had one of those "lightbulb" moments. Already a homebrewer, he decided to experiment with brewing beer with Yerba mate, keeping hops character low to produce a bitter balance. That's how he hit upon his first MateVeza beer, a name that combines "mate" with the last part of the Spanish word for beer, *cerveza*.

Determined to turn his passion into a viable business, he took the intensive brewing course at the University of California's Davis campus, known informally as UC Davis. He used his recipes to start contract brewing, and for a number of years, he's been working with Mendocino Brewing in Ukiah for all of the company's bottled products. For the first few years, MateVeza was a one-man operation, and Woods concentrated on building his brand at the retail level, trying to get his bottles into retail stores and restaurants and kegs into bars. But he always wanted a space of his own, though building a big production brewery

Beers brewed: Year-round: Black Lager, Yerba Mate IPA, and Morpho Herbal Ale (a collaboration with Mill Valley Beerworks).

The Pick: You could easily dismiss MateVeza's creations as novelty beers, but the fact is the concept works. Mate and hops work well together and provide a unique flavor. Whether or not you like the tea, you'll probably like the beer—it's bigger than the sum of its parts. I like the IPA, because although it's hoppy, the mate shines through and gives the beer its distinctive flavor. It's not dry or overly bitter but is nicely balanced.

seemed out of reach.

Instead, Woods partnered with longtime friend Matt Coelho, who was a veteran bartender in San Francisco, and they looked for a smaller space that they could call their own. Last year, they settled on a funky little corner space across the street from Dolores Park, which they named Cervecería de MateVeza. Inside, the décor is decidedly eclectic, with window seats, a curio cabinet, a reclaimed lumber bar, and a giant chandelier they found on craigslist. The chandelier was in Southern California, so to transport it to the Bay Area, they got it into a car coming this way through rideshare. On the walls hang paintings of Elvis Presley on velvet, and the brewpub's signs are made using the cards from the 1960s Parker Brothers game Probe.

The nanobrewpub carries all of MateVeza's beers, which are certified organic, along with a number of guest taps of local beers. A four-door cooler holds a nice selection of around a hundred different local and imported bottled beers. In keeping with its South American roots, the brewpub also serves half a dozen different handmade empanadas from San Francisco's El Porteño, along with a selection of dessert treats. But perhaps its most important feature is the 20-gallon pilot brewery that allows Woods to keep experimenting with new beers and have immediate feedback to help decide which recipes work and which don't. If you're lucky enough, perhaps you'll have a chance to try the next great MateVeza beer.

Cervecería de MateVeza

Opened: Brewpub, April 7, 2012; contract brewery, November 2006.

Type: Brewpub, contract brewery for packaged beer.

Owners: Jim Woods and Matt Coelho.

Brewer: Jim Woods.

Guild membership: SFBG.

System: 20-gallon MoreBeer Tippy Brewsculpture, 60 barrels annual capacity; packaged beer brewed under contract with Mendocino Brewing Company (see page 246).

Annual production: 60 barrels at brewpub; 500 barrels packaged beer.

Packages available: Growlers at the brewpub; four-packs of 12-ounce bottles, 22-ounce bottles, and 5- and 15.5-gallon kegs at retail.

Tours: Yes; no reservations needed.

Hours: Tuesday through Saturday, noon to 10 p.m.; Sunday, noon to 6 p.m.

Food: Limited to tasty Argentinian-style empanadas. Varieties include carne, pollo, jamón y queso, and champiñones, with alfajores and empanaditas for dessert.

Extras: Located directly adjacent to Dolores Park, with outdoor seating.

Gift shop: T-shirts and bottle openers are available for purchase.

Magnolia Gastropub & Brewery

1398 Haight Street, San Francisco, CA 94117
(Magnolia Gastropub & Brewery)
2505 Third Street, San Francisco, CA 94107
(Dogpatch Brewpub and production brewery)
415-864-7468 • www.magnoliapub.com
Twitter @magnoliapub
Facebook.com/pages/Magnolia-Gastropub-
Brewery/62902472652

The corner of Haight and Ashbury in San Francisco is one of the city's most famous destinations, with a storied past that originated in the colorful sixties counterculture. The original hippie denizens that made it famous now exist uneasily side by side with chain stores and gift shops that cater to the many tourists that flock to the neighborhood every year.

The Magnolia Gastropub & Brewery is just one block away from the famous intersection, at the corner of Haight and Masonic, in a 1903 building that used to house a restaurant owned by Magnolia Thunder-pussy, a local burlesque dancer and well-known personality. There's a certain symmetry to the location, as McLean credits the beginnings of his love for beer to the Grateful Dead, who lived in the area during the heady days of the sixties. As a student at Boston University, McLean had his first taste of West Coast beer in the parking lot of one of their shows and was immediately hooked. After graduating, it was an easy decision to move closer to his passions, so McLean left the East Coast and his native Pittsburgh, Pennsylvania, and the young man went west.

In San Francisco, McLean started homebrewing and wanted to create his favorite beer at the time, Mendocino's Red Tail Ale. He took microbiology extension courses at UC Berkeley, eventually enrolling in the brewing curriculum at UC Davis in 1993. By that time, his career path had taken something of a detour, and he dreamed of opening his own brewpub. In 1995, he found the Haight Street building and knew it was the perfect location. Although it had been a restaurant and at one time a Rexall drugstore, fitting in the brewery proved quite difficult. The basement had to be lowered to fit the brewing equipment, and it took two years to carry out the dirt in buckets and install the brew-house and fermenters. Even so, it's one of the most cramped breweries you'll ever visit, but somehow it works.

When the original brewpub opened in 1997, its décor featured psychedelic murals any Deadhead would be proud of. And while that served the brewpub, and the neighborhood, well for many years, the inside was renovated a few years ago and has a much more upscale look and feel these days. It's no less eclectic but better suits the quality of the food and beer. It's more cozy and comfortable now. I suppose it's not so much a renovation as part of the evolving and maturing of the brewery that's now been open fifteen years.

You'll generally see at least ten Magnolia beers available at any given time, along with another two to four on cask. The selection also frequently includes a guest cask. Always start with the cask selection. Nothing can beat fresh cask ale, and this beer is brewed downstairs in the basement. You'd be hard-pressed to find fresher cask beer than that. As good as the beer is, the emphasis put on the menu is nothing short of fanatical. All of the food is locally sourced and carefully chosen to pair with the selection of beer. And it's delicious, too. Taking a cue from the brewpub's English influence, the staff often refer to Magnolia as a gastropub, which is loosely defined as a pub that places a special emphasis on the quality of the food they serve. I can think of few brewpubs more deserving to be called a gastropub.

You can also find Magnolia's beers on tap a few blocks away down Haight, at the Alembic Bar, which McLean opened in 2006. In addition to the draft beer and an extensive bottle list, the Alembic has a full bar and specializes in spirits and inventive cocktails. There's also a small but creative menu that's completely different from what you'll find at Magnolia. It's currently a cozy little place, which makes it an ideal location to close an evening's festivities. McLean will soon be taking over the space next door, which housed the Red Vic Theater, and renovating it to include retail space, an event center, and almost 500 more square feet of seating inside the Alembic Bar.

Beers brewed: Year-round: Kalifornia Kolsch, Proving Ground IPA, Blue Bell Bitter, Bonnie Lee's Best Bitter, New Speedway Bitter, Sara's Ruby Mild, Spud Boy's IPA, Cole Porter, Stout of Circumstance, and Big Cypress Brown. Seasonals: Old Thunderpussy Barleywine, Winter Warmer, Barking Pumpkin, Saison de Lily, Rosebud, Tweezer Tripel, and Weekapaug Gruit.

The Pick: I love a good mild, and Dave's Ruby Mild was modeled after a fine English mild that he discovered during a vacation many years ago. Milds don't get the recognition they deserve. They're relatively low-alcohol beers with—no pun intended—mild flavors that don't hit you over the head. Though it may sound contradictory, they are still full-flavored. Sara's Ruby Mild hits all the marks and is a great beer that many people will pass on in favor of the bigger beers that Magnolia makes, which, I should add, are also terrific beers. But this is a delicate beer with subtle, nuanced flavors that you can drink all night long. What's not to love?

In a nearby neighborhood, or more properly a microhood, known as Dogpatch, a new production brewery is being built. This brewery will brew Magnolia beers for bottling and kegging and will also include a public space for people to enjoy a pint, with or without a meal, which Dave believes will be some type of barbecue or other casual fare.

Magnolia Brewing Company

Opened: November 11, 1997.

Type: Brewpub, plus a newly opened brewpub and production brewery at a separate location.

Owner: Dave McLean.

Brewers: Dave McLean (brewmaster) and Ben Spencer (head brewer).

Guild membership: BA, CCBA, SFBG, NCBG.

System: 7-barrel Quality Stainless, 1,000 barrels annual capacity. Production brewery estimated to have 7,000 barrels annual capacity.

Annual production: 1,000 barrels, brewpub.

Packages available: Growlers and 5- and 15.5-gallon kegs at the brewpub. Magnolia also produces cask versions of many of the beers. The production brewery will produce bottled beer, but sizes have yet to be determined.

Tours: Brewpub by appointment only. At Dogpatch, tours will be available, but the details are not yet determined.

Hours: Brewpub: Monday through Thursday, 11 a.m. to midnight; Friday, 11 a.m. to 1 a.m.; Saturday, 10 a.m. to 1 a.m.; and Sunday, 10 a.m. to midnight. Dogpatch most likely will be open seven days a week, 11 a.m. to midnight.

Food: The brewpub on Haight offers seasonally appropriate, locally sourced gastro-pub fare, with an emphasis on serving unique versions of inventive comfort food designed to match the beer perfectly. The cooks practice nose-to-tail butchery, and their most popular dish is the organic Prather Ranch burger. Separate menus are available for lunch, dinner, and brunch, which is served only on the weekends. The lunch menu includes satisfying nibbles divided into snacks, meat, cheese, starters, and house sausages, along with an eclectic selection of burgers and sandwiches and very tasty desserts. It's hard to pass up a fried doughnut, and the frites are top-notch. Dinner, during which a few heartier dishes are added to the menu, is served until midnight. Dogpatch brewpub and production brewery menu is still being finalized but will most likely offer sustainably sourced nondenominational barbecue.
Extras: The brewpub has outdoor seating on the sidewalk. Both breweries are family-friendly.

Gift shop: A variety of brewery merchandise is available at both locations and also may be ordered online.

Pacific Brewing Laboratory

334 South Van Ness, San Francisco CA 94103
415-937-7843 • www.pacbrewlab.com
Twitter @PacBrewLab • Facebook.com/PacBrewLab

Pacific Brewing Laboratory, or PacBrewLab, is one of San Francisco's newest breweries. Started by a pair of avid homebrewers, the contract brewery has made waves from the get-go, with a sense of whimsy, fun, creative marketing and concepts—and most important, by making very good beer.

The two mad scientists who founded the Laboratory are Patrick Horn and Bryan Hermannsson. Hermannsson is a Bay Area native who dabbled in biomedical engineering before finding brewing. When I say dabbled, I mean he has a BS in the subject and has been a chemist in the wine industry and studied human bones at UCSF. So that's some serious dabbling. His business partner, Patrick Horn, hails from South Carolina. Horn had spent a decade as a lobbyist in Washington, DC, when he felt he needed a change of scenery. After moving to San Francisco and discovering homebrewing, he decided to use his business acumen in pursuit of something he actually enjoyed. The pair met as a part of the city's homebrewing community and realized they were kindred spirits with a shared dream of opening a brewery.

It took about two years to launch the brewery, which entailed a lot of experimentation in a garage. While they were getting up and running, they invited friends, neighbors, and interested parties to sample their early efforts for free in now-legendary garage parties. It was guerrilla marketing at its purest and helped spread the word about their beer and their brand even before they formally opened the doors.

They've also been experimenting with unusual ingredients. In addition to their current lineup of beers, they've played around with chamomile, lemongrass, Szechuan peppercorns, and even soaking their beer in wine and wine barrels. When

Beers brewed: Year-round: Squid Ink (black IPA) and Nautilus (Hibiscus saison). Seasonals: Red Triangle California Red Ale (with kelp and rose hips; fall), and The Kraken (winter).

The Pick: It's hard not to love a beer called Squid Ink. But besides having a great name, it's a solid black IPA, with great chocolate and toasty malt aromas. The chocolate continues through the flavors, with big hops character up front, along with a mélange of fruit notes and a spicy finish.

serving beer at beer festivals, Bryan and Patrick wear lab coats and surround themselves with the props you'd expect to find in a mad scientist's laboratory. It's a great gimmick that works well, especially since they can back it up with great beer.

Changes are afoot for PacBrewLab: more beers, more of a presence in the brewing community, more creativity, and—without a doubt— more great beers on the horizon. The future looks quite bright; it's a good thing the partners are wearing shades with their lab coats.

Pacific Brewing Laboratory

Opened: December 2011.
Type: Contract brewery.
Owners: Patrick Horn and Bryan Hermannsson.
Brewer: Bryan Hermannsson.
Guild membership: BA, CCBA, SFBG.
System: See Hermitage Brewing (page 150).
Annual production: 400 barrels (2012 estimate).
Packages available: 5-gallon and 50-liter kegs.
Tours: By appointment only.
Gift shop: Merchandise is available online.

Pine Street Brewery

1270 Pine Street #1, San Francisco, CA 94109
415-744-4062 • www.pinestreetbrewery.com
Twitter @pinestreetbeer
Facebook.com/pinestreetbrewery

Pine Street Brewery is another of San Francisco's newest breweries. But homebrewer Jay Holliday has been dreaming and brewing since at least 2009, having developed at least ten beers for his portfolio in that time. So the brewery has been ready for its close-up for years now. It's only the devilish details that have prevented it from opening sooner.

Holliday made some of his first beers in a kitchen on Pine Street and knew at once that this was something he wanted to do professionally. Originally from Ohio, he earned multiple degrees from Ohio State before taking a job with a bank in Southern California. After transferring to San Francisco, he began his plans for making Pine Street Brewery a reality.

If all goes according to the script, by now you should be able to find Holliday's beer throughout San Francisco in both kegs and six-pack bottles. For the first couple years, Holliday will brew with Pine Street's partner at Devil's Canyon, with an eye toward building a small brewery all his own sometime during or after year three.

Beers brewed: Year-round: Atom Splitter (West Coast Red IPA), Menagerie (Farmhouse Ale), Black Bay Oyster Stout, La Flama Blanca (white ale), Guardian Double, Red Head Raspberry Blonde, Smoked on the Water Rauchbier, Brown Bag, Walter (Double IPA), Glory (Scotch Ale), and SF Lager. Seasonals: All Hallows Eve Pumpkin Porter (fall).

Pine Street Brewery

Opened: Fall 2012.

Type: Alternating proprietorship.

Owner: Jay Holliday.

Brewer: Jay Holliday.

Guild membership: SFBG.

System: See Devil's Canyon Brewing (page 132).

Packages available: 12-ounce bottles, in six-packs, and 5- and 15.5-gallon kegs.

The Pick: Since all ten beers are not available all the time, I've only had half of Pine Street's offerings, but from among those, I really like Holliday's take on saison with the Menagerie. It has great spicy, fruity—mostly lemon—notes and is clean and zesty, with a spicy finish. Also, you can't go wrong with the Atom Splitter, a hoppy red ale.

Shmaltz Brewing Company

Est. 1996

912 Cole Street #338, San Francisco, CA 94117
www.shmaltzbrewing.com
Twitter @shmaltzbrewingw
Facebook.com/shmaltzbrewing

San Francisco native Jeremy Cowan started out with a great gimmick, playing off his faith with He'Brew: The Chosen Beer. For Hanukkah his first year, 1996, he delivered a hundred hand-bottled cases using his grandmother's car. His early efforts were imbued with great wit and playful cleverness. In the nearly two decades since then, Cowan's brewing has become so much more than that, in a way outgrowing its novelty roots.

Cowan's original vision was to tap the Jewish market everywhere, as he figured that 10 percent of any given urban market was probably Jewish. He strived to have fun with He'Brew, drawing on pop culture and Jewish history. The first offering, Genesis Ale, also included pomegranate, one of the "seven sacred species from the land of milk and honey." Others were barley, wheat, and figs, which were used in a later He'Brew release, the Rejewvenator Dopplebock . . . Shmopplebock.

After initially brewing in California, Cowan eventually moved production to the Mendocino Brewery in Saratoga Springs, New York. And that's when things really started to change. During the early years, walking softly but using a big shtick, he ended up getting He'Brew into some of the best beer bars in most major cities in over half the states, selling, as he puts it, "a little beer in a lot of places." And almost by accident, that's been the secret to his success. "It's been really cool for the past few years," he says, "pushing the quality using innovative recipes. The more we do that, the more the best beer drinkers respond to us."

As the "English major behind the brewmaster," Cowan describes exactly what he wants, and then he and brewer Paul McErlean "taste an enormous array of beers" to find the next He'Brew. That's how they started making extreme beers—like Jew-

Beers brewed: Year-round: He'Brew Genesis Dry Hopped Session Ale, Messiah Nut Brown Ale, Hop Manna IPA, Origin Pomegranate Strong Ale, Bittersweet Lenny's R.I.P.A., Coney Island Lager, Coney Island Albino Python, Coney Island Sword Swallower, and Coney Island Human Blockhead. Seasonals: Coney Island Variety 12 Pack (June), Coney Island Freaktoberfest (September), He'Brew Jewbelation Series (November), He'Brew Chanukah Gift Pack (November), Reunion: A Beer for Hope (Terrapin Beer Company/SBS Imports collaboration; July), and the Shmaltz Barrel Aged Series (ongoing).

belation and Bittersweet Lenny's R.I.P.A. "It's just a bummer that contract brewing got a bad name," he says. "It's really not that different in the scheme of things than the owner of a brewery who doesn't know how to brew."

These days, Cowan splits his time between his two biggest markets, San Francisco and New York City. In New York, he launched a second brand, the Coney Island line of lager beers, with provocative labels by artist Matt Polacheck and a Brooklyn tattoo artist. When an interviewer asked if he was selling out, Cowan summed up his philosophy: "Well, if circus freaks are more mainstream than Jews, then I guess we're going mainstream. I'm proud of sticking to my goal of digging deeper into the cult personality of the brand, using ingredients, shtick, and themes that are close to the original vision for Genesis Ale."

And that's what has made Shmaltz so successful and such a cult favorite. When Jeremy set aside the shtick in favor of just making great beers, big beers that might not sell everywhere but would be welcomed in select accounts across the country, things started to click and have been doing so ever since. It's a unique approach that has worked wonders and allowed Cowan to grow the brand—now brands—well beyond the Bay Area and much farther than he originally had thought possible. After being a one-man show for many years, he has finally been successful enough to hire some staff and take a little pressure off his shoulders. These days, you can find He'Brew beers almost everywhere, especially in the Bay Area.

Shmaltz Brewing Company

Opened: 1996.

Type: Contract brewery.

Owner: Jeremy Cowan.

Brewer: Paul McErlean.

Guild membership: SFBG.

Annual production: 15,000 barrels (2011).

Packages available: 12-ounce bottles in six-packs and four-packs, 22-ounce bottles, and 5- and 15.5-gallon kegs.

Gift shop: Merchandise is available online.

Social Kitchen & Brewery

1326 Ninth Avenue, San Francisco, CA 94122
415-681-0330
www.socialkitchenandbrewery.com
@socialbrewery
Facebook.com/SocialKitchenandBrewery

For a long time, it was tempting to think of the space where Social Kitchen & Brewery is located as cursed. The first brewery to open there, in 1997, was Golden Gate Park Brewery, but it closed the following year. In 2001, it opened again as Eldo's Grill & Brewery, followed by Wunder Brewing in 2007, which lasted until 2009.

It may seem odd to begin talking about all the failures that have beset the location of another new brewery, but that's because I so firmly believe that this time the owner and brewers got everything right. Social Brewery & Kitchen opened in the spring of 2010, and its first brewer was Rich Higgins, one of only four master cicerones (the beer equivalent of a sommelier) in America and a terrific brewer. He not only created some truly memorable, tasty beers, but also worked closely with the chef so that the dishes and beers worked perfectly as a team.

The initial offerings of beer were a neat mix of traditional styles and unique offerings, and though one of the limitations of the brewery had always been an unwillingness to update or modify the brewing equipment—which, unusually, is also owned by the landlord—Higgins managed to do just that and in the process gave the space its first fighting chance in over a decade.

It's a beautiful, comfortable place, with nooks and crannies in which to enjoy a meal or share a drink, plus there's a long, spacious bar. The food is quite tasty, especially the Kennebec fries, and is priced reasonably, especially for the Inner Sunset neighborhood. Higgins left last year, but Kim Sturdavant, who cut his teeth brewing at Marin Brewing, has ably stepped in as brewmaster. He's kept

Beers brewed: Year-round: SKB Pilsner, Beach House Blonde, Ramsgate Rye PA, SF Session Ale, Irving Street Pale Ale, Skimmer's ESB, Ramsgate Rye PA, West Side IPA, The Smell IPA, Waterfront Porter, and Rapscallion. Seasonals: Anniversary Brune (May) and Citradora Elegans (July).

The Pick: I really love the Rapscallion, which is Rich Higgins's take on a strong Belgian-style golden ale. I was pleased that Kim kept that one on the menu when he took over. At 7.2 percent ABV, it's definitely a sipping beer, and it's served in an appropriate tulip glass designed just for that. It's nicely spicy, with coriander, ginger, and hints of pepper.

some of the beers that Rich introduced but also has put his own stamp on the lineup of beers. He employs a deft hand with hops, and it shows in his big but surprisingly delicate IPA, among others. I think Social Kitchen & Brewery is, unlike so many of its predecessors, here to stay.

Social Kitchen & Brewery

Opened: May 2010.

Type: Brewpub.

Owner: Ed Bernardo.

Brewer: Kim Sturdavant.

Guild membership: SFBG.

System: 15-barrel Liquid Assets, 500 barrels annual capacity.

Annual production: 450 barrels (2012 estimate).

Packages available: Growlers and 5- and 15.5-gallon kegs.

Tours: No tours are available, although you can see into the brewery from the balcony.

Hours: Monday through Thursday, 4 p.m. to midnight; Friday, 4 p.m. to 2 a.m.; Saturday, 11:30 a.m. to 2 a.m.; and Sunday 10:30 a.m. to midnight.

Food: Social Kitchen offers a total beer and food experience. The food menu weaves in beer ingredients, and the beer is all food-friendly. Depending on how hungry you are, the menu is divided into "smaller" and "larger" dishes, with the smaller side including a wealth of appetizer-like items to share or snack on. The pork belly sliders and sweet potato tempura are particularly tasty. You can also get salads, soup, and a selection of sandwiches. Brunch is available on Sundays, and happy hour beer prices and food specials are offered weekdays from 4 to 7 p.m.

Extras: Once a month, there's a Brewmaster's Dinner featuring a prix fixe beer and food pairing menu hosted by both brewmaster Kim Sturdavant and chef Chris Wong.

Gift shop: Limited merchandise is available at the brewpub.

Southern Pacific Brewing

620 Treat Avenue, San Francisco, CA 94110
415-341-0152 • www.southernpacificbrewing.com
Twitter @SoPacBrewing
Facebook.com/pages/Southern-Pacific-Brewing/
  152542374781013

One of San Francisco's newest breweries, Southern Pacific has its roots in another local favorite. Both founder Chris Lawrence and brewmaster Andy French once worked for Speakeasy, which is where they met. Andy was Speakeasy's second brewer and was there during its formative years, from 1999 to 2006. After seven years, he left Speakeasy and worked for a number of years at Zeitgeist, a great nearby beer bar. Chris originally worked in sales at Speakeasy, but he left to take a job with Matagrano, a local beer distributor.

The two were roommates when Chris decided he wanted to open a brewery. Knowing Andy's skill as a brewer, he hired him as employee number one to brew the beer. A native San Franciscan, Chris wanted his brewery to be located in the city and researched local history, discovering a number of rail lines near the brewery's present location, which was originally a machine shop known as Metkin Tool & Die. Metkin even did work for the brewery's namesake, Southern Pacific Railroad. Apparently a lot of rail activity took place around the present location of the brewery, and the industrial feel of the area and the brewery's building harks back to an earlier era of the city's history.

Andy French grew up in the Washington, DC, area, where he learned to homebrew before heading west to San Francisco in the early 1990s. His beers tend to be very clean and hew toward traditional styles. I've always liked his beers. They're no-nonsense, not flashy, but always consistent and well made. His brewery is behind the scenes—and behind a chain-link fence—around the back of the open seating area, where there's plenty of room for

Beers brewed: Year-round: California Blonde, Pale Ale, India Pale Ale, Extra India Pale Ale, Black Lager, Porter, Belgian Wit, and Hefeweizen. Seasonals: French will be doing seasonal offerings roughly each quarter, though not following any pattern or schedule.

The Pick: In the short time the brewery has been open, the California Blonde has proven to be the most enduringly popular beer, and it's a nice mild beer with muted hops character, a light body but tons of flavor. But it's the IPA that I find to be spot-on, with big grapefruit character but no bitterness. It's the perfect antidote for a foggy or hot day on the city.

expansion. It's a beautiful copper-clad brewhouse, so it's a bit of a shame that it's not more visible.

Southern Pacific tends to be packed on evenings and weekends, but because the space is so cavernous, with dual levels and bars, along with lots of windows, it rarely feels overcrowded, even when it actually is. The clean industrial lines were left intact while the entire building was modernized with all new water, power, and gas. Original art lines one wall, bringing welcome bright colors to the industrial grays and blacks and polished wood that fill the hall. The art changes at least monthly, so no matter how often you go, you're likely to find a new artist's works hanging in the brewery. A gigantic fan that looks like a propeller for a large airplane hangs from the ceiling.

Despite being a new brewery, Southern Pacific already appears to be a fixture of the vibrant San Francisco beer scene. With such experienced veterans at the helm, I expect Southern Pacific Brewing to be around a long time and to just keep getting better.

Southern Pacific Brewing

Opened: January 27, 2012.

Type: Brewpub.

Owner: Chris Lawrence.

Brewer: Andy French.

Guild membership: SFBG.

System: 15-barrel Specific Mechanical, 1,800 barrels annual capacity.

Annual production: 1,200 barrels (estimated).

Packages available: Growlers and kegs available.

Tours: No tours currently available.

Hours: Sunday through Wednesday, 11 a.m. to midnight; Thursday through Saturday, 11 a.m. to 2 a.m.

Food: Besides terrific french fries, the small but varied menu includes tasty, high-end versions of salads, pizza, sandwiches, and burgers, perfectly complementing the beer. There's a nice selection of "bar bites," such as a jar of pickles, house-cured charcuterie, and crispy brussels sprouts. It's hard to beat the bacon ricotta pizza, but there are several other interesting pizzas too. One of the most interesting burger choices is a lentil and spent grain burger with fontina cheese and grilled onion jam. To satisfy your sweet tooth, there's also a satisfying mix of desserts.

Extras: There's outdoor seating in front, and inside there are bars on two levels, so that even indoors the brewery has an outdoor feel. A number of guest tap beers are also available.

Gift shop: T-shirts, hats, and hoodies are available from the wall near the entrance.

Southpaw BBQ & Southern Cooking

2170 Mission Street, San Francisco, CA 94110
415-218-0197 • www.southpawbbqsf.com
Twitter @southpawbbqsf
Facebook.com/southpawbbq

The founders of Southpaw BBQ grew up loving southern barbecue for one simple reason: they both grew up in the Deep South, Elizabeth Wells in Alabama and Edward Calhoun in North Carolina. The two friends met in college, and by 2001 they were living in Nashville but looking for a change. Stints working in New Orleans and Colorado gave them experience in the food and beverage industry, and Wells also worked in product development, sustainable international development, and with local communities—and worked a memorable big beer festival along the way—before relocating to San Francisco.

When they hit upon the plan to open a restaurant, they knew it would revolve around their home cooking of southern barbecue but also envisioned a bar concept with beer and moonshine. After talking with local homebrewers, they were determined to create a community-based brewing space where collaborations could take place. John Wunder, who had opened the short-lived Wunder Brewing (where Social Kitchen & Brewery is now located), built the small brewery system shortly after the restaurant opened. It's a tight squeeze behind and to the left of the bar, where patrons can watch the brewing taking place from almost anywhere they sit.

Veteran brewer Phil Cutti is now the head brewer. Cutti learned homebrewing from Speakeasy cofounders, Steve and Mike Bruce, and has since also brewed at Mill Valley Beerworks and the Pacific Brewing Laboratory. He is a member of the Night Train Swimmers, a world-renowned open-water swim team that raises money for charity, and has been a research scientist with NASA. Expect to see big things from Cutti as he expands Southpaw's beer offerings. He's planning a rye porter and some smoked beers.

Beers brewed: Year-round: Summer Session Ale, Match Head Red, Sucker Punch Stout, Van Damme Good Belgian-Ale Style, and Mild at Heart. Seasonals: The style of beer brewed changes with each batch.

The Pick: The Mild at Heart is my current favorite, though it's such a new brewery that I haven't tasted everything yet. But I'm a sucker for milds, and Phil Cutti is brewing up a tasty one.

I love the feel of the place, very warm and inviting despite the sparse interior. There's a brick wall on one side, a long well-stocked bar on the other, and simple tables and chairs in between. It's all you need. The emphasis is on the food, the beer, and other drinks.

Southpaw BBQ & Southern Cooking

Opened: November 11, 2011.

Type: Brewpub.

Owners: Elizabeth Wells and Edward Calhoun.

Brewer: Phil Cutti.

Guild membership: SFBG.

System: 7-barrel Pacific Brewing Systems, 120 barrels annual capacity.

Annual production: 100 barrels (2012 estimate).

Packages available: Draft only, but growlers will likely be available in the near future.

Tours: The brewhouse is on display in the open on one side of the brewpub, so tours are self-guided.

Hours: Monday, 5 to 11:30 p.m.; Wednesday through Friday, 5 to 11:30 p.m.; Saturday and Sunday, 3 to 11:30 p.m. Closed Tuesday.

Food: BBQ and Southern regional cuisine. Appetizers, salads, and side dishes change often and seasonally, and there are weekly specials. Some unique dishes include smoked pulled goat with salsa verde, house pickles, fry bread, and smoked pork belly and P. E. I. mussels with crispy sweet potato and Match Head Red broth, not to mention Frogmore Stew, which consists of poached gulf shrimp, marble potatoes, and red corn with house-smoked ham (a whole braised hamhock) and egg noodles, shishito peppers, and mustard cream. The most popular dishes are the smoked and pulled pork shoulder, ribs (especially the dry-rubbed), and beef brisket. The menu includes many vegetarian, vegan, and gluten-free options. I particularly loved the warm potato chips and the hush puppies.

Extras: Southpaw may soon offer a bluegrass brunch once a month, as well as monthly classes on food, beer, and cocktails.

Speakeasy Ales & Lagers

1195 Evans Avenue, San Francisco, CA 94124
415-642-3371 • www.goodbeer.com
Twitter @speakeasybeer
Facebook.com/SpeakeasyBeer

Speakeasy was founded in 1997 by Forest Gray along with Steve Bruce, who now runs the iconic Toronado Pub. The brewery was originally closer to downtown, but around 2000, it was relocated to its present location in Hunter's Point. Now that more than a decade has gone by, I think we can safely say the move was a good one, as it's allowed the brewery to grow—and keep growing—as the popularity of its big beers with an attitude has skyrocketed.

As the brewery has grown into the space, more and more events take place there, with regular open hours every Friday and Saturday. Food trucks are generally parked outside, and free concerts are often held on the grounds. Sometime in 2013, the brewery will be opening a new taproom and is planning to be open from Tuesday through Saturday. Keep an eye on the website and Facebook page for current information on the days and times the brewery is open to the public, as well as for the occasional special event.

The brewery was named for that peculiar institution of Prohibition. Back in those dark days when beer was illegal, what made the Roaring Twenties roar was the speakeasy—an illicit bar where one needed to "speak easy" to gain admittance, usually with a password. Inside these dark, seedy rooms flowed bathtub gin, homemade hooch, and beer of questionable quality. They also usually served food and had entertainment, often jazz bands and even burlesque shows. The police either were paid to look the other way or did so willingly, especially in big cities, where the speakeasy flourished. Before and during Prohibition, the nation was split along urban and rural lines. At that time, when the United States was still mostly agrarian, a rural majority was able to get Prohibition passed. So in the big cities, where almost everyone opposed it—includ-

Beers brewed: Year-round: Big Daddy IPA, Prohibition Ale, The Witness, Payback Porter, and Double Daddy IIPA. Seasonals: Butchertown Black Ale, Scarlett Red Rye, Vendetta IPA, Scarface Imperial Stout, Betrayal Imperial Red, Tallulah India Pale Lager, Dolores Pale Ale, Old Godfather Barleywine, and Anniversary Triple IPA. New occasional releases: the Bootlegger Series, the Syndicate Series of barrel-aged beers, and the Brewer's Reserve Series (draft-only offerings).

ing many police officers, judges, and government officials—they were tacitly allowed to exist. By one estimate, as many a hundred thousand speakeasies flourished in New York City alone.

When Gray opened his brewery sixty-four years after Prohibition ended, he wanted to bring back San Francisco's rich brewing traditions and also have some fun with the clichés and traditions of the speakeasy. All of Speakeasy's beers are named for some aspect of the Prohibition era, using jazz era slang, mobster lingo, and bootlegger jargon. As the brewery has increased production, it has also expanded distribution, and its beers are now available throughout California and five additional states, including a few on the East Coast.

Between the wonderful regular beers and the several seasonal and special series that head brewer Kushal Hall is creating, it's certainly a good thing you no longer need to know the password to get to the beer.

Speakeasy Ales & Lagers

Opened: August 25, 1997.

Type: Production brewery, with taproom.

Owner: Forest Gray.

Brewer: Kushal Hall.

Guild membership: BA, CCBA, SFBG, NCBG.

System: 15-barrel single infusion mash tun, with 20-barrel steam-fired kettle, 30,000 barrels annual capacity.

Annual production: 18,500 barrels (2012 estimate), increasing to an estimated 27,500 in 2013.

Packages available: 12-ounce bottles in six-packs, 22-ounce bottles, and 5- and 15.5-gallon kegs. Growlers are also available, but only at the taproom.

Tours: Speakeasy's brewmaster leads a free tour most Fridays around 4:30; call ahead first to ensure that he'll be leading a tour.

Hours: Friday and Saturday, 4 to 9 p.m.; plans are afoot to expand their hours.

Food: Food trucks park at the brewery every Friday, providing food for hungry patrons. You also may bring in your own food, if you prefer.

Extras: Free concerts and events regularly take place at the brewery; check out the website for up-to-date details. The taproom is family-friendly, and there's ample seating and an outdoor smoking patio.

Gift shop: Shirts, hats, sweatshirts, bottle openers, and pint glasses are available online and at the brewery.

Thirsty Bear Brewing Company

• EST. 1996 •

661 Howard Street, San Francisco, CA 94105
415-974-0905 • www.thirstybear.com
Twitter @thirstybearbrew
Facebook.com/pages/ThirstyBear-Brewing-Company

Thirsty Bear's founder, Ron Silberstein, was grinding out a living as an immigration attorney, feeling that he was doing good work but it was not exactly making him a happy camper—or in his case, happy brewer. He'd been homebrewing for several years, and dreaming of switching careers, when a headline in the local newspaper caught his eye: "Thirsty Bear Bites Man for Cold Beer." That was 1991. He clipped out the article and hung it on his refrigerator as an inspiration for the next phase of his life. When he finally opened his brewery five years later, in 1996, he named it Thirsty Bear after that incident, which had involved a circus bear in Ukraine that, according to the story, bit a patron on the hand and made off with his beer. Police found the bear sleeping it off in a nearby park that same night.

Silberstein opened his brewpub with a simple philosophy: he wanted to combine two of the most social foods and beverages, beer and tapas, or appetizers. Having lived in Madrid for a few years, he found that Spanish cuisine was a perfect fit, because the tradition for small plates to be shared was a natural for his concept of beer as a social lubricant. It was also as far as possible from the typical "pub grub" that so many other brewpubs were offering at the time. Since opening, Silberstein has continued to place great emphasis on the quality of the food, and the entire brewery and restaurant is certified organic; in fact, Thirsty Bear was San Francisco's first brewery to achieve this. And it shows, as Thirsty Bear's food is a cut above the average, with everything on the menu being well thought out, using local ingredients whenever possible, and most important, tasting delicious.

Brenden Dobel, who trained as a brewer in both

Beers brewed: Year-round: Polar Bear Pils, Golden Vanilla Ale, Valencia Wheat, Brown Bear Ale, Meyer ESB, Kozlov Stout, and Howard St. IPA (all certified organic by the CCOF). Seasonals: Black Bear Lager (spring), Edelweiss Hefe-Weizen (summer), Golden Hallucination (summer), Full Belly Ale (fall), Wet Hop Ale (fall), Oktobearfest (fall), Hibernator Doppelbock (winter), and Bearley Legal Barley Wine (winter). Throughout the year, they release barrel-aged and soured beers in their Stave Series. Bottled Gluten Free Beer is also available, and cask-conditioned ales are dry hopped in the firkin each day.

California and Germany, joined Thirsty Bear more than ten years ago and has really put his mark on the beer. Although he's a native San Franciscan, his mother is German, and as a result, he spent some time as a child living in Germany and also worked in Bavarian breweries for a year before returning to brew in the Bay Area. While Dobel brews a variety of beers in different traditions, what sets him apart is his German-style lagers, which few brewpubs take the time to make, along with the cask-conditioned beers that are served at the brewery restaurant. His beers are all food-friendly and seemingly designed to pair perfectly with the eclectic menu.

The Pick: I'm partial to Dobel's Black Bear Lager, a nutty, smooth schwarzbier with toasted malt and lightly chocolate notes. Unfortunately, it's only available in the spring.

Everything about Thirsty Bear is unique—the beers, the extensive and tasty menu, the entertainment available, the whole experience—and it's unlike any other brewpub I know of. I think that's because Silberstein's approach is a little different. He thought first about the experience people visiting his place should have and has designed the elements within his control to give people something different. It's not just your average brewpub, and in this case that's a very good thing.

Thirsty Bear Brewing Company

Opened: September 13, 1996.

Type: Brewpub.

Owner: Ron Silberstein.

Brewer: Brenden Dobel.

Guild membership: BA, SFBG, CCBA.

System: 15-barrel Liquid Assets, approximately 1,500 barrels annual capacity.

Annual production: Approximately 1,485 barrels in 2011.

Packages available: 2-liter growlers to go, along with 7.5- and 15.5-gallon kegs.

Tours: Available by reservation only.

Hours: Restaurant: Monday through Thursday, 11:30 a.m. to 10 p.m.; Friday, 11:30 a.m. to 11 p.m.; Saturday, noon to 11 p.m.; Sunday: 5 p.m. to 10 p.m. Bar: Open until last call daily.

Food: Authentic Spanish cuisine, which the brewpub describes as Mediterranean style from Spain. The menu features tapas and paellas and a great selection of artisan cheeses, chosen to pair with the beers. The menu changes every four to eight weeks based on seasonal availability of produce and other products. The most popular dishes include the patatas bravas, empanadillas, and paella Valenciana.

Extras: A full bar features sangria, local wines, and cocktails. There's a large banquet space upstairs. Each Sunday is a live flamenco show, with no cover.

Gift shop: T-shirts, hoodies, caps, and logo glasses are available at the brewpub.

Triple Voodoo Brewing

No public address at present, office only in San Francisco, CA
415-390-1070 (sales); 415-598-8811 (customer inquiries)
www.triplevoodoobrewing.com
Twitter @TripleVoodoo • Facebook.com/TripleVoodoo

Longtime craft beer aficionado Greg Kitchen, along with two friends, decided to turn pro in 2010 and launched Triple Voodoo during SF Beer Week 2011. They made their original deliveries to distributors in their pickup truck and continue to self-distribute in San Francisco. They've been doing brisk business in both draft and bottled beer and have gotten their beer into nearly a thousand bars, restaurants, and retailers throughout the Bay Area, concentrated in San Francisco, but also in Sacramento and parts of Southern California.

The business is located in San Francisco, but brewing is done at Devil's Canyon Brewing on the Peninsula, in Belmont, where Triple Voodoo has an alternating proprietorship license that allows its brewers to take over the brewery to create their beers using Devil's Canyon's equipment. In addition to a number of popular inventive beers that are brewed year-round, they've also started working with barrel aging and doing collaborations with other local brewers. With some of the more special barrel-aged releases, they've brewed only limited amounts, in some cases as few as thirty-six cases. For the barrel-aged version of the Grand Cru, only nineteen cases were released. As a result, some of the beers are incredibly rare and sought after. The website includes a beer finder, listing the accounts where you can find Triple Voodoo beer.

While at this point you can't visit a Triple Voodoo brewery, they have announced they'll be opening a brewery and tap room in San Francisco sometime in 2013, to be located in the Dogpatch,

Beers brewed: Year-round: Inception Belgian Style Ale, Triple Voodoo Grand Cru, Kraken Imperial Stout, and Witopia. Seasonals: White IPA (collaboration with Knee Deep Brewing), Vermilion Red IPA, Angel Honey Pale Ale, Filth Pig Oak Aged Imperial IPA, Witopia, and Kaleidoscope smoked black lager (collaboration with nine different breweries).

The Pick: As a new brewery, Triple Voodoo is trying to make a name for itself with unique interpretations of traditional Belgian styles, among other beers. The brewers have succeeded handsomely with their Belgian-style tripel, Inception, which was brewed with black currants, giving a nice intangible tartness to the sweetness, light spiciness, and big hops presence.

at 2245 Third Street, although there's no estimate when exactly it will open. Until then, you can and should find the beer at numerous California locations, both in 22-ounce bottles and on tap.

Triple Voodoo Brewing

Opened: February 2011.
Type: Alternating proprietorship.
Owners: Greg Kitchen and Aaron Chan.
Brewers: Greg Kitchen and Devin Stephens.
Guild membership: BA, CCBA, SFBG.
System: See Devil's Canyon Brewing (page 132).
Annual production: 550 barrels (estimated).
Packages available: 22-ounce bottles and 5.2- and 13.2-gallon kegs.
Gift shop: Merchandise is available on the website.

21st Amendment Brewery & Restaurant

563 Second Street, San Francisco, CA 94107
415-360-0900 • www.21st-Amendment.com
Twitter @21stAmendment
Facebook.com/21stAmendment

It's been eighty years since the 21st Amendment to the U.S. Constitution repealed Prohibition in 1933. Of the few dozen breweries that existed in San Francisco before brewing was outlawed, very few successfully reopened after Repeal. By the time of the microbrewery revolution in the early 1980s, only Anchor remained.

At that time, both Shaun O'Sullivan and Nico Freccia lived in Los Angeles. Freccia was a struggling actor, bartender, and restaurant manager. O'Sullivan was a paralegal at a large law firm. Both were homebrewers and dreamed of turning pro. Independent of one another, they both moved to the Bay Area in the early nineties to pursue their goal because of the burgeoning beer community that was brewing in and around San Francisco.

Freccia first got work at some local restaurants as a waiter and bartender, eventually moving up to manager. He also began writing about beer for the Celebrator Beer News, becoming its Bay Area correspondent, where he familiarized himself with the local breweries and learned about San Francisco's rich brewing heritage.

Meanwhile, across the Bay, Shaun O'Sullivan, a freshly scrubbed émigré from the Southland, became assistant brewer at Triple Rock Brewery in Berkeley under John Paxman. In his new capacity as Celebrator correspondent, Freccia visited Triple Rock in early 1995 and met O'Sullivan, who'd been tapped to give the brewery tour. The two kept running into each other at local beer festivals and other beer events. Then that summer, both attended the two-week brewing course at UC Davis, and during the laboratory week, they became lab partners, solidifying their friendship and sealing their fate. That fall at the Great American Beer Festival, they began talking about their mutual desire to open a brewpub. Since they couldn't both be brewers, they decided that because Shaun had professional brewing experience, he would brew, and since Nico had restaurant experience, that side of the business would fall to him.

At least, that's Shaun's version of the events; Nico remembers it differently. In his version, shortly after attending brewing school, he stopped by Triple Rock, where Shaun was working, to hang out, and it was there that the idea was first proposed over a frosty beverage in the manner of an Andy Hardy movie. "Hey, let's open a brewpub. You do the brewing and I'll do the restaurant." That was 1995, and it took five more years to bring their dream to fruition. During that time, Freccia managed the opening of a restaurant in Ghirardelli Square, while O'Sullivan became head brewer of Steelhead Brewery's new place in Fisherman's Wharf, where he learned to install a brewery system from scratch. They found a great location on Second Street near South Park and signed a lease. Then fate smiled upon them. A June 1997 vote approved the same area as the location for a new baseball stadium for the San Francisco Giants. In hindsight, it makes their decision seem almost prophetic, since the area in 1997 was mostly a wasteland of abandoned buildings and few residences.

As a brewery slowly took shape in the back, they stayed afloat by continuing to operate a coffee shop in the front that had been run by the previous tenant. Then finally, on a hot August day in 2000, their five years of planning, sweat, and hard work paid off as the 21st Amendment Brewery & Restaurant opened its doors.

The first few years were tough going, though the 21st Amendment fared better than a lot of other restaurants, many of which went under during the dot-com bust. By year five, the partners' heads were above water, and they started to relax and look for their next challenge. That turned out to be putting their beer in cans, and in 2008 the 21st Amendment became only the third California craft brewery to use cans. Initially the IPA and the popular Watermelon Wheat were hand-canned in the small brewpub brewery. But demand quickly outstripped the brewery's ability to keep up, so it has since outsourced can production to Cold Springs Brewery in Minnesota, where brewmaster O'Sullivan spends so much of his time these days

Beers brewed: Year-round: Draft only: Amendment Pale Ale, Double Trouble Imperial IPA, General Pippo's Porter, Potrero ESB, and South Park Blonde. In cans: Brew Free or Die IPA, Bitter American Extra Pale Ale, and Back in Black. Seasonals: Draft only: Lower de Boom Barley Wine, Opening Day IPA, Oyster Point Oyster Stout, and Saint Patrick O'Sullivan's Irish Red. In cans: Fireside Chat Winter Spiced Ale, Hell or High Watermelon, and Sneak Attack Cardemon Saison. Limited Release: In cans: Allies Win the War, Hop Crisis Imperial IPA, Marooned on Hog Island Oyster Stout, Lower the Boom Barley Wine, and Monk's Blood Belgian Dark Ale.

The Pick: It's tough to pick just one, because Zambo makes some terrific beers. During the summer, it's hard to beat the popular Watermelon Wheat, made with real watermelon juice and served with a watermelon wedge. Even if you're not a fan of fruit beers, this is a great beer. The watermelon is not overpowering and adds a subtle fruity character to the wheat beer. My other favorite is the heartier Back in Black, one of the best examples I've tasted of a black IPA, with nice roasted notes balancing the big hops profile.

that they gave him his own office there, while brewer David "Zambo" Zamborsky takes care of the beer at the brewpub.

Most of the names of the regular beers pay homage to the local area and its brewing heritage. On tap most days you'll find South Park Blonde, Amendment Pale Ale, Potrero E.S.B., General Pippo's Porter, and Double Trouble Imperial IPA. But brewpub-only beers change frequently, and dozens are offered throughout the year, especially in February and November. In February, the 21st Amendment works with the nearby Magnolia Gastropub for Strong Beer Month, with each offering six different—and often new—beers throughout the month. Similarly, in November, in what they call the BRU/SFO Project, each brewpub creates six new Belgian-style or Belgian-influenced beers. In addition, the 21st Amendment has several guest taps at any given time, usually local favorites, and a hard cider too. The brewery is also very active in community beer events and is a cofounder of SF Beer Week, which takes place each February.

21st Amendment Brewery & Restaurant

Opened: August 2, 2000.

Type: Brewpub, and contract brewery for the canned product.

Owners: Nico Freccia and Shaun O'Sullivan.

Brewer: David "Zambo" Zamborsky.

Guild membership: San Francisco Brewers Guild, CCBA.

System: 12-barrel Pacific Mechanical, four 12-barrel fermenters, 1,200 barrels annual capacity.

Annual production: 850 barrels at the brewpub.

Packages available: 12-ounce six-pack cans and 5- and 15.5-gallon kegs.

Tours: By appointment or walk-in when not busy.

Hours: Monday through Thursday, 11:30 a.m. to midnight; Friday and Saturday, 11:30 a.m. to 1 a.m.; Sunday, 10 a.m. to midnight.

Food: With separate lunch and dinner menus, the restaurant offers high-end pub food that includes gourmet pizza, Niman Ranch burgers, specialty sandwiches, soups, salads, and a variety of entrées that change each season. The house-made Kennebec fries are particularly good.

Extras: Kids are welcome. Upstairs in the balcony, there is a box of toys for children, and the balcony is also available for private parties. Beer School takes place each month in the balcony, and each session tackles a different beer style, providing samples and education. Check the website for scheduled times and cost.

Gift shop: T-shirts and other items are sold at the brewpub and online.

Anchor Brewing
America's Original Craft Brewer

The history of craft beer in California, and indeed the entire nation, begins in 1965, in the heart of San Francisco. On a warm day in late September, recent Stanford graduate Fritz Maytag—heir to his family's appliance empire—was having dinner at the Old Spaghetti Factory and learned that the Anchor Brewery was on the verge of going out of business. A fan of its Steam Beer, Maytag visited the brewery the next day and, for a modest investment, bought a controlling interest in the ailing business.

Fritz Maytag's importance to craft beer today cannot be overstated. When he bought the Anchor Brewery in 1965, it was one of dozens of similar regional breweries struggling against the competition from national beer brands building empires across the country.

Over the next few years, Maytag learned all there was to know about brewing and its rich traditions. He traveled to England and visited breweries there. He studied old texts. He investigated steam beer, one of America's few unique beer styles, and pieced together as best he could how it was made before Prohibition. For a full account, see "A word about . . . Steam Beer" on page 257.

Throughout the 1970s and early 1980s, Anchor Brewing introduced a number of firsts into the dwindling American beer scene. In 1971, Maytag bottled Anchor Steam Beer for the first time in modern times, though the initial bottling was just two hundred cases. It was the beginning of a prolific decade of innovation. Three years later, in 1974, the brewery first bottled its Anchor Porter, a beer style that had almost completely died out in its native England.

On April 18 of the following year, Anchor released Liberty Ale to commemorate the two hundredth anniversary of Paul Revere's ride. It was also one of the first beers to use Cascade hops, which today is the most popular hops variety used by craft brewers.

That same year saw the introduction of the first seasonal beer in modern times, Anchor Christmas beer, officially called "Our Special

Ale." For the first few years this was a brown ale, but then the brewery began creating a new recipe each year, along with a new hand-drawn label featuring a tree for each year's release, a practice that continues to this day.

In 1976, the brewery debuted Old Foghorn, the first American barleywine-style ale in modern times. The brewery was moved to its present location on Mariposa Street in 1979. That's also when Anchor began working on special projects, like the Sumerian Beer Project to make Ninkasi Beer and a spruce beer based on colonial recipes. Anchor continued to innovate, and in 1984, its Summer Beer was the first American wheat beer since Prohibition.

Anchor's reputation then, as now, was one of absolute integrity. When people considered opening microbreweries beginning around 1980, they all visited Anchor Brewery. There was simply nowhere else to go, and Maytag opened his brewery to the inquisitive, inspiring many early breweries that are still with us today, which in turn inspired the next generation of brewers. And that is why so many people consider Maytag to be the father of craft beer.

Beyond beer, Anchor began distilling in 1993, kicking off the microdistilling craze. Maytag also opened York Creek Vineyards around the same time, making wine with grapes grown on his property in the Napa Valley.

Through his commitment to quality and tradition and his numerous innovations, Fritz Maytag proved that Americans were ready for a different kind of beer—beer with flavor, diversity and history. His Anchor Brewery became an inspiration to the massive craft beer industry, which today numbers over two thousand breweries—more than at any other time in America since before 1900.

The North Bay

The North Bay is the region just above San Francisco. It's where the Golden Gate Bridge out of the city takes you, though there are also other bridges and other ways to get there. For the purposes of this book, the North Bay region includes the counties of Marin, Napa, and Sonoma. In addition to having a lot of great beer, this region is also the heart of wine country.

The three counties of the North Bay are about the same size as the island of Puerto Rico, or about one-third as big as the state of Vermont. The region has only a slightly larger combined population than the city of San Francisco, where many people commute each morning, especially from Marin. If you won't be needing your car, a great, scenic way to get to Marin is by the ferry that runs from San Francisco to Sausalito and Larkspur. If you're heading farther north, however, you will find the going much easier if you have a car. Highway 101 is the main thoroughfare coming over the Golden Gate Bridge, connecting Marin and Sonoma, and heading north.

Marin boasts a wealth of open spaces, hiking trails, and parks, not to mention Muir Woods, a family-friendly place to go for a spiritual walk among the redwoods. It was the first national park created in an urban setting, which allows easy access and pleasant, nonstressful walks through the groves of trees. Mount Tamalpais overlooks the county where, until recently, George Lucas's Skywalker Ranch was located, and the Marin County Civic Center was one of the last buildings created by famed architect Frank Lloyd Wright. Farther west are Point Reyes National Seashore and Stinson Beach.

The two outermost counties, Napa and Sonoma, are much better known for their many wineries, especially in other parts of the country.

But as the saying goes, it takes a lot of beer to make good wine, so no wonder the wine is so good, because there are plenty of wonderful breweries in this same region. Though arguably not as well known as Napa, Sonoma nonetheless is the largest producer of wine in California and is home to more than 250 wineries.

Napa is due east from Sonoma but is a little harder to get to because there are no big highways that can take you to Napa, only small, slower roads. A decade after the California gold rush, Napa had a smaller silver rush, but it didn't last very long. Before the First World War, local farmers were growing nuts and fruit, especially prunes and pears, but by the turn of the century, over 90 percent of the crops planted in Napa were wine grapes.

Before Prohibition, California grew more hops than any other state, and the area still has remnants of that long-gone industry. There's the town of Hopland in Mendocino County, for instance, and in this region you'll find Sonoma's Hop Kiln Winery, housed in an old building where hops were dried after being picked.

Baeltane Brewing

401-B Bel Marin Keys Boulevard, Novato, CA 94945
415-328-1373 • www.baeltanebrewing.com
Twitter @BaeltaneBrewing
Facebook.com/pages/Beltane-Brewing/
236136683132235

Baeltane is one of the Bay Area's newest nano-breweries, a modest brewery and tasting room in the Bel Marin Keys neighborhood of Novato. Its founder and brewer, Alan Atha, turned his homebrewing hobby into a second life, a new career, bringing into a commercial setting that spirit of experimentation that often causes homebrewers to produce interesting and unique beers. A lot of his beers are creative twists on traditional styles, many with a Belgian inspiration, while others are purely his own inventions. He has roughly ten on at any given time, along with other local breweries on guest tap.

That same creative spirit is evident in the small, cozy tasting room, which was designed to keep people engaged and interacting. To further that goal, book clubs are encouraged to meet there, and there's live music that's acoustic so that conversation continues to be king. The space has an antibrewery feel, with very little breweriana. Instead, it's decorated in a comfortable chic that's sparse but inviting. You'll know your neighbors. Tables and chairs are made from recycled materials, and a bench seat in the window is a cozy spot to sit and take it all in. It's like going over to a friend's house for a beer in his rec room.

The brewery was named for Baeltane, or Beltane, the Gaelic festival held May 1 in ancient Ireland, Scotland, and the Isle of Man to mark the traditional start of summer. It's still observed today in certain new age circles, but it is celebrated each and every day at Baeltane Brewing.

Beers brewed: Year-round: Automne Eve, Black Moria Black Double IPA, Corsair Dark Strong Ale, En Suite Saison, Fleuret Golden Ale, The Frog That Ate the World, Luminesce Tripel, Meritage Session IPA, Paleo Belgo, Rumplestiltskin, Sable Black IPA and Venus in Blue Jeans. Seasonals: Beleriand Barleywine, En Suite Saison Sauvage, and Friar Tuck Sour.

The Pick: Almost of all of Baeltane's beers are unique, making a favorite a tough choice. But Alan's Rumplestiltskin, an Imperial IPA made with New Zealand hops, easily gets my vote.

Baeltane Brewing

Opened: December 15, 2012.

Type: Production brewery, with tasting room.

Owners: Alan Atha and Cathy Portje.

Brewer: Alan Atha.

Guild membership: CCBA.

System: 3-barrel brewhouse with two 1.5-barrel fermenters, two 3-barrel fermenters, and one 6-barrel fermenter, 300 barrels annual capacity.

Annual production: 200 barrels (2013 estimate).

Packages available: Growlers and 5- and 15.5-gallon kegs, with bottles scheduled to be added to production in late 2013.

Tours: No tours are available, but you can see most of the brewery from your seat at the bar.

Hours: Monday through Thursday, 3 to 9 p.m.; Saturday, 1-10 p.m.; and Sunday, 2-7 p.m.

Food: No food is available in the tasting room, but you can bring your own or order out for delivery or pickup. Food trucks are parked outside at various times throughout the week.

Extras: One of the extras at Baeltane is that something is missing that's found in many beer places: there are no TVs in the tasting room. That's because, according to Atha, "camaraderie is the key!" You can enjoy a small outdoor patio, weather permitting, and from time to time, acoustic music and poetry and book readings take place in the tasting room.

Gift shop: T-shirts and glassware are available in the tasting room.

Bear Republic Brewing Company

Brewpub: 345 Healdsburg Avenue, Healdsburg, CA 95448
Production brewery: 110 Sandholm Lane, Suite 10,
    Cloverdale, CA 95425 (not open to the public)
Brewpub: 707-433-2337; brewery: 707-894-2722
www.bearrepublic.com
Twitter @brbcbrew (brewpub) / @bearrepublic (brewery)
Facebook.com/bearrepublic

There are a lot of great people in the brewing community. You'll hear me, and most everybody I know, say that all the time about almost every brewer. But even among the rarefied crowd of great beer people, Rich Norgrove stands out as one of the warmest, nicest people you could ever want to meet. All that might be enough, but he's also an amazing brewer, and because of the exemplary way he treats everyone around him, he has created an environment that includes a talented brewing staff from top to bottom, especially head brewer Peter Kruger. And it's that very attitude and atmosphere that has allowed Bear Republic to make such great beer.

In addition to brewing, Rich also served as a volunteer fireman and races stock car, all in his spare time. Both his brewing and racing passions show themselves in the names of many of Bear Republic's beers, like Racer 5—featured ever so briefly in the 2008 feature film *Speed Racer*—as well as Racer X and Hop Rod Rye.

The brewpub was founded in 1996 and is a true family affair, with two generations of Norgroves running the business. After a stint in the U.S. Army, Rich returned home to Healdsburg and began homebrewing, and the Norgroves eventually decided to open their own brewery. Since the family has been in Sonoma County for at least four generations, there was never any discussion about where to open the brewery. Over time, they've developed a deserved reputation for hoppy West Coast beers, and any trip to downtown Healdsburg will satisfy even the most diehard hophead's cravings for *Humulus lupulus*.

The brewpub is a very comfortable place, like a vacation home where you feel okay putting your feet up and just relaxing for a few pints and a meal. It's laid-back but efficient, and you feel like you never want to leave and never feel hurried. I like that about Healdsburg in general, but it is especially so in Bear Republic's brewpub. Even if the brewery had been making mediocre beer all this time, I think it still would have been a fun place to go for a drink, as the Norgroves have created an atmosphere for success in the way they've run the place. But Bear Republic has never made anything less than exceptional beer, and the brewpub didn't stay a secret for long, if in fact it ever was. Anytime you're near Healdsburg, it's hard to avoid its pull. It's just that good.

At the Great American Beer Festival in 2006, Bear Republic was thrust even more into the limelight when it was awarded the Small Brewery of the Year and Rich Norgrove was named Small Brewer of the Year. The brewery's beer has received many such accolades over the years.

In 2007, having maxed out their capacity at the downtown location, the Norgroves opened a new production brewery in nearby Cloverdale, allowing them to vastly increase the amount of beer they can make. This in turn has allowed them to expand the business into nearly thirty states, and they also have a few international accounts, like Japan and Great Britain. This keeps them racing around the country, with more plans for expansion in the works.

The Bear Republic name comes from a nickname for the original California Republic, which involved a small group of American settlers in the Bay Area declaring themselves independent from Mexico, shortly before the Mexican-American War reached the region. After the United States prevailed and what today is Sonoma County became part of America, California's state flag adopted the bear from the banner the revolutionaries used.

With their two locations, I think the Norgroves have struck just the right balance. They have managed to keep the feel of the original brewpub intact, while the production brewery has allowed them to grow well beyond the sleepy wine town of Healdsburg and make their beer available around the entire country. It's the best of both worlds,

Beers brewed: Year-round: Racer 5 IPA, Red Rocket Ale, Hop Rod Rye, Peter Brown Tribute Ale, Big Bear Black Stout, and XP Pale Ale. Seasonals: Altered Beast, Apex, Black Racer, Café Racer 15, Carburetor, Cher Ami, Crazy Ivan, Crystal Wheat, Das Koma, Double Aught, Double Rocket, El Oso, Endeavor IPA, Grand Am, Heritage Ale, Jack London ESB, Late Harvest Lager, Lucha Libre Lager, Maibock, Mach 10, Monkey High Five, Nor Cal Ale, Old Baba Yaga, Olde Scoutter's Barleywine, Racer X DIPA, Rebellion, Roggenbier, Ryevalry, Speed Bump, Stickball Alt, Volksbier, and Wine Country Wheat. Barrel-aged beers: Cuvee de Bubba, Clobberskull, Sour Crazy Ivan, Barrel Aged Heritage Ale, and Tartare.

The Pick: The Red Rocket was the first beer I ever had from Bear Republic, and I can still recall being blown away by how it was so big and hoppy yet remained well balanced. It was, and continues to be, quite a feat. In terms of popularity, Red Rocket has been eclipsed by the other hoppy offerings, like the equally delicious flagship Racer 5 IPA or the Racer X Double IPA, but I always return to the Red Rocket.

often a cliché, at its elegant best. Bear Republic has created its own peaceful revolt and in the process has been a big part of creating a California Beer Republic in Sonoma County. Viva la beer!

Bear Republic Brewing Company

Opened: January 27, 1996.

Type: Brewpub and production brewery.

Owners: Richard Norgrove Sr., Richard Norgrove Jr., Sandy Norgrove, and Tami Norgrove.

Brewer: Richard Norgrove Jr.

Guild membership: BA, CCBA, NCBG.

System: Brewpub: 17-barrel Liquid Assets; production brewery: 50-barrel JV Northwest, 75,000 barrels annual capacity.

Annual production: 55,000 barrels.

Packages available: 12-ounce six-packs, twelve-packs, and four-packs; 22-ounce bottles; 5- and 15.5-gallon kegs; plus casks and firkins of select beers.

Tours: Brewpub tours are available, but call to make a reservation ahead of your visit. The production brewery in Cloverdale is not open to the public or for tours.

Hours: Monday through Thursday, 11 a.m. to 9:30 p.m.; Friday through Sunday, 11 a.m. to 10 p.m.

Food: The brewpub carries an extensive menu of California pub-centric cuisine, that including numerous vegetarian options and dishes that are prepared with the brewery's beer. In addition to a few entrées, there are a number of inventive sandwiches and burgers, along with soups, salads, and a selection of appetizers for sharing. Look for the daily specials.

Extras: Downtown Healdsburg is a popular wine country destination, making it easy to lose an afternoon ambling around the neighborhood. The brewpub has an outdoor patio, and the entire restaurant is kid-friendly.

Gift shop: Swag is available at the brewpub and online.

Broken Drum Brewery & Wood Grill

BROKEN DRUM
BREWERY & WOOD GRILL

1132 Fourth Street, San Rafael, CA 94901
415-456-HOPS (4677) • www.brokendrum.com
Twitter @BrokenDrumBrew
Facebook.com/brokendrum

Broken Drum's name came from a joke told by the ninety-eight-year-old grandmother of the brewpub's founder. Why a broken drum? Because it can't be beat. Ba-dum-bum-ching. But that's also an apt description, because Broken Drum has everything you want in a downtown neighborhood bar and brewpub.

Noah Beery, who's also the brewer, started out like many brewpub owners, as a homebrewer. He had experience with restaurants and loved bringing people together, and he thought that adding beer was the best way to put all three of his passions together. So he attended the American Brewers Guild to become a professional brewer and opened Broken Drum.

The brewpub sits along a busy thoroughfare in downtown San Rafael, right in the heart of the city. Inside, you'll find mostly booth seating or you can sit at the bar. Floor-to-ceiling windows ensure that it's very bright during the day. As you'd expect, actual broken drums have been collected on ledges around the ceiling, and vintage alcohol posters hang on the walls.

But the best seat in the house is actually outside, on the patio. Covered with a canvas awning, it has a short glass enclosure that keeps out the wind but allows unimpeded people-watching. Diners can enjoy the warm weather that so often occurs in San Rafael at least nine months of the year.

Food is plentiful and uniformly tasty, with the namesake wood grill used to great advantage for most dishes. Whether for lunch, dinner, or a happy hour snack, you won't leave hungry . . . or thirsty.

Beers brewed: Year-round: Schwartz Lager, I.P.A., Bock, Whamber, Pale Ale, Wheat, and Terrifico. Seasonals: Summer Golden Ale.

The Pick: I suspect it's not their most popular, but I really like the Whamber, which is essentially a dark wheat beer. The aroma is all wheat and biscuits with hints of sour lemon. It's a little bigger than most, at 7.2 percent, and it gives you a warming glow with rich caramel malt flavors and subtle fruit character.

Broken Drum Brewery & Wood Grill

Opened: July 2, 1997.

Type: Brewpub.

Owners: Noah Beery.

Brewer: Noah Beery.

System: 7-barrel DME, 1,200 barrels annual capacity.

Annual production: 800 barrels (2012 estimate).

Packages available: Growlers and 3-, 5-, 7.75-, 13.2-, and 15.5-gallon kegs.

Tours: Limited to when the brewer is available.

Hours: Seven days a week, 11 a.m. to 1 a.m.

Food: Broken Drum has a big menu of pub food, with plentiful appetizers like nachos and beer-battered onion rings. The menu also features meal-worthy salads, burgers and sandwiches, several kinds of tacos and quesadillas, and some larger entrées like Achiote Mahi-Mahi Tostada and Jerk Chicken Pesto Pita.

Extras: Happy hour takes place every day from 3:30 to 6:30 p.m., with $4 beers, well drinks, and appetizers. Kids eat free seven days a week. There's a different special each day of the week: Monday has selected beers for $3, Taco Tuesday features $2.50 chicken tacos and $4 margaritas and sangria, Wednesday is trivia night with a competition for cash prizes, Thursday has a farmers' market with a live DJ beginning at 8 p.m., Friday and Saturday feature live music starting around 7 p.m., and Sunday offers Bloody Mary specials.

Gift shop: T-shirts and glassware are sold at the brewery.

Calistoga Inn Restaurant & Brewery (Napa Valley Brewing Company)

CALISTOGA INN
RESTAURANT & BREWERY

1250 Lincoln Avenue, Calistoga, CA 94515
707-942-4101 • www.calistogainn.com
or napabeer.com
Facebook.com/CalistogaInn

The original building that encompasses the Calistoga Inn was completed in 1882 and sits along the main street of downtown Napa's tourist area. The street is lined with galleries, shops, restaurants, and theaters, along with salons and day spas, several of which are on the same street as the brewpub. While many tourists flock to Napa for its wine, not everybody is a wine lover or wants wine all the time, and the Calistoga Inn has taken advantage of that by being the only brewery in town.

Downtown Napa has a lot to recommend it and makes a great weekend getaway. Many visitors park their cars and never start them up again until they're ready to leave for home. In addition to all the daytime attractions, there are a number of quaint bed-and-breakfasts both on the main street and down side streets. But if you're a beer lover, only one allows you to order freshly made beer and take it to your room.

UC Davis graduate Michael Dunsford, along with his mother, Rosie, opened the Calistoga Inn in 1987, and it was the first commercial brewery in the entire county since before Prohibition. The brewery is located in a separate building in the back, in what was originally the water tower. All the beer produced is sold at the inn, in one of its two full bars, an air-conditioned pub and a patio bar, or in 22-ounce bottles sold only on the premises.

The eighteen-room inn is a charming European-style hotel, which means that while there are sinks in every room, guests share a community bathroom and shower. Each room is clean, quirky, and perhaps most important, comfortable. The décor

Beers brewed: Year-round: Wheat Ale, Pilsner, Calistoga Red Ale, and Calistoga Porter. Seasonals: A.S.B. (American Special Bitter), Barley Wine, Dugan Oatmeal Stout, Diplopia D.P.A., English Best Bitter, Saison du Calistoga, Belgian Tripel, Abbet Style Dubbel, R.I.P.A. (Red India Pale Ale), German Kolsch, Patriotic Pale Ale, Purple Haze, Pumpkin Witbiere, Belgian Pale Ale, RyeP.A., India Pale Ale, Oktoberfest, and Blitzen I.P.A.

The Pick: The Porter that Napa Valley Brewing makes is a really nice example of the style, with bittersweet chocolate and dry coffee notes. It also has some great complexity—earthy, roasty, bitter flavors with hints of tobacco, leafy herbs, and black tea.

is rustic chic, with lots of turn-of-the-century antiques. The room rate is modest for the area and includes a continental breakfast. The sunny restaurant has seating both indoors and on the patio outside, next to the brewery. The patio overlooks the Napa River, which runs past the inn's backyard.

In late August 2012, an electrical fire broke out in the middle of the night, damaging the roof, the upper floors, and other parts of the building to the tune of half a million dollars. The hotel, restaurant, and brewery closed temporarily while the entire building was repaired and refurbished. The Calistoga Inn is now open again and looks better than ever, with the same beer brewed out back.

Calistoga Inn Restaurant & Brewery (Napa Valley Brewing Company)

Opened: 1987, incorporated May 5, 1989.

Type: Brewpub.

Owners: Michael Dunsford and Rosie Dunsford.

Brewer: Brad Smisloff.

Guild membership: BA, CCBA.

System: 7-barrel brewhouse.

Annual production: 450 barrels.

Packages available: 22-ounce bottles and draft only at the brewpub.

Tours: Brewery tours are available Monday through Friday, but please call in advance to make a reservation.

Hours: Sunday through Tuesday, 8 a.m. to 11 p.m.; Wednesday, 8 a.m. to midnight; Thursday through Saturday, 8 a.m. to 11 p.m.

Food: The restaurant has separate lunch and dinner menus. The lunch menu has a selection of sandwiches and luncheon plates like fish tacos, risotto, and pasta. The dinner menu features a nice variety of both small plates, such as pot roast, baby back ribs, and steamed clams and mussels, and large plates, including chicken, duck breast, and lamb shank. Both menus also offer starters and greens. Brunch is served from 10 a.m. to 3 p.m. each Saturday and Sunday, with breakfast entrées as well as most of the lunch menu items.

Extras: The grounds have banquet space for a variety of private events. Live jazz music is featured on the patio during the warmer months. The inn also hosts special dinners on select holidays throughout the year. Check the website for details.

Dempsey's Restaurant & Brewery

EST. 1991

50 East Washington Street, Petaluma, CA 94952
707-765-9694 • www.dempseys.com

Dempsey's is a hidden gem. Because of where it's located, it's tucked out of sight, around the corner on the end of the Golden Eagle Center, a shopping center in downtown Petaluma. But once you round that corner, you find a picturesque other world, with outdoor seating that overlooks the Petaluma River. You can escape for a meal right in the middle of town.

Inside, there's a spacious bar and restaurant area to your right, with a smaller, more intimate hallway with additional seating to your left. You can see the brewery behind glass from the hallway. But if the weather is right, your best seat is outside. I always choose to sit outside when it's warm enough, which is most of the time.

While Peter Burrell, who's been the owner and brewer there for more than twenty years, makes a nice array of beers, what really sets the place apart is just how good the food is. It surprises me whenever I eat there and is a treat every time. Dempsey's is such a casual, unassuming looking place, but whatever you order will blow you away. In that sense, it's also a figurative hidden gem.

Many of the ingredients used in the dishes come from cofounder Bernadette Burrell's Red Rooster Ranch, a biodynamic farm that grows organic produce and keeps chickens too. The rest are locally sourced from nearby farmers. So while this is a great place to go for a beer, also make sure to stay for the food.

Beers brewed: Year-round: Sonoma Irish Ale, Red Rooster Ale, Petaluma Strong Ale (PSA), Ugly Dog Stout, Rusty Rye, Biere DeMunck, and Petaluma Pale Ale. Seasonals: Sonoma Mountain Wheat (spring/summer), Anniversary Barleywine (winter, aged versions on at brewer's choice), 707 Wet Hop Ale, Pale Bock, American Bock, Riverside Rye, Tank #9 Barley Wine, Winter Wheat, Weizenbock, IPA, and Golden Ale.

The Pick: My go-to beer here is the PSA, the Petaluma Strong Ale, which, despite its name, is just a little over 7 percent ABV, putting it in range of the average IPA. And while it has a nice hops character, the generous pale malts give it good balance and complexity.

Dempsey's Restaurant & Brewery

Opened: December 7, 1991.

Type: Castro brewpub.

Owner: Peter Burrell.

Brewer: Peter Burrell.

Guild membership: BA, CCBA.

System: 14-barrel JV Northwest, 2,000 barrels annual capacity.

Annual production: 500 barrels.

Packages available: 22-ounce bottles, growlers, and kegs.

Tours: Self-guided tours are available; just look through the windows to see the brewery.

Hours: Sunday through Thursday, 11:30 a.m. to 9 p.m.; Friday through Saturday, 11:30 a.m. to 2 a.m.

Food: All of the food is made with fresh, local ingredients. The menu changes with the seasons, and there are new special menu items daily for both lunch and dinner. The menu includes something for everyone, with numerous salads and vegetarian dishes, wood-fired pizza, burgers, sandwiches, pork chops, chicken, and fresh fish, along with Asian and Mexican cuisine. And don't miss the unique starters, like Dave's red chili pretzels, beer-spiked olives, or the "best darn pickles."

Extras: There is picturesque outdoor seating overlooking the Petaluma River. The restaurant is family-friendly.

Gift shop: T-shirts, sweatshirts, hats, and pint glasses are available from the bar.

Divine Brewing Company

www.divinebeer.com

Kevin Robinson is an old-school brewer who focuses on one thing only—brewing beer. He doesn't care for the term *brewmaster*. As he modestly puts it, "I am a brewer. That is all." Robinson has brewed for a number of Bay Area breweries, including Speakeasy and Lagunitas. He also spent some time making wine at the V. Sattui Winery, an experience he's brought into the sphere of his beermaking. He currently brews at Russian River Brewing, while moonlighting with his own Divine Brewing enterprise. His license is an alternating proprietorship, which allows him to brew on the system at Sonoma Springs, owned by his friend Tim Goeppinger, whom he met when they both worked at Lagunitas.

All of Kevin's beer is bottled. He has no plans to keg his beer. If you want to know why, buy him a beer. He claims it's a not too long but boring story, involving the way kegs are treated when they leave the brewery. Currently he brews two beers, one on each equinox, and plans to add a summer and winter beer for each solstice. The two beers, Teufelweizen and Engelen Tarwe, each use three strains of yeast, including one wine yeast. As a result, they don't hew to any specific style. The Teufelweizen is closest to a German weizenbock, while the Engelen Tarwe resembles a Belgian-style tripel or similar strong beer. His beers are designed to be aged, unlike most beers. He wants them to be at home on a white linen tablecloth. That's why the black labels are as simple and unbeerlike as possible.

Robinson is searching for a location for a Divine Brewery, but he's not in any hurry. As the brewery's motto, "Refuse to compromise," suggests, there will be a new brewery only when he's found the perfect spot.

Beers brewed: Engelen Tarwe (spring) and Teufelweizen (fall).

The Pick: The Teufelweizen is brown with a complex aroma of vinous character coupled with fruit, nuts, and a German-style hefeweizen yeast's signature banana and clove undercurrent. Surprisingly, these disparate components meld together handsomely. Pitted fruits, roasted malt, and bittersweet chocolate lead to a satisfying dry finish. The mélange of flavors is equally harmonious.

Divine Brewing Company

Opened: September 23, 2011.

Type: Alternating proprietorship.

Owner and brewer: Kevin Robinson.

System: See Sonoma Springs Brewing (page 113).

Annual production: 25 barrels (2012).

Packages available: 750-milliliter bottles.

Downtown Joe's Brewery & Restaurant

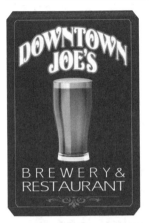

902 Main Street, Napa, CA 94559
707-258-2337 • www.downtownjoes.com
Twitter @DTJoeNapa • Facebook.com/dtjoes

The Oberon building in downtown Napa was constructed in 1894 and has been an entertainment center ever since. Since 1993, it's been the site of a brewpub originally started by Joe Ruffino and Joe and Nancye Peatman. Ruffino's grandmother Grace had opened Ruffino's Restaurant in 1944, which was located on nearby First Street. The Peatmans bought out Ruffino in 2004 and have run Downtown Joe's alone ever since. Joe Peatman's family first came to the Napa Valley from Italy in the 1800s to make wine, and Joe is fifth-generation Napa.

The brewpub is located along the Napa River right next door to Veterans Memorial Park. From the back outdoor patio, overlooking the river, you can bird-watch and enjoy the sunshine. There's also a side patio that borders the park.

The restaurant is an American grill with a changing menu of traditional dishes, including vegetarian and gluten-free choices. Chefs Bernabe Leon and Gaspar Montoya have been creating the food there since the beginning. The restaurant and the full sports bar have separate entrances. If you want to have a beer and watch TV, the street entrance is what you want. If you're hungry, enter on the side, by the park.

The brewery is located in the center of the building, between the bar and a back dining room that's slightly raised over the outdoor patio and also overlooks the river. Much of the brewery was recently retrofitted and refurbished, although the custom-built copper brewhouse is still intact. It was originally built in 1988 by Moonlight Brewing's Brian Hunt and Chuck Ankeny, a descendant of the Hamm's beer dynasty of Milwaukee. Hunt

Beers brewed: Year-round: Lazy Summer American Wheat, Golden Ribbon Pale Ale, Tail Waggin' Amber Ale, Golden Thistle Very Bitter Ale, Tantric IPA, Overdue Porter, Double Secret Probation IPA, and one stout, either Worthy's Leprechaun Stout or Old Magnolia Oatmeal Stout. Seasonals: Catherine the Great Imperial Stout, Double Indemnity IPA, Lou Paine's Pale Ale, James Brown Ale, Harvest Ale, Oberon Altbier, Dancing Feet Red Wheat, What She's Having Pilsner, I'll Be Bock, Raspberry Blonde Ale, Past Due Dark, DIX ESB, Smooth Operator Malt Liquor, Temptation Dark Ale, Slip Knot Imperial Stout, Victory Dark Ale, Maggie May Bock, Ruddy Mutton Irish Red, High Five Celebration Ale, Sunset Red Lager, and Tripple Dog Dare You!

left in 1999 to start Moonlight, and the brewing fell to Lance McGlaughlin, who hired Colin Kaminski to brew part-time over the summer.

By 2003, Kaminski became brewmaster and overhauled the recipes. He began using British malts, since the brewery was originally conceived as an English alehouse. He keeps between ten and thirteen house beers on at any given time. Six of them are usually the same, and throughout the year he rotates a wide variety of changing beers. He coauthored a book with well-known homebrewing expert John Palmer, titled *Water: A Comprehensive Guide for Brewers*, scheduled to be published in 2013 by Brewers Publications.

The brewpub has become a downtown institution for locals as well as many tourists who come to Napa for the wine and look for something else while they're there. You couldn't ask for a better location, and it helps that Kaminski makes beer that's every bit as good as Napa's wine.

Downtown Joe's Brewery & Restaurant

Opened: January 20, 1993.

Type: Brewpub.

Owner: Joe Peatman.

Brewer: Colin Kaminski.

Guild membership: BA.

System: 7-barrel hand-built brewhouse, with Zaft Copper Works kettles, six fermenters, and eighteen aging tanks; 1,200 barrels annual capacity.

Annual production: 800 barrels (2012).

Packages available: Draft only at the brewpub.

Tours: Brewery tours are available when the brewer is there. Ask if he's around, and he'll be happy to show you the brewery if he has the time.

Hours: Monday through Friday, 8 a.m. to 1 a.m.; Saturday and Sunday, 8 a.m. to 2 a.m.

Food: A full menu of American cuisine includes "pub fare," such as Buffalo wings and fish and chips, as well as burgers, sandwiches, salads, seafood, and other entrées like rosemary polenta, lemon chicken fettuccini, and a smoked pastrami Rueben. There's also a separate kids' menu and a selection of desserts. Happy hour takes place every weekday, and daily specials include Meatloaf Monday and Wing Ding Tuesday.

Extras: Live music and DJ Nights. Twelve big-screen TVs are tuned to various sporting events. Downtown Joe's also hosts special events during holidays and prominent sporting events. The bar carries a selection of local craft beers on guest tap and in bottles.

Gift shop: T-shirts, hats, and more are available at the brewpub and online.

Healdsburg Beer Company

1670 Stirrup Loop, Healdsburg, CA 95448
707-385-9385 • www.healdsburgbeercompany.com
Twitter @Healdsbrew
Facebook.com/pages/Healdsburg-Beer-Company/
    105257845911

The Healdsburg Brewing Company defines what it means to make handcrafted, artisan beers. It's essentially a one-man operation that Kevin McGee runs out of his home, or more accurately, his detached garage. You'd be hard-pressed to find a smaller commercial brewery. And he's been brewing there since 2007, making him one of the first in the new class of nanobrewers, whose numbers have been steadily increasing over the last few years.

Back in 2007, the idea of operating so small a brewery was still a novel concept, and few understood it or believed it could be viable. At the time, McGee was an attorney for Kendall-Jackson vineyard and winery, working directly with founder Jess Jackson. After several difficult and frustrating weeks trying to figure out the best way to restructure the business more efficiently, McGee—who'd been an avid homebrewer for several years—went home and penciled out a business plan to put a brewery in his garage. The next day at work, he jokingly told Jackson, whom he counted as a friend, that the solution to the winery's business was to make beer. And then he showed him the hastily made business plan. They spent the talking about beer and the brewery business. At the end of the day, Jackson told McGee that he really should start the brewery. Jackson was convinced it could be done.

And that's exactly what he did. By day, McGee continues his life as a typical Sonoma County attorney holding down a job and feeding his family. By night and weekends, however, his passions emerge and he toils in his makeshift brewhouse making English-style cask beer right smack dab in the middle of hophead heaven. He does it to set himself apart from the pack, and also because it's what he likes to drink. As he puts it, he "sweats the details on every pint," and it shows. These are true handcrafted beers.

Beers brewed: Year-round: The Alexander Cask (English-style IPA), The Lytton Cask (porter), The Fitch Cask (California golden ale), and The H3 (an anniversary ale). Seasonals: McGee's Green Beer, an organic pale ale available for St. Patrick's Day, and The Brown & Sexy Ale, brewed whenever he's in the mood.

McGee's beer is available only on draft and can be found at about a dozen select area restaurants, most in the downtown Healdsburg area, as close to the source as possible. That's because he firmly believes beer's highest purpose is to be enjoyed with good food. Seven regular accounts make up the core of the brewery's business. Each place is one that McGee loves walking into and seeing the people there. The people at every one of them either were already friends when he started or have become friends since he began delivering beer. That's what it means to be an artisanal nanobrewery.

Healdsburg Brewing Company

Opened: November 2007.

Type: Production nanobrewery.

Owner: Kevin McGee.

Brewer: Kevin McGee.

Guild membership: BA, CCBA.

System: Custom built 1-barrel brewhouse, 365 barrels annual capacity.

Annual production: 25 barrels.

Packages available: 5-gallon casks only.

Gift shop: T-shirts, sweatshirts, hats, and stickers are available online.

The Pick: I like the antidote to West Coast hops bombs, the Alexander Cask, an IPA that bucks the trend so common here that if some hops are good, then more hops are always better. The Alexander is in the British tradition of having just slightly more pronounced hops than a pale ale, giving it a more subtle tang. Healdsburg's version hits all the right notes, though it's a touch more perfumy in the nose. But its big malt backbone gives it a nice balance, and the English hops—Fuggles and East Kent Goldings—shine in the finish and leave you wanting more.

HenHouse Brewing Company

HENHOUSE
BREWING COMPANY
PETALUMA, CALIFORNIA
henhousebrewing.com

133-D Copeland Street, Petaluma, CA 94952
707-762-4769 • www.henhousebrewing.com
Twitter @HenHouseBrewing
Facebook.com/pages/HenHouse-Brewing-Company/
211269008902745

You might not know it to walk the streets of Petaluma today, but there was a time when it was the egg capital of the world. The egg incubator was invented there in 1879, and chickens and eggs were once its main source of income. Although most of that business has since flown the coop, the area remains deeply rooted in dairy and agriculture, and the remnants of its past linger everywhere you look.

Unlike most of the Bay Area, Petaluma was relatively unharmed by the great earthquake of 1906, and as a result, the downtown area has a large number of pre-earthquake and Victorian buildings. The brewery, although in an old manufacturing facility, is right in the heart of town, just a short walk from its shopping district. In fact, the building now occupied by one of Petaluma's newest breweries, HenHouse Brewing Company, used to be the home of an egg processing plant.

Unfortunately, it's not currently open to the public, so trying to walk to it will do you no good. But the beer is available in local markets and bars. And maybe, just maybe, someday in the far future—if the owners have their way—it will morph into a brewpub. They're also launching both a barrel program and a sour program, but it will be some time before the fruits of those efforts are brought to market. One of the first they'll likely release will be a sour saison.

For now, the three Petaluma founders are content just selling what they can make, with three beers regularly appearing in bottles, which they also self-distribute. All of the bottling is done by hand, a very labor-intensive process. The brewing equipment harks back to an earlier time, when

Beers brewed: Year-round: Belgian Golden Ale, Saison, and Oyster Stout. One-offs: Imperial Stout.

The Pick: I personally love the Saison, a spicy beer brewed with black pepper and coriander. It's nicely effervescent and zesty, and in addition to the expected pepper and coriander, there are aromas of lemon citrus, flowers, and Belgian yeast. The flavors are equally complex and refreshing, and I suspect this beer would pair nicely with many challenging food dishes. The spicing is what really sets it apart, and it also has a great dry finish that leaves you wanting more.

new brewing equipment was impossible to find and brewers made do with what they could find and make. The mash tun used to be an essential oil extractor, and the boil kettle was originally used for root beer syrup in the 1950s but has been completely refurbished for beer.

The brewery shares space with Rogue Research, a company that makes dietary supplements, cosmetics, and soap. Two of HenHouse's founders, Shane Goepel and Scott Goyne, work for Rogue and subleased space there, where they can brew only on the weekends. The brewing equipment is locked up behind bars, in two caged areas mandated by the California ABC, and some of the equipment, notably the mash tun, kettle, and fermenters, are rolled out during brew times.

Goyne is a certified herbalist and is the self-styled mad scientist of the trio. Goepel is more analytical, agonizes over the recipes, and is reputed to be a walking brewing encyclopedia. And although all three pitch in to do the brewing, Collin McDonnell has the most experience. During the week, he works as a professional brewer at Drake's in San Leandro. He interned with Brenden Dobel at Thirsty Bear, before working at Devil's Canyon and then part-time simultaneously at 21st Amendment and Beach Chalet, an experience that left him well prepared for brewing at HenHouse and Drake's concurrently.

But all three have been friends since they were kids and grew up in the Petaluma area. They're firmly committed to making HenHouse a local institution, one bottle at a time. Honestly, they're off to a great start, and this should be a brewery to watch . . . and drink their beers.

HenHouse Brewing Company

Opened: January 24, 2012.
Type: Production brewery.
Owners: Shane Goepel, Scott Goyne, and Collin McDonnell.
Brewers: Shane Goepel, Scott Goyne, and Collin McDonnell.
System: 2-barrel custom built brewhouse, 80 barrels annual capacity.
Annual production: 80 barrels.
Packages available: 22-ounce bottles and kegs (wholesale only).
Tours: No brewery tours are available at this time.
Gift shop: T-shirts and glassware are available online.

Iron Springs Pub & Brewery

763A Center Boulevard, Fairfax, CA 94930
415-485-1005 • www.ironspringspub.com
Twitter @ironspringspub
Facebook.com/ironspringspub

The Iron Springs Pub & Brewery was born when Mike and Anne Altman bought the Ross Valley Brewing Company in 2004 and transformed it into today's brewpub. Altman grew up on Long Island, New York, but moved to Portland, Oregon, to brew at McMenamins Edgefield, and then spent seven years brewing in Boulder, Colorado, at the Mountain Sun Pub & Brewery.

For the first few years, Altman did all the brewing himself, but in 2008, he hired former Triple Rock brewer Christian Kazakoff as head brewer. Kazakoff had caught the brewing bug shortly after spending several years aboard U.S. Navy aircraft carriers. His first job was in the kitchen of the Berkeley brewpub Triple Rock Alehouse & Brewery. In no time, he began homebrewing and volunteering in the brewpub brewery. After a trip to the Oregon Brewers Festival, he realized that brewing was his true calling and immersed himself in learning all he could. He completed the American Brewers Guild brewing course and also became Triple Rock's head brewer in 1999.

Between Kazakoff and Altman, plus assistant Phil Meeker, they've considerably improved the small brewpub's beers. Iron Springs has started bottling four of its popular beers and created a real ale program of cask beers. It has also launched a Chocolate Beer Month at the brewpub, as well as Brewed and Cultured in Marin events, pairing its beer with local artisan cheese. The equipment has been upgraded over the years, including the

Beers brewed: Year-round: Kent Lake Kolsch-style Ale, Alsatian Pale Ale, Chazz Cat Rye, JC Flyer I.P.A., Casey Jones Imperial I.P.A., Epiphany Ale, Anne Marie's Amber, Flashover Porter, Fairfax Coffee Porter, and Sless' Oatmeal Stout. Winter seasonals: Black Magic Rye, Late Seasonal Draught, and Edwin's Winterscotch. Spring seasonals: The Crippla' Double Pale Ale, Honey Blonde Ale, Thriller Mai Bock, and Helles Angels Lager. Summer seasonals: El Jefe Hefeweizen and Czechered Past Pilsner. Fall seasonals: Dark Path Lager, Oktoberfest Lager, and Harvest Epiphany Ale. One-off beers: Revolutionary Garde, La Guillotine, Bing Cherry Bourbon Stout, Chardonnay Barrel Rye Ale, Chardonnay Barrel Rye Ale with Candy-Cots, Bourbon Barrel Aged Bear's Deadicale English-Style Barleywine, Platypus Spiced Ale, Mocha Porter, Chocolate Stout, and an *altbier.*

recent replacement of the open fermenters with brand new conical fermenters.

One of the most unusual features of Iron Springs can often be seen making deliveries throughout Marin County: the Ambrewlance, a former ambulance that Altman bought and converted into a rolling taphouse and beer delivery van that runs on vegetable oil from the restaurant. At local beer festivals, Iron Springs beer is served from the taps built into the side of the van.

The Pick: Kazakoff's Casey Jones Imperial I.P.A. is a favorite, with a big floral, spicy, and citrus nose and big grapefruit and tart flavors, and a quiet malt backbone that stays in the shadows and lets the hops shine brightly.

The brewpub recently became a Green Certified Business by the Marin County Community Development Agency, and in 2008 it was voted one of the top ten Green Businesses in the Bay Area. All of its food is likewise made with fresh, local ingredients, using no trans fat. The bread is baked locally every day, and all of the sauces and dressings used in the restaurant are made from scratch. But the best reason to visit Iron Springs is the beer.

Iron Springs Pub & Brewery

Opened: October 8, 2004 (the original brewery opened in 1998).

Type: Brewpub.

Owners: Michael and Anne Altman.

Brewers: Christian Kazakoff (head brewer) and Phil Meeker (lead brewer).

Guild membership: BA, CCBA, NCBG.

System: 10-barrel Specific Mechanical, 1,600 barrels annual capacity.

Annual production: 1,400+ barrels (2012 estimate).

Packages available: 22-ounce bottles, growlers, and 5-gallon kegs.

Tours: Brewery tours are available by appointment only.

Hours: Monday and Tuesday, 4 to 10 p.m.; Wednesday through Sunday, noon to 10 p.m.

Food: Serves what it aptly calls "refined pub food with a Latin and Asian slant." The menu includes a dozen appetizers and really good fries. There are also bigger entrées like Par Roasted Chicken and Miguel's Famous Poc Chuc, and weekly specials include fish and chips and oysters. Iron Springs also offers kid-friendly fare and quick "hop sack lunches" that can be made to go. Each hop sack includes a ready-made dish, such as an avocado roll-up or grilled meatloaf Reuben.

Extras: Live music on Wednesday and Saturday afternoons. The pub is family-friendly and has dog-friendly heated outdoor seating. There are televisions for big games, but the sound is turned off. Daily specials include Give Back Tuesday, when a portion of the day's proceeds are donated to a local charity; and both Cask Thursday and T-Shirt Thursday, with happy hour pricing if you wear your Iron Springs T-shirt.

Gift shop: T-shirts, hoodies, and glassware are sold exclusively at the brewpub.

Lagunitas Brewing Company

1280 North McDowell Boulevard, Petaluma, CA 94954
707-769-4495 • www.lagunitas.com
Twitter @lagunitasbruhws (brewhouse) /
  @lagunitasT (owner Tony Magee)
Facebook.com/LagunitasBrewingCo /
  Facebook.com/LagunitasTapRoom

One of the fastest-growing brands in the country, Lagunitas has been growing by leaps and bounds over the last few years. The Lagunitas brewery of today bears almost no resemblance to the one where founder Tony Magee made the first batch of Lagunitas beer nearly twenty years ago, in his kitchen in the sleepy bedroom community of Lagunitas. Magee originally considered calling the brewery West Marin Brewing but feared that the residents of East Marin would snobbishly refuse to drink his beer. He believed no one would know where Lagunitas was, plus he liked the way it sounded, so he decided it was the right name. Magee was also aware that no one but locals would be able to correctly pronounce Lagunitas, which is why every bottle, even to this day, includes the helpful "Say lah-goo-KNEE-tuss" on the label.

Tony Magee grew up in a Chicago suburb, and his first love was music. He played the piano and saxophone but briefly studied design in college, before winning a music contest. Inspired by the win, he transferred to Northern Illinois University, where he studied music. He later worked for an ad agency, writing advertising jingles, and orchestrated jingles for Philadelphia Cream Cheese, Pizza Hut, Hallmark Greeting Cards, and even Bud Light.

When that job didn't seem to be going anywhere, he took some time off and drove out to visit his father, who at that time was living in Los Angeles. Almost by accident, during that trip he was offered a job with a printing company in San Francisco, having never set foot in Northern California. When the the printing business in general, and the company he was working for, more specifically, fell on hard times, he got the idea to open his own brewery.

The initial idea came from Magee's brother, who worked for a brewpub in the Pacific Northwest, something Tony had never given any thought to before that time. He started frequenting Marin Brewing and tried making a steam beer, a California common, for no better reason than that he loved Anchor Steam Beer and it was winter, so he believed it would be easier to lager. Apparently, it didn't taste very good. The next batch, a pale ale, turned out much better. Encouraged, he rented some space down the street from his kitchen brewery, and the Lagunitas Brewing Company was born.

Ron Lindenbusch, who worked for local beer distributors in the early 1990s, stopped by the brewery and was immediately hooked, becoming one of the earliest Lagunitas employees. Today, apart from Tony and his wife, Carissa Brader, Lindenbusch has been here the longest of any Lagunitas employee, followed closely behind by Robin McClain, who is the controller.

The brewery quickly outgrew its space in Lagunitas and found a larger space in nearby Petaluma. The business changed fairly rapidly after the initial move, as the focus on pale ale shifted to IPA. Magee saw IPA as an underserved market, with few people really focusing on the style in the early 1990s, and worked to market his IPA as "the" IPA, which has been at least in part why the brewery has been so successful.

Beers brewed: Year-round: IPA, PILS, New Dog Town Pale Ale, CENSORED, Little Sumpin' Sumpin', Maximus, Imperial Stout, and Hop Stoopid. Seasonals: The Hairy Eyeball, Imperial Red, Wilco Tango Foxtrot, Undercover Investigation Shut-Down Ale, Lucky 13.alt, Lagunitas Sucks, Little Sumpin' Wild, DayTime Ale, Brown Shugga', and Cappuccino Stout. The taproom also has a rotating selection of one-off and special releases, many of which can only be found there, though a few show up at better beer bars in limited quantities.

While growth of the brewery has been steady, nearly since the beginning, in recent years it has accelerated significantly. A couple years ago, Lagunitas upgraded to an 80-barrel brewhouse, and last year he replaced that with a 250-barrel one. The past two years have again seen record growth, with sales volumes over 160,000 barrels. Initial forecasts for 2012 were a growth rate of 30 percent, but actual sales have been double that.

Lagunitas announced in 2012 that the company would be building a second brewery in Chicago, equal in size to the one in Petaluma, and the plan was for it to open in the summer of 2013. Once open, it will be Chicago's biggest brewery. Although Tony Magee continues to steer the ship, along with Lindenbusch and McClain, more experienced businesspeople have been added to strategic positions, like COO and CFO, to help Lagunitas as it grows ever larger. However, Magee is committed to keeping the same rebel sensibilities that got the brewery this far.

As Lagunitas has become a force to be reckoned with, the beer is still about telling stories. Founder Tony Magee may have handed off certain parts of the business to specialists, finance people, and even his brewmaster, Jeremy Marshall, who did a great job making Lagunitas beer more consistently good in the years he's been there, but Magee continues to write the quirky story about each beer that appears on every label and gives each beer a lot of its unique character.

Visiting the brewery has become an experience in and of itself, and it's the equal of much bigger brewery tours. If you haven't been to Lagunitas in a while, or if you've never visited it, you should, because it's one of the most amazing breweries in Northern California. It used to be housed in just two buildings, an office and the brewery, but it's now taken over quite a bit more of the industrial park on North McDowell Boulevard. What was once the office is now the taproom, with a kitchen and square central bar, where you can get a meal and all of Lagunitas's beers plus many unique ones only available there five days a week. Outside the taproom, adjacent to the brewery's business office, is a big outdoor space with large picnic tables and other seating. It's partially covered and has heating lamps scattered about for those times when the weather decides to actually turn cool or rainy.

The brewery itself has grown exponentially larger. They literally raised the roof to accommodate the new brewhouse, and the entire bottling line was moved into a large warehouse next door, where all of the beer is now pumped through pipes that run overhead. The office has taken over a two-story building, and a separate gift shop is open different hours every day of the week. Both walking tours and tasting tours are given at regular times throughout the week.

During one of the construction projects, the tons of extra dirt were used to build a small sloped amphitheater between the offices and taproom, and concerts are held here from time to time. The brewery also hosts several other functions throughout the year, the most impressive one being the Lagunitas Beer Circus, which is a spectacle to behold. The dates of this event change from year to year, so watch the Facebook page or website for details.

The Pick: Brown Shugga' is my favorite Lagunitas beer, partly because of the story behind how it came to be. It was the happiest of happy accidents. When an inadvertent brewing error in the middle of the night nearly ruined a batch of beer, the brewers cleaned out every twenty-four-hour grocery store of every package of brown sugar they could find and rescued the beer, creating what's become the brewery's annual holiday beer, Brown Shugga'. It's sweet and chewy, with big hopping and complex notes of cherries, caramel, and butterscotch cookies, but what's so remarkable is its balance and just how enjoyable it is to sip a glass of it. But it's available only at the end of each year, so during the rest of year, my pick is the wonderfully named Hop Stoopid. Originally almost a joke to see how big they could make it, the brewers managed to make one of the biggest, hoppiest beers possible, while at the same time keeping it balanced and tasting amazing. The IPA is a great everyday beer, as is Daytime, but if you want hops, hops, and more hops, go with Hop Stoopid.

Lagunitas is, to my mind, simply one of the most impressive breweries in all of Northern California. It's not the biggest, or the most well-known, or even the flashiest, but it has managed to remain true to its counterculture roots, even as it has grown large enough to be considered a respectable business, something that has crushed the spirit of many small companies as they've grown. But founder Tony Magee's unflinching commitment to remain true to his unique vision has kept Lagunitas on the right path, and that it's managed to be so successful is almost just a bonus. I'd place Lagunitas among the top two or three Northern California breweries you need to visit. Missing it would make any tour of the region's breweries incomplete. It's just that good.

Lagunitas Brewing Company

Opened: 1993.

Type: Production brewery, with taproom and beer sanctuary.

Owner: Tony Magee.

Brewer: Jeremy Marshall.

Guild membership: BA, CCBA.

System: 250-barrel Rolec brewhouse, 80-barrel Rolec, 750,420 barrels annual capacity.

Annual production: 230,420 barrels (2012 estimate).

Packages available: 12-ounce bottles in six-packs, 22-ounce bottles, growlers (in the taproom), and 7.75- and 15.5-gallon kegs.

Tours: Tasting tours are available Monday through Friday at 3 p.m. Walking tours, which do not include any tasting, are available Wednesday through Friday at 5 p.m. and Saturday and Sunday at 1, 3, and 5 p.m. No reservations are required for any of the tours, but you need to have an ID for the tasting tours.

Hours: Office: Monday through Friday, 9 a.m. to 5 p.m. Taproom: Wednesday through Friday, 2 to 9 p.m.; Saturday and Sunday, 11:30 a.m. to 8 p.m.; closed Monday and Tuesday.

Food: Lagunitas features a limited but well-chosen menu of appetizers, salads, and panini sandwiches, along with tasty desserts, including the Imperial Stout Ice Cream Float.

Extras: Live music in the taproom and beer sanctuary Wednesday through Sunday. Both dogs and kids are welcome in the outdoor beer garden.

Gift shop: A separate retail store called the Schwag Shop, located on the brewery grounds, carries a wide variety of logo merchandise. It has separate hours when it's open: Monday and Tuesday, 9 a.m. to 5:30 p.m.; Wednesday and Thursday, 9 a.m. to 8 p.m.; Friday, 9 a.m. to 9 p.m.; Saturday and Sunday, 11 a.m. to 8 p.m. Lagunitas merchandise is also available online.

Lucky Hand

530 Alameda Del Prado #304, Novato CA 94949
415-272-7788 • www.luckyhandbeer.com
Twitter @LuckyHandBeer
Facebook.com/luckyhandbrewingcompany

Bill Jablon was originally a winemaker but decided to try his luck with beer. It began as a joke, but when he made a faux website for a fictitious brewery, his friends didn't laugh; instead, they encouraged him to actually do it.

The 100 percent organic Lucky Hand beers were originally brewed at Linden Street, but Jablon later moved production to Uncommon Brewers (see page 176). Since Uncommon was already an organic certified brewery, it was an easy fit. Adam Krammer also came on board as head brewer. In addition to brewing, Krammer is a beer docent, consultant, and certified cicerone. He's often the face of the company, doing sales, marketing, presentations, and festivals as well. He changed the beer recipes when the brewery relaunched them, and his beer won an impressive bronze medal at the World Beer Cup in 2012. The brewery currently only makes two beers, Cali Common and Black Lager, a schwarzbier. Lucky Hand is available in all Whole Foods grocery stores and many other independent markets and select restaurants in the Bay Area.

One of the most important issues for Bill Jablon is childhood poverty and hunger. As Lucky Hand's success grows, Jablon plans to start a charity called Helping Hands, which will build and operate a commercial kitchen to provide healthy breakfasts to children in need.

Lucky Hand

Opened: August 2009.
Type: Contract brewery.
Owner: Bill Jablon.
Brewer: Adam Krammer.
Guild membership: BA.
System: See Uncommon Brewers (page 176).
Annual production: 1,200 barrels (2013 estimate).
Packages available: 22-ounce bottles and 30-liter kegs.
Gift shop: E-mail the brewery to purchase T-shirts.

Beers brewed: Cali Common Lager and Black Lager.

The Pick: The Cali Common Lager has fresh baked bread aromas, a generous pillowy head, and a yeasty tang. There are lightly sweet notes and some herbal hops character, with just a touch of fruity apples on toast.

Marin Brewing Company

1809 Larkspur Landing, Larkspur, CA 94939
415-461-4677 • www.marinbrewing.com
Twitter @MarinBrewingCo / @BrendanMoylan
Facebook.com/marinbrewingcompany /
Facebook.com/brewco

Marin Brewing was the county's first microbrewery when it was opened by Brendan Moylan in 1989. Moylan grew up in San Francisco and is an alumnus of St. Mary's College. He started homebrewing early in life and also managed the Jug Shop, worked for a beer importer, and was a draft technician and merchandising director for Spaten West. He attended UC Davis for the brewing program, then opened his first brewpub with the late Craig Tasley. He later opened the eponymous Moylan's Brewing (see page 93).

Brewmaster Arne Johnson has been making beer at Marin for nearly twenty years, having attended the American Brewers Guild and interned under Grant Johnston, Marin's first brewer. In that time, Johnson's picked up an amazing wealth of awards, including four gold medals in one year at the Great American Beer Festival. At home, he also dabbles in winemaking, cheesemaking, and many other similar pursuits. Johnson makes a number of regular beers but an even more impressive range of seasonals, one-offs, and special beers. There's always something new to discover when you visit Marin.

The brewpub is located across the street from the ferry that takes commuters to and from San Francisco. The brewery inside is a comfortable space that feels like an Irish pub, with wood everywhere, custom art on the walls, and even a full-size kayak and surfboard. There are long tables and booths to accommodate large groups or intimate dinners. I've never gotten anything less than a stellar meal here.

If you prefer a sunnier spot, try the back of the pub, where sunshine streams through large picture windows. There's also an outdoor patio in the back, overlooking the courtyard, which is ideal on warm Marin days. The patrons there on any given day are a mix of friendly locals and out-of-towners. In that same courtyard, beginning in 2000, Marin Brewing launched one of the best-attended beer festivals in the Bay Area, the Breastfest, which raises money each year for low-income women suffering from cancer. It has since outgrown the space behind the brewpub and now takes place each July at Fort Mason in San Francisco.

The brewery itself, or at least the brewhouse, is a small room to your left when you come in the front door. On brew days, you can watch Arne Johnson or one of the other brewers going about the business of making your next pint. The rest of the brewing takes place behind the scenes, in a warren of rooms that snake up and around behind the open restaurant and the bar.

If you're not having a meal, sidle up to the very long bar and order a beer. That's assuming you can make up your mind. There's likely to be as many as a dozen options, plus another on cask, probably including something you've never seen there before.

Marin Brewing Company

Opened: April 1, 1989 (no fooling).

Type: Brewpub.

Owner: Brendan J. Moylan.

Brewer: Arne Johnson.

Guild membership: BA, CCBA.

System: 14-barrel Pub Brewing system, two-vessel brewhouse combined with ten 14-barrel fermenters, eight 10-barrel serving tanks, and a 7-barrel bottling tank, 2,800 barrels annual capacity.

Annual production: 2,692 barrel (2011).

Packages available: Growlers, 22-ounce bottles, casks, and kegs are available at the pub and retail stores.

Tours: Tours depend on staff availability.

Hours: Saturday through Thursday, 11:30 a.m. to midnight; Friday, 11:30 a.m. to 1 a.m.

Food: Pub food menu includes appetizers ("beer buddies"), soup, salads, sandwiches and giant burgers, pasta, and terrific wood-fired pizza. The most popular dish is the fish and chips, with fresh cod dipped in batter made with Mt. Tam Pale Ale. The menu also includes traditional items such as bangers and mash, and my personal favorite, the meatloaf sandwich. Every Monday is Fish Taco Night, and barbecued oysters are served on Wednesday nights during the summer.

Extras: The brewpub has a 42-foot bar, the longest in town, darts, and outdoor seating in the beer garden. Events take place at the pub most days.

Gift shop: T-shirts and other merchandise are available at the pub and online.

Beers brewed: Year-round: Albion Amber, Blueberry Ale, India Pale Ale, Mt. Tam Pale Ale, Point Reyes Porter, Raspberry Trail Ale, San Quentin's Breakout Stout, Tiburon Blonde, and Weiss Beer. Seasonals: 3 Flowers IPA, Altar Boy, Abbey Special, Brass Knuckle Imperial IPA, Chocolate Airporter, Dirty Blonde, White Knuckle Eldridge Grade Double IPA, ES-Chi, Hefe Doppel Weizen, Hefe Weiss, Hoppy Holidaze X-Mas Ale, Orange & Black Congrats, Preservation Ale, Left End Pale Ale, Late for Dinner Belgian Single, Cuvee Roge, Saint Brendan's Irish Red, Saison de Revolution, Starbrew Tripel Wheat Ale, Stinson Beach Peach, Old Dipsea Barleywine, Bourbon Barrel Aged Old Dipsea Barleywine, Tripel Dipsea Belgian Style Ale, Belgian Quad, Platypus Venom Imperial Stout, Duck Goose Gose, and Witty Monk.

The Pick: I really love Marin Brewing's Point Reyes Porter, a smooth porter with creamy vanilla and caramel notes, bursting with chocolate syrup and molasses flavors.

Mill Valley Beerworks

173 Throckmorton Avenue, Mill Valley, CA 94941
415-888-8218 • www.millvalleybeerworks.com
Twitter @mvbeerworks
Facebook.com/millvalleybeerworks

The Beerworks is tucked away in a corner of Marin County, in a suburban downtown area loaded with upscale shops, restaurants and cafés. But if you love beer, Mill Valley Beerworks is the only place in the area you need to visit. In addition to offering its own beer, it has more than a hundred great bottled beers, mostly from nearby local breweries or from Belgium and other international beer destinations, but in a wide range of styles.

Beer-loving brothers Tyler and Justin Catalana, who grew up in Mill Valley, returned home after college with an eye toward starting their own business. Their original plan was to open a production brewery, but as they looked at the business plan, they realized they'd need a way to serve the public too, so they came up with the idea of having a café bar as a way to sustain the brewery.

The décor of the brewery is amazing: it's both modern and rustic at the same time, with old wood, clean lines, and a spartan feel. And given how small the footprint is, that's really the only way it would work. If the brothers had tried to cram too much in, it would have looked cluttered. The decorations can best be termed minimalist. One wall is all shelves, glassware, and bottles behind a long, wooden bar with high-backed chairs. The tiny brewery is along the wall in the very back.

Last year, the Beerworks expanded, taking over the space next door and adding a second bar; a few more tables, including some community tables; and a full kitchen with a menu of constantly changing California cuisine emphasizing seasonal ingredients, most of which are sourced

Beers brewed: Year-round: Black, Porcelain IPA, Treble Hook Rye, Westfalia, Shipshape, Botanical, Sweetwater Kolsch, and Zeppelin Society. Seasonals: Drinkin' in the Park (summer) and Drinkin' in the Dark (fall). There are also occasional limited releases, like Saison Scribe, Tea Time Bitter, Phil in the Blank, and Four Brothers. Follow the brewery on Twitter for newly released beers.

The Pick: Like the food, the beer available changes frequently too, in part because of the small batches brewed. I've generally enjoyed the Botanical offering, which is brewed with juniper and bay leaves. The spicing is subtle and adds a nice refreshing quality to the beer, and it's a food-friendly beer. The Morpho Herbal Ale collaboration is equally tasty and can be found in bottles throughout the area when available.

locally from nearby farms. When the brothers added the kitchen, they brought in chef David Wilcox, who'd made a name for himself at Gjelina, in Venice, an upscale restaurant near Los Angeles. They also added a morning espresso bar in partnership with Blue Bottle Coffee. There was a time when you could walk in most evenings and find a seat, but those days are gone, as the popularity of the Beerworks has soared. If you're planning an evening visit, especially on the weekends, call for a reservation.

There are usually six housemade beers on tap, with several regulars and a rotating selection of seasonals and other one-off beers. Mill Valley also brewed a collaboration beer, Morpho Herbal Ale, brewed with Jim Woods of MateVeza (see Cervecería de MateVeza on page 32). The beer is made with hibiscus flowers, organic bay leaves, and Yerba mate and is available in limited quantities in 22-ounce bottles.

Mill Valley Beerworks

Opened: May 2011.

Type: Brewpub.

Owners: Tyler and Justin Catalana.

Brewer: Mike Schnebeck.

Guild membership: BA, CCBA.

System: 3-barrel Premier Stainless direct-fire two-vessel brewhouse, 350 barrels annual capacity.

Annual production: 222 barrels (2012) to 350 barrels (2013 estimate).

Packages available: 12-ounce bottles in six-packs, 22-ounce bottles, growlers, and kegs.

Tours: No organized tours are available, but you are encouraged to say hello and watch during the morning brewing sessions.

Hours: Seven days a week, 7 a.m. to midnight. Espresso bar: Every day, 7 a.m. to 3 p.m. Lunch: Weekdays, 11:30 a.m. to 3 p.m. Dinner: Sunday through Wednesday, 5 to 10:30 p.m.; Friday and Saturday, 5 to 11 p.m. Brunch: Saturday and Sunday, 10 a.m. to 3 p.m.

Food: The restaurant offers a full lunch and dinner menu, along with brunch on the weekends. The menu changes constantly based on seasonal availability of ingredients. There's generally a selection of nibbles and small plates for sharing; several full entrée dishes, such as confit rabbit, short ribs agridolce, and pan-seared pork chop with cranberry beans; and plenty of vegetarian fare. You won't find any obvious pub food on the menu, in part because Wilcox likes it that way and wants to be free to create unique flavors in his dishes. Keep an eye on the Facebook page, where new menu items are posted as they're added.

Extras: When it's warm outside, two outdoor tables are set up during the day. Children are welcome, but only until 9 p.m.

Gift shop: Shirts and glassware are available at the brewpub.

Moonlight Brewing Company

Production brewery: Box 6, Fulton, CA 95439
   (not open to the public)
Growler fill station: 3350 Coffey Lane, Suite A,
   Santa Rosa, CA 95403
415-528-2537 • www.moonlightbrewing.com

Moonlight founder Brian Hunt was born in a log cabin near Sacramento and walked 10 miles to school, uphill—both ways—through blizzards in winter and punishing heat in summer. Okay, I made up everything in that last sentence, except Sacramento. But Hunt is such an iconic figure in the local beer community that his past just cries out to be remade as a mythic fable. I love hearing his story.

Hunt started college at UC San Diego as a biochemistry major but soon realized that most of his fellow students were pre-med, a path he decidedly was not interested in pursuing. So he transferred to UC Davis to study fermentation sciences, with an eye toward becoming a winemaker. Fate stepped in when he was randomly assigned Michael Lewis as his advisor. Needing income, he ended up working in Lewis's laboratory, where it was easy to be persuaded to concentrate on beer instead of wine. "Beer just seemed more enjoyable," Hunt says.

After graduating with a degree in fermentation sciences in 1980, Hunt relocated to the heart of early brewing—Milwaukee, Wisconsin—to take a job at the Schlitz Brewery. He loved the history of the brewery, and it was all around him. Hunt spent about eighteen months working for Schlitz. There were no computers in the place. Every step was done manually, so he learned the reasons why he did certain things, and he could extrapolate the logic to subsequent steps as well. He credits that experience with setting the tone for the rest of his career.

He moved back to California in 1981, brewing at the now long gone Berkeley Brewing Company, making ales and lagers on a 40-barrel system. After that venture went belly-up, he consulted on several brewing projects throughout the Bay Area, ending up at Acme Brewing in Santa Rosa in 1985. After that, he had a brief stint at the early Anderson Valley Brewing Company in Boonville, where he formulated two beers (whose recipes have since changed) and helped lay out the brewery.

In 1988, Brian finally opened his own place in Napa with a descendant of the Hamm's brewing family. He had a one-third share of Willett's Brewing Company (now Downtown Joe's) from sweat equity and $1,100 of his own money. But by 1992, a get-rich-quick lawsuit brought by one of the brewpub's employees forced Willett's into bankruptcy. Brian Hunt saw the writing on the wall, and when someone phoned him to offer a hundred Hoff-Stevens kegs, he bought them for himself and began . . . well, moonlighting.

Brian built the original Moonlight brewery in a barn behind the house he was renting, financing the whole enterprise with credit cards and a $20,000 personal loan. He cobbled together the entire system himself using equipment from a variety of sources. When Sierra Nevada Brewing Company opened a larger brewery in Chico and sold off some of the old equipment, quite a number of these items found their way into Moonlight's brewery barn, including fermenters and a keg washer. The initial brewhouse included a 7-barrel system.

The original name was going to be Old Barn Brewery, but it never sounded quite right. New Moon Brewing was also an early contender among the hundreds of names brainstormed. But once the name Moonlight was floated, there was no turning back. It worked on so many levels, and seemed to mean different things to different people, a quality Hunt relished.

For the first two and a half years, beginning in 1992, Brian slept only five-and-a-half nights a week. He was working two jobs: at the newly opened Downtown Joe's, where the bankrupt Willett's brewpub had been, and at his own place in the barn. This continued until he could afford to concentrate on just Moonlight Brewing. But only a few years into the new venture, his landlord decided he wanted the house Brian and his family lived in for his own son and told the Hunts they had to go. Luckily, he let Brian keep the brewery in the barn until it could be moved. In 1999, Brian moved to his present location. It would take another four years until all the permits were in place and the new brewery was built. The new 21-barrel-system was the original Hart Brewing system, which Brian bought from the Thomas Kemper brewery on Bainbridge Island in Washington. The present setup has pieces from at least fifty different breweries, ones that either went out of business or upgraded.

Neither the original nor the new brewery has a computer of any kind in it, and that's by design. It's because of one of Hunt's favorite quotes,

Beers brewed: Year-round: Bombay by Boat IPA, Death & Taxes Black Beer, Lunatic Lager, Reality Czeck Pils, and Twist of Fate Bitter. Seasonals: Boney Fingers (Halloween), Homegrown Fresh Hop Ale, Winter Tipple Ale, Toast (Slightly Burnt). Occasional unique beers: Artemis, Left for Dead Sour Black Ale, Misspent Youth, Sour Mash Wheat, Two Weeks Notice, and Working for Tips.

The Pick: The black lager Death & Taxes is a sparingly light-bodied beer but full-flavored with nice roasting, chocolate notes, and great bittering that finishes dry.

by Albert Einstein: "Imagination is more important than knowledge." Hunt feels that one of the most important aspects of brewing is creativity and thinks of himself more as a tinkerer of sorts. And, as he puts it, "You can't see what's happening if you're just pushing buttons."

The first three beers Moonlight brewed are still being made: Lunatic Lager, Death & Taxes, and Twist of Fate. The fourth beer Hunt made was Bombay by Boat IPA, also in 1992, and was one of the first IPAs made in America. At that time, very few brewers really made one, and those few who did didn't call it an IPA.

Hunt's original plan was to try to make a living in Sonoma County selling whatever he brewed. Though his net is now spread slightly wider than he had anticipated, it's not by much, and he has remained true to his initial vision. "I don't find success by selling a lot," he says. "I find it by selling to people who respect [Moonlight beer] or appreciate it." As long as that's the case, we won't be seeing Moonlight beer in grocery stores nationwide or even bottled locally. Brian is just not looking for that kind of success. He's content doing what he wants in his own way, an iconoclast to the end.

One concession he has made is the opening of a growler station in Santa Rosa, giving his fans an opportunity to finally enjoy it in their own homes. Those who know how good Moonlight's beer is will travel great distances to get some. Hunt is a true unsung hero of sorts, a brewer's brewer, whose reputation is unparalleled among those in the know. You may not be able to go to the source of the beer, but you can find it all over Sonoma County and beyond, at least throughout the Bay Area.

Moonlight Brewing Company

Opened: August 28, 1992.

Type: Production brewery.

Owner and brewer: Brian Hunt.

Guild membership: BA, CCBA, NCBG.

System: 21-barrel system from assorted manufacturers, including a kettle from Alaskan Copper & Brass and a copper mash tun from Quality Stainless Tanks, 2,000 barrels annual capacity.

Annual production: 2,000 barrels.

Packages available: Growlers and 5-, 7.75-, and 15.5-gallon kegs.

Tours: Tours are not available.

Hours: See website for growler station hours.

Gift shop: T-shirts, hooded sweatshirts, and hats are available through the website.

Moylan's Brewery and Restaurant

15 Rowland Way, Novato, CA 94945
415-898-4677 • www.moylans.com
Twitter @MoylansBrewery / @BrendanMoylan
Facebook.com/moylans

Moylan's Brewery is the second brewpub opened by Bay Area native Brendan Moylan. His first, Marin Brewing (see page 86), was opened in 1989, and six years later he opened Moylan's. After the success of his first brewery, he wanted to build another one closer to where he lived. With Moylan's, he made the brewpub more Irish, which is his family's background. Moylan's mother is from Wexford, and his father was from Tipperary, although he grew up in the Sunset district of San Francisco.

Moylan's has had a number of excellent brewers over the years—Paddy Giffen and James Costa, for example—but the brewery seems to have really clicked under Denise Jones, who's been there for the last seven years. She brewed in Nevada and in Tahoe City before becoming the brewer at Third Street Aleworks, where she first made a name for herself. After brewing there for a number of years, she left to work on a historic brewery in San Francisco, but that project was ultimately abandoned. Happily, she found a home in the Novato brewpub.

Jones learned her craft at the American Brewers Guild and has also gone to the Siebel Institute of Technology in Chicago and studied brewing in Munich, Germany. She tends to concentrate on fresh beer rather than big, aged beers. She's well known for her dark beers and makes some wonderful stouts. But she's equally at home with hoppy beers, and Moylan's has some terrific hops monsters. Jones usually has as many as twenty different beers on tap at any given time.

The brewpub is located conveniently just off the main road in the area, U.S. Route 101, and if you're heading almost anywhere between San Francisco and the North Coast, you'll undoubtedly take that road at some point. The brewpub is a

Beers brewed: Year-round: Celts Golden Ale, Chelsea Moylan's Porter, Danny's Irish Red, Dragoon's Irish Dry Stout, Extra Special Bitter, Hopsickle Imperial IPA, Kiltlifter Scotch Ale, Moylander Double IPA, Moylan's Special Bitter, Nor Cal India Pale Ale, Old Blarney Barleywine, Pomegranate Wheat, Ryan O'Sullivan's Imperial Stout, Tipperary Pale Ale, and Unfiltered Wheat. Seasonals: Barrel Aged Wet Hopsickle, Bjor Nagal Lager, Double Kilt-Sickle Reserve, Harvest IPA, Hell Export Lager, Hop Craic XXXX IPA, Hopgarten Pilsner, Moylan's Oktoberfest, Orange & Black Congrats Ale, Sommer Kolsch Bier, and White Christmas Spice Lager.

stand-alone building that was built specifically to house Moylan's.

There's a very long bar to your right as you enter the restaurant; in fact, it's the longest in the entire county. The brewery is behind it, and you can catch a glimpse through windows along the wall behind the bar, but you'll need to go back there to get a good look. The restaurant at Moylan's is fairly large, and you can sit on the outside patio on warm days. Beyond the end of the bar, there's a small room with a large fireplace and a basket of toys and books for the kids.

Moylan's has a setup where you can buy someone a pint of beer even if he or she is not there. You pay the bartender, who writes the name of the person you designate on a chalkboard behind the bar. There's nothing quite like walking in and discovering someone bought you a pint. And that's indicative of the type of place Moylan's is—one where friends can share a pint of a great beer.

Moylan's Brewery and Restaurant

Opened: August 18, 1995

Type: Brewpub.

Owner: Brendan J. Moylan.

Brewer: Denise Jones.

Guild membership: BA, CCBA.

System: 20-barrel Pub Brewing system, 2-vessel brewhouse combined with eight 40-barrel fermenters, eight 10-barrel serving tanks, three 7-barrel serving tanks, and a 20-barrel bottling tank, 4,400 barrels annual capacity.

Annual production: 4,303 barrels (2011).

Packages available: Growlers, 22-ounce bottles, casks, and 5- and 15.5-gallon kegs.

Tours: Brewery tours depend on staff availability; it's best to make a reservation.

Hours: Saturday through Thursday, 11:30 a.m. to midnight; Friday, 11:30 a.m. to 1 a.m.

Food: An extensive menu of Irish pub food includes appetizers, sandwiches and burgers, pasta, terrific wood-fired pizza, and Irish lamb stew. The most popular dish is the fish and chips, made from fresh cod dipped in batter made with Moylan's beer. There are daily specials, including taco specials on Monday, salmon and chips on Thursday, and corned beef and cabbage, San Francisco-style, on Saturday.

Extras: The brewpub has a 54-foot bar, the longest in Marin County, and darts, a beer library, and outdoor seating in the beer garden. The brewery hosts several holiday-themed parties throughout the year; of course, St. Patrick's Day is the biggest.

Gift shop: T-shirts and other merchandise are available at the pub and online.

Napa Smith Brewery

1 Executive Way, Napa, CA 94558
707-254-7167 (brewpub) 707-255-2912 (brewery)
www.napasmithbrewery.com
Twitter @Napa_Smith
Facebook.com/NapaSmithBrewery

Napa Smith was originally founded by a winemaking family in Napa—the Smiths, of course. And they acquired the former Hakasan Saki building at the intersection of State Routes 12 and 29, colloquially known as the "gateway to Napa Valley," for their Napa Smith Brewery. Napa Smith also operates a winery, but wine is made there one day a year, while brewing beer is a daily enterprise.

One of the most important aspects of Napa Smith Brewery is the involvement of Don Barkley, who was coaxed out of retirement to help start the Napa brewery, and he's been there ever since. Barkley is nothing short of a brewing legend, having been the assistant brewer at the New Albion Brewery in Sonoma, which was the first modern microbrewery in America when it opened in 1977 (see "A word about . . . New Albion, America's First Modern Microbrewery" on page 120). When New Albion closed in 1983, Barkley moved the brewhouse equipment to Hopland and helped found Mendocino Brewing (page 246), where he created its flagship Red Tail Ale and the iconic Eye of the Hawk, among many others.

But now he's at the helm of another brewery and making some more fine beers. The regular year-round lineup consists of four solid everyday beers—a pilsner and a wheat beer, along with both an amber and a pale ale. But it's in the special releases that the brewery shines. From the outrageous Hopageddon Imperial IPA to the Bonfire Imperial Porter to the Grateful Dog Barleywine, Napa Smith has created a stable of impressive big beers.

Beers brewed: Year-round: Amber Ale, Pale Ale, Ginger Wheat, and Pilsner. Signature Series: Organic IPA and Lost Dog American Red Ale. Special Series: Hopageddon Imperial IPA and Grateful Dog Barleywine. Seasonals: Bonfire Imperial Porter, Cool Brew Hop Ale, Ewan Paine Scottish Ale, and Crush Beer Amber Lager.

The Pick: The Hopageddon, an oak-aged Imperial IPA, is just plain humungous, weighing in at 9.2 percent ABV and with listed IBUs at an impossible 144! The most surprising thing you'll notice after taking in those stats is just how drinkable the beer really is. It's loaded with citrus, pine, and a mélange of hops superlatives that carry through to its massive flavor profile. You know its balance is there only because of how drinkable it is, because it's hops, hops, and more hops from start to finish.

In late 2010, Napa Smith was purchased by drinks company Pelican Brands (now Paddington brands) and considerably expanded its market into more than thirty states. It also opened a separate tasting room, known as the brewpub, in late 2011. The brewpub is open extended hours from the production brewery and functions as a public space that features Napa Smith beers as close to the source as possible. Special events are hosted here, the tours start and end here, and it's just a great place to escape from Napa's wine-centric worldview. They say it takes a lot of great beer to make great wine, and here is where you can find it.

Napa Smith Brewery

Opened: March 2008.

Type: Production brewery with a brewpub.

Owner: Paddington Brands, LLC.

Brewer: Don Barkley.

Guild membership: BA, CCBA.

System: 15-barrel Pub Brewing system, 7,500 barrels annual capacity (with tanks added recently to double production for 2013).

Annual production: 4,500 barrels (2012).

Packages available: 12-ounce bottles in six-packs, 22-ounce bottles, growlers, and 5- and 15.5-gallon kegs.

Tours: Brewery tours are available; please call the brewpub to make a reservation.

Hours: Seven days a week, 11 a.m. to 7:30 p.m.

Food: There are usually just snacks at the tasting room, although for special events a food truck is often parked outside, serving food to take into the tasting room.

Extras: Growler fills are $4 off on Wednesday. The brewpub regularly hosts music and other special events; the schedule can be found on the Napa Smith website under "events."

Gift shop: Merchandise is available at the brewpub.

Old Redwood Brewing Company

9000 Windsor Road, Suite A, Windsor, CA 95492
707-657-7624 • www.oldredwoodbrewing.com
Twitter @oldredwoodbrewing
Facebook.com/oldredwoodbrewing

Although the beautiful corner building in Old Town Windsor that houses this brewery has every appearance of being a historic structure from the turn of the last century, it actually dates from closer to the turn of *this* century and is less than fifteen years old. It was part of the downtown area's redevelopment project and was based on the old Windsor Hotel, which stood on the exact same spot in the 1800s. An architect studied photographs of the old building to re-create it as closely as possible. It certainly works, because you'd never know this was a new building.

And it's proven to be an ideal spot for the Old Redwood Brewing Company, the brainchild of four local area friends who built a small membership club brewery in the heart of wine country using some of the same methods that boutique wineries use. The membership club has no fees, but just asks prospective members to commit for one year to buying three, six, or twelve bottles each month. Each month, members pick up their bottles and also have first dibs on new releases. After all members get their beer, whatever is left over is sold in the tasting room.

The tasting room is modeled after area wine-tasting spaces. It's light and airy, sparsely decorated, and looks nothing like the average brewery. Also, you can only buy samples of the beer. The brewery doesn't sell pints or kegs, and there's no food either. If you like the beer, you can either join the membership club or purchase bottles of whatever is available. The original brewery is also on display, but you may not recognize it. It was made out of what look like oil drums, and in a way they were, although they actually first held cinnamon oil. The partners quickly outgrew the 1-barrel brewery and replaced it with a 3-barrel brewhouse. Everything is hand done, from brewing to

Beers brewed: Year-round: The Fulton Imperial Wheat (brewed with honey), The Windsor Wit (brewed with raspberries, coriander, and orange peel), The Colonel, Trippel, The Burl Dubbel, The Arrow Pomegranate Wheat Ale, The Stack Smoked Imperial Porter, The Shilellagh Irish Red Ale, The Fortress Russian Imperial Stout, The Highway Old India Pale Ale, The Compromise Belgian IPA, and The Picker's Saison (brewed with chardonnay). Seasonals: Naughty and Nice Holiday Spiced Belgian.

bottling and sticking on the labels. The brewers use an old six-head wine filler and a hand labeler that was handmade just for this purpose.

Two of the partners, Bobby Anderson and Mike Stewart, do the brewing. Both have been home-brewing for many years, Stewart since he was seventeen, twenty years ago. Anderson's the hophead, while Stewart prefers Belgians and maltier beers. One of their best beers is called The Compromise, a Belgian IPA that nicely encapsulates their differences in one beer. But it works for them. Each one's strengths are the other's weaknesses, and they end up making better beer because of it.

Each month, a new beer is released. Some have proven wildly popular, while others not as much, but so far everything's been well received. And the brewers get real-time, immediate feedback. They learn what tweaks can improve a beer and which ones to make again. As they learn what works, undoubtedly favorites will emerge that will be made every year. Until then, it's a treat to see what new beer each month brings.

The Pick: Since the beers change regularly and you may not see the same beer twice, it's hard to recommend a particular beer. But of the half dozen or so I've had so far, I can say they're all pretty good. The Shilellagh has proven to be one of the most popular so far, although I think I prefer The Compromise, a Belgian IPA. It starts with a nice yeasty nose that reminds me of a Belgian golden, but with tart, spicy hops aromas. Using four common American hops, and dry-hopping with Amarillo and Cascades, the two brewers melded their styles seamlessly into a beer that's more than the sum of its parts.

Old Redwood Brewing Company

Opened: August 5, 2012.

Type: Nanobrewery, with tasting room.

Owners: Adam Derum, Bobby Anderson, Mike Stewart, and Dominic Foppoli.

Brewers: Bobby Anderson and Mike Stewart.

Guild membership: CCBA.

System: 3-barrel Stout Tank system, 200 barrels annual capacity.

Annual production: 150 barrels (2012 estimate).

Packages available: 750-milliliter bottles with swing-tops.

Tours: Brewery tours are available on request; please call for an appointment.

Hours: Winter: Wednesday through Sunday, noon to 6 p.m.; closed Monday and Tuesday. Summer: Seven days a week, noon to 8 p.m.

Food: No food is available in the tasting room.

Extras: Old Redwood Brewing operates a beer tasting room that specializes in alternative ales. The brewery offers flights of its beer along with personalized tasting for each customer and does not serve pints or fill growlers. However, it does offer a beer club membership for both locals and fans nationwide and will even make beer specifically for its members. It also offers private "members only" events.

101 North Brewing Company

1304 Scott Street, Suite D, Petaluma, CA 01051
707-778-8384 • www.101northbeer.com
Twitter @101NORTHBREWING
Facebook.com/pages/101-North-Brewing-
    Company/112643938842239

With the name 101 North Brewing, this brewery is exactly where you'd expect it to be, just a chip shot from U.S. Route 101, in Petaluma. But to get to it, you have to get off the exit and make a couple right-hand turns into an industrial park. Happily, it's a quick trip from the highway to the brewery.

The new brewery is the brainchild of veteran brewer Joel Johnson, who's been brewing professionally since 1997. His first big gig was a few miles up the road on 101 at Bear Republic Brewing in Healdsburg, where he was responsible for a few of the early beers, including Racer 5 and Hop Rod Rye. Johnson also created the label artwork for the rye beer. After a couple years, he was named head brewer, a position he held until 2005. For the next five years, he ran brewing operations at Mount St. Helena Brewing Company in Middletown, which is still open as a restaurant but is no longer brewing.

Then two years ago, his dream to open his own brewery grew tangibly closer when a 15-barrel Jacob Carl Brewhaus system arrived that summer from Lake Placid, New York, and was delivered to the 4,000-square-foot warehouse just off Route 101 North. For the next two years, Johnson, with a little help from his partners, family, and friends, began the long process of installing the equipment.

Last fall, 101 North released its first beer, Heroine IPA, at the grand opening. Weighing in at 7.2 percent ABV and 61 IBUs, it's a decidedly hoppy beer primarily made with Pacific Northwest hops varieties, including Cascade, Summit, and Tomahawk, balanced with British Crystal and Caramel Malts. The label shows a comic book–worthy costumed superheroine by local artist Leslie Hiromi Hotchkiss. It will undoubted-

Beers brewed: Year-round: Heroine IPA, Golden Naked Ale, Stigmata Red Rye and Sancho (Mexicali lager). Seasonals: For winter, the brewery released Naughty Aud, a Russian imperial stout.

The Pick: This is an easy one. The Heroine IPA is a beautiful hops monster, well balanced but with a pronounced hops character that never lets you forget it's an IPA.

ly be the brewery's flagship, as it slowly begins to release additional beers.

With Johnson's experience and track record, expect great things from this brewery. So far, everything he's brewed, both before his new venture and at 101, has been great. Expect that trend to continue along Route 101 North.

101 North Brewing Company

Opened: August 23, 2012.

Type: Production brewery.

Owners: John Brainin, Jacob Johnson, Joel Johnson, and Johnnie Johnson.

Brewer: Joel Johnson.

Guild membership: BA, CCBA, NCBG.

System: 20-barrel Jacob Carl, 1,200 barrels annual capacity.

Annual production: 1,020 barrels (estimated).

Packages available: 22-ounce bottles and kegs (15.5 and 5 gallon).

Tours: Tours will be available one day a week, most likely on Friday, when the tasting room is anticipated to be open to the public.

Hours: Currently open Friday only, 1 to 5 p.m., but check the website or Facebook page for updates, as the hours will be extended once the tasting room is open to the public.

Food: Details are still being worked out for the tasting room, but food trucks or light snacks will likely be available.

Extras: Check online for special events to be held at the brewery from time to time.

Gift shop: Merchandise is sold online and at the brewery, when the tasting room is open.

Petaluma Hills Brewing Company

1333 North McDowell Boulevard, Petaluma, CA 94954
707-484-6911 • www.petalumahills.com
Twitter @petalumahills • Facebook.com/petalumahills

JJ Jay, his real name, had been homebrewing for twenty-two years before deciding to open his own brewery. Originally from the Midwest, he spent the first decade homebrewing in the kitchen, making extract beer, and was perfectly content with the results. During that time, he worked as a computer scientist, specializing in graphics, and relocated to the Bay Area sixteen years ago to accept a job offer from Pixar.

After settling in Petaluma, he continued homebrewing but progressed to all-malt beers, taking his hobby increasingly seriously. In the meantime, he started working for Dreamworks, assisting on the first two *Madagascar* films, *Monsters vs. Aliens*, and the final two *Shrek* films, along with other projects, and these days is a character technical director supervisor while he builds his new brewery.

The production brewery, which is still a work in progress, is located on a corner building along North McDowell Boulevard, directly across the street from Lagunitas. It's a prime spot, becoming the third brewery within a few hundred yards of one another (the other being Highway 101 Brewing), making visiting the trio of breweries an easy affair.

When finished, it should be a great space, with an L-shaped bar separating the taproom from the brewery, but open to it so that anyone in the taproom can watch the brewing take place. JJ wants visitors to be connected to the process, to be able to see and smell and taste the beer in its industrial natural state.

All of JJ's beers, with the exception of the more personal Tripel J, are named for local aspects of Petaluma, and he expects that will always be the focus of the brewery. For now, kegs will be the focus, though down the line, you may see cans of Petaluma Hills beer. Until then, check out the brewery, have a growler filled, and enjoy a pint there at the source.

Beers brewed: Year-round: Old Adobe Stout, Porterluma, East Side Bitter, River Town Brown, Big House Blonde, Tripel J, Kinahan Red Ale, Lamppost Ale, Date Night Ale, and Northern English Brown. Seasonals: Traffic Jam Pumpkin Maze Ale (fall).

Petaluma Hills Brewing Company

Opened: Summer 2013.

Type: Production brewery, with taproom.

Owner: JJ Jay.

Brewer: JJ Jay.

Guild membership: BA, CCBA.

System: 10-barrel Premier Stainless, 1,920 barrels annual capacity.

Annual production: 220 barrels (2013 estimate).

Packages available: Growlers and kegs.

Tours: Brewery tours will be available; check the website for updates.

Hours: Thursday through Sunday evenings, but check the website for specific hours and open days.

Food: JJ plans to have snacks available in the taproom.

Extras: The taproom will feature some amenities, including a private room and the ability to watch the brewing process from your bar stool.

Gift shop: Merchandise is available online and at the brewery taproom.

Pizza Orgasmica & Brewing Company

The Original Sin

812 Fourth Street, San Rafael, CA 94901
415-457-BEER (2337) • www.pizzaorgasmica.com
    or www.pizzaorgasmica.net
Twitter @PizzaOrgasmica
Facebook.com/We.Never.Fake.It.SanRafael /
    Facebook.com/WeNeverFakeIt

The mythic story is that Pizza Orgasmica co-founder Taylor Maia grew up in Brazil, dreaming of one day creating his own brand of orgasmic pizza, and when he was old enough, he left South America to seek his pizza fortune in San Francisco. True or not, he and his wife and partner, Gina Gochez, have created their own pizza empire, which they describe as "a sensuous and hedonistic place."

When Maia decided he wanted to add his own beer to the menu—primarily because pizza and beer are a match made in heaven—he visited the Brewcraft homebrew store in San Francisco looking for help. There he met Rev Jackson, who'd started homebrewing in North Beach years before. Jackson had been brewing with some friends almost every weekend, and his hobby had gotten so out of hand he was working at the homebrew store. The two hit it off, and Jackson began creating beers at a local brewery for Pizza Orgasmica, which started serving its own exclusive beers in July 2004.

The brewpub in San Rafael had originally opened as Willow Street Brewery and later operated as the Limelight, and then as Rafter's before that closed. But when Pizza Orgasmica discovered that the former pizza restaurant with a brewery was available, it seemed like a natural fit, perfect for what it was already successfully doing: bringing great beer and pizza together.

The Pizza Orgasmica brewpub is located at the end of the main street in downtown San Rafael,

Beers brewed: Year-round: Golden Ale, I.P.A., Peach Pale Ale, Amber Ale, Porter, 4 Grain Hefeweizen, Raspberry Hefeweizen, Blueberry Best Bitter, Orgasmica Pale Ale, and Kolsch. Seasonals: Orgasmica Barley Wine.

The Pick: I like both Rev's Porter and his I.P.A. The Porter is lightly toasty, with great cocoa powder and caramel flavors, with some licorice and dark fruit thrown into the mix. There's a touch of bitter coffee as well, along with the chocolate and toffee notes, and a crisp mouthfeel. The IPA is also a good West Coast example, with big grapefruit and pine aromas, big hops flavors, a good earthy malt balance, and a touch of sweetness from midpalate to the finish.

and it's a big restaurant. There's a large bar in the main room, with the brewery behind glass on the opposite wall. On hot days, the front of the brewpub can be open to the sidewalk. There's another large room in the back, and that's also where they have a kids' play area. It's been entirely redecorated to have the same look and feel of the Pizza Orgasmica world, and I especially love how they "fixed" the giant wall mural.

I think the space has finally found the right owners to inhabit it, and Pizza Orgasmica seems to have just the right vibe to fit here. Rev Jackson is a fine brewer and makes some terrific beers. The beer he makes is sold not only at the San Rafael location, but also exclusively at all the other Pizza Orgasmica restaurants.

In addition to the San Rafael brewpub, there are four more Pizza Orgasmica restaurants, all of them in San Francisco. The other locations are at 823 Clement Street, 2 Embarcadero Center, 3145 Fillmore Street, and 3157 Fillmore Street. As the slogan suggests, "Be Happy! Eat Pizza! Eat Pizza Orgasmica!" To that should be added "And Drink Pizza Orgasmica Beer!"

Pizza Orgasmica & Brewing Company

Opened: Pizza restaurant, 1996; San Rafael brewpub, February 2, 2011.

Type: Brewpub.

Owners: Gina Gochez and Taylor Maia.

Brewer: Rev Jackson.

System: 15-barrel JV Northwest, 1,500 barrels annual capacity.

Annual production: 1,000 barrels (2012).

Packages available: Draft only at the five Pizza Orgasmica restaurants.

Tours: You can see the brewery when you're sitting in the restaurant, but if you want to know more, ask if the brewer is available. If he's not too busy, he'll come out and tell you about the brewery and the beer he makes.

Hours: Sunday through Wednesday, 11 a.m. to 10 p.m.; Thursday, 11 a.m. to 11 p.m.; Friday and Saturday, 11 a.m. to midnight.

Food: Pizza, of course, is the raison d'être here, and the place makes outstanding pizza. In addition to at least twenty-eight specialty pizzas, you can make your own with either a thin cornmeal crust, a thick Sicilian crust, or as a calzone for two. You can then choose from among seven different cheeses, a dozen meats, seven sauces, five different seafood toppings, and twenty vegetable toppings. If that's not enough, there are also salads, Brazilian appetizers and entrées, and desserts. Monthly specials are posted on the website.

Extras: Happy hour, with discounted pints, is Monday through Friday, 3 to 6 p.m. and 10 p.m. to close. Also check the website for online coupons before you visit.

Gift shop: Shirts and hats are available online, and some merchandise is available at the restaurants.

Russian River Brewing Company

721 Fourth Street, Santa Rosa, CA 95404
707-545-BEER (2337) • russianriverbrewing.com
Facebook.com/russianriverbrewing

Vinnie Cilurzo, the prodigious brewer of Russian River Brewing, is living his dream. He's almost always wanted to be a brewer, and although he grew up working at the family winery in Temecula, north of San Diego, he decided he wanted to brew beer after making his first batch of homebrew with some friends shortly after high school. After that, all his energies and focus in college were on that ultimate goal, and he threw himself into meeting it while continuing to homebrew and hone his brewing skills. Even then, he focused on his favorite kind of beer: hoppy IPAs.

The only distraction occurred on his twentieth birthday, when he went on his first date with Natalie, whom he had met while she was working at a neighboring winery. Natalie likes to joke that on their first date, she had to buy the beer. They married shortly thereafter, and she continued working in the wine industry while he pursued his passion for brewing.

At twenty-four Vinnie opened his first brewery, the Blind Pig Brewing Company in his hometown of Temecula. Russian River's popular India pale ale is named for that first brewery. It was also then, in 1994, that Vinnie brewed Blind Pig Inaugural Ale, believed to be the very first double IPA. Although the brewery enjoyed some modest success, it was ahead of its time. After a few years, Cilurzo sold the company and the couple moved to Healdsburg, in Sonoma County. They had gotten to know the Sonoma area after several visits to Vinnie's sister in Napa and felt it was the place where they wanted to live. After they moved north, Natalie continued working in the wine business at such well-known wineries as Silver Oak and Kendall-Jackson.

At that same time, craft beer was beginning to catch the attention of some bigger companies, and two large wineries in the area were considering adding brewing operations to their portfolios. Cilurzo interviewed with both Benzinger and Korbel. He took the job with Korbel Champagne Cellars and opened Russian River Brewing in May 1997.

It was during this time that Cilurzo began experimenting with Belgian-inspired beers and both barrel aging and creating sour beers, something he discovered while traveling in Europe in the early 1990s. A day trip to Belgium turned into a week, as he was introduced first-hand to the endless possibilities of using wild yeast. That experience eventually led to the brewery's series of beers in which each name ends in the suffix "-tion," like Damnation and Temptation. These beers were inspired by Cilurzo's Belgian brethren, but as he's quick to point out, they are not exactly Belgian-style beers. They're unique beers that use a mix of traditional brewing techniques and ingredients but also have his original stamp on them.

Russian River Brewing took off, and it succeeded both commercially and in terms of reputation. It was operating at capacity after just the first year. Two years after opening, Russian River was named Small Brewery of the Year at the 1999 Great American Beer Festival. Despite the considerable accomplishments of the brewery, Korbel lost interest, and in 2002, it generously offered the Cilurzos the chance to determine their own destiny and sold them the rights to the brewery.

It was an uncertain time, but Natalie left her winery job and partnered with Cilurzo to reopen Russian River Brewing on their own terms. They secured a prime location on Fourth Street in downtown Santa Rosa, the former Old Vic bar, which had been a local institution, and in the spring of 2004, they opened the doors of the brewpub.

The brewpub features a very long wooden bar, bench seating, and as much other seating as they could comfortably fit in. There's also a small side room, with a few tables overlooking one of the barrel rooms, and patio seating out front. Breweriana hangs on the walls and sits on shelves high above near the ceiling. The jewel in the crown is the original sign for New Albion Brewery, America's first modern microbrewery. The New Albion sign hangs behind the bar and was recently signed by Jack McAuliffe, who founded the Sonoma brewery in 1977. (See "A word about . . . New Albion, America's First Modern Microbrewery" on page 120.)

In one corner of the main dining area is a small stage, where live music is performed on weekends and for special occasions. Above the

Beers brewed: Year-round: Blind Pig IPA, Pliny the Elder, and Damnation. Barrel-aged beers: Beatification, Consecration, Supplication, and Temptation. Belgian-inspired ales: Damnation 23, Defenestration, Erudition, Mortification, Perdition, Redemption, Rejection, Sanctification, Salvation, Benediction, and Little White Lie. Seasonals, limited releases, and pub-only beers: Aud Blonde, Framboise for a Cure, Gaffers, Happy Hops, Hopfather IPA, HopTime Harvest Ale, Janet's Brown Ale, O.V.L. Stout, Row 2 Hill 56, Russian River IPA, Russian River Porter, Segal Select, Toronado 25th Anniversary Ale, and Pliny the Younger (released the first Friday in February).

bar, a colorful chalkboard lists the available beers, and it's always an extensive list, with the "-tion" line of beers on the right-hand side and the hoppy and other beers on the left. You can order food from any seat in the house, and all of the menu items pair nicely with the beers, as you'd expect. At certain times of day and on weekends, the brewpub can get crowded, and at dinnertime it's not uncommon to have to wait for a table. It's worth the wait, though, and happily, you can order a beer while you wait in most cases. Except during some special events, the service is brisk and moves quickly.

After the couple had operated the brewpub for a few years, it became clear that they needed a way to brew more beer, so they started putting together the plans for a new production brewery. Located less than a mile from the brewpub, it opened in May 2008 and has been running at capacity ever since. They also installed a bottling line and began putting Blind Pig IPA and Pliny the Elder in 16-ounce bottles, and all of the "-tion" series cork-and-cage bottles are now done there as well. The production brewery also boasts a barrel room where all of the "-tion" beers are aged. It is not open for tours or to the public, however.

As far as I know, this is the only brewery anywhere with a double IPA as its flagship. Pliny the Elder accounts for a little over 50 percent of all the beer Russian River sells. Pliny has been voted or rated as the best beer in America several times over the years by popular ratings websites and polling. Since opening, the brewpub has been named the Large Brewpub Champion at the World Beer Cup twice, in 2004 and again in 2006, and Vinnie Cilurzo won the highly coveted Russell Schehrer Award for Innovation in Brewing in 2008.

Each year on the first Friday in February, the brewery releases Pliny the Younger, its highly sought-after triple IPA. It's usually gone within two weeks. The best place to try it is at the brewpub, although a few select accounts do get a keg of it, often opening them during SF Beer Week, which takes place in mid-February. If you're planning a pilgrimage to Russian River Brewing, that's a good time to visit, although expect bigger-than-usual crowds.

Russian River Brewing Company

Opened: April 3, 2004 (current brewpub; original brewery opened in May 1997).

Type: Brewpub and production brewery.

Owners: Natalie and Vinnie Cilurzo.

Brewer: Vinnie Cilurzo.

Guild membership: BA, CCBA, NCBG.

System: 20-barrel Criveller, annual capacity 3,000 barrels. Production brewery: 50-barrel Pub Systems brewhouse, 11,000 barrels annual capacity.

Annual production: 14,000 barrels (2012).

Packages available: 375-, 500-, and 750-milliliter bottles and growlers. Kegs are not available for purchase by consumers.

Tours: Tours are not available, though you can see the barrel room and portions of the brewery from windows in the brewpub. The production brewery is not open to the public.

Hours: Sunday through Thursday, 11 a.m. to midnight; Friday and Saturday, 11 a.m. to 1 a.m.

Food: The brewpub has a full menu of beer-friendly dishes, including a terrific selection of appetizers. The beer bites are my favorite. Described as "crispy bits of dough topped with mozzarella and garlic," they're like bite-size pizzas and are available with additional ingredients, like pepperoni or oregano and Parmesan. The menu also includes sandwiches, meal-size salads, calzones, and an inventive collection of nearly twenty different pizzas.

Extras: Happy hour is from 4 to 6:30 p.m. Monday through Friday and all day on Sunday. There's also live music on Saturday and Sunday.

Gift shop: T-shirts, hoodies, hats, glassware, and more are available at the brewpub and online.

Ruth McGowan's Brewpub

131 East First Street, Cloverdale, CA 95425
707-894-9610 • www.ruthmcgowansbrewpub.com
Twitter @ruthmcgowans
Facebook.com/ruthmcgowans

Ruth McGowan was a feisty lady from New London, Wisconsin, who was still mowing her own lawn and shoveling snow off her walk at the ripe old age of ninety-six. She was also a favorite of her grandson, Mike Brigham, who, along with his wife, Mary Ann, opened Ruth McGowan's Brewpub in her honor on Saint Patrick's Day in 2002. His grandmother would have been proud.

They got no less a brewing rockstar than Vinnie Cilurzo to design the initial lineup of beers, who at the time was still installing his present Russian River brewpub in Santa Rosa (see Russian River Brewing Company on page 105). Bear Republic's head brewer, Peter Kruger, also made beer there for a time but now works at Cloverdale's only other brewery. These days, Timothy Gallagher works the pipes and valves behind the bar to make all of the beer.

Ruth McGowan's is located in the downtown Cloverdale area, which is dotted with shops, restaurants, bars, and parks. Walking around the downtown area, you may feel as if you've stepped back in time. Things are slower here, and the hum of the nearby highway is just white noise. From time to time you'll see a modern reminder that it is indeed the twenty-first century, but not before you've slowed your pace and allowed yourself to saunter for a time, relaxing under the spell. Give in to it. Take a deep breath and go for a pint.

Inside, the brewpub is clean and well lit, and there are no barflies here. When founding Ruth McGowan, Mary Ann had a goal of creating a space that was female-friendly, something that can be a rarity in many male-oriented drinking estab-

Beers brewed: Year-round: Floyd IPA, Caroline's Blonde Ale, Cloverdale Ale, Monster Brown, McGowan's Dry Irish Stout, Citrus Wheat, and Mighty Shillelagh Belgian Triple. Seasonals: Acapulco Rock (spring), Drinko de Ryeo (summer), and the Oatmeal Raisin Cookie (winter holidays).

The Pick: The Floyd IPA is a really complex hops monster, with a mélange of grassy, herbal, grapefruit, and sweet onion aromas, bitter but never astringent. Try it; you'll like it. If you happen to be there during the holidays, don't miss the delightfully subtle and spicy Oatmeal Raisin Cookie.

lishments. Surveying the number of families here on any given day tells you she's succeeded handsomely.

The brewpub serves large portions of comfort food that seems home-cooked and makes you feel right at home, especially if you live in a brewery. Every time I've been there, locals dot the bar stools, and it's one of those small-town places where everybody does indeed seem to know everybody's name. But even as the stranger, I've always felt welcome. You will, too. That's just the atmosphere the Brighams have created.

Ruth McGowan's Brewpub

Opened: March 17, 2002.

Type: Brewpub.

Owners: Mike and Mary Ann Brigham.

Brewer: Timothy Gallagher.

System: 12-barrel brew system, 650 barrels annual capacity.

Annual production: 400 to 450 barrels (estimated).

Packages available: Growlers and 5- and 15.5-gallon kegs, as well as 22-ounce bottles of five of the beers.

Tours: Available on written request.

Hours: Monday through Thursday, 3 to 9 p.m.; Friday and Saturday, 11:30 a.m. to 10 p.m.; Sunday, 11:30 a.m. to 9 p.m.

Food: The menu is classic American pub food, with an extensive starters list that includes not just old favorites, but also such eclectic items as Irish nachos and Fritto Misto, buttermilk-battered and fried rock shrimp, calamari, artichoke hearts, fennel, and asparagus. The dinner menu includes burgers, sandwiches, and fish and chips, along with a selection of soups and salads.

Extras: There's usually live music on Saturday nights, and the brewpub has a shuffleboard table and darts. The first and third Thursday of each month, from 6 to 9 p.m., is Session Night—patrons bring their acoustic instruments to the brewpub and take part in a neighborhood jam session that includes as wide a variety of music styles as there are musicians. A number of guest taps from local craft brewers are also available. Outdoor seating is available, where smoking is permitted.

St. Florian's Brewery

7704-A Bell Road, Windsor, CA 95492
707-838-BREW (2739)
www.stfloriansbrewery.com
Twitter @stfloriansbrew
Facebook.com/stfloriansbrewery

St. Florian is the patron saint of firefighters, who, "legend has it, used water set aside for the next day's brew to extinguish a catastrophic fire," securing his place as a hero and a saint. This description of the third-century Roman soldier appears on every label of St. Florian's Brewery beer. Some believe that the shield on some fire department logos is derived from a Florian cross. The brewery's cofounder, Aron Levin, a captain with the Windsor Fire Department, has never experienced anything worse than minor burns, but he knows others who weren't as fortunate, which led him to choose St. Florian as the name for his brewery and to commit to donating at least 5 percent of the brewery's profits to fire-related and community-based local charities.

The new Sonoma County production brewery is run by a husband-and-wife team whose goal is for their brewery to have the "happiest customers and most delighted imbimbers." Amy Levin, who spent a decade in software sales, oversees sales, marketing, and the business side of things, while Aron, who has been making beer in his home for more than twenty years, brews all the beer and bottles it with their Maheen bottling line.

The brewery is in an industrial park near U.S. Route 101 just north of Santa Rosa. For the near term, it's a production-only space, with no public facilities, but the Levins may convert the front office to a tasting room in a couple years. For now, they are concentrating on brewing and selling the beer.

Beers brewed: Year-round: Brown Ale, Cali Common, and India Pale Ale (IPA). Seasonals: To be announced.

The Pick: The IPA is a nice, more restrained version of a West Coast IPA, with great malt notes and good hopping that never hits you over the head. The nose is predominately citrus and grapefruit, with aromas of pine and floral aromas. The hops are thick and chewy in the taste but buoyed by a sweet caramel malt presence. The result is a big IPA that's very drinkable and won't wreck your palate.

St. Florian's Brewery

Opened: January 2013.

Type: Production brewery.

Owners: Amy and Aron Levin.

Brewer: Aron Levin.

Guild membership: BA, CCBA.

System: 15-barrel Premier Stainless, 1,500 barrels annual capacity.

Annual production: 1,500 barrels (2013 estimate).

Packages available: 12-ounce bottles in six-packs, 22-ounce bottles, and 5- and 15.5-gallon kegs.

Tours: Brewery tours are available by appointment only. St. Florian's Brewery is also available for tours through North Bay Brewery Tours (northbaybrewerytours.com).

Hours: Check the website or Facebook page for current hours.

Gift shop: A range of apparel is available at the brewery. More items will be added and merchandise will be sold online in the near future.

Sonoma Springs Brewing Company

750 West Napa Street, Sonoma, CA 95476
707-938-7422 • www.sonomaspringsbrewery.com
Facebook.com/sonomaspringsbrewingco

Like many young brewers, Tim Goeppinger developed a passion for great beer while in college. He got a degree in engineering from Northwestern University, at the Chicago campus, not too far from where he grew up in central Illinois. After graduating in 1998, he got a job with a brew-on-premises (BOP), which taught him how to create beer recipes. After a year at the BOP, he got what he considers his first real job in the brewing industry, at Goose Island Brewing in Chicago, where he worked with Matt Brynildson from 1999 on.

When Brynildson came to California to take the head brewer's job at Firestone Waker Brewing, he discovered he needed some help in the brewhouse. So he asked his friend Tim Goeppinger if he'd be interested in coming out to work there too. After a lifetime of Chicago winters, Tim jumped at the chance to brew in California and spent a couple years brewing with Brynildson at Firestone Walker. He then moved north to Sonoma County and has been there ever since. He worked for a time at Lagunitas Brewing, then for a local winery, and finally at Russian River Brewing, before starting his own brewery in 2008.

Goeppinger founded Sonoma Springs with two of his brothers, Tom and Toby Goeppinger, who also fled the Midwest for Northern California. Tim comes from a family of five, and he has two more brothers also making plans to head west. Sonoma Springs is a true family business, and it's not uncommon for the Goeppinger brothers' mom to answer the phone when you call there, because she too has made the western trek to work at the brewery. Tim's wife, Ann, is also a partner in the brewery and can be found behind the bar as well.

The brewery is located along State Route 12, which makes its way through downtown Sonoma, where a rustic wooden sign announces Sonoma Springs' presence. The place is next door to a bakery, and the brewery is small and clean. A modern

Beers brewed: Year-round: Lil' Chief Pale Ale, Uncle Jack's Kolsch, and Enchanted Forest Black IPA. Seasonals: SlowNoma Saison, 'Noma Coma Imperial IPA, Mission Bell Sour Wheat, New Bavaria Roggenbier, Oktobock Lager, Green Purl Herbal Tonic, Noma Weiss Hefe-Style, Oktopotomus Dark Lager, Isis, FREUDE Fig Lambic, ONYX Double Black IPA Whiskey Barrel Aged, and Wolf House Double Black IPA.

bar is on one side, but it feels more as if you're in somebody's home. The copper brewhouse is in the back and sits out in the open, with wine barrels used for aging tucked away wherever they'll fit.

The biggest problem facing Sonoma Springs these days is keeping up with demand. It has already outgrown its location and needs to expand. The family is currently in the process of scouting around for a new place to move the brewery. It's not too surprising, because even though Sonoma Springs flies under the radar somewhat, Goeppinger is really a terrific brewer, and everything he's making is pretty tasty. He likes to focus on German-style beers, especially the lesser-known, top-fermenting kind like roggenbier. He also has a deft hand with sour beers and more traditional West Coast hoppy beers. So the range you'll find on tap at any given time is surprisingly vast. How good they all taste, on the other hand, is no surprise at all.

The Pick: It's hard to beat a good roggenbier—it's a favorite style of mine—and Sonoma Springs' version, New Bavaria Roggenbier, is quite good. It's got a Bavarian wheat nose, but with zesty rye spicing and bread dough malt flavors. The mouthfeel is chewy and rich. If that's not available, take a trip to the Enchanted Forest, the brewery's black IPA. It's a great version of the emerging style, with pine and citrus hops aromas, and chocolate malt as well. With flavors of molasses and toast, plus a hint of espresso or mocha and chocolate, it's a rich beer with really nice synergy between the hops character and the dark malt.

Sonoma Springs Brewing Company

Opened: April 2008.

Type: Production brewery, with tasting room.

Owners: Tim, Tom, and Toby Goeppinger.

Brewer: Tim Goeppinger.

Guild membership: BA, CCBA.

System: 10-barrel Bohemian Systems brewhouse, 1,000 barrels annual capacity.

Annual production: 500 barrels (2012 estimate).

Packages available: Growlers, specialty bottles, and 13.2- and 15.5-gallon kegs.

Tours: Brewery tours are available; no reservations are necessary.

Hours: Monday and Wednesday through Saturday, 1 to 9 p.m.; Sunday, 1 to 6 p.m. Closed Tuesday.

Food: No food is available at the brewery, other than for some special events and occasions, but visitors are welcome to bring their own food.

Extras: There's an outdoor area with a few tables out in front of the brewery where you can sit and enjoy a beer. It's not a beer garden exactly, but it's comfortable enough. Happy hour is from 4 to 6 p.m. each day. On most weekends you can enjoy live entertainment, usually local bands and solo artists. Check the Facebook page for details and scheduled events.

Gift shop: T-shirts, hoodies, hats, and pint glasses are sold at the brewery.

Stumptown Brewery

15045 River Road, Guerneville, CA 95446
707-869-0705 • www.stumptown.com
Facebook.com/pages/Stumptown-Brewery/244542762268119

Situated on a sloping hill above the Russian River, the Stumptown Brewery offers picturesque views. While the bar inside is mostly wood and has the comfortable feel of a roadhouse, complete with pool tables, it's the large outdoor patio you should explore. That 3,500-square-foot balcony is where the views are, and with plentiful 9-foot tables, there's seating for more than two hundred.

Australian ex-pat Peter Hackett starting thinking about opening a brewery in the early 1990s, but after a few misstarts and bureaucratic hurdles, the first beer was brewed in June 2001. The original brewer was Peter Kruger, who went on to become the head brewer at Bear Republic, but not before teaching Hackett everything he knew about brewing. Since 2005, Hackett has brewed all of the beer himself.

The brewpub is just down the road from the Korbel Winery in Guerneville, a rustic tourist destination, and during the summer and on weekends, it's packed with out-of-towners, though regulars can be found at the bar all year long. The area is also a great place for a bike ride or taking a kayak down the Russian River.

One of the highlights of beer festival season is Stumptown's Russian River Beer Revival & BBQ Cookoff, a terrific food and beer festival held each year in late summer, usually mid-August. Directly below the brewpub, the banks of the Russian River are filled with brewery tents and barbecue teams (at least thirty of each), who smoke and cook their meat right there at the festival. The number of people who can attend is purposely kept small, in part because of the fixed space where the event takes place, but also to maximize the enjoyment of everybody who does attend by keeping it full but not overcrowded. As a result, it always feels like a big outdoor party, but one where you can move around, dance to the live music, and enjoy your beer in the warm sun. The

Beers brewed: Year-round: Rat Bastard Pale Ale, Bootlegger IPA, Bush Wacker Wheat, Donkey Punch Lager, and Blimey the Wanker IPA.

The Pick: The flagship Rat Bastard Pale Ale is the perfect beer to sip on the outdoor patio overlooking the river. It's a light, refreshing pale, with grassy and herbal hops aromas. Nicely balanced with sweet malt character and fresh herbal hops, it's an easy-drinking beer.

event sells out quickly, and usually only advance tickets are available, so plan accordingly.

Stumptown Brewery & Smokehouse

Opened: June 2001.

Type: Brewpub.

Owner: Peter Hackett.

Brewer: Peter Hackett.

Guild membership: BA, CCBA.

System: 7-barrel Quality Stainless brewhouse.

Packages available: Draft only at the brewery.

Tours: A short brewery tour may be available if the brewer is around.

Hours: Sunday through Thursday, 11 a.m. to midnight; Friday and Saturday, 11 a.m. to 2 a.m. Kitchen hours: Most days, 11 a.m. to 9 p.m.; closed Tuesday. Hours change seasonally, however, so it's best to call for current days and times.

Food: Stumptown offers a full menu of roadhouse food, with sandwiches and burgers, along with BBQ ribs and fish and chips. You can also order the "boat load" of fries. I love the slow-smoked pulled-pork sandwich, which is simmered in Stumptown's house BBQ sauce. On the weekends, you can also get Drakes Bay oysters.

Extras: In addition to its own beers, Stumptown also offers around five guest taps from local breweries. There's live music, and happy hour is 4 to 7 p.m. weekdays, when beers are $1 off.

Third Street Aleworks

BREWERY & EATERY

610 Third Street, Santa Rosa, CA 95404
707-523-3060 • www.thirdstreetaleworks.com
   or 3rdstbrewery.com
Twitter @3rdStBrewery
Facebook.com/3rdStBrewery

When it comes to beer travel, many people come to Santa Rosa with one destination in mind, and that's just one street over. And that's something of a shame, because the older Third Street Aleworks is nothing like its more well-known neighbor Russian River, but that's not at all a bad thing. In fact, the Third Street Aleworks has much to recommend it, and it deserves the attention that locals give it. It's just off the Old Courthouse Square in the heart of downtown Santa Rosa.

It may be more of a traditional brewpub, with a nice range of beers and an extensive menu of pub food, but the food is delicious, plentiful, and reasonably priced. Oh, and the beer is quite tasty too. Randy Gremp has been the capable brewer at Third Street since November 2005, when he left his brewing job at the Calistoga Inn after thirteen years. Originally from Chicago, Gremp moved to the Bay Area in 1981, where he worked primarily as a carpenter and also did some outdoor landscape gardening before he began homebrewing, about four or five years before starting his brewing career in Napa.

The brewpub is quite large, at around 7,000 square feet, and is very well lit, with big windows giving an airy feel to the space, especially in the upstairs balcony. Despite its industrial look, it still has a warm feeling inside. There's a large, long bar when you enter the restaurant, with seating all around. The cramped brewery is behind the bar, partially hidden, but it can be seen behind the large windows that dot the wall behind the full bar. On nice days, you can also sit outside on the small but wonderful patio. The brewpub is family-friendly at all times of the day and night.

Gremp keeps at least ten different beers on, and often more than that. In addition to the regulars, he brews seasonal offerings and a rotating assortment of one-offs and special releases throughout the year. Many of these are brewed only once. Third Street also recently starting bottling some of the beer, and at any given time, you can find three of its beers in 22-ounce bottles, both at the brewpub and at many area retailers.

Third Street Aleworks may be one of the hidden gems of Santa Rosa, but it deserves to be much more than that.

Third Street Aleworks

Opened: March 8, 1996.

Type: Brewpub.

Owners: Todd Hedrick, Chris Hagan, and additional investors.

Brewer: Randy Gremp.

Guild membership: BA, CCBA.

System: 14-barrel Pub Brewing system, 1,500 barrels annual capacity.

Annual production: 1,400 barrels (2012).

Packages available: 22-ounce bottles, growlers, and 5-, 7.75-, and 15.5-gallon kegs.

Tours: No formal tours are available, but if you ask, the brewer will be happy to show you around if he's not too busy making the next batch of beer.

Hours: Sunday through Thursday, 11:30 a.m. to midnight; Friday and Saturday, 11:30 a.m. to 1 a.m. Kitchen closes Sunday and Monday at 10 p.m.; Tuesday through Thursday at 11 p.m.; and Friday and Saturday at 11:30 p.m.

Food: The menu includes a nice mix of dishes, with a number of tasty starters, especially the sliders and beer-battered zucchini sticks, as well as soups and salads, burgers and sandwiches, and pizza. Other entrées include tacos, bratwurst, macaroni and cheese, fish and chips, and my favorite, the shepherd's pie. There's also a separate kids' menu.

Extras: Happy hour is 3 to 6 p.m. on weekdays, and there are daily food specials for both lunch and dinner. On Tuesday, you can get discounted beers and bratwurst. On Wednesday, kids eat free with one meal per adult entrée. There's also a billiard table on the second floor. Third Street also puts on the occasional beer dinner, so keep an eye on the Facebook page or website for details.

Gift shop: T-shirts, hats, and glassware are available at the brewpub.

Beers brewed: Year-round: Annadel English Style Pale Ale, Bombay Rouge, Puddle Jumper Pale Ale, Cherry Springer, American Wheat Ale, Cascadian Dark, Blarney Sisters Dry Irish Stout, Bodega Head IPA, and Stonefly Oatmeal Stout. Seasonals: Kalamity Kolsch, Brass Parachute Barley Wine, Double Standard India Pale Ale, Melissa's Cream Ale, Hedrick and Hagan Bitter, Jeckyll's Best Bitter, and Stepchild Red Ale. Gremp also brews a bewildering number of special beers that he often makes just once, so you never know what you might encounter during a visit there.

The Pick: The Blarney Sisters Dry Irish Stout is one of the best-tasting dry stouts you're likely to encounter outside of Ireland. It's a spot-on version, with great roasted notes and chocolate character. It also has a subtle fruit component, some licorice, and a touch of smokiness. It's very complex despite its overall mellowness. The mouthfeel is smooth and silky, and it goes down easy.

Warped Brewing Company

6790 McKinley Street, Unit 155, Sebastopol, CA 95465
www.warpedbrewing.com
Twitter @warpedbrewing • Facebook.com/WarpedBrewing

Warped Brewing is a new brewery being built by Noah and Mirjam Bolmer, the owners of the popular Occidental beer bar Barley and Hops Tavern. The brewery is less than 10 miles from the pub in nearby Sebastopol and is expected to open in August 2013.

Longtime homebrewers, the Bolmers had the brewhouse custom-built in Northern California. With a 10-barrel brewing system, 20-barrel hot liquor tank, and four jacketed fermenters, Noah Bolmer will create local beer for his pub and operate a tasting room for people to sample his beer.

Their tavern, Barley and Hops, is located in a yellow Victorian house in downtown Occidental. All of Warped's beers will be available there, among the tavern's thirteen taps and sixty bottled craft beers. There may be no food at the brewery, but the delicious food served at the Bolmer's tavern more than makes up for this.

Warped Brewing Company

Opened: August 2013.

Type: Production brewery, with tasting room.

Owners: Noah A. and Mirjam Bolmer.

Brewer: Noah A. Bolmer.

Guild membership: BA, CCBA.

System: 10-barrel custom-built brewing system, designed and built by Dan Schulte of Cazadero, 1,200 barrels annual capacity.

Packages available: Growlers and 5- and 15.5-gallon kegs.

Tours: Walk-in tours will be available, though it will be such a small brewery there won't be too much to see.

Hours: Check the website or Facebook page for current hours.

Food: No food will be available at the brewery, but you can get delicious, made-from-scratch, high-end comfort food at their Barley and Hops Tavern in Occidental, less than 10 miles away.

Extras: You can enjoy a pint of Warped beer on the large outdoor patio.

Gift shop: Shirts, swag, and growlers will be available at the brewery.

New Albion
America's First Modern Microbrewery

Among the numerous pioneers of craft beer who blazed the trail that has allowed today's brewers to make some of the best beer anywhere in the world, one who goes largely unheralded is a former navy engineer named Jack McAuliffe. On October 8, 1976, McAuliffe incorporated America's first modern microbrewery, New Albion Brewery. With the stamp of the clerk's seal on the papers being filed, the first modern microbrewery was launched. By the following year, McAuliffe was brewing and selling his beer out of a small, unassuming corrugated tin building in Sonoma.

While Fritz Maytag turned the old Anchor Brewery into a model of modern brewery, reintroducing new styles and in essence creating the first craft brewery as we understand that term today, New Albion blazed a different path, equally important to the building of an entirely new industry of small breweries. What I believe makes Jack McAuliffe's accomplishment so important is that he was the first person to build a brewery from scratch, almost entirely by himself, scouring salvage yards for scrap metal, discarded dairy tanks, and anything he could use to build a brewery. In those days, there were no domestic brewing equipment companies from which you could simply order what you needed. You had to make do with what you could find.

The homemade brewery McAuliffe built was a tiny one-barrel system, also perhaps making New Albion the original nanobrewery, a term that's recently become popular to describe breweries making very small batches. The beers were hand-bottled and delivered in wooden crates.

That was, I believe, Jack's biggest contribution: showing that you could build a brewery on the cheap, with limited resources but tons of gumption, determination, and hard work. Dozens of new microbrewers in the early 1980s followed McAuliffe's example and built ramshackle breweries with whatever equipment they could find or build themselves. Many of these early breweries failed, but others are still with us today.

For example, following New Albion's example, Ken Grossman, living at the time in Chico, took night classes to learn how to weld in order to build Sierra Nevada's first brewhouse. Though the brewery has moved on from that first handmade system, today it's still churning out great beer at Mad River Brewing in nearby Blue Lake.

Unfortunately, New Albion was a bit ahead of its time, and McAuliffe was unable to secure the financing he needed to grow his brewery. When I asked Jack about that experience, he told me, "They just didn't know what to make of me or the very idea of a microbrewery." Disheartened by New Albion's untimely closure Jack went back to his earlier career in engineering, refusing to stay involved in the fledgling beer industry. After several years no one in the brewing community knew where Jack was, and until recently he remained an elusive figure. Then in 2005, Maureen Ogle, a historian and writer from Iowa who was researching a book on the history of beer in America, tracked him down. While looking for McAuliffe on the Internet, she came across Jack's daughter, Rene DeLuca, who put Ogle onto his trail. Jack, who by then was living in Las Vegas, opened up to Ogle about his brewing experiences, and a chapter in her book *Ambitious Brew: The Story of American Beer*, published the following year, became one of the first accounts of New Albion Brewing's history and legacy.

But Jack himself remained out of the limelight. At the Craft Brewers Conference in Austin, Texas, in 2007, McAuliffe was honored with their Recognition Award, but he declined to attend and his former assistant brewer, Don Barkley, received the award on his behalf.

It's often said that history is written by the winners, and until recently, few people knew New Albion's story, which is not at all surprising when you consider that it was in business a mere seven years and distributed its beer only around the Bay Area. After it shuttered its doors, Barkley bought the brewing equipment and, along with some investors, founded Mendocino Brewing Company.

After the Craft Brewers Conference was held in San Francisco in 2011, I had lunch with Jack McAuliffe at the Russian River Brewery in Santa Rosa, where the original sign for the New Albion Brewery now hangs. The following day, McAuliffe escorted me, along with Vinnie and Natalie Cilurzo, to the site of the original brewery in Sonoma. We drove to the old Ninth Street location, and Jack showed us around the small, nondescript corrugated steel warehouse building where New Albion Brewery first made pale ale, amber ale, and a porter, along with the occasional special release.

Although it's now used as a warehouse, it looks almost the same as it does in the few surviving photos of the brewery. Not much has changed. Jack walked us around the building, pointing out where various pieces of equipment used to be and showing us the loft he had made to sleep in by pushing up a portion of the roof. There should be a historical marker at the site, and perhaps one day there will be.

In 2009, McAuliffe was in a serious car accident and has since relocated to San Antonio, Texas, where he now lives with his sister. He's been going to the meetings at a local homebrew club and helping out the next generation of brewers. I don't know if the young homebrewers he's tutoring are aware of his place in the history of craft beer in America. Like many beer lovers, they might not even know who Jack is, but they really should. He was a pioneer who helped put Northern California on the map as the undisputed birthplace of craft beer.

The South Bay

The South Bay is, as you might expect, the region just below San Francisco.
Drive south from the city down the Peninsula and you're in the South
Bay, which takes you to Silicon Valley. For the purposes of this book,
the South Bay region includes the counties of San Mateo, Santa Clara,
and Santa Cruz. San Mateo and Santa Cruz Counties border the Pacific
Ocean on their western edges, and Santa Clara borders both of them
on its own western border. The region is about half the size of Connecticut but has a population slightly larger than the entire state of
Nevada, with three times as many people as San Francisco.

San Francisco is nestled at the northern tip of a peninsula that sepa-
rates the San Francisco Bay from the Pacific Ocean. South of the city,
that area is known as the Peninsula and includes most of San Mateo
County. The Peninsula is filled with suburban communities and, like
Marin in the north, is a place from which many people commute to the
city each day. There's very little undeveloped land on the Peninsula,
and you encounter city after city as you work your way down one of the
main arteries, Highway 101 or Interstate 280. The San Francisco International Airport is actually located here and not within the city limits.

There are some ocean communities down Highway 1 that are somewhat removed from the more urban communities, and here you can
find one of the most famous surfing spots in California: Mavericks.
Since 1999, a big wave surfing contest has been held annually at the
site near Half Moon Bay. Along the same stretch of ocean, San Mateo
also includes a dozen state beaches, and farther inland it has an equal
number of state parks.

Farther south and slightly east is Santa Clara County, which is both
the most populous county in the Bay Area and, thanks to its high-tech

industry, one of the most affluent—not just in California, but in the whole United States. If the name Santa Clara is unfamiliar, you most likely know it by its more famous nickname: Silicon Valley.

It's an apt name, with around sixty-five hundred high-tech companies in the county. Some of the most famous names in computers and technology are headquartered there, including Apple, eBay, Facebook, Google, Hewlett Packard, Intel, and Yahoo, to name just a few. Although San Jose installed a light rail system in the late 1980s and has continued to increase its reach, you'll most likely still need a car, as it's difficult to get around the congested South Bay without one.

Just below San Mateo and Santa Clara Counties, just south of the well-known San Andreas Fault, is Santa Cruz County, which is decidedly more laid-back than the other two. The tourist beach towns that cozy up to the ocean draw heavily from people around the area as long weekend and vacation destinations. The southern portion of the county encompasses the northern half of Monterey Bay.

The Santa Cruz Boardwalk, an oceanfront amusement park reminiscent of old Atlantic City, has one of those classic wooden roller coasters, called the Giant Dipper. The once famous Cocoanut Grove is there too. In the thirties and forties, some of the biggest names in big-band jazz performed there, but today it's an event space people rent for weddings, dances, and the like.

Armstrong Brewing Company

330 Littlefield Avenue, South San Francisco, CA 94080
415-745-2739 • www.armstrongbrewing.com
Twitter @armstrongbrew
Facebook.com/ArmstrongBrewing

South San Francisco is known as "the Industrial City," and it's been home to numerous industries, from the Western Meat Company, the very first in 1894, to Fuller Paint and two U.S. Steel mills. Today the biggest industry is Genentech, though United Airlines employs the most people. But Armstrong Brewing Company, which opened in early 2013, is the first brewery in South San Francisco.

Armstrong Brewing was founded by Nick Armstrong and Pat Hinterberger, both homebrewers with years of experience before going pro. Nick, the Armstrong in the brewery name, has been homebrewing for more than a decade and has a degree in bioprocessing and food science. He's worked for breweries as well as some beer and flavor labs, and he continues to work at Genentech in addition to the new brewery. Hinterberger's been homebrewing for five years and is also a certified cicerone.

Along with business partner Ben Colombo, they found a 900-square-foot space in an industrial park and installed a small brewing system. In addition to the tasting room and kegs at local bars and restaurants, Armstrong Brewing also offers another way to purchase its beer: through a membership club. Membership is available in three types, for annual fees currently ranging from $30 to $75. Members receive various exclusive opportunities to purchase the brewery's limited releases before they're available to the public at large, and each level provides increasing benefits. See the website for full details on membership options.

One amazing project that Armstrong is undertaking is to figure out a better process to make a great-tasting gluten-free beer, something of a holy grail for celiac sufferers. He's partnered with a group of senior students in food science and bioprocessing at North Carolina State University to develop a new process for removing or separating

Beers brewed: Year-round: South City Brown, Mo's Gose, ESB, and Belgian. Membership specials: Chocolate Cherry Stout, Traditional Lambic and Rye Whiskey Porter. Seasonals: ESB, Saison, and Coffee Stout.

gluten proteins from the beer, yet still use 100 percent barley to brew it, something that's currently not possible. If successful, it would be a major breakthrough.

While production is currently very limited, plans for the future include canning the brewery's beer, most likely starting with the gose. Unless you stop by the brewery on Friday night or purchase a membership, finding the beer may prove difficult, though Armstrong and Hinterberger are making some very interesting beers, and I suspect they'll be highly sought after once word gets around.

Armstrong Brewing Company

Opened: February 2013.

Type: Production brewery, with taproom.

Owners: Nick Armstrong, Pat Hinterberger, and Ben Colombo.

Brewers: Nick Armstrong and Pat Hinterberger.

System: 2-barrel brewhouse, 200 barrels annual capacity.

Annual production: 150 to 200 barrels (estimate).

Packages available: Cans, growlers, and pints in the taproom, in addition to beer offered exclusively to club members.

Tours: The brewery can be seen during open hours on Friday.

Hours: Friday, 5 to 11 p.m.

Food: No food is available at the brewery.

Extras: The taproom has a big-screen television.

Gift shop: T-shirts and glassware, as well as brewery memberships, are available online.

Ass Kisser Ales

1027 South Seventh Street, San Jose, CA 95112
www.asskisserales.com
Twitter @asskisserales
Facebook.com/pages/Ass-Kisser-Ales/
136206689742166

The Ass Kisser brand is a family-owned company making irreverently named beers. But there's no joking when it comes to the beers themselves. The company has partnered with Hermitage Brewing and has even leased warehouse space right next door to Hermitage in order to increase production over the next two years, and it plans to install its own tank farms to ferment the beer after it's brewed.

Ass Kisser offers four year-round beers and a rotating mix of inventive seasonals. You can find them throughout California and beyond. In just a few short years, the company has spread the distribution of its beer into a number of states throughout the country.

Beers brewed: Year-round: Vanilla Pale Ale, Tight Ass Hefeweizen, Kick Ass Double IPA, and Porter Pounder Smoked Porter. Seasonals: Bourbon Barrel Aged Smoked Porter, Berry Nice Ass Belgian Style Strawberry Wit, Vanilla Pale Ale, and Chocolate Box Dark Oatmeal Stout.

Ass Kisser Ales

Opened: June 2010.

Type: Production brewery.

Owner: Franc Rocca.

Guild membership: BA.

System: See Hermitage Brewing (page 150) for brewery details.

Annual production: 3,000 barrels (2012 estimate).

Packages available: 12-ounce four-packs and 22-ounce bottles.

Gift shop: Brewery merchandise is available at the Facebook page.

The Pick: I really like the Porter Pounder Smoked Porter; it's very rich, with chocolate, vanilla, and caramel notes, and of course, big smoked aromas and flavors. The amount of smoke in the beer hits the Goldilocks spot—it's just right. That's the key to a good smoked beer, as far as I'm concerned.

Boulder Creek Brewery and Café

13040 Highway 9, Boulder Creek, CA 95006
831-338-7882 • www.bouldercreekbrewery.net
Facebook.com/bouldercreekbrewery

Boulder Creek is a small town tucked into the San Lorenzo Valley, surrounded by trees. It was built as a logging town, and today about four thousand people live in this rural oasis among the redwoods. The main part of town is the Highway 9 thoroughfare, which runs from Saratoga in the north to the Pacific Ocean and Santa Cruz. State Route 9 cuts through Castle Rock State Park and skirts nearby Big Basin Redwoods State Park, the same route that loggers once took to get the trees to the wharf, where they could be loaded onto ships.

The roadside café is an oasis among the trees, where travelers can stop for a few pints and a good meal. Behind its unassuming façade, you'll find a treasure inside, and the small brewpub equipment is put to amazing use, brewing a wide array of different styles of beer. Most of the brewery is situated behind a bar, in its own room to your left as you walk in, and there are a few tables in there too. You can watch brewer Joe Yuhas doing his job while enjoying the fruits of his labor at the same time. If you didn't feel guilty, you could easily sit there all day.

San Lorenzo Valley native Michael Demers had been the brewer at Boulder Creek for nearly fifteen years, but he left last year to be part of a new brewing venture in Santa Cruz called Discretion Brewing (see page 134). Joe Yuhas, a longtime homebrewer, had been interning at the brewpub and was thrilled to step up and turn pro. He's been nicely carrying on the tradition of great beers left by Demers.

There's also a separate dining area on the right as you enter the building. Either here or in the brewery, you can be assured of an amazing meal and some fine beers. It takes some effort to travel to Boulder Creek, but it's definitely worth the trip

Beers brewed: Year-round: Bloom Grade Blonde, Harvest Wheat, ESB, Aptos Pale Ale, Redwood Ale, Loch Lomond Scotch Ale, San Lorenzo Porter, Black Dragon Stout, Dragon's Breath IPA, and Double Dragon DIPA. Seasonals: Galena Pale Ale, Summit Pale Ale, Cluster Fuggle Pale Ale, Golden Girl Pale Ale, Aptos Pale Ale, Fall Creek Pale Ale, Zythos IPA, Ohlone Ale, Black Magic CDA, Belgian Wit, Belgian Abbey, Belgian Tripel, Winter Warmer, Christmas City Ale, Irish Red(wood) Ale, Skyline Amber, Gambrinus Extra Pale, 1892 Smoke Ale, Black Brett, and Saison Brett, along with numerous one-offs and special beers throughout the year.

through some beautiful country. Boulder Creek Brewery beers can also be found at the Surfrider Café in Santa Cruz, which has the same owners as the brewpub.

Boulder Creek Brewery and Café

Opened: December 1989.

Type: Brewpub.

Owner: Stephen Wyman.

Brewer: Joe Yuhas.

System: 7-barrel JV Northwest, modified, 700 barrels annual capacity.

Annual production: 500 barrels (2011 estimate).

Packages available: Growlers and 5- and 15.5-gallon kegs.

Tours: Brewery tours are available. No reservations are necessary, but weekdays during the day are the best times to ask for a tour.

Hours: Monday through Thursday, 11:30 a.m. to 10 p.m.; Friday and Saturday, 11:30 a.m. to 10:30 p.m.; Sunday, 11:30 a.m. to 10 p.m.

Food: Curiously, Boulder Creek is billed as a café and refers to itself as a sandwich shop and burger joint, but that's really false modesty. Because despite that and the appearance of a rustic roadhouse, the food is top-notch, and in addition to sandwiches and burgers, you can enjoy such dishes as pan-seared sea scallops beurre blanc, Kahlua pig and waffles, Welsh rarebit, blackened gulf shrimp Caesar salad and Parmesan tuile, sautéed Mediteranean mussels, and a bewildering selection of ever-changing specials. Keep an eye on the Facebook page, which is regularly updated with both new menu items and new beers on tap.

Extras: Blues music is performed Thursday and Saturdays. Check the Facebook page for details.

Gift shop: T-shirts are available at the brewpub.

The Pick: The Dragon's Breath IPA is a really nice hoppy beer, perfect on a hot day surrounded by woods, since its nose is grassy, pine, and herbal. It's well balanced with some treacly sweet malt and sticky hops character. Yuhas was also experimenting with brett beers the last time I was there, with some interesting results. If that's still going on, be sure to give some of those a try too.

Campbell Brewing Company

200 E. Campbell Avenue, Campbell, CA 95008
408-866-2699 • www.campbellbrewing.com
Twitter @CampbellBrewing
Facebook.com/CampbellBrewingCompany

When the space that now holds the Campbell Brewing Company first opened in 2002, it was the second location of Stoddard's Brewhouse and Eatery, and it took four years and $8 million to build. The bank that used to occupy the corner lot was torn down for the two-story brewery building. It started out like gangbusters but quickly fizzled, and by late 2003 it had closed.

New owners made major renovations and reopened the following summer under the current name. But just a few months later, it was closed again. The San Jose restaurant Sonoma Chicken Coop moved it but continued to run the brewery as a quasi-separate business under the same roof.

The brewery and bar are located on the left-hand side of the building, somewhat segregated from the restaurant. The brewpub resembles a sports bar, with big-screen televisions showing a variety of sports. Tall tables and bar stools fill the open floor plan, although there's a partition running parallel to the bar. The bar has an angled shape, with a row of windows running along the back and side through which you can see into the brewhouse.

Four years ago, Jim Turturici took over the brewery. Turturici began homebrewing at the tender age of sixteen. He got his first adult brewing job at the Front Street Pub in Santa Cruz, brewing under Scotty Morgan, and later brewed at the Rock Bottom in Campbell. His style hews toward traditional and authentic English-style recipes—nothing too extreme, just solid, well-made beers. He changes the hops in each batch of India Pale Ale, so it's always a little different every time you order one.

Beers brewed: Year-round: Kolsch, IPA, ESB, and Scottish Ale. Seasonals: Hefeweizen, Porter, Summer Ale, American Strong Red, Barleywine, Imperial Stout, and Barrel Aged Big Brown Ale, to name a few.

The Pick: Kolsch is a deceptively difficult beer to make well, but the Campbell Brewing version is quite nice. It's clean and refreshing, with clear straw color, delicate spicing, and lemon citrus aromas. With subtle fruit character and light, biscuity, cracker flavors, it's a crisp beer that finishes with a soft tang.

Management and ownership of the brewery recently changed once more, earlier this year, and the name is firmly Campbell Brewing Company once again as it began focusing more on the beer. Turturici will be experimenting with beer in firkins, making more seasonal and rotating beers, and generally trying to shake things up. It will be fun to see what he brews up.

Campbell Brewing Company

Opened: July 1, 2004.

Type: Brewpub.

Owner: Jerry McDougal.

Brewer: Jim Turturici.

Guild membership: BA, CCBA, BBG.

System: 20-barrel JV Northwest, 3,000 barrels annual capacity.

Annual production: 1,600 barrels (2012).

Packages available: Draft-only and 5- and 15.5-gallon kegs.

Tours: Reservations are recommended for brewery tours, but if the brewer is available, he'll be happy to conduct a quick tour.

Hours: Sunday, 9 a.m. to 9 p.m.; Monday through Wednesday, 11 a.m. to 9 p.m.; Thursday through Saturday, 9 a.m. to 10 p.m.

Food: Sonoma Chicken Coop, which shares the space with the brewery, has a menu of salads and starters, pizzas and grilled items, pasta, sandwiches, and Roost-tisserie Chicken. There's also a separate weekend brunch menu.

Extras: Happy hour is Monday through Friday, 2 to 6 p.m., with discounts on pints and on select appetizers. The brewpub also hosts a beer dinner every month. Check the website and Facebook page for details.

Gift shop: Shirts, hats, and glassware are available at the brewpub.

Devil's Canyon Brewing Company

935 Washington, San Carlos, CA 94070
650-592-2739 • www.DevilsCanyon.com
Twitter @devilscanyon
Facebook.com/devilscanyon

For a little over a decade, Devil's Canyon organically grew, little by little, in its own corner of Belmont on the Bay Area Peninsula. When you visited the place, it looked a little like Willy Wonka's Chocolate Factory might have looked, if Wonka had made beer. But it just kept growing, with the owners building what they needed as they went along; the result was equipment tucked here and there, wherever it would fit, with blind corridors and dead ends. It was the brewing equivalent of the Winchester Mystery House. Yet it worked.

Devil's Canyon started out as a brew-on-premises (BOP), making beer with groups of people, and then did contract brewing—creating as many as thirty different private-label beers for other businesses to sell under their own names—before it started making a name for its own beer too. So much so, in fact, that it outgrew the Belmont facility and recently moved to much larger quarters, more than doubling its space.

The new location is in nearby San Carlos, about 2 miles due south along U.S. Route 101, in an industrial park just off Industrial Road. It has about 11,500 square feet of brewing space and another 10,000 for a concert hall, plus another building dedicated for cold storage and barrel aging the beer. The BOP equipment will still be available for corporate parties and educational demonstrations.

Founder Chris Garrett grew up in New Mexico but came to the Peninsula to attend college and stayed in the area after graduation. He began homebrewing in 1990, and a love affair with brewing kept growing while he worked in high-tech for companies like Disney and a Microsoft subsidiary. He also spent some time in the Pacific Northwest and pitched in at breweries such as Full Sail, Hood River, and Deschutes. While there, he worked at Admiralty Beverage with the legendary Jim Kennedy, whom his sister married, and Kennedy tried to talk Garrett out of going onto the beer business but eventually came to support his decision.

Garrett made the final decision one morning, while facing another day in the high-tech world of Silicon Valley and deciding he was "not stoked." He turned to his wife, Kristiann, whose relatives in the Czech

Republic had been brewers for generations, and told her of his plans to open a brewery. She not only enthusiastically agreed but also became his biggest supporter, working with him in the business from the very beginning. It got its name from the canyon that runs through today's Belmont and San Carlos, which was called La Canada del Diablo, or Devil's Canyon, prior to the 1780s.

The concert hall space at the new location also includes a beer tasting room and is supported by a bowstring truss roof, giving it a cathedral-like vibe, with a 14-by-22-foot stage and thirty taps. Devil's Canyon will continue to host Beer Friday and live music events. Additional concerts will take place on a regular schedule that's still being developed. The events started at the new location in April, with the brewing transitioning planned a little later, likely sometime in July or August.

It's great to see the success of Devil's Canyon after some tough early years. It has finally gotten more of the recognition it deserves and has built a loyal group of followers and customers. With the new brewery location, you now have even more reasons to stop by and check out what's brewing.

Beers brewed: Year-round: Full Boar Scotch Ale, California Sunshine IPA, Deadicated Amber Ale, Silicon Blonde Ale, Lager Diabla, Belle Biere Brut California Sparkling Ale, Kaleidoscope Black Ale, and Devil's Canyon Brand Root Beer.

The Pick: The Belle is a sparkling beer that comes in both a 750-milliliter bottle and a can, for which the brewery gets bonus points. As you'd expect, it has wonderful effervescence, dancing lightly on the tongue, with a sweet nose of lemon zest, malt grain, grassy hops aromas, and a hint of apples. The flavors are similarly zesty, with some delicate spicing, like ginger and lemongrass, and a refreshingly dry finish.

Devil's Canyon Brewing Company

Opened: September 2001.

Type: Production brewery.

Owners: Chris Garrett, Kristiann Garrett, and Dan Curran.

Brewer: Chris Garrett.

Guild membership: BA, CCBA.

System: 45-barrel custom-built brewhouse, 14,000 barrels annual capacity.

Annual production: 10,000 barrels (2012 estimate).

Packages available: 12-ounce bottles in six-packs, 750 ml bottles, 16-ounce cans, growlers, and 5.16-, 13.2-, and 15.5-gallon kegs.

Tours: Brewery tours are available by reservation only.

Hours: Office: Monday through Friday, 9 a.m. to 5 p.m. Brewery: Friday from 4 to 6 p.m.

Food: Food trucks and food vendors; pizza kitchen planned for 2014.

Extras: Beer Friday events are held on the last Friday of each month, when pints of Devil's Canyon beer are served. Families and dogs are welcome at these events.

Gift shop: Merchandise is available online and when the brewery is open.

Discretion Brewing

2703 41st Avenue, Suite A, Soquel, CA 95073
831-316-0662 • www.discretionbrewing.com
Twitter @DiscretionBrew
Facebook.com/DiscretionBrewing

Discretion Brewing is one of the newest breweries in the Santa Cruz area, having just opened in March 2013. It's a family-owned company with deep roots in the area. After founders Rob and Kathleen Genco's son Lars began homebrewing—and sharing the enjoyable results with his parents—they began talking seriously about opening their own brewpub. Their goal from the beginning was to create "a relaxed yet sophisticated space in which to enjoy great beer and food, as well as a local product that the whole community can be proud of."

The name Discretion refers to the family's desire to "be wise and full of care as they brew and serve their beer, interacting with each other and those that they come in contact with." The logo defines discretion as "Wisdom. Wit. Kindness. Beer," and their slogan urges people, "Choose goodness. Have Discretion." That's their overriding philosophy.

Discretion's head brewer, Michael Demers, also grew up in the Santa Cruz area, in the nearby San Lorenzo Valley. Demers was the brewer at Boulder Creek Brewing for nearly fifteen years, before joining the Genco family to open Discretion Brewing. Demers's beers at his other brewery were quite tasty, and the lineup at Discretion looks equally interesting.

The tall red building that houses the brewery and taproom was brand new, and the Gencos built everything inside from scratch. There's a bar made from hundred-year-old pickle barrels and an 11-foot-long redwood community table. From the long wooden bar, you can see into the brewhouse behind it. All of the chairs have been painted blue, and the tables are covered with fabric, giving the

Beers brewed: Year-round: Shimmer Pils, A Song in Your Heart (Dark Mild), Uncle Dave's Rye IPA, Schwarzbier, and Pale Ale. Seasonals: Good Faith Strong Ale, Rosemary Saison, Triple, Abbey, Stout, and various cask-conditioned ales.

The Pick: Besides having a great name, Uncle Dave's Rye IPA is my favorite Discretion brew. It pours a bright ruby amber color with a vegetal nose of onion and grapefruit aromas. There's a touch of heat and tart spices in the flavor profile, balanced with bready malt character. A very satisfying IPA.

interior space a homey feel. There are no televisions in the brewery, with the aim of encouraging "relaxing, story-telling and convivial togetherness," a worthy goal. There's also a small outdoor garden area with handmade log benches.

Discretion Brewing

Opened: March 2013.

Type: Brewpub.

Owners: Rob and Kathleen Genco.

Brewer: Michael Demers.

Guild membership: BA, CCBA, BBG.

System: 10-barrel Global Stainless brewhouse, 1,200 barrels annual capacity.

Annual production: 600 barrels (2013 estimate).

Packages available: Growlers and 5.17- and 15.85-gallon kegs.

Tours: No reservations are necessary for tours. Just ask someone, and most times he or she will give you a tour.

Hours: Seven days a week, 11:30 a.m. to 8 p.m.

Food: Main Street Garden & Café, a local restaurant less than a mile away, also runs the brewpub's kitchen, specializing in Italian countryside cuisine. The menu is tailored to be seasonal cicchetti, or "small bites," in the style of southern European tapas bars, using only fresh, local ingredients. All of the vegetables, fruit, pork, chicken, and eggs will be sourced from Fogline Farms, less than 4 miles from the brewpub. The food runs the seasonal gamut and includes such dishes as arancini, seasonal vegetable dishes, house-made beer sausage, beer chili, burrata, and salami plates. To make sharing easier, every dish can be ordered in two sizes, regular and small. For dessert, there are housemade sweets.

Extras: Outside the brewery, there's a spacious beer garden with redwood log benches and an arbor, and it's dog-friendly. The brewpub provides free Wi-Fi and has a kids' corner for families with young children, complete with books, puzzles, and games.

Gift shop: Logoware, T-shirts and sweatshirts, and other items are sold in the taproom.

El Toro Brewing Company

Brewpub: 17605 Monterey Street, Morgan Hill, CA 95037
Production brewery: 17370 Hill Road, Morgan Hill, CA 95037
408-782-2739 (brewpub) / 408-778-2739 (brewery) • www.eltorobrewing.com
Facebook.com/pages/El-Toro-Brewpub/142406249444

When Geno and Cindy Acevedo were first planning to open a brewery, the initial location was in Southern California. But some big problems with the space, and some of the people involved, stopped that plan in its tracks before it began.

In the end, however, perhaps that was good for us, because they instead came back home, to where they'd grown up and, more importantly, their family had some land. That was the summer of 1992, and after a lengthy planning phase, Geno built the brewery in early 1994 on a rural part of his family's land in Morgan Hill. The brewery is in the shadow of a small peak, a hill technically, at 1,289 feet, known simply as El Toro. It is believed to have been named by writer Bret Harte, who supposedly climbed it only to find a pair of bulls fighting near the top.

That first year, El Toro took home its first gold medal from the Great American Beer Festival, for Geno's Oro Golden Ale in the category for English Pale Ale. In the intervening years, the brewery continued to package and sell its beer. To my mind, Geno Acevedo is one of the unsung brewers in California. All of his beers are terrific, yet he rarely gets the acclaim he deserves.

Over a decade later, the original vision of the Acevedos was finally realized when they opened the separate brewpub in downtown Morgan Hill, a little less than 3 miles from the production brewery, but on the other side of U.S. Route 101. It's located

Beers brewed: Year-round: Poppy Jasper Amber Ale, Oro Golden Ale, Negro Oatmeal Stout, Awesome India Pale Ale, and Deuce Imperial IPA. Seasonals: Gena's Honey Blonde, William Jones Wheat, Herman's Hefe, Airmet R Red IPA, ABC Wheat IPA, Ghost Chili Golden Ale, Porter, Blarney O'Toro's Irish Stout, Yo Barleywine (including several past vintages at the brewpub), Amigo Poquito Lager Mo Hill Pils, Marzen, Barker's Kolsch, Morgan Hill Centenni-Ale, Whiskey Barrel-aged Stout, Olde Mack Imperial Stout, El Toro IPL, Peach Lambic, Raspberry Wheat, Black Raspberry Ale, 500 Barleywine, Bravo 500 Barleywine, Paolo's OL #56 Winter Wheat Wine, El Toro X Tenth Anniversary Ale, and Yo Winter Brew. Specialty releases: assorted versions of Extra Hoppy Poppy Jasper dry hopped with different hops varieties, including Apollo Bravo, Cascade, and some experimental hops.

on the corner of Main Street and has a parking lot in the back, by the outdoor bar, as well as a pizza oven made out of an old brewing fermenter.

The two-story building was originally a bank, and the vault is still there, complete with the giant steel door. Inside the vault is a private dining room. Because of the upstairs balcony, the center portion of the restaurant is large, light-filled, and airy. The main bar is the world's only bar made of poppy jasper, a type of quartz found only in and around Morgan Hill. It consists of over 45 feet of inlaid and polished poppy jasper rock. Behind the mirrored bar are up to twenty-five different El Toro beers. The brewery also makes its own soda, which is on tap.

The brewpub system is out in the open, to the right of the bar. The 100-gallon copper pilot brewery makes experimental and seasonal brews just to be served right there in the brewpub.

The Pick: I've always thought that El Toro's Negro Oatmeal Stout is Acevedo's best beer. It's black as night, with a thick, dense tan head. The nose is milk chocolate with espresso aromas in the background. The flavors include oats, strong roasted coffee, and a touch of tobacco, with a creamy mouthfeel and a very long, bitter finish.

El Toro Brewing Company

Opened: April 30, 1994; brewpub opened November 25, 2006.

Type: Brewpub and separate production brewery.

Owners: Geno and Cindy Acevedo.

Brewer: Geno Acevedo.

Guild membership: BA.

System: 3-barrel Pub Brewing system at the brewpub, and a 20-hectoliter Newlands brewhouse at the production brewery, 5,000 barrels annual capacity.

Annual production: 1,000 barrels (2012).

Packages available: 12-ounce bottles in six-packs, cask, and kegs.

Tours: The production brewery is not open to the public, but tours may be arranged.

Hours: Sunday through Tuesday, 11:30 a.m. to midnight; Friday and Saturday, 11:30 a.m. to 1 a.m.

Food: Pub fare, with appetizers, soups, salads, sandwiches and burgers, wood-fired pizzas, and entrées including chili in a sourdough bread bowl, and Baja fish tacos. The unique El Toro Famous Original Dog Tacos are a particular treat. There are also desserts, like an oatmeal stout float, and a separate kids' menu.

Extras: Happy hour is Tuesday through Thursday, 3 to 5 p.m. The brewpub has foosball, beer pong, a pool table, and shuffleboard. It also occasionally features live music, and karaoke. There's an outdoor patio bar, with a firepit, that's pet-friendly and seats a hundred.

Gift shop: Shirts, hoodies, hats, logo glassware, and stickers available at the brewpub.

Faultline Brewing Company

1235 Oakmead Parkway, Sunnyvale, CA 94085
408-736-2739 • www.faultlinebrewing.com
Twitter @FaultlineBrew
Facebook.com/FaultlineBrewingCo

Faultline was one of the earlier South Bay brewpubs and the first to open in Sunnyvale. It's equally focused on the food and the beer, and chef Basilio Mariscal has created a fusion menu that includes both unique dishes, like his famous tempura ahi roll, and more traditional ones, as described below.

The building is a modern concrete structure with a squat roof and vines climbing up the sides. Considering how it looks out front, it's surprising how spacious and high the ceilings are inside. With wood columns and beams partitioning the restaurant into different sections, there's room for quite a few diners. Floor-to-ceiling windows along the back allow the picturesque duck pond and gardens behind the brewpub enhances your dining experience. There's also outdoor seating by the pond, which features a fountain in the center.

Windows also run the length of the long metal bar with high-backed wooden bar stools, revealing the brewery behind the scenes, where you can watch veteran brewmaster Peter Catizone at work, creating your next pint of beer. Catizone has been brewing at Faultline for ten years and makes roughly twenty-five different beers each year. He makes only traditional, time-honored styles and avoids using any fruit, vegetable, or candy flavorings. Peter started homebrewing in the late eighties and took a job bartending at Boulder Creek Brewing, working his way up to head brewer in 1993. He held that position for a decade before joining Faultline in July 2003. He's a graduate of Rensselaer Polytechnic Institute, with a BS in physics, and is a member of the Master Brewers Association of the Americas (MBAA).

Beers brewed: Year-round: Kolsch, Hefe Weizen, Pale Ale, Best Bitter, IPA, and Stout. Seasonals: Brown Ale (spring/summer), Burton Ale (spring/summer), Belgian Abbey (late winter/early spring), Belgian Blonde (late winter/early spring), Spring Bock (spring), Irish Red (spring/summer), Golden Ale (spring/summer), Belgian White (summer), Pilsner (summer), Oktoberfest (fall), Dunkelweizen (fall), London Porter (winter), and Holiday Strong Ale (winter).

The modern setting of the large restaurant and bar is really impressive, and Faultline understandably does a big happy hour business. With tasty food and uniformly great beer, you'll be hard-pressed to find fault with the Faultline.

Faultline Brewing Company

Opened: December 1, 1994.

Type: Brewpub.

Owners: Steve and Ted Geiszler.

Brewer: Peter Catizone.

Guild membership: BA, CCBA, BBG.

System: 20-barrel Triple AAA brewhouse, with Newlands fermenters, 1,000 barrels annual capacity.

Annual production: 874 barrels (2011), 900 barrels (2012 estimate)

Packages available: 5-liter minikegs and 5- and 15.5-gallon kegs, with forty-eight hours notice.

Tours: Available only for groups of eight or more; reservations required.

Hours: Monday through Friday, 11 a.m. to 9:30 p.m.; Saturday, 5 to 9 p.m. Closed Sunday.

Food: Starting daily at 3:15 p.m., there's an extensive bar menu that's as big as any regular dinner menu, with more than enough to satisfy all but the hungriest person. Overall, the food is upscale pub grub that mixes unique dishes, such as tempura ahi roll and Thai orange roughy, with traditional fare like pot roast in pearl onion pan sauce. The lunch menu includes a few big salads, along with sandwiches, burgers, pasta, and entrées such as Louisiana seafood gumbo and ale-battered fish and chips. The dinner menu adds entrées of pork, chicken, steak, and seafood.

Extras: There's outdoor seating overlooking a small duck pond, a private banquet dining room, and twenty-three flat-screen televisions with a seasonal sports package. Happy hour is from 3 to 6 p.m. throughout the week, with specials on pints and selected appetizers. On Friday and Saturday evenings, there's live music at the brewpub. The restaurant is family-friendly, and kids eat free on Monday and Friday nights from 5 to 9:30 p.m.

Gift shop: T-shirts and pint glasses are sold at the brewpub.

The Pick: Overall, I'm really impressed with the quality of Peter's beers, making the pick all that more difficult. His Best Bitter is spot-on, with mild hops character, crisp fruit notes, and a touch of caramel. It's malt forward, but very refreshing. The Hefe Weizen is a good example of a Bavarian-style wheat beer, and the IPA is English-style, with restrained hops, good bittering but no astringency. It doesn't hit you over the head but just gives you a little extra hops character in a clean, soft beer.

FireHouse Grill & Brewery

111 South Murphy Avenue, Sunnyvale, CA 94086
408-773-9500 • www.firehousegrill.com
Facebook.com/FireHouseGrillBrewery

Although the address at 111 South Murphy Avenue opened as the FireHouse Grill & Brewery in 2005, a brewery had been there long before. Stoddard's Brewhouse had opened there in 1993 but closed in 2004. FireHouse took over the space, renovated much of it, and reopened the following year.

The brewpub is going for a firehouse look, but the overall feel of the place is that of a neighborhood sports bar, with all that implies. There are big-screen plasma televisions showing multiple sporting events, and bottles of mainstream beer and popular regionals like Sierra Nevada and Blue Moon share the bar with the brewery's own housemade beers. It's also a full bar, so in addition to beer, wine and a cocktail menu are available. The servers wear a somewhat Hooter-esque uniform, with very short plaid skirts, black V-neck FireHouse T-shirts, and knee-high black boots.

The brewery is in a backroom, hidden from view. Brewer Eric Brown used to brew at the Westminster Rock Bottom in Colorado, before relocating to the Bay Area to replace Steve Donahue, who in turn has moved on to open his own brewery.

The brewpub is in a prime location in the heart of Silicon Valley's historic district, and Murphy Street is now a closed street mall, lined with shops and restaurants. It's also conveniently located across the street from the Sunnyvale Caltrain station. There's also a second FireHouse location in East Palo Alto (1765 East Bayshore Road, Suite A, 650-326-9700, in the shopping center with Home Depot and Ikea), which is identical in concept and

Beers brewed: Year-round: Hefeweizen and Pale Ale. Seasonals: Red Ale, Porter, Meaghan's Maibock, Cody's Crib Kolsch, Golden Wheat, Oktoberfest, Hops on Rye, Scotch Ale, Abbey Dubbel, Brewer's Whim, St. Eve's Belgesque Goldish Strong Revolutionary Ale, OTIS (One Tun Imperial Stout), Brettaweizen, and many other special beers throughout the year.

The Pick: The Hops on Rye, originally developed by former brewer Steve Donahue, is one terrific beer. One of the first rye IPAs, and certainly one of the best, it has a citrus- and pine-filled nose and that whiff of spicy tartness that a touch of rye gives beer. Grapefruit notes come out in the flavors, balanced by caramel sweetness and sourdough breadiness, with a dry, tart finish. But if hops aren't your thing, both the Pale Ale and Hefeweizen are really nice examples of those styles, light and refreshing beers.

serves all of the FireHouse beers. The only difference is that there's no brewery at that location.

If you're a sports fan, this is a terrific spot to watch a game. If your friends are not yet fans of craft beer, there are enough other choices here that everyone can find something to like, a big plus if you often have trouble finding a place everyone can agree on. But regardless of why you go, you'll find some tasty beers and big plates of satisfying food, with enough people-watching and sports to keep almost everybody happy.

FireHouse Grill & Brewery

Opened: 2005.

Type: Brewpub.

Owner: Ehab Yousef.

Brewer: Eric Brown.

Guild membership: BA, BBG.

System: 22-barrel JV Northwest, 2,500 barrels annual capacity.

Annual production: 1,800 barrels (2012 estimate).

Packages available: 22-ounce bottles, growlers, and 5- and 15.5-gallon kegs.

Tours: Brewery tours are available when the brewer is there and has some free time.

Hours: Sunday and Monday, 11 a.m. to 9 p.m.; Tuesday, 11 a.m. to 10 p.m.; Wednesday through Saturday, 11 a.m. to 11 p.m.

Food: The menu is huge, with a full page of delicious-sounding appetizers, including sampler platters of their most popular ones, as well as soups, salads, burgers, wraps, and sandwiches. There are also wood-fired pizzas, fish and chips, cioppino, grilled swordfish, and oven-roasted jumbo prawns, to name just a few of the vast menu items available. Entrées include steaks, seafood, and pasta dishes. It could take you a while to decide—the menu's that big. There are also separate kids' and dessert menus.

Extras: Happy hour features $2 pints of select FireHouse beers, Monday through Friday, 2 to 4 p.m. But that's almost a pre–happy hour, because from 4 to 7 p.m. Monday through Friday, FireHouse pints are $3, pitchers are $12, select national brands are $4, and there are more than a dozen $5 appetizer specials. There are additional daily specials each day of the week; check the website for details. The brewpub features special sporting events on its TVs and hosts events surrounding these. There are private rooms for corporate and other private events, with a separate catering menu, an outdoor patio for when the weather's warm, and free Wi-Fi.

Gift shop: T-shirts and other brewery gear are available at the brewpub.

Freewheel Brewing Company

3736 Florence Street, Redwood City, CA 94063
650-365-BEER (2337) • www.freewheelbrewing.com
Twitter @freewheelbrew
Facebook.com/pages/Freewheel-Brewing-Company/
  147505355281208

Lamenting the lack of real, cask-conditioned ales, in the United States, four friends decided to do something about it. One of them, Pete Krausa, an Englishman, knows how ubiquitous cask beer is on his side of the pond. He befriended Malcolm McGinnis when they worked together at a biotech startup. McGinnis met the other two Freewheel partners, Gary Waymire and Larry Bucka, when their three sons played lacrosse together.

McGinnis has a PhD in biochemistry and had been homebrewing for twenty years, so he was tapped to be the new company's brewer. To learn more about the practical aspects of cask beer, he interned for a year at Magnolia, where some of the beers are cask-conditioned. The goal was to be able to found a brewery dedicated to making cask beer.

As for the rest of the team, Gary Waymire owns a marketing consulting business and provides marketing for the brewery. Larry Bucka works the sales angles and by day continues in his role with a manufacturers' rep firm. And Krausa, who moved back to the UK and lives in Gloucestershire, in southwest England, has been making contact and working with collaborators there and has set up two English brewing partners so far: Ironbridge Brewery in Telford and Green Jack Brewery in Lowestoft.

The Freewheel brewpub is located in a Redwood City shopping center adjacent to the Key Market and near Marsh Road. I'm a huge fan of cask beer, so I support any effort to introduce more "real ale" to Northern California. If any brewery or bar offers a beer on cask, I almost always make a point of ordering it. Real ale allows so many more flavors of the beer to come through that are often dampened down by the carbonation in noncask beer. As new breweries increasingly specialize in a particular style or method, it's wonderful to see someone bring an English-style all-cask brewery to our shores.

Freewheel Brewing Company

Opened: December 29, 2012.

Type: Brewpub.

Owners: Malcolm McGinnis, Pete Krausa, Gary Waymire, and Larry Bucka.

Brewer: Malcolm McGinnis.

Guild membership: NCBG, BBG

System: 8.3-barrel custom-built for brewing "real ale" by Vincent Johnson of Johnson Brewing Designs, Bury, Lancashire, UK, 1,500 barrels annual capacity.

Packages available: Cask and growlers, with plans to offer kegs and possibly cans in the future.

Tours: Brewery tours are available without reservations; just ask at the bar.

Hours: Monday, 4 to 8 p.m.; Tuesday through Thursday, 11 a.m. to 9 p.m.; Friday and Saturday, 11 a.m. to midnight. Closed Sunday.

Food: The menu is British-inspired California-style pub food, featuring a regular lineup of pasties or hand pies, such as steak and stout or butternut squash. There are also snacks, including pretzels, hand-made crisps (a.k.a. potato chips), chips (a.k.a. french fries), beer-braised sausages, and specials like fish and chips, meatloaf, ale mac and cheese, curries, and pulled pork sandwiches. The menu also includes salads and burgers. The food is designed to pair well with the beer, and even daily specials include a suggested beer pairing. As much of the produce, cheeses, and meats as possible is from local suppliers. There's also a separate kids' menu.

Extras: In addition to the brewery's own cask beers, guest beers are on cask as well. The brewpub does private events for groups, such as office parties, school fundraisers, game-watching events, or whatever people ask for. The walls of the brewpub are decorated with art from local artists, which will be constantly rotating. There's also outdoor seating for around fifty people. Live music may be featured at a future time. Check the Facebook page for updates on events at the brewpub, along with daily menu specials.

Gift shop: T-shirts, hats, glassware, and other merchandise will be available at the brewpub.

Beers brewed: Year-round: Ironbridge Gold, Ironbridge Stout, Ironbridge Killer 48 IPA, Green Jack Hybrid Bitter, Big V Amber, and Big D Bitter. Seasonals: A rotating seasonal will be on tap each month at the brewpub.

The Pick: Freewheel is so new that I've only had an opportunity to try a few of its beers, but of the ones I've had, the Green Jack Hybrid Bitter is a fave. It's brewed to the more restrained English-style India pale ale but uses American hops varieties: Cascade, Centennial, and Willamette. So it has the aromatics of an American IPA, though more subtly, with tangerine and marmalade aromas. It's also relatively low in alcohol for an IPA, at 5.2 percent ABV, but still full flavored and refreshing. And like all cask beer, it's smooth and still, allowing all of the flavors of the beer to shine.

Gordon Biersch Brewing Company (Production Brewery)

357 East Taylor Street, San Jose, CA 95112
408-792-1500
www.gordonbiersch.com/brewery
Twitter @GBbrewingCo
Facebook.com/gordonbierschbrewingco

A large brick building that takes up an entire city block along East Taylor Street in San Jose looks as if it could hold just about any industrial enterprise. But the sign above the entrance announces its true purpose: the Gordon Biersch Brewing Company. When it opened in May 1997, Gordon Biersch was already a well-known name, having opened several successful brewpubs in California. The production brewery was built to make beer to sell outside of the brewpubs, in bottles and kegs.

Dan Gordon, the Gordon in the name, is the brewing side of the company. His partner, Dean Biersch, ran the restaurant side until he retired from the business after management of the brewpubs was taken over by Big River, a national restaurant chain, and the two companies became separate, although they both continue to market beer under the Gordon Biersch name. (For more about the brewpubs, see the Gordon Biersch Brewery Restaurant entry on page 146.)

From the production brewery in San Jose, Gordon created bottled beer for retail and kegs for other bars and restaurants. Originally an economics major at Berkeley, he spent a year in Germany, discovering that it was possible to get a degree in brewing, and decided to change his career path. After that, he spent a year working at the Anheuser-Busch brewery in Fairfield, and then applied to Germany's oldest brewing school, the Technical University Munich's brewing department at Weihenstephan. When he graduated from the five-year program—becoming at the time the first American to do so in more than fifty years—he was offered jobs at both Anheuser-Busch and Coors, but he decided instead to start the Gordon Biersch brewpub chain with Dean Biersch.

Beers brewed: Year-round: Märzen, Pilsner, Blonde Bock, and Hefeweizen. Seasonals: Maibock (February–April), Sommerbrau (May–July), Festbier (August–October), and Winterbock (November–January). Braumeister Selekt Series: Imperial Pilsner Brau, Weizen Eisbock, and Eisbock. Uberbier Series: Zwickel Bock Unfiltered Lager and Zwickelpils.

After successfully building, operating, and training brewing staff at half a dozen brewpubs, Gordon Biersch decided to build a production brewery, believing packaged beer would increase its brand awareness for the brewpubs. In order to fund the expansion plans, in 1995 a Las Vegas investor acquired a controlling interest in the company, and the 114,000-square foot brewery was built and opened in 1997. Two years later, in 1999, the brewpub restaurants were sold off and the company began concentrating on its production brewery.

The Pick: I've long thought the Gordon Biersch Dunkelweizen is the best beer Dan Gordon makes, but it's only made as a seasonal, and not even every year. Of the year-round offerings, the Hefeweizen is a nice Bavarian-style wheat beer with the signature clove and banana character, though it leans more heavily on the clove spices. Gordon's new line of big-bottle beers, the Braumeister Selekt series, shows great promise, with the Imperial Pilsner Brau being a delightfully big, hoppy pilsner brewed with tons of noble hops.

The brewery is massive by small-brewery standards, and state-of-the-art equipment abounds. It's an impressive sight, thoroughly modern and fully automated. Dan Gordon is justly proud of his brewery and what it can do. It's strictly a working brewery, and although it does tours, it isn't set up as a tourist destination like some other breweries, and there's no gift shop or other diversions. You'll see the brewhouse, a tank farm of fermenters, and the bottling line. Everything you'd expect to see at an even larger brewer is there. It's really the best of both worlds, a big little brewery in the heart of San Jose.

Gordon Biersch Brewing Company (Production Brewery)

Opened: May 23, 1997.

Type: Production brewery.

Owner: Dan Gordon.

Brewer: Dan Gordon.

Guild membership: BA.

System: 185-barrel Huppman brewhouse, with Nerb automation, twenty 550-barrel fermenters, Krones filler and laveler, 110,000 barrels annual capacity.

Annual production: 103,000 barrels (2011).

Packages available: 12-ounce bottles, in six-packs, twelve-packs, and twenty-four-packs; 16-ounce plastic bottles; 750-milliliter swing-top bottles; 5- and 15.5-gallon kegs; and 20-, 50-, and 90-liter unfiltered wooden kegs.

Tours: Tours of the production brewery are available during regular office hours, Monday through Thursday; reservations are necessary by email, at tours@gordonbiersch.com.

Gift shop: Merchandise is available online.

Gordon Biersch Brewery Restaurant

Palo Alto: 640 Emerson Street, Palo Alto, CA 94301
San Jose: 33 East San Fernando Street, San Jose,
  CA 95113
650-323-7723 (Palo Alto) • 408-294-6785 (San Jose)
www.gordonbiersch.com
Twitter @Gordon_Biersch / @GBPaloAlto /
  @GBSanJose • Facebook.com/GBPaloAlto /
  Facebook.com/GBSanJose

The Palo Alto Gordon Biersch brewpub was the first opened by Dan Gordon and Dean Biersch, and it was one of the first small breweries to concentrate on making lagers. While Gordon ran the brewery, Biersch brought his restaurant management experience to the partnership.

The Palo Alto location was an immediate hit, and two years later, the partners opened their second location in downtown San Jose. A third brewpub was opened in San Francisco but closed last year, in 2012. After that, additional locations were added outside the Bay Area and in other states. To fund expansion, a Las Vegas investor acquired a controlling interest and in 1999 sold the brewpub portion of the business to a Chattanooga, Tennessee company, Big River, which specialized in operating brewery restaurants, while Gordon Biersch concentrated on its production brewery business. The two companies became separate, although they both continue to market beer under the Gordon Biersch name. (See page 144 for the production brewery.)

Big River also operated additional brewpubs under the name Gordon Biersch Brewery Restaurant Group, Inc. In 2010, Big River merged with the brewpub chain Rock Bottom and changed the name of the new entity to CraftWorks Restaurants and Breweries. Today the company operates thirty-two Gordon Biersch locations in eighteen states, along with thirty-seven Rock Bottom brewpubs, as well as Big River Grille, A1A Ale Works, Seven Bridges Grille & Brewery, the ChopHouse & Brewery, and the Walnut Brewery, among others. In addition, CraftWorks operates nearly one hundred Old Chicago Pasta & Pizza restaurants.

Beers brewed: Year-round: Marzen, Czech Pilsner, Schwarzbier, Hefeweizen, and Golden Export. Seasonals: Maibock, Winterbock, Sommerbrau, and Festbier.

The Pick: While most of the regular offerings tend to be solid beers, based on recipes Dan Gordon wrote and perfected years ago, I generally gravitate toward the seasonals, especially the fall Festbier.

Dean Biersch's original vision for the Gordon Biersch restaurants was for the food to be different from the usual pub fare, essentially white table linen food, but served with beer. In 1988, that too was innovative, and people flocked to a place with fine dining and fresh beer made right there in front of them.

Years later, the beer remains quite good, at least in the two original brewpubs in San Jose and Palo Alto. John Tucci was one of Gordon Biersch's earliest brewers and for many years was the head brewer at the San Francisco location. After it closed, he relocated to the original brewpub in Palo Alto.

These two Gordon Biersch brewpubs continue to operate in the Bay Area, but there's also a Gordon Biersch Tavern near Sacramento, in Roseville (1151 Galleria Boulevard, #9211, 916-772-2739), that's essentially a Gordon Biersch restaurant without a brewery.

Gordon Biersch Brewery Restaurant

Opened: July 6, 1988 (Palo Alto); 1990 (San Jose).

Type: Brewpub.

Owners: CraftWorks Restaurants and Breweries, Inc.

Brewers: John Tucci (Palo Alto); Jeff Liles (San Jose).

System: Palo Alto: 1965 Nerb Bavarian brewhouse, 1,800 barrels annual capacity; San Jose: 1988 JV Northwest, 2,000 barrels annual capacity.

Annual production: Palo Alto: 700 barrels (2011); San Jose: 1,300 barrels (2011).

Packages available: Growlers and on-premises draft.

Tours: Brewery tours are available on request; no reservations are necessary.

Hours: Sunday through Thursday, 11:30 a.m. to 11 p.m.; Friday and Saturday, 11:30 a.m. to 1 a.m.

Food: An extensive menu of dishes, described as "featuring bold, international flavors." The popularity of the classic garlic fries appetizer helped fuel the brewpub's early success. It was created by Dan Gordon, based on experiences he had with a visiting garlic professor while attending brewing school in Germany. The menu offers a wide selection of soups and salads, pizzas and flatbreads, pastas and stir fries, steaks and seafood, as well as a selection of lighter fare, tacos, and several house specialties, like a gorgonzola bone-in ribeye and lobster and shrimp mac and cheese. Tempting desserts include a sampler of four miniature-size desserts in case you can't decide.

Extras: Happy hour Monday through Friday, 4 to 6 p.m. and an evening happy hour Sunday through Thursday, 9 p.m. to close.

Gift shop: Shirts, sweatshirts, hats, and glassware are sold at the brewpub and online.

Half Moon Bay Brewing Company

390 Capistrano Rd., Half Moon Bay, CA 94019
650-728-BREW (2739) • www.hmbbrewingco.com
Twitter @hmbbrewingco
Facebook.com/pages/Half-Moon-Bay-Brewing-
    Company/68771224360

Right by the water of the Half Moon Bay Harbor, just off State Route 1 a little south of Half Moon Airport, you'll find a perfect little spot to enjoy a pint of beer and watch the boats sail by. Half Moon Bay Brewing Company is in a building resembling a beachside cottage, with a large outdoor patio at the entrance. Outside, there's a wind guard and heat lamps around the many tables, chairs, and benches to help keep patrons warm, as well as a fire pit with a ring of wicker seats surrounding it. The door has a beautiful stained-glass re-creation of the brewpub's logo.

Inside, the large restaurant includes several separate dining areas, some with views of the bay, others more interior, with a large aquarium in the center of one of the rooms. A few of the bay windows have bench seating. Another room holds a large, rectangular bar ringed with bar stools. There's more seating around the bar, along the windows, and a couple of big-screen televisions there too.

Adjacent to the brewpub is the Inn at Mavericks, where you can make a weekend of it by staying in one of the half-dozen oceanside rooms. Each room is a little different, named after one of the famous nearby beaches, and all have a view of the surrounding area. A good time to stay at the inn might be one of the several events that the brewpub hosts throughout the year, such as the annual Pumpkin Harvest Festival, a local event that's been held for more than forty years every October, the weekend after Columbus Day.

The brewery was originally installed and manned by local legend Alec Moss, who recently retired. James Costa became the brewmaster in late 2012. Costa is a nearly twenty-year veteran of the Bay Area beer scene, having started brewing

Beers brewed: Year-round: Mavericks Amber Ale, Princeton-by-the-Sea IPA, Pillar Point Pale Ale, Sandy Beach Blonde Hefeweizen, Bootleggers Brown Ale, and Big Break Ale. Seasonals: Cherry Brown Ale, Tunitas Trippel, and Sweetwood Saison (spring); Devil's Slide Summer Ale (summer); Oktoberfest, Pumpkin Harvest Ale, and MacMavericks Scotch Ale (fall); Old Winter Ale, Moon Glow Barleywine, and Wipeout Imperial Stout (winter). During election years: Presidential Alection (Pillar Point Pale Ale).

with Bear Republic when it opened in 1996. He's also brewed at 20 Tank, Black Diamond, Marin Brewing, and Moylan's, before beginning to plan his own place, Oakland Brewing Company (see page 209). As progress for his Oakland venture has been slow, Costa's been brewing at Half Moon Bay. Costa is known for his big, hoppy beers, and I expect to see more hoppy one-off specials to start showing up soon.

Half Moon Bay Brewing Company Restaurant & Brew Pub

Opened: July 2, 2000.

Type: Brewpub.

Owner: Lenny Mendonca.

Brewer: James Costa.

Guild membership: BA, CCBA.

System: 15-barrel Pub Brewing system, 1,200 barrels annual capacity.

Annual production: 1,000 barrels (2012 estimate).

Packages available: 22-ounce bottles, growlers, and 5- and 15.5-gallon kegs.

Tours: Brewery tours are available by request, but reservations are appreciated.

Hours: Monday through Friday, 11:30 a.m. to 9 p.m.; Saturday and Sunday, 10 a.m. to 11 p.m. Closing time may vary on the weekends.

Food: The restaurant serves world-class food, with an extensive menu of seafood, soups, salads, burgers, and sandwiches. Other entrées include Medallions à la Oscar, Cochinita Pibil, and Garden Harvest Ravioli. There are also daily specials, even for desserts, and a separate kids' menu. You can go fancy for an evening out or stay casual and eat at the bar. Either way, you'll find tasty food with beer pairing suggestions for each dish.

Extras: The brewpub hosts several weekly specials. Happy hour is Monday through Friday, 4 to 7 p.m., with bar bites and drink specials. On Monday, growler refills are $9. On Tuesday, pints are $3.50 all day, and from 5 to 7 p.m., chef Gaston Alfaro hosts Pampered by the Chef, being available in the bar to meet customers and offering free previews of upcoming appetizers. Wednesday features one-third off bottles of wine, and on Threaded Thursday, you'll get 10 percent off your bill by wearing Half Moon Bay logo clothing. Each month on the first Thursday, from 6 to 8 p.m., Half Moon Bay hosts Brews & Views, an open political discussion with a different speaker each time. Check the website for details.

Gift shop: Hats, T-shirts, and sweatshirts are available at the brewpub.

The Pick: Now that Costa has signed on as brewmaster at Half Moon Bay, I fully expect that their stable of hoppy beers will get better and better; not that they were bad to begin with, but James is justly known for his skill with hops. Of the old recipes, I still think the underrated Mavericks Amber Ale is one fine example of underappreciated style. It has a bright copper color, and the nose is malt forward, with aromas of fruit and caramel. The flavors show good complexity, with sweet malt dominating but kept in check nicely by some nutty, floral, pine, and fruity character, with slightly chalky notes and a sweetish finish.

Hermitage Brewing Company

Hermitage
Brewing Company

1627 South Seventh Street, San Jose, CA 95112
408-291-0966 • www.hermitagebrewing.com
Twitter @hermitagebrews
Facebook.com/hermitagebrewing

I have something of a soft spot for the Hermitage Brewery's brewhouse, originally used in the Tied House Brewpub, which was located in downtown San Jose in San Pedro Square. Many years ago, my wedding reception was held there, and my favorite wedding photo is of my wife and me on the stairs of the brewhouse. It's the only personal picture that hangs in my office.

Years later, the recession hit, and Tied House made the difficult decision to close one of its two brewpubs, choosing to shutter the San Jose location in May 2009. When the brewpub closed, the brewing equipment was moved to the old Langendorf Bakery building on Seventh Street, near Spartan Stadium, and Hermitage Brewing was born.

Peter Licht, who for many years was the original brewer at Coast Range Brewery in nearby Gilroy, came to work at the San Jose Tied House and moved with the equipment to Hermitage's new location. Licht is originally from Rochester, New York, but moved to California to attend the Master Brewers Program at UC Davis in 1994. He's been brewing in the South Bay ever since.

Hermitage makes several lines of beers for the Tied House, along with a number of different beers under the Hermitage label, under a variety of brand names, most of which can be found at Bay Area stores like BevMo, including its private label Coastal Fog. While the range of beers Licht brews is vast, I really like his Ale of the Imp, a big imperial IPA, and the Ale des Dieux, a biere de garde, which is similar to a saison but slightly sweeter and richer flavored.

Beers brewed: Year-round: Hoptopia DIPA, Maltopia Scotch Ale, Ale of the Imp DIPA, Ale of the 2 Tun Imperial Stout, Ale of the Hermit IPA, and Menage a Singe Black IPA. Seasonals: Fruit Crate Pumpkin Ale, Ale des Dieux Biere de Garde, One Door Saison, One Door Quadrupel, and "H" Series Single Hop IPA; 2012 releases were Citra, Sorachi Ace, Nelson Sauvin, and Admiral.

The Pick: Licht is a wonderful, often underrated brewer. His Ale of the Hermit imperial IPA is one huge double, mathematically weighing in at 99.9 IBUs. Despite that monstrous amount of hops, it's still very well balanced, with an equally big malt backbone that makes it surprisingly drinkable.

Hermitage also brews beer for several startup breweries on a contract basis. While many of them work hard to build their own breweries, they brew their beers at Hermitage so they can get them into the hands of consumers and begin making a name for themselves. Many of those brands can be found elsewhere in this book.

As a result, the brewery is a very busy place, doing several brews a day, and it seems to be perpetually brewing, with almost no downtime. The brewery is in a strictly industrial part of town, and it's not set up for tours at all. That's a shame, because I love seeing a working brewery that's so devoid of any pretense. It has just one purpose: brewing beer. It's an open, well-lit warehouse space, with equipment on all sides and very few comforts. Music blares as the brewers work, and it's cranked up loud so it can be heard over the clanking bottling machine and boiling kettle. I can only assume the beer likes the music too, because it not only has good taste, but also tastes good.

Hermitage Brewing Company

Opened: November 8, 2009.

Type: Production brewery.

Owners: Lou Jemison and Ron Manabe.

Brewers: Peter Licht (brewmaster) and Greg Filippi (brewer).

Guild membership: BBG.

System: 25-barrel Pub System, with six 25-barrel fermenters and four 50-barrel ones, and Tree Floyds old bottling line.

Annual production: 7,000 barrels (2012).

Packages available: 12-ounce six-packs, 16.9- and 22-ounce bottles, and 750-milliliter bottles.

Tours: The brewery is not open to the public, and no tours are available.

Extras: During the annual SF Beer Week, Hermitage hosts a festival called Meet the Brewers, which has become the biggest event in the area and celebrates the small local brewers of the Silicon Valley and Monterey Bay.

Gift shop: Merchandise is available at Hermitage's sister brewery, the Tied House.

Highway 1 Brewing Company

5720 Cabrillo Highway, Pescadero, CA 94060
650-879-9243 • www.highway1brewing.com
Twitter @Highway1Brewing
Facebook.com/pages/Highway-1-Brewing-Company/
    124098964406578

Highway 1 Brewing is exactly where you'd expect it to be, straddling the ocean with the Cabrillo Highway in the front yard and the Old Coast Highway in the backyard. The brewpub is roughly halfway between Santa Cruz and Half Moon Bay, around two dozen miles up or down the road from either. It's at the northern border of Año Nuevo State Reserve and just 8 miles south of Pescadero State Beach.

The California state park at Año Nuevo is home to the largest mainland breeding colony of elephant seals. The nearby state beach is also adjacent to the Pescadero Marsh Natural Preserve, a great spot for birders and nature lovers. Some of the wildlife that can be seen in the preserve includes blue herons, kites, foxes, and deer.

After a long day of hiking and taking in the natural wonders of the Pacific Ocean in Northern California, you're going to build a powerful thirst. Happily, husband-and-wife team Jeff and Melissa Page have created a solution: the Highway 1 Brewing Company. The Pages are experienced caterers and home brewers, and they recently renovated an old grill and created a clean space out of wood and metal for their brewpub. The cozy beach house serves a full lunch and dinner menu along with house beers and several guest taps.

Inside, the cafe looks great, warm and inviting. There are essentially three main rooms. A dining area in the front overlooks the ocean. An L-shaped bar in the middle has a fireplace and comfy chairs around it. And the back room houses the working brewery, which you can watch on your way to the back door. Out back, you'll find a spacious beer garden with picnic tables, a fire pit, and outdoor games. And the views are spectacular, making this a perfect place to sit and watch the ocean, beer in hand.

Highway 1 Brewing Company

Opened: February 15, 2013.

Type: Brewpub.

Owners: Jeff and Melissa Page.

Brewer: Jeff Page.

Guild membership: CCBA.

System: 3-barrel Electric brewhouse with 3-barrel Stout Tanks & Kettles fermenters, 270 barrels annual capacity.

Annual production: 216 barrels (2013 estimate).

Packages available: Growlers.

Tours: Brewery tours are available by appointment or based on brewer availability.

Hours: Thursday through Monday, 11 a.m. to 9 p.m. Closed Tuesday and Wednesday, but check the website for updated hours.

Food: Highway 1 serves American cuisine using local coastal ingredients and fresh beer. The menu features burgers, American-style grilled pizzas, small plates, unique salads, and desserts. The menu will vary throughout the year based on the availability of seasonal vegetables and other ingredients.

Extras: From the dining and bar areas, there are relaxing ocean views, especially from the beer garden, which has a planned summer opening and will also be pet-friendly. Local musicians will perform at the brewpub on Friday and weekend evenings.

Gift shop: Shirts, hats, growlers, stickers, and other brewery-related items are for sale at the brewpub.

Beers brewed: Year-round: 1PA, A Pepper in the Rye, Amberdextrous, French Mexican War, Black Pug Ale, Rock Queen, and Through Wit Work. Seasonals: Knuckle Down Brown and Strawberry Blond Belgian. Other seasonal releases will be determined by customer input.

The Pick: I like Jeff's Rock Queen, his Pale Ale. It's a solid beer, with lightly tart aromas and flavor, and just a touch of spiciness in the mix. It's a clean, well-made beer with a lingering chewy hop finish.

Los Gatos Brewing Company

130 North Santa Cruz Avenue, Los Gatos, CA 95030
408-395-9929 • lgbrewingco.com/losgatos/
Twitter @LosGatosBrewSJ
Facebook.com/LosGatosBrewingCompany

The Los Gatos Brewing Company may be a brewpub, but the owners prefer to think of it as a "diner's pub," and it shows in the way they do everything here. The building was originally constructed in 1926, and for more than thirty years, it was the site of a car dealership. It was later home to a yacht company, a photography studio, and finally a Noodle Palace, before the brewpub opened in the early 1990s.

The space is gorgeous, with dark mahogany wood everywhere, as well as lots of glass and brass railings. The bar in particular is just beautiful, and its huge mahogany arches were originally part of a St. Louis brothel. Behind the bar is a glass wall through which the entire brewery is on display. At night it's an especially awesome sight. The brewpub has both booths and regular tables, and the tables are separated by short wooden fences, creating privacy in an open floor plan. Bavarian flags hang from the tall vaulted ceiling, and a ceramic pizza oven is in one corner of the restaurant. There are also at least six big-screen televisions, with one above the bar and the rest scattered around.

Kent Wheat has been the brewmaster for more than seven years, having originally brewed at the Rock Bottom brewery in Campbell. Like many brewers, he started as a homebrewer and attended the American Brewers Guild to become a professional brewer. In addition to a regular lineup of classic styles, he has free rein to brew a wide range of seasonals and special release beers throughout the year, so you never know what you'll find beyond the usual suspects.

Beers brewed: Year-round: Lexington Lager, Cougar Town IPA, Dog Tale Pale, Hue Hefe, El Gatoberfest Oktoberfest, Black Perle Porter, and Scuttlebutt Stout. Seasonals: Scottish Ale, Coquettish Blonde Kolsch, Maibock, Summertime Ale, Classic Pale Ale, Exhibition Ale, Doppelbock, and Sherman Stout.

The Pick: While Kent Wheat makes a nice range of beers, his namesake wheat beer, the Hue Hefe, is my favorite. It's a Bavarian-style hefe, with the signature banana and clove aromas, a creamy mouthfeel, and flavors of lemon sprite, citrus, banana, and light spices, especially in the finish. It's a very refreshing beer that's soft and well rounded.

There's a big emphasis on the food too, and while it's casual dining, it's a cut above the usual brewpub fare, both in choices and presentation. The California cuisine is hearty, and every dish I've had has been terrific.

There's also a second Los Gatos Brewing Company location in downtown San Jose, in San Pedro Square (163 West Santa Clara Street, 408-600-1181). The restaurant is located in a historic building, built for Masson-Lefranc Winery in 1883 by Theodore Lenzen, a famous local architect at that time. Although that location does not have a brewery, it does serve all of the beers made at Los Gatos. The menus are similar, but not exactly the same.

Los Gatos Brewing Company

Opened: 1991.

Type: Brewpub.

Owners: Andy Pavicich and Jim Stump.

Brewer: Kent Wheat.

Guild membership: BA, BBG.

System: 15-barrel JV Northwest, 1,500 barrels annual capacity.

Annual production: 1,000 barrels (2013 estimate).

Packages available: Draft only at the brewpub and at the San Jose location. Some of the beer is also on cask.

Tours: Brewery tours are available by reservation or if the brewer is there and has time.

Hours: Monday through Thursday, 11:30 a.m. to 9 p.m.; Friday and Saturday, 11:30 a.m. to 10 p.m.; and Sunday, 10 a.m. to 9 p.m.

Food: The lunch menu includes numerous things to share, along with pizza, salads, burgers and sandwiches, and entrées like housemade bratwurst, Bolognese and other pasta dishes, Tunisian chickpea stew, and ocean trout, as well as several vegetarian options. The dinner menu includes most of the lunch items plus some additional heartier entrées, such as char-grilled swordfish, Hampshire pork chop, and prime strip steak. There's also a separate dessert menu, plus a pub menu that's just for ordering food at the bar and during happy hour. On Saturday and Sunday, breakfast is served until 2 p.m. and has a separate menu.

Extras: Happy hour is from 4 to 6 p.m. on weekdays. In addition to the house-brewed beers, guest beers are available in bottles and on draft, and there's also hard cider. The brewpub hosts occasional special events during holidays and sporting events, and it also features live music from time to time. Check the Facebook page for details.

Gift shop: Merchandise is available at the brewpub.

Mavericks Beer Company

P.O. Box 874, El Granada, CA 94108
650-720-4450 • www.mavericksbeer.com
Twitter @MavericksBeer • Facebook.com/mavericksbeer

Mavericks Beer is a new company dedicated to bringing session beers to Northern California. A session beer is a craft beer that is low in alcohol but still full-flavored. The average beer is between 5 and 6 percent alcohol by volume, but the brewery's first three beers are each a mere 3.75 percent ABV, yet without sacrificing any flavor.

Each one is available in both 12-ounce cans and kegs. They're being brewed, kegged, and canned at Half Moon Bay Brewing Company. The initial three offerings are Pace Setter Belgian Style Wit Beer; Back in the Saddle Rye Pale Ale, brewed with Maris Otter and rye malts, along with Cascade and Centennial hops; and Pit Stop Chocolate Porter, which has cocoa and vanilla added to the brew.

The company is a collaboration between Half Moon Bay Brewing Company and Pete Slosberg, founder of Pete's Wicked Ales and a pioneer in the craft beer industry. Slosberg has also recruited Will Shelton, one of the brothers in Shelton Brothers Importers, a well-known beer importer that brings to the U.S. such beers as Cantillon and many other brands. Rounding out the team is Alex Slosberg.

They're calling their line of beers "not yet world famous session beers," but it's easy to see them having to change that in short order.

Beers brewed: Pace Setter Belgian Style Wit Beer, Back in the Saddle Rye Pale Ale, and Pit Stop Chocolate Porter.

Mavericks Beer

Opened: February 8, 2013.

Type: Production brewery.

Owner: Lenny Mendonca.

Brewer: James Costa

Guild membership: BA, CCBA.

System: 15-barrel Pub Brewing system, 1,200 barrels annual capacity.

Packages available: 12-ounce cans in six-packs and 5- and 15.5-gallon kegs.

The Pick: Back in the Saddle Rye Pale Ale is bright gold, with a zesty tart hops nose and a creamy mouthfeel. The delicate spicy rye peaks through a good hops presence, which lingers long through a tart, delicious finish. There's so much flavor it's hard to believe it's only 3.75 percent ABV.

Palo Alto Brewing Company

PALO ALTO BREWING COMPANY

1080-B La Avenida Street, Mountain View, CA 94043
www.paloaltobrewing.com
Twitter @PaloAltoBrewing
Facebook.com/pages/Palo-Alto-Brewing-Company/
309231062452840

The original Palo Alto Brewing Company was one of the earliest microbreweries in America but was very short-lived. Opened by Ken Kolence in 1983 with a 7-barrel brewing system, and taken over by Bob Stoddard in 1985, it only lasted until 1987 before closing. It's also notable as the brewery that made the first Pete's Wicked Ales, under contract with Pete Slosberg. After it closed, Stoddard opened Stoddard's Brewhouse in Sunnyvale, which today is the FireHouse Grill & Brewery (see page 140).

The new Palo Alto Brewing Company was started by the Syed family, whose son Kasim and his wife, Guldem, own and operate the Rose & Crown Pub in Palo Alto (547 Emerson Avenue, 650-327-7673). The Rose & Crown was for many years just another British-style pub, but since Syed bought it in 2006, he's turned it into much more of a beer destination, with twenty-five taps of mostly craft beer and as many as a hundred bottles. Syed, who was originally in real estate, was also working part-time at the Palo Alto pub when the owner was looking to get out of the business and offered him a chance to buy it.

The Syeds have certainly kept the look and feel of an English pub, and it still looks like an Elizabethan alehouse from the time of Shakespeare. The menu of pub food is equally authentic, with such dishes as rarebit, ploughman's lunch, bangers and mash, fish and chips, and my favorite, shepherd's pie. And when his family started up the Palo Alto Brewing Company, with Kasim as brewmaster, it was only natural that the Rose & Crown became the brewery's de facto taproom.

Beers brewed: Year-round: Hoppy Ending Pale Ale, Barley Legal Coconut Porter, Atlas Double IPA, Cool Beanz Coffee Porter, and Nice Lacing Belgian Rye IPA (brewed in Belgium). Seasonals: Onoskelis Barleywine and Rye P.A.

The Pick: I really love the Atlas Double IPA, the biggest of Palo Alto's hoppy beers. It's a beast of a beer, with citrus aromas of grapefruit, pineapple, and peaches, along with some grassy, vegetal, and pine notes. It's thick, with big hops flavors and a caramel and biscuity malt background keeping it balanced. There's a warming heat and a long, lingering bitter finish.

All of the beers are contract brewed at Hermitage Brewing, although one beer, the Nice Lacing Belgian Rye IPA, Syed brewed at De Proef in Lochristi, Belgium.

Palo Alto's beers are interesting and inventive variations on popular styles, and Kasim has a good feel for his recipes. For example, he's had four versions of his porter, one made with coffee, a regular coconut one, a coconut porter with added chocolate, and another coconut porter that's sour and aged in bourbon barrels. His hoppy beer are all big but well balanced. Bottles and kegs can be found not only at the Rose & Crown, or even in just the South Bay, but at area stores, bars, and restaurants throughout the Bay Area.

Palo Alto Brewing Company

Opened: March 18, 2009.

Type: Contract gypsy brewery.

Owners: The Syed family.

Brewer: Kasim Syed.

Guild membership: BA.

System: See Hermitage Brewing on page 150 for brewery details.

Annual production: 1,000 barrels (2013 estimate).

Packages available: 12-ounce bottles in six-packs, 22-ounce bottles, and 5- and 15.5-gallon kegs.

Hours: A separate company office is located in Mountain View and is not open to the public. You can taste all of the beers at the Rose & Crown, which opens at 11:30 a.m. seven days a week. Closing time varies depending on how busy the pub is in the evening, although the kitchen closes each night at 9 p.m.

Food: The Rose & Crown offers a full menu of English-style pub food.

Extras: The Rose & Crown hosts a trivia night every Tuesday, beginning at 8 p.m., when there are also drink specials. The last Wednesday of each month is Brewery Night, when the pub offers eight to fifteen beers from a single featured brewery, several of which are not ordinarily available.

Red Branch Brewing Company (Rabbit's Foot Meadery)

1246 Birchwood Drive, Sunnyvale, CA 94087
408-747-0770 • www.rabbitsfootmeadery.com
@rabbitsfootmead
Facebook.com/rabbitsfootmeadery

The Red Branch Brewery is one of the most distinctive breweries in Northern California. It's a meadery first, a cider and cyser (another fermented apple beverage) maker second, and a brewery that makes beer and braggots third. But it's the braggots that are the reason that their secondary name has brewery in the name. Braggots are an ancient hybrid between beer and mead, made from beer and honey brewed together (see the Glossary for more about braggots).

Founder Mike Faul makes several meads under the Rabbit's Foot brand and recently relaunched a line of ciders under the brand Red Branch Cider. He also makes cyser, a honey and apple blend that's fermented together. The diversity of products Faul makes is remarkable, and everything he offers is more impressive than the last. His family owns several acres in Northern California where they grow their own apples and also keep bees to produce honey.

I've never been much of a fan of mead, but Faul's meads are in a different class from almost everything else I've tasted. His Grand Reserve, known as "the Mead of Poetry," is believed to be the first strong mead similar to port ever made. It's aged in oak for at least seven years and can be aged up to ten or even fifteen years. The Melia, a dessert mead, is made from orange blossom honey. You can sample what Faul makes a few days a week, when the tasting room is open.

His beer and braggots alone are worth the trip. You've most likely never tasted anything like them. The Honey Stout and Honey Red are beers

Beers brewed: Year-round: Diabhal (Belgian golden style), Biere de Miel (Kolsch style), Honey Red (Irish red style), and Honey Stout (imperial stout). Seasonals: Hel (saison) and Honey Wheat (wheat beer).

The Pick: Every one of Faul's beers and braggots is unique, and I recommend trying them all if you can. The Honey Stout is the one I'll go with if you press a gun to my head, because it's probably the most unusual but also manages to deliver great roasted flavors with a honeyed sweetness that all works together seamlessly.

made with an unusual amount of honey, which adds more texture than sweetness and gives them both delicate, soft flavors. The Diabhal is a braggot that has a Belgian golden as its base beer, and the Biere de Miel has a Kolsch base. The seasonal Hel is based on a saison, and it can only be described as sublime.

The tasting room is nothing fancy, but it's comfortable and often crowded with regulars. You pass through an entryway with a side table on which are samples of all of the different Rabbit's Foot Meadery and Red Branch Brewing products, along with the many awards and ribbons Faul has accumulated. Inside is the tasting room, with a small bar, and dollars bills attached to the ceiling. But the magic happens in the back, where Faul makes so many tasty beverages whose only common thread is the honey. How sweet it is.

Red Branch Brewing Company (Rabbit's Foot Meadery)

Opened: January 5, 1995.

Type: Production brewery, with tasting room.

Owners: Mike and Maria Faul.

Brewer: Mike Faul.

Guild membership: BA.

System: 15-barrel CBC mash/partial mash; 100 barrels (beer), 6,000 gallons (mead), and 6,000 barrels (cider) annual capacity.

Annual production: 100 barrels of beer (2012).

Packages available: 500-milliliter bottles, growlers, and kegs.

Tours: Brewery tours are available; reservations are not necessary.

Hours: Tuesday through Thursday, 2 to 7 p.m.; Friday, 2 to 8 p.m.; Saturday, 1 to 5 p.m. (closed some Saturdays, so call first). Closed Sunday and Monday.

Food: Food is not available in the tasting room.

Extras: Red Branch has a Mug Club with limited membership. It throws annual Halloween and New Year's parties and hosts several cook-offs throughout the year.

Gift shop: Some merchandise is available in the tasting room.

Rock Bottom Restaurant & Brewery

1875 South Bascom Avenue, #700,
Campbell, CA 95008
408-377-0707 • www.rockbottom.com
Twitter @rockbottom
Facebook.com/RBCampbellCA /
Facebook.com/RockBottomRestaurant

The first Rock Bottom brewpub opened in downtown Denver in 1991, and by 1994, it had an IPO and began opening additional locations, opening eight new brewpubs the first year. In 1999, it became a private company again, but in 2010, it merged with Big River Breweries, which also owned the Gordon Biersch chain of brewpubs, and the newly created entity was named CraftWorks Restaurants and Breweries. Craft-Works also operates Old Chicago, Big River, the ChopHouse, A1A Aleworks, Seven Bridges Grille & Brewery, and the Walnut Brewery brewpubs, in addition to the Rock Bottom and Gordon Biersch chains.

Today there are thirty-four Rock Bottoms in seventeen states. The Campbell Rock Bottom opened in February 1997, in the Pruneyard shopping center. The brewpub is located toward the back, on a corner. It's big, with an impressively large outdoor beer garden in the front that can comfortably accommodate up to a hundred people. At night, the garden is illuminated by large red neon lights on the roof and white bulbs strung from poles above the outdoor patio. A larger-than-life unused fermenter is on the corner of the property and is also lit up at night.

Inside, the brewery has high-beamed ceilings and a large bar against a wall, behind which you can see the serving tanks on two floors through a series of large windows. The brewhouse is off to the side of the bar, and the back of it can be seen through another set of windows. Even during the day, the interior is an escape from the sun, and between the dark wood and lack of exterior windows, it's a shadow world, with a plethora of ceiling lamps lighting each table and giving it a private ambience even with the open floor plan. Above the bar is a really cool drawing of the inside of the brewpub with some of its patrons enjoying themselves, and several big-screen televisions hang above the bar and dot the interior.

Beers brewed: Year-round: Kolsch, White Ale, Red Ale, and India Pale Ale, a dark beer, a rotating featured beer, and a brewmaster's choice. Seasonals: Robust Porter, Brown Bear, Vanilla Stout, Fire Chief Ale, Imperial IPA, Seismic Saison, Holidaze Belgian Dubbel, Blitzen Belgian Tripel, The Angry Brewer Barley Wine, Rotating Stout Imperial Oatmeal Stout, and many more.

Brewmaster Russell Clements is originally from New Jersey and studied philosophy in college. While working as a baker in Asheville, North Carolina, in a bakery that was located above a brewery, he began helping out in the brewery too, since he was already the yeast wrangler for the bread. One thing led to another, and before he knew it, he was brewing beer instead of baking bread. He worked at the Rock Bottom in La Jolla, in the San Diego area, and developed a deft hand with hoppy beers, winning several medals at the Great American Beer Festival. Two years ago, Clements moved north to take over brewing at the Campbell location.

Rock Bottom Restaurant & Brewery

Opened: First Rock Bottom opened in 1991; Campbell location opened February 16, 1997.

Type: Brewpub.

Owners: CraftWorks Restaurants and Breweries, Inc.

Brewer: Russell Clements.

Guild membership: BA, BBG.

System: 10-barrel JV Northwest, 2,100 barrels annual capacity.

Annual production: 2,100 barrels (2012).

Packages available: Draft only at the brewpub, plus a couple beers on cask most times.

Tours: Brewery tours available on request, if the brewer is there and has free time.

Hours: Sunday and Monday, 11 a.m. to 10 p.m.; Tuesday through Thursday, 11 a.m. to 11 p.m.; Friday and Saturday, 11 a.m. to midnight.

Food: Rock Bottom restaurants have a dizzying number of choices, beginning with a dozen and a half starters. The menu also includes salads, steaks, burgers, sandwiches, pizza, and "house favorites," such as bacon chicken mac and cheese, turkey meatloaf, hazelnut crusted chicken, and Creole jambalaya. There's also a dessert menu and a separate kids' menu. Throughout the year, a selection of featured menu items changes, including choices like chipotle agave salmon, jalapeno sticks, and Fire Chief Pork Chop, designed to go with one of the brewery's seasonal beers, the Fire Chief Ale. Special dishes are also posted on the Facebook page.

Extras: Happy hour is weekdays 3 to 6 p.m. and from 10 p.m. to close, although it takes place all day on Wednesday. Rock Bottom has a mug club or Rock Rewards loyalty program you can join, which provides special discounts and rewards. You can find details at www.rbmugclub.com.

Gift shop: Merchandise is sold at the brewpub.

Santa Cruz Ale Works

150 Dubois Street, Suite E, Santa Cruz,
   CA 95060
831-425-1182 • www.santacruzaleworks.com
Twitter @S_C_AleWorks
Facebook.com/santacruz.aleworks

The "Works" part of Santa Cruz Ale Works defines what the brewery does: it's a no-frills production brewery. If you want to stop by and see it working, call first. The tasting room and tours are available by appointment only. Most of the time, that's because the brewer is simply busy in the back brewing beer.

Founder, owner, and brewer Marc Rosenblum was bitten by the homebrewing bug around 1992, while attending Sonoma State. He eventually studied brewing at the University of Sunderland, which is near Newcastle in Great Britain. He spent six months immersed in brewing in the northeast of England, using weekends to travel the countryside and intern in local cottage breweries.

After returning to California, he worked at both large and small breweries, including Lagunitas, Pyramid, and Seabright, before founding his own brewery in Santa Cruz, where he makes three regular beers in kegs and bottles, plus the occasional seasonal. He makes no-nonsense beers that simply taste good.

Santa Cruz Ale Works

Opened: January 2008.

Type: Production brewery.

Owner: Marc Rosenblum.

Brewer: Marc Rosenblum.

System: 15-barrel DME, 4,000 barrels annual capacity.

Annual production: 1,500 barrels (2012).

Packages available: 22-ounce bottles, growlers, and 20- and 50-liter kegs.

Tours: Brewery tours are available by appointment only.

Hours: No public hours; the tasting room is open by appointment only.

Gift shop: The tasting room has some merchandise for sale.

Beers brewed: Year-round: Hefeweizen, IPA, and Pale Ale. Seasonals: Cruz Control Red, Dark Night Oatmeal Stout, and Saison Dubois.

The Pick: I like Marc's take on IPA. It starts with a big citrus nose, aromas of grapefruit, oranges, and lemons, along with earthy pine and spicy notes. The mouthfeel is on the lighter side, making it easy drinking and a great summer IPA, though it stands up any time of the year. The finish is slightly dry, with a sweet aftertaste.

Santa Cruz Mountain Brewing

402 Ingalls Street #27, Santa Cruz, CA 95060
831-425-4900 • www.scmbrew.com
Facebook.com/santacruzmountainbrewing

All of Santa Cruz Mountain's beers are certified organic. Most are available in bottles, but there are some great one-offs and seasonals you can get only by visiting the brewery's taproom. In addition to the brewery's seven flagship beers on tap there, and the seasonals, the brewers also make their own hard ciders using local apples.

The small production brewery is next door to a little taproom, and there's acozy beer garden outside in the front. Behind the bar is one of many curiosities to be found here: a large copper tree appears to be growing out of the back wall and into the ceiling. Branches hang down, and mugs are hung from hooks in the tree. There's an ATM machine next to a rack of brewery T-shirts and other items, and original works by local artists hang on the walls. A stuffed mallard duck flies under a ceiling lamp, and what looks to be a gazelle that's suffered a similar fate is on an interior wall, looking over the brewpub patrons.

Food is available from Kelly's French Bakery, which is adjacent to the brewery. There's a small but adequate amount of seating, including a bench seat along one wall below the resident gazelle, tables and chairs in the middle, and bar stools along the L-shaped bar. The place has a funky but comfortable feel to it, and you feel right at home, even among strangers.

The idea to open the brewery was hatched when cofounder Emily Thomas was in college in that other Mecca of beer: Portland, Oregon. After her uncles helped along her education of brewing and loving beer, she in turn passed that pas-

Beers brewed: Year-round: Amber Ale, Pale Ale, Wilder Wheat, Organic IPA, Devout Stout, People's Porter, and Dread Brown Ale. Seasonals: Olallieberry Cream Ale (July and August), Daddy's Little Helper Double IPA, O'Berry, Fresh Hopped Black IPA, Black Swan Imperial Stout (February), Nicky 666 Red Ale (January), Rakau Singular Sensation, Pumpkin Ale (October), Nectar de Festivus (a.k.a. Emily's Winter Warmer), and Ginger's Winter Warmer.

The Pick: The chocolaty Devout Stout is sinfully good, with a powdered chocolate nose and milk chocolate flavors throughout. Did I mention there's chocolate? There's also rich toffee, roasted coffee, and a touch of spice and vanilla.

sion on to cofounder Chad Brill, and the pair launched the brewery in 2005.

In addition to regular events throughout the year, each February during SF Beer Week, Santa Cruz Mountain hosts what it calls Strong Women Brew Day, a day for learning about homebrewing and a chance for people to help out with the brewing of a beer. Plans are also afoot to open a second location with a full restaurant in the summer of 2013. The new place will be called the Brewers Kitchen.

Santa Cruz Mountain Brewing

Opened: January 2005.

Type: Production brewery, with beer garden and taproom.

Owners: Emily Thomas and Chad Brill.

Brewers: Chad Brill, Emily Thomas, Tommy Mills, and Pepe Palacious.

Guild membership: BBG.

System: 7-barrel, direct fire kettle (with most equipment dug out of a friend's back yard), 1,500 barrels annual capacity.

Annual production: 1,200 barrels.

Packages available: Growlers, 22-ounce bottles, and 5- and 15.5-gallon kegs.

Tours: No tours are available.

Hours: Seven days a week, noon to 10 p.m. Food is available each day from noon until 7 p.m., or 8 p.m. on Friday.

Food: Food is served from the restaurant next door to the production brewery, Kelly's French Bakery. The menu includes appetizers, such as a bowl of fries and a Bavarian pretzel with mustard; salads and sandwiches, both hot and cold; and heartier dishes like chicken pot pie, lasagna, and roasted eggplant.

Extras: Kid- and dog-friendly, with games, Wi-Fi, special events, and good company. Throughout the week, there are various specials. On Monday and Tuesday, pints of the regular offerings (not the seasonals) are $3.50 all day long, and Wednesday through Sunday, happy hour is 5 to 6 p.m. (7 p.m. on Friday), with $3.50 pints. On Der Weenie Wednesday, liters (not including seasonals) are $8 all day. On Thank You Thursday, $1 of every pint sold is donated to a local nonprofit.

Gift shop: T-shirts, glasses, gift boxes, hats, key chains, stickers, and beer Thermoses are available at the brewpub and online.

Sante Adairius Rustic Ales

SANTE ADAIRIUS
RUSTIC ALES

103 Kennedy Drive, Capitola, CA 95010
831-462-1227 • www.rusticales.com
@santeadairius
Facebook.com/santeadairius

The first time I met Tim Clifford, we were both helping Brian Hunt harvest hops at his small hopyard at Moonlight Brewing. Back then, Clifford was a beer writer for the Northwest Brewing News, a co-owner of the Seven Bridges Cooperative homebrew store, and an avid homebrewer.

The next thing I knew, he was set to open his own brewery with his wife, Adair Paterno. Eventually, in the spring of 2012, Sante Adairius Rustic Ales opened its doors. The small brewery is located on an access road just off State Route 1, though there's no direct route and you will need to backtrack slightly. Apparently some GPS systems get the address wrong, so unless you're a local, be prepared to make a wrong turn or two. Though the address is on Kennedy Drive, it's at the corner of Rosedale Avenue, where one road turns into the other at an elbow curve. The brewery is housed in a fairly unassuming, nondescript building, and it's the middle unit. So keep your eyes peeled, or you may miss it. Luckily, it's worth the effort.

Inside, you'll find a clean, modern, and somewhat rustic tasting room, with wooden barrels for tables and bar stools all around. The brewery is behind closed doors beyond the tasting room. All of the equipment once had another use and has been recycled, repurposed, and reimagined into a working brewery. That's where the magic happens. Although the brewery has been open less than a year at the time of this writing, the brewers have already created a dizzying number of beers. Unless you're a regular, there's no way you could try everything they brew.

Clifford is clearly a talented brewer, and his reputation is understandably growing by leaps

Beers brewed: Year-round: Anais (Belgian-style saison with spelt), Chavez (rye porter), 831 IPA, The Professor (Belgian-style imperial stout), Saison Bernice (saison with brett), and West Ashley (barrel-aged saison with apricots). Seasonals or occasional releases: 1894, A Blackened Eye, Adjunct Professor, Amber Oak, And You Me, Barrel-Aged Professor, Big Lou, Brewer's Beard, Chavez, Cocoa Vanilla Joe, Farmhouse IPA, Farmhouse Ron, Fumare, Golden Bell, Golden Rye, Group Trip, Harvest Blonde, HopDrink, Joe Chavez, Kermit's Ennui, Last Friday, Lazy Day, Love's Armor, Maiden Fields, McGrath's Stash, Nonna's Blend, Northern Influence, Professor White, SARA Loves Brett, Simple: Citra, The Sum and Its Parts, There She Gose, Tripod Tripel, Two Pilots, Vanilla Joe, We(e) Hop, West Ashley, Winkyface ;), and Adairius (American wild ale).

and bounds. The brewery has only limited hours for now, so choose the time of your visit carefully, as more and more people are crowding the small tasting room with each passing month. But don't let that deter you either. If your schedule is flexible, Thursday and Sunday aren't quite as busy as the other days, so they may be your best bet. Sante Adairius Rustic Ales is making an amazing array of terrific beers. And you'll find something new with every visit.

Sante Adairius Rustic Ales

Opened: May 2012.

Type: Production brewery, with tasting room.

Owners: Tim Clifford and Adair Paterno.

Brewers: Tim Clifford and Jason Hansen.

Guild membership: CCBA.

System: 7-barrel repurposed dairy and tea-manufacturing equipment.

Packages available: 750-milliliter bottles, growlers, and 5-gallon kegs (kegs are not available for purchase by consumers).

Tours: No tours are currently available.

Hours: Thursday and Friday, 4 to 8 p.m.; Saturday and Sunday, 1 to 7 p.m.

Food: On weekends, food trucks often park outside the brewery's tasting room.

Extras: Dogs are welcome, but children are not permitted at the brewery.

The Pick: It's particularly difficult to choose just one from among so many different unique and tasty beers, so I won't. The Saison Bernice is really terrific, a tart, refreshing farmhouse beer with citrus and spicy notes, and it's brewed with *Brettanomyces*. Its doppelganger, Anais, a saison without brett and brewed with spelt, is very spicy and zesty, with a honeyed sweetness and a dry finish. If you prefer something hoppy, the 831 IPA is a big hops blast of tangerine, pine, and herbal character. Want something bigger? The Professor, an imperial stout with chocolate and smoky goodness, is also tart and spicy, and there's a barrel-aged version of this beer too.

Seabright Brewery

519 Seabright Avenue, Suite 107, Santa Cruz, CA 95062
831-426-2739 • www.seabrightbrewery.com
Facebook.com/pages/Seabright-Brewery/ 40798702665

In the late 1980s, Charlie Meehan was a home-brewer, and his friend Keith Cranmer had recently sold his silversmith business. Meehan had been winning homebrew competitions, and the pair decided that a brewpub might be an exciting venture. It turned out they were right, and the brewpub celebrated its silver anniversary earlier this year.

The brewpub is located in a shopping center and occupies a good portion of one end. Inside, it's all light wood, with a wooden bar that hugs one side of the open restaurant. Several big-screen TVs are mounted above it and throughout the brewpub. Between the bar and the rest of the seating—booths and tables—there's a long, tall table with high-backed stools circling it.

There's also a large outdoor patio, with tables surrounding a clever fountain. It's usually crowded. Dogs are allowed on the patio, but if you want to bring your dog, the brewery has some specific rules you should read on the website first. The main ones are a limit of two dogs per owner, on only nonretractable leases, and dogs get the night off on Tuesday and Friday, when those evenings they have to go home at 6 p.m.

Brewmaster Jason Chavez started homebrewing on his family's kitchen stove while still in high school. He's a graduate of the American Brewers Guild and has been brewing at Seabright since 1999. In addition to a regular lineup of year-round beers, he keeps three to eight seasonals on at any given time. The brewery is in a side room but is visible through a series of windows above the booth seating. Look for the pink stuffed elephant inside the brewery.

Beers brewed: Year-round: Pelican Pale, Seabright Amber, The Blur IPA, Oatmeal Stout, and Sacrilicious Ale. Seasonals: Chavez keeps a rotating series of beers on, in addition to the regular lineup. Some previous offerings have included Dog Nose Porter, Red Beard Bitter, Gringo's Gold, Say Hey Wheat, Tasty Green, Hopnotic, Mt. Walker Winter Warmer, Penguin ESB, Old Okole, Leroy Barleywine, Jackalope Dark Wheat, Plonker Pale Ale, Alpha-Bet Ale, Double Wide IPA, Hopnoxious, Sour Donkey, and Hot Foot Ale.

The food at Seabright is tasty and plentiful, and with the range of beers that Chavez brews, you'll easily find something to like. It's actually more likely that you won't be able to pick just one. The crowd tends to consist of lots of locals, with a smattering of out-of-towners, especially during the summer months, when the beach draws people from all over the state and beyond. It's easy to see why Seabright has endured and remained popular for more than twenty-five years.

Seabright Brewery

Opened: May 14, 1988.

Type: Brewpub.

Owners: Charlie Meehan and Keith Cranmer.

Brewer: Jason Chavez.

Guild membership: BA, CCBA.

System: 7-barrel JV Northwest, 1,200 barrels annual capacity.

Annual production: 1,000 to 1,100 barrels (2012 estimate).

Packages available: Growlers, cask, and draft only at the brewpub; 12-ounce cans are also being added to the lineup.

Tours: Brewery tours are available if the brewer is around; just ask if he's there.

Hours: Seven days a week, 11:30 a.m to 11:30 p.m.

Food: Seabright offers an extensive menu of pub fare, with a great selection of appetizers, such as beer-battered onion rings, baked brie and caramelized roasted garlic, steamed clams, and french fries seven ways. The menu also includes a long list of soups, salads, burgers, sandwiches, and pub favorites, like Jiggy's Pub Club, salmon fish and chips, and Mediterranean wraps. There's also a separate kids' menu.

Extras: Happy hour is 3 p.m. to 6 p.m. Monday through Friday, except Tuesday, called Neighborhood Night, when happy hour runs until closing time. Wednesday features specials on fish tacos, and Thursday is Brewer's Night, with special pricing on a featured beer and some food specials too. Friday has live music from 6:30 to 10 p.m. The brewpub has six big-screen TVs and a dog-friendly patio, though, as they're fond of saying, "Kids must be leashed." That's a joke, of course, but be sure to read the rules regarding dogs on the website.

Gift shop: T-shirts, sweatshirts, and hats are available at the brewpub.

Steelhead Brewing Company

333 California Drive, Burlingame, CA 94010
650-344-6050
www.steelheadbrewery.com/burlingame.htm

The first Steelhead Brewing Company opened in Eugene, Oregon, in early 1991. The brainchild of five local businesspeople from diverse backgrounds, the first one was successful enough that a few years later, in 1995, two more opened in California: the Burlingame brewpub and one in Irvine, both of which are still open today. Later, two additional California brewpubs, one in San Francisco and another in Fresno, also opened but have since closed.

When it first opened, the brewpub in Burlingame was known as the Burlingame Station Brewing Company because it's located across the street from a train station and train tracks run right past the brewery, where CalTrans trains chug up and down the Peninsula. Though technically it's now the Golden State Brewing Company d.b.a. the Steelhead Brewery at Burlingame Station, most people just call it Steelhead or the Steelhead Brewery.

When it opened in 1995, Steelhead was part of the downtown area's revitalization project and is in a historic old brick building. The building's front door is the one across from the railroad tracks, but I suspect more people come in through the back, which is closer to parking and provides a better view coming in. That's also where a small outdoor patio beer garden is, in the shadow of a large silo with the Steelhead logo emblazoned on it.

Inside, the brewpub looks a little bit like an airplane hangar, with 33-foot-high ceilings that give it a very open feel. It's quite large and seats around two hundred. The kitchen is also open to the restaurant, and there's a granite bar along part of one wall. In between the bar and the kitchen is a brick pizza oven that resembles a castle turret. Only the brewery is partially hidden, but it can be seen through three arched windows behind the bar.

Beers brewed: Year-round: Hairy Weasel Hefeweizen, Broadway Blond, Raging Rhino Red, and Bombay Bomber IPA. Seasonals: Pumpkin Pie Ale, Half Moon Porter, McFadden's Oatmeal Stout, and Station Square Imperial Stout. Roughly once a month, a new seasonal is added, and there are usually two different ones on at any given time. Recent specialty beers: Hopasaurus Rex, Doubleplay IPA, Wee Heavy Scotch Ale, Pacific Crest Porter, Terrapin Ale, Hearthside Wheat Wine, Heat Miser, Doppelbock, Oaxaca Chocolate Stout, Iron Brewer, Nigel's Extra ESB, Starchild Unfiltered Pale Ale, Little Pookies Old Ale, and Guava-licious IPA.

A separate backroom has its own bar and six full-size pool tables. The tables can be rented by the hour and are ideal for small parties or any group getting together for an evening of fun and beer. You can also rent all or half of the room for private parties or banquets.

Brewmaster Emil Caluori is a graduate of the American Brewers Guild and first apprenticed at the Brew Brothers, the brewpub inside the Eldorado Hotel and Casino in Reno, before getting a job at the Eugene Steelhead. Fifteen years ago, he moved to Burlingame to brew, and for the last ten years, he's been the only brewer there, doing all of the brewing himself. He makes all of the standard Steelhead beers, as well as a number of seasonal and one-offs that are constantly changing.

Steelhead Brewing Company

Opened: The first Steelhead opened January 22, 1991; the Burlingame location opened March 8, 1995.

Type: Brewpub.

Owners: Corydon Jensen and the Connors Brothers.

Brewer: Emil Caluori.

Guild membership: BA.

System: 14-barrel JV Northwest, 2,366 barrels annual capacity.

Annual production: 850 barrels (2012 estimate).

Packages available: Draft only at the brewpub.

Tours: Brewery tours are available, but reservations are necessary.

Hours: Sunday and Monday, 11:30 a.m to 9 p.m.; Tuesday through Thursday, 11:30 a.m. to 10 p.m.; Friday and Saturday, 11:30 a.m. to 11 p.m.

Food: A big list of appetizers, such as beer-steamed clams, beer-battered onion rings, and a literal "mound o' fries," as well as soups and salads, burgers and sandwiches, wood-fired pizza, and entrées like popcorn shrimp tacos. And that's just the lunch menu. For dinner, the menu also includes several pasta dishes and some heartier steak choices. There's a separate kids' menu, and Steelhead also brews its own root beer.

Extras: There's a separate poolroom in the back of the brewpub, and on Friday and Saturday evenings, it stays open later than the restaurant. There are usually two beers on cask. The brewpub is also set up to handle very large groups and banquets.

Gift shop: Merchandise is available at the brewpub; look for the jam-packed cases in front and another in the back near the poolroom.

Strike Brewing Company

640 Leaf Court, Los Altos, CA 94022 (office address)
650-714-6983 • www.strikebrewingco.com
Twitter @strikebrewingco
Facebook.com/strikebrewingco

Strike Brewing debuted in mid-December of the year before last, but has been a long time coming for its founders, Jenny and Ben Lewis, along with brewmaster Drew Ehrlich. Over a birthday pint at a Giants game in 2008, the trio decided they should start a brewery and began taking steps to realize that goal. Jenny went back to Rice and got her MBA while Drew worked on the recipes, all with an eye toward creating a brewery business.

Both Ben and Drew had been baseball pitchers, Lewis for San Jose State and Ehrlich for Stanford and the Red Sox minor league farm system, so the goal of throwing strikes translated well when it came to picking a name too. Jenny, who's the CEO, is a swimmer, and the owners decided to make Strike's beers with athletic pursuits in mind. The majority of their beers are part of what they call the Session Series and are full-flavored beers under 5 percent ABV, based on the idea that session beers make more sense after exercise and sports. They also have their own running club and work with a number of athletic partners. Every Wednesday evening at 6:30 p.m., club members meet at Los Gatos High School track field and set off on a run along the Los Gatos Creek Trail. The runs are led by fitness advocate and certified personal trainer Lori Beveridge, who is also the owner of Couture Conditioning. As Strike Brewing T-shirts promise, "You Get Beer When It's Over."

Strike's owners are actively seeking a spot in San Jose to build a brewery of their own, but in the meantime, they're happy making beer at Hermitage. They're hoping to find a location from which they can start and end a run. To find where Strike's beer is being sold, check the website, which has a list of retailers carrying its bottles and kegs.

Beers brewed: Year-round: Strike Blonde, Strike Brown, Strike Wit, Strike IPA, Strike Stout, and Strike Imperial Red. Seasonals: Strike Porter. The Strike Blonde, Wit, Brown, and seasonal Porter are all part of the Session Series of beer.

The Pick: The Strike Brown ale is a refreshing, clean beer that's malty sweet, with nutty and caramel aromas. The flavors are similarly sweet, with a touch of brown sugar and chocolate powder notes. It's a very easy drinking beer, with full flavors and a slightly nutty finish.

Strike Brewing Company

Opened: December 15, 2011.

Type: Contract brewery currently, but Strike is actively raising funds to build a production brewery with tasting room.

Owners: Jenny Lewis and Drew Ehrlich.

Brewer: Drew Ehrlich.

Guild membership: BBG.

System: 20-barrel brewhouse is planned for the new production brewery. Currently brewing at Hermitage (see page 150).

Annual production: 800 barrels (2012 estimate).

Packages available: 12-ounce bottles in six-packs and kegs (15.5 and 5 gallon).

Tours: Tours will be available by appointment once the new production brewery opens.

Food: No food will be available at the brewery, but the owners plan to bring in food trucks on weekends and for special events, and customers will be welcome to bring their own food to the tasting room.

Extras: Strike has offered to be a meeting place for other triathlon, cycling, and running clubs. The owners are hoping to be able to have outdoor seating as well.

Gift shop: Merchandise is currently available online.

Tied House Brewery & Café

954 Villa Street, Mountain View, CA 94041
650-965-2739 • www.tiedhouse.com
Twitter @tiedhouse • Facebook.com/TiedHouseBrewing

In 1987, there was only a handful of brewery restaurants in the entire country, but California had more than its fair share. Sensing a trend and an increasing demand for craft beer, Lou Jemison and Ron Manabe decided that they too would open a brewpub. Although neither was a brewer, Manabe had traveled and tried different beers all over the globe, and he knew the potential beer had.

From the very beginning, they focused on making great beer. Their first brewer was Chuck Tom, who'd brewed for Anheuser-Busch and also spent thirty years as the brewer at San Miguel Brewery in Hong Kong. Manabe, already very interested in beer as a consumer, learned everything he could from the experienced Tom and also attended the Siebel Institute for formal brewing instruction, earning his certificate in 1995. He's since taken over as brewmaster and now makes all of the beer.

The building was built from scratch to house the brewery restaurant, and the brewhouse is behind the scenes, although it's on full view from behind the long wooden L-shaped bar. Next to the bar, the clubhouse wall is filled with hooks on which hang more than 150 numbered ceramic mugs, which belong to the members of the Tied House's mug club. The main part of the restaurant is in a large, open space, with high ceilings. A massively giant screen hangs above the entrance, and more televisions are scattered around the inside.

One of my favorite Tied House stories involves the space shuttle and a beer coaster. A group of NASA astronauts visited the brewpub in the 1990s and took one of its coasters with them into space. When they returned to Earth, they brought the

Beers brewed: Year-round: Amber Light, Alpine Gold, Cascade Amber, New World Wheat, Oatmeal Stout, and Ironwood Dark. Seasonals: Mai Bock and Oktoberfest, with a rotating selection of one-off and seasonal beers that changes frequently.

The Pick: I love Ron's Oatmeal Stout; it's a very smooth beer with good chocolate notes, as well as a touch of sweetness, a dash of bittersweet, and some lightly burnt toffee. It's appropriately thin-bodied and has a toasty dry finish. If you're more in the mood for something lighter in color, you can't go wrong with the popular and sweeter Cascade Amber, a light-bodied, malt-forward beer.

well-traveled coaster back and presented it the brewery. If you search the walls, you can find it hanging in a place of honor, framed with a letter and signed photo from the space shuttle personnel.

My favorite part of the brewpub may be the covered outdoor patio in the back of the building. It's the best of both worlds, with fresh air and covered warmth. The space also includes very long tables, which are ideal for large groups, as well as a separate bar. If you want to be all the way outside, there's a side patio with small tables and chairs, plus heat lamps for cool evenings.

The Tied House is a Mountain View and South Bay institution, one of the originals, and it still does things right. You'll find great food, with big portions, and a terrific mix of beers. For these and many other reasons, it's a popular hangout for locals. But since you'll feel welcome there even on your first visit, it's worth coming to the Tied House no matter where you live.

Tied House Brewery & Café

Opened: January 5, 1988.

Type: Brewpub.

Owners: Lou Jemison and Ron Manabe.

Brewer: Ron Manabe.

Guild membership: BA, CCBA, BBG.

System: 20-barrel Custom built brewhouse, 3,000 barrels annual capacity.

Annual production: 3,000 barrels (2012).

Packages available: 22-ounce bottles, growlers, and 5-, 7.75-, and 15.5-gallon kegs.

Tours: Brewery tours are available with a reservation.

Hours: Monday through Wednesday, 11:30 a.m. to 10 p.m.; Thursday, 11:30 a.m. to 10:30 p.m.; Friday, 11:30 a.m. to 11 p.m.; Saturday, 11:30 a.m. to 10 p.m.; Sunday, 11:30 a.m. to 9 p.m.

Food: Pub fare includes an extensive variety of appetizers, salads and soups, burgers and sandwiches, pasta, and meat and seafood dishes, such as panko-crusted fish and chips. There are also choices from the smoker, like the house-smoked baby back ribs; smoked platters of chicken, fish, or ribs; housemade sausages; and wild game burgers.

Extras: Happy hour is 4 to 6 p.m. on weekdays, with selected appetizers for half price and discounted prices for pints of beer. Thursday, beginning at 9 p.m., is Half Pint Night, with all regular pints (not high-alcohol beers) for half price. On weekends, there's a "3 for $3 Sampler" special. Check the website for current specials. The Tied House has a mug club, and for an annual fee, you'll have a numbered ceramic mug waiting for you whenever you stop by, as well as larger pours, various discounts, and invitations to special events. Banquet and catering services are also available.

Gift shop: Merchandise is available at the brewpub.

Uncommon Brewers

303 Potrero Street, Suite 40H, Santa Cruz, CA 95060
831-621-6270 (voicemail only)
www.uncommonbrewers.com
Facebook.com/pages/Uncommon-Brewers/244982068151

Uncommon Brewers certainly lives up to its name. Nothing that the brewery makes is ordinary or traditional—not the types of beer, not the packaging, and not the way the beer is brewed, which is 100 percent organic. So far, Uncommon has brewed beer with coriander, kaffir lime, lemongrass, bacon, poppy seeds, licorice root, star anise, mushrooms, and maple sugar, and one beer was aged on redwood. It was also the first brewery to can a nonalcoholic craft beer, and it made the strongest beer ever put in a can.

Founder Alec Stefansky started homebrewing while in college in 1996, and by 2002, he was in graduate school and working on recipes for the brewery that even then he was planning on opening. He grew up among olive trees, as his family owns and operates an olive oil business, and this gave him an appreciation for agriculture and for handcrafted products. That made his decision to make Uncommon Brewers a certified organic brewery an easy one.

Stefansky's vision has been the same during the years it took him to open the brewery, as well as in the years since he's been in business. He wanted to create an organic brewery in the tradition of the Slow Food movement. The brewery is operated using both traditional Belgian brewing methods and contemporary West Coast techniques.He chose the name Uncommon Brewers, saying, "Our goal is to make uncommon beers for uncommon people."

Beers brewed: Year-round: Siamese Twin Ale, Golden State Ale, Baltic Porter, Bacon Brown Ale, and Scotty K (nonalcoholic). Seasonals: Rubidus Red Ale and American Special Bitter.

The Pick: The Siamese Twin Ale is the first beer I ever had from Uncommon, and it's still my favorite. The Belgian-style dubbel is flavored with coriander, kaffir lime, and lemongrass, and while the combination isn't obvious, it really works well, especially with certain types of food, such as Asian cuisine, salads, and curries. The complex nose of spices and fruit aromas gives way to a refreshing malty sweetness, balanced with the herbal flavors of the coriander and Thai spices. Even with its considerable heft, it's very drinkable, though sipping is the best approach to take.

In that goal, he's succeeded magnificently, and the lineup has continued to grow more adventurous and more inventive, with each new beer as delicious as the last. You can now find Uncommon beers in ten states, along with Washington, D.C., and the cans have also traveled to Canada, Japan, and Denmark.

Uncommon Brewers

Opened: August 2007 (first batch brewed), May 2008 (first beer sold).

Type: Production brewery.

Owner: Alec Stefansky.

Brewer: Alec Stefansky.

Guild membership: BA, CCBA, BBG

System: 30-barrel Stromberg brewhouse, heavily modified, 6,000 barrels annual capacity.

Annual production: 2,000 barrels (2012 estimate).

Packages available: 8- and 16-ounce cans and 20- and 30-liter kegs.

Tours: Brewery tours are available by appointment only.

Hours: The brewery is not open to the public.

Gift shop: T-shirts and sweatshirts are sold online, during private brewery tours, and at some beer festivals.

Three of America's First Five Brewpubs

A brewpub is a brewery that has a restaurant on the premises. Most of the beer is brewed to be sold right where it's made, at the restaurant and bar. In America, the brewpub is a fairly new phenomenon—the first one in the United States was opened in 1982. The Yakima Brewing & Malting Company, founded by Bert Grant, opened Grant's Brewery Pub in Yakima, Washington. Over the next few years, more brewpubs opened across the country. Three of the first five brewpubs in the United States, or three of the next four, were all opened in Northern California.

The year after Grant's opened, when Jack McAuliffe's New Albion Brewery went out of business, assistant brewer Don Barkley, along with Michael Laybourn and Norman Franks, bought the brewing equipment and used it to found a brewpub in the nearby town of Hopland, so named because hops were grown there before Prohibition. When Mendocino Brewing Company opened on August 14, 1983, it was the first brewpub in California, and the second to open in the United States.

Barkley created the brewpub's flagship beer, Red Tail Ale, which is still popular today. Its seasonal Eye of the Hawk, then brewed just twice a year, achieved cult status. The brewery became very successful, and in the early 1990s, a much larger brewery was built in Ukiah, near Highway 101, a dozen miles north of Hopland. In 1997, Vijay Mallya, who also owned the Indian beer brand Kingfisher, bought a controlling interest in Mendocino Brewing. In 2010, the original Hopland brewpub was closed when the landlord declined to renew the lease.

On September 9, 1983, almost a month after Mendocino Brewing opened, California's second brewpub (and America's third) was opened by Bill Owens in Hayward. Buffalo Bill's Brewery brewed one of the first pumpkin beers, now a common fall sight, and its Alimony Ale was cheekily declared "the bitterest beer in America." Owens, who also published *American Brewer* magazine and *Beer: The Magazine* briefly, sold the brewpub to its current owner, Geoff Harries, in 1994.

California's third brewpub (and the fifth in the country), then known as Roaring Rock, opened its doors on March 14, 1986, though brothers John and Reid Martin brewed their first batch of beer on Christmas Day 1985. The Pennsylvania brand Rolling Rock (now owned by Anheuser-Busch InBev and brewed in New Jersey) took issue with the similar-sounding name Roaring Rock and took the Martins to court, where they lost their legal battle. As a result, they had to change the name of their brewpub, settling on Triple Rock Brewery & Alehouse. Some of the possible names they rejected at the time included Foamy Rock and Roaring Duck. Today Triple Rock is still owned and operated by its original founders, John and Reid Martin.

In between Buffalo Bill's and Triple Rock, toward the end of 1984, the fourth U.S. brewpub to open was Manhattan Brewing Company in New York City. It closed in 1991. Today more than two thousand breweries are open in the United States, of which nearly eleven hundred are brewpubs. Northern California alone has around seventy, more than most entire states.

The East Bay

The East Bay is the region due east from San Francisco. Drive across the Bay Bridge from the city, on either the Dumbarton or San Mateo-Hayward Bridge from the Peninsula in the South Bay and you'll arrive in the East Bay. For the purposes of this book, the East Bay region includes the counties of Alameda and Contra Costa. Though it consists of just two urban counties, the region is slightly larger than Rhode Island, with almost as many people as Jamaica and more than the entire state of New Mexico. Contra Costa means "opposite coast" and was so named because it's across the bay from San Francisco. Part of Contra Costa County was spun off to become Alameda in 1853, and the split resulted in the two counties as they are today.

If you're starting out in San Francisco, most places in the East Bay can be reached by BART, the Bay Area Rapid Transit, which operates trains extensively throughout this area.

Alameda County is more urban, with Oakland as its center, and most of the county is filled with overlapping urban and suburban communities. It also includes the college town of Berkeley, home to the oldest university in California. Berkeley is also famous for its liberal leanings, and at least one study ranked it as the third most liberal city in the nation.

The county also includes an island of the same name, Alameda Island, across from the Bay Area's second-largest airport, the Oakland International Airport. It was originally a peninsula, but eventually became a separate island. There used to be a naval station on the island, but it's been decommissioned since 1997. The former naval base is still home to a floating museum, a World War II–era aircraft carrier, the USS *Hornet*.

Oakland is the third-largest city in the Bay Area and has a small but excellent art museum. Jack London Square, named for the author of *The Call of the Wild*, who grew up in Oakland and lived there on and off throughout his life, is a popular tourist destination and includes a number of restaurants, shops, and a multiplex movie theater.

Contra Costa, by contrast, is more separate, owing in part to its physical separation. The most common way to reach the county is via the Caldecott Tunnel, which acts as a natural barrier so that on the other side of urban Alameda County, Contra Costa is far more suburban, with more open land, though one end of the county includes a fair amount of heavy industry, notably Chevron, Shell, and other oil refineries.

Mount Diablo is the most visible landmark in the county and can be seen rising above from most vantage points. It's an isolated peak at the end of the Diablo Range of hills. At least three major faults run through the area: the Hayward Fault, Calaveras Fault, and Concord Fault. As a result, it is considered a high-risk area in the event of a bigger earthquake.

Ale Industries

975 Detroit Avenue, Concord, CA 94518
925-470-5280 • www.aleindustries.com
Twitter @AleIndustries
Facebook.com/pages/Ale-Industries/86191682727

Ale Industries founder and brewmaster Morgan Cox knew he wanted his own brewery from the first beer he ever made. He started homebrewing after a homebrewing neighbor gave him a copy of Charlie Papazian's book *The Complete Joy of Homebrewing* for his eighteenth birthday, underlining the part in the preface stating that it was legal to brew your own beer in the United States once you turned eighteen. When Cox smelled that first batch, he knew that's what he wanted to do with his life. He immediately fell in love with the art and science of brewing.

When he was twenty-two, he washed kegs and cleaned up for Dave Heist at his HopTown Brewery in Pleasanton, but he got his first brewing job with E. J. Phair Brewing. In the eight years he was there, going from keg washer to brewmaster in the process, he learned everything he needed to know to open his own brewery. That's also where he met his business partner, Stephen Lopas, who was also working at E. J. Phair. When E. J. Phair expanded, it moved from its original location, and Cox and Lopas bought the equipment, starting Ale Industries in the same spot where they'd worked. Ale Industries is currently located in Concord, in the warehouse right next door to the well-known homebrew supply store More Beer!

But with the success of Ale Industries, that's probably going to be changing soon. Cox is currently searching for larger quarters, possibly as far away as Oakland, but he's hoping to find a place closer to home where he can move the brewhouse and add more fermenters to increase

Beers brewed: Year-round: Golden State of Mind (formerly Orange Kush), Rye'd Piper, and Uncles Jesse's. Seasonals: Bliss, Grand Cru, East Bay IPA, Fall Down Brown, Agent Ned, Leroy, B.B. Le Roy, Funky Le Roy, Fuzzy Snowbeck, Fysus, Double Albino Cascadian Ale, and Evolution.

The Pick: The brewery's most popular offering is its session beer Golden State of Mind, which used to be called Orange Kush, and it's a great beer made with chamomile, orange peel, and coriander. But my favorite is the Rye'd Piper, which is essential a hoppy red ale with a touch of rye malt. It has all the best elements of a hoppy red, with grapefruit and pine hops aromas and bready malt character. The flavors are similar to a typical red ale, but with a zesty spiciness from the rye that makes it pop.

production dramatically. Because the company's roots are Concord, he plans to maintain a tasting room there too, though most likely not where the brewery is now.

Ale Industries is making some unique, delicious beers, and the owners are staying true to their vision by making only beers they like to drink. So far, it's a winning combination, and I expect that to continue even as Ale Industries grows larger.

Ale Industries

Opened: March 3, 2009.

Type: Production brewery, with taproom.

Owners: Morgan Cox and Stephen Lopas.

Brewer: Morgan Cox.

Guild membership: NCBG.

System: 15-barrel Specific Mechanical, and three 20-barrel fermenters, 1,800 barrels annual capacity. Cox plans to add some 40- and even 60-barrel fermenters in the new location.

Annual production: 1,400 barrels (2012).

Packages available: 22-ounce bottles and kegs.

Tours: Brewery tours are available during normal taproom hours.

Hours: Monday, Thursday, and Friday, 4 to 9 p.m.; Saturday, 2 to 9 p.m.; Sunday, 2 to 7 p.m. Closed Tuesday and Wednesday.

Food: No food is served in the brewery, but visitors are welcome to bring their own. In addition, several times a month, food trucks are available in front of the taproom. Check the Facebook page for details.

Extras: Thursday night is Open Mic Night, and on the first Saturday of the month, the brewery hosts Artist's Marketplace, where local artists bring their latest creations to show off and sell. Both events also feature live music. If you look hard enough, you can find a dartboard and chessboard too.

Gift shop: T-shirts and pint glasses are available in the brewery taproom.

Altamont Beer Works

2402 Research Drive, Livermore, CA 94550
925-443-BEER (2337)
www.altamontbeerworks.com
Twitter @AltamontBW
Facebook.com/pages/Altamont-Beer-Works/
 310137182336613

Billed as the first brewery in Livermore since prohibition, Altamont Beer Works is the brainchild of two homebrewers, Greg Robles and Stephen Sartori. Sartori is a recent homebrewer, having started four years ago, while Robles has been making his own beer since 1987. They've been working on their dream of opening a brewery since late 2010. Both are longtime Livermore residents and wanted to create something local. Sartori's experience and education are in business, while Robles's are in mechanical engineering.

They found a great space for their brewery among Livermore's many local wineries, just two minutes from the Altamont Pass, the well-traveled mountain pass through which I-580 runs and that's lined with numerous wind turbines taking advantage of the windy conditions of the valley. Unfortunately, a delay in the delivery of their 20-barrel brewhouse and brewing equipment forced them to make beer on a much smaller pilot system for the first several months, beginning in May 2012. Until then, they were brewing as fast as they could and were delivering beer themselves throughout the Livermore area.

Finally, the new brewhouse arrived and was installed, and the brewery's official grand opening took place in February 2013. The brewery can be seen through windows and a glass door from the tasting room. It's a spacious 3,200 square feet, and the majority of the building is used for brewing. The smaller tasting room has a simple handmade, U-shaped wooden bar, with a row of taps along the back wall, separating it from the brewery. There's

Beers brewed: Year-round: Left Coast Session, Rich Mahogany, Shelter IPA, Hella Hoppy, Cerveza Espumosa, and Birra Bianco. Seasonals: Ganja Juice Double IPA, Dirty "D" Brown Ale, and Smooth Operator Oatmeal Stout.

The Pick: I think the hoppy beers are generally outstanding, but it's the Rich Mahogany I find myself returning to time after time. In addition to the great hops character, mostly floral and grapefruit, the sweet caramel malt flavors give it a rich mouthfeel and balance, making it a beer that I can drink and drink throughout an evening's festivities.

a colorful painted mural on the far wall, decorated with brewing scenes of equipment and ingredients.

Altamont makes eight different beers, though it's been difficult to keep up with demand for most of them so far. It's an IPA world we're living in, so it's little surprise that the Shelter IPA is the one everybody wants. But the Cerveza Espumosa is worth finding and gets points just for its concept. It's a sparkling wheat beer, very effervescent, and is brewed with blackberries. It's meant to be a wholly original take on Berliner Weisse, which is often a sour and tart beer. Another great beer is the Rich Mahogany, whose name is a playful take on Will Ferrell's character Ron Burgundy from the film *Anchorman*. It's a hoppy red ale with a sweet, hoppy nose and rich flavors. You can find Altamont's beer at various places in and around Livermore, and the brewery's Facebook page offers timely tips about where it's available.

Altamont Beer Works

Opened: February 6, 2013.

Type: Production brewery, with tasting room.

Owners: Greg Robles and Stephen Sartori.

Brewers: Brewmasters: Greg Robles and Stephen Sartori.

Head Brewer: Chris Norberg.

Guild membership: CCBA.

System: 20-barrel brewhouse, 40-barrel hot liquor tank, with one 40-barrel and three 20-barrel fermenters.

Annual production: 3,500 barrels (2013 estimate).

Packages available: Growlers, growlettes, and 5.17- and 13.2-gallon kegs.

Tours: Tours are available if people are interested in seeing the brewery and getting a feel for the process, as long as the brewer is not busy.

Hours: Wednesday and Thursday, 4 to 8 p.m.; Friday through Sunday, noon to 6 p.m. Closed Monday and Tuesday.

Food: Pretzels are available in the tasting room, though food trucks will be available in the parking lot during events and at select times.

Extras: The tasting room will feature live music from time to time. Check the Facebook page for details.

Gift shop: Shirts, hats, and other items are sold in the tasting room.

Bison Brewing

ORGANIC BEER

No public address at present; business office only in Berkeley
510-697-1537 • www.bisonbrew.com
Twitter @bisonbrew • Facebook.com/bison

Bison Brewing Company was originally a brewpub on Telegraph Avenue in downtown Berkeley, just a few blocks from the university, when it opened in 1989. But when brewer Daniel Del Grande bought it in 1997, the restaurant was having a few problems, and he decided to close the brewpub and concentrate on brewing the beer.

Del Grande had graduated from Berkeley with a degree in civil engineering and later got an MBA from nearby Saint Mary's in Orinda. He also attended UC Davis to learn brewing and today is a part-time instructor at the American Brewers Guild, a brewing school in Vermont, where he continues to put his engineering degree to good use. By 2008, Del Grande had outgrown the brewing space in Berkeley but was unable to expand there because of zoning restrictions.

Del Grande's focus in both his brewery and his personal life has been his passion for conservation, and the biggest change since he took over the brewery is that for the last few years, all Bison beer is 100 percent organic, and the brewery where he makes his beer has also been certified organic by both the USDA and California Certified Organic Farmers (CCOF). He's an advocate for sustainable and ecologically sound food production, and he makes his own biodiesel from used cooking oil, which he uses to power both the Bison Brewing Company van and his own car.

The status of organic beer has generally improved considerably in recent years. These days, beer can be organic as well as unique and tasty, and Bison's range of beers proves this with every sip. The Honey Basil Ale, made with whole leaf organic basil and infused with organic clover honey, has a one-of-a-kind taste, and the seasonal

Beers brewed: Year-round: Chocolate Stout, Honey Basil Ale, and Strong Pale Ale (formerly Organic IPA). Seasonals: Gingerbread Ale (fall/winter), Saison de Wench (spring/summer), and the Anniversary Series (in yearly rotation).

The Pick: The Chocolate Stout is one seriously delicious beer, with big chocolate and roasted malt flavors. It's creamy and rich, with aromas of cocoa powder and mocha, and the finish is dry.

Gingerbread Ale, a porter brewed with ginger, nutmeg, and cinnamon, is as close to a liquid cookie as you're likely to ever find.

All of the Bison beers are very food-friendly, and the website includes extensive suggestions and recipes for cooking with the brewery's beers, as well as recipes for cocktails made with the beers. Bison also promotes going one day a week without meat for the health and environmental benefits, and to encourage people to participate, the website provides a large number of beer-friendly and tasty meatless recipes, adding a new recipe every couple weeks.

Bison Brewing

Opened: February 1989.

Type: Contract brewery.

Owner: Daniel Del Grande.

Brewer: Daniel Del Grande.

Guild membership: BA, CCBA.

System: See Mendocino Brewing Company (page 246) for brewery information.

Annual production: 3,000-4,000 barrels (2012 estimate).

Packages available: 12-ounce bottles in four-packs and six-packs, 22-ounce bottles, and 5- and 15.5-gallon kegs.

Tours: No tours are available.

Extras: The brewery is certified CCOF Organic and USDA Organic.

Black Diamond Brewing Company

2470 Bates Avenue, Suite C, Concord, CA 94520
925-356-0120 • www.bdbrewing.com
Twitter @bdbrewingco
Facebook.com/pages/Black-Diamond-Brewery/
196220291070

Black Diamond used to be a small brewpub just off the highway in Walnut Creek, but in 2005, after a decade there, it moved to much larger quarters a few miles up the road in a Concord industrial park. It's now a production brewery with a small taproom. The brewery concentrates on bottled product, as well as selling kegs to the trade, a 180-degree shift from its original business model. But the plan is definitely working, and the brewery is now distributing in a dozen states, as far away as Maine.

Black Diamond takes its name from a little-known feature of the area's history. Contra Costa County used to be known for its coal, and in the nineteenth century, only Pennsylvania had larger coal deposits. In 1860, the Black Diamond coal mine was started in Nortonville, a nearby town that no longer exists and is now the Black Diamond Mines Regional Preserve, a part of the East Bay Regional Park District. During the nineteenth and early twentieth centuries, the mine produced nearly four million tons of coal, a nickname for which was "black diamonds." Mining was hard work, and according to the brewery's website, "occasional celebrations were important to help sustain the dedicated miners, and beer became a favorite beverage."

After graduating from Texas A&M, brewer Derek Smith was visiting England when he got a job working for Mark Dorber at the famous White Horse Pub on Parsons Green in London. The beer that specifically caused his epiphany was Rose de Gambrinus, a framboise lambic from Cantillon. Between that and the English cask ales he drank and served every night, by the time he returned to Texas, fate had changed his career path. His first American beer job was with Two Rows Restaurant & Brewery, first at its Houston location, and later in Dallas. He enrolled in the master brewers course at UC Davis and afterward became the assistant brewer with Black Diamond. Two and a

Beers brewed: Year-round: Jagged Edge IPA, Free Style Belgian Blond, Steep Trail Amber Ale, Rampage Imperial IPA, Fracas Imperial Red Ale, Pale Ale, and Wheat Ale. Seasonals: Peak XV Imperial Porter (January–March), Wheat Wacker (April–July), Saison (July–September), Harvest Ale (September–October), The Deuce (October/December), and The Twelve (February/March).

half years later, he was made brewmaster, a position he's held ever since.

The brewery takes up quite a bit of space and is all behind the scenes. The brand new taproom is adjacent to it. It's set up to resemble an old saloon, with a mix of brewery paraphernalia and historic photos of miners and coal mines from around the area. There's a modest-size bar at one end, with a Black Diamond logo mirror behind it and a single big-screen TV in the corner. Several tables and chairs take up the middle.

The taproom has limited hours, but it's a great place to try all of Black Diamond's beers, as well as a few surprises. For instance, Smith has added a barrel aging program, with beers aged in bourbon and wine barrels, and many can be sampled before they're packaged. He's also been brewing with Scharffen Berger cacao nibs, using them in his Imperial Porter. It's certainly a worthwhile spot to sit down, drink a few beers, and find a few nuggets . . . or even some black diamonds.

The Pick: I love Derek's Rampage Imperial IPA. The nose is redolent of the tropical fruit section of your local grocer, with citrus, grapefruit, and pineapple aromas that just won't quit. You can get a whiff from across the room. The flavors are equally strong, again with monstrous hops character. There's nothing subtle about it, which is as it should be. You only know the balance is there because it quietly keeps the beer together, doing its job without asserting itself, letting only the hops juice be the star of the show. Toward the end, you may start to notice some heat, but the long, lingering finish turns slightly dry.

Black Diamond Brewing Company

Opened: December 31, 1994.

Type: Production brewery, with taproom.

Owners: Joe Garaventa and Tim Bredbenner.

Brewer: Derek Smith.

Guild membership: BA, CCBA, NCBG.

System: 15-barrel Liquid Assets brewhouse, 7,500 barrel annual capacity.

Annual production: 3,550 barrels (2011).

Packages available: 12-ounce bottles (six-packs), 22-ounce bottles, 5- and 15.5 gallon kegs, and growlers, available at the taproom.

Tours: Available Wednesday and Thursday, 2:30 p.m.; reservations recommended.

Hours: Brewery: Monday through Friday, 9 a.m. to 5 p.m.; taproom: Monday through Friday, 3:30 p.m. to 8 p.m.

Food: Only light snacks like pretzels or chips are served in the taproom, but people are welcome to bring their own food.

Extras: Occasional special-release parties, barbecues, and an annual ladderball tournament.

Gift shop: T-shirts, women's shirts, polo shirts, baseball hats, and hoodies available in the taproom.

Buffalo Bill's Brewery

1081 B Street, Hayward, CA 94541
510-886-9823 • www.buffalobillsbrewery.com
Facebook.com/BuffaloBillsBrewery

Buffalo Bill's Brewery was one of the first brewpubs in America, and the Bill in the name was Bill Owens, a photographer and Guggenheim Fellowship winner. His best-known work was a collection of suburban photos called *Suburbia*, published in 1973. Owens turned Buffalo Bill's into a local institution and ran it for more than ten years before selling the brewpub to its present owner, Geoff Harries, in 1994. Harries has continued that tradition ever since.

The brewpub is in a corner building in downtown Hayward, surrounded by shops and across the street from the movie theater. The front of the building has sliding glass doors that can be opened during good weather onto an outdoor patio, surrounded by an iron fence, where you can sit outside. Inside, the bar is to the left, with a stuffed buffalo head hanging over it, looking down on the brewpub. In the rear corner behind the bar, to the right as you're looking at it, is the brewery where all of the beer served in the brewpub is made. Between the end of the bar and the brewing equipment, there's a great old sign advertising "Buffalo Bill's Micro Brewery," showing a buffalo drinking a beer and with a tagline saying, "Don't say beer, say 'Buffalo.'"

The brewery also contracts additional bottled beer, in six-packs, which can also be purchased there or at retail stores throughout the state. Buffalo Bill's effectively started the modern trend of pumpkin beers for Halloween and Thanksgiving with its six-packs of Pumpkin Ale, which debuted in 1985, and its Alimony Ale was humorously declared "the bitterest beer in America," back at a time when hoppy beers were the exception rather than the rule.

The restaurant interior is spartan, with brick walls and tall ceilings with fans, banners, and

Beers brewed: Year-round: Alimony Ale India Pale Ale, Tasmanian Devil, Buffalo Bill's Beer, Ricochet Red, Johnny Midnight Oatmeal Stout, and Hayward Hefe. Seasonals: Orange Blossom Cream Ale (March–August), Strawberry Blonde Ale (June–October), America's Original Pumpkin Ale (August–November), Blueberry Oatmeal Stout (November–February), and Extra Special Reserve Barley Wine (February).

The Pick: The Tasmanian Devil, Buffalo Bill's strong ale, is my go-to beer here. It's a sweet, malty beer with caramel notes, a spicy tang, and a touch of warmth. Despite being malt-forward, it has a complex hops character and a dry finish.

lamps hanging down. It's a warm and friendly place that does a brisk lunchtime business with both families and happy hour singles mixing seamlessly for dinner and drinks. The food is beer-friendly fare, with really great pizza and sandwiches, which is a good thing, because there's plenty of beer.

Buffalo Bill's Brewery

Opened: 1983.

Type: Brewpub.

Owner: Geoff Harries.

Brewer: Mike Manty.

Guild membership: BA, CCBA

System: 10-barrel customized Bohemian, 1,200 annual capacity.

Annual production: 1,200 barrels (2012).

Packages available: Growlers and 12-ounce bottles in six-packs.

Tours: No formal tours are available, but the brewery is out in the open and can be seen when it's open.

Hours: Seven days a week, opens at 11 a.m.; Sunday through Thursday, the kitchen closes at 10 p.m. and the bar at 10:45 p.m.; Friday and Saturday, the kitchen closes at 11 p.m. and the bar at 11:45 p.m.

Food: The menu is fairly extensive, with some very tasty choices, like homemade potato chips, soups and salads, and a dozen specialty rustic pizzas. There's an entire page of sandwiches, dividing them into grilled, cold, and burgers. The dessert menu changes daily.

Extras: In the warmer months, there's outdoor seating for 120 people. Inside, there's a 20-foot shuffleboard game and TV screens at the bar. The brewpub hosts seasonal beer release parties throughout the year, as well as a Cinco de Mayo party. On the third Thursday of June, July, and August, you can find folks dancing in the streets at the brewery's summer street parties. The brewpub is within walking distance of the Hayward BART station.

Gift shop: T-shirts, hats, bottle openers, and other merchandise are sold at the restaurant.

Calicraft Brewing Company

2700 Mitchell Drive, Building B, Walnut Creek, CA 94598
925-478-8734 • www.calicraft.com
Twitter @calicraft • Facebook.com/calicraftbeer

Most fourteen-year-olds want to be cowboys or baseball players, but seven years before he could legally taste his first beer, Calicraft founder Blaine Landberg had already decided that one day he wanted to start a brewery. He grew up in a family of homebrewers but didn't start homebrewing himself until he started college at UC Berkeley.

After graduating, although he continued to hone his brewing skills, Landberg took a job with the startup company Honest Teas and was one of its first employees. He helped build that brand into a powerhouse, selling it from the back of his car. He's now putting that experience to work for himself, with his one-man brewery.

While he's currently brewing on other people's equipment, his ultimate goal is to build his own brewery and tasting room in Walnut Creek and things are moving briskly in that direction. He is already bringing in his own ingredients, locally or sourced in California wherever possible, such as Klamath Basin malt and Lake County hops.

His beers to date have been uniformly excellent, and perhaps more important, they manage to stand out in an increasingly crowded marketplace, not by being extreme, but by each one having a little twist, a variation on a theme. The Oaktown Brown, for example, is a brown ale brewed with organic Cascade hops and aged in oak barrels, making it a brown ale yet not a brown ale—something slightly more.

I expect big things from Calicraft in the coming years. For now, look for the beers in Bay Area retail stores, but also keep an eye out for the brewery and tasting room to be open soon.

Beers brewed: Year-round: Buzzerkeley Sparkling Ale, Oaktown American Brown with Oak, and Cali Coast California Kolsch-Style Ale. Seasonals: Chez Panisse Farmhouse Ale (April–May), Wild Wit (April–July), Chez Panisse Pale (August–October), and Wobblies, a wet hops ale (August–September).

Calicraft Brewing Company

Opened: May 2012.

Type: Gypsy contract brewery.

Owner: Blaine Landberg.

Brewer: Blaine Landberg.

System: 25-barrel brewhouse, 5,000 barrels annual capacity.

Annual production: 2,500 barrels (2013 estimate).

Packages available: 11.2-ounce (330-milliliter) bottles, 22-ounce bottles, 375- and 750-milliliter bottles, growlers, and 5- and 15.5-gallon kegs.

Tours: Once the tasting room is complete, tours will be available.

Hours: Monday through Friday, 8 a.m. to 5 p.m.

Food: Locally made snacks will be available in the tasting room.

Extras: The brewery will feature live music and outdoor seating on the lawn.

Gift shop: Brewery merchandise is available online.

The Pick: Besides having a great name, the Buzzerkeley is a fine beer too. Blurring the line between beer and sparkling wine, it's brewed with two yeasts, champagne and ale, along with California star thistle honey. The sparkling ale is bubbly and effervescent, with a very creamy and rich mouthfeel. The nose is a complex mélange of yeasty notes, with citrus and floral aromas. The flavors are clean and refreshing, with zippy fruit character and vanilla, a honeyed sweetness, and spicy pepper and doughy bread notes. The finish is dry, and it's a worthy addition to the canon of champagne-like beers.

JP DasBrew

44356 South Grimmer Boulevard, Fremont, CA 94538
415-517-8100 • www.dasbrewinc.com
Twitter @JPDasBrew • Facebook.com/JPDasBrew

Brewer Jan Schutze was born in Germany and grew up drinking German lagers. His family included vintners and brewers, and he was very familiar with the brewing process even before life took him to Canada for his education and eventually to Northern California, where he settled with his wife and business partner, Priscilla La Rocca. For nearly three decades, he homebrewed on the side while building an environmental consulting business as a geologist. The decision to turn pro was apparently an easy one, as everyone who tasted Jan's beer urged him to do so. His original plan was to keep the brewery small and neighborhood-friendly. Since German-style beers were his favorites, he initially believed these would be the focus, but he found it hard to ignore Northern California's love for hoppy beers and also started making an imperial IPA and a black IPA. DasBrew beers are currently available at several Fremont and surrounding area restaurants and bars, or at the source, in the brewery's tasting room.

JP DasBrew

Opened: August 2009 (first beer sold July 2010).

Type: Production brewery, with tasting room.

Owners: Jan Schutze and Priscilla La Rocca.

Brewer: Jan Schutze.

Guild membership: CCBA.

System: 7-barrel brewhouse, 400 barrels annual capacity.

Annual production: 100 barrels (2012).

Packages available: Growlers and 5- and 15.5-gallon kegs.

Tours: Tours can be conducted, but call for reservations.

Hours: Monday through Thursday, 5 to 8 p.m.; Friday through Sunday, noon to 5 p.m. Check the website to confirm the days and hours.

Gift shop: T-shirts, bottle openers, hand-etched growlers, and other glassware are available at the brewery.

Beers brewed: Year-round: Buxom Blonde Ale, Knotty Red Ale, Monkey Fist Hefeweizen, Eye Crosser IPA, and Triple Blitz IPA (a.k.a. Triple Black IPA). Seasonals: Red Sled Holiday Ale.

The Pick: I think Schutze's hoppy beers are his best, especially his newest, the Triple Blitz IPA—it's sort of a black IPA, but at 12 percent ABV, it's something else too. There are loads of chocolate notes, citrus hops, a caramel sweetness, and just a touch of saltiness. It may not be everybody's cup of hops, but it's a really interesting take on dark, strong, hoppy beers.

Drake's Brewing

1933 Davis Street, Building 177, San Leandro, CA 94577
510-568-2739 • www.drinkdrakes.com
Twitter @DrakesBrewery
Facebook.com/Drakesbrewing /
    Facebook.com/DrakesBarrelHouse

Drake's was originally known as Lind Brewing for its original owner and brewer Roger Lind. When he opened the brewery in 1989, it was one of the few draft-only production breweries. For several years, it was a one-man operation, with Roger Lind doing everything and slowly building a solid reputation. After nearly a decade, he decided he needed a change and returned to college to get his teaching credentials, selling the brewery to the business next door, a coffee company owned by the Rogers family. With Lind gone, they renamed it Drake's Brewing and added a bottling line, doubling production.

The Rogers family also entered into a business relationship in 2002 with Triple Rock's John Martin (see page 222), who needed to find a home for the recently closed Twenty Tank equipment. The brewhouse, along with fermenters and other paraphernalia, was installed at Drake's, and the two companies shared the equipment. That worked well for a few years, but eventually the Rogers family wanted to get out of the beer business, so John Martin and Roy Kirkorian bought Drake's in 2008. Every year since then, business has shot up at least 50 percent, and the brewery has been in a near-constant expansion phase.

The brewery is almost hidden from sight, around the back of a Walmart in the West Gate Center shopping mall, just off I-880 in San Leandro. You have to drive around the back, and it isn't obvious that you're even allowed to drive there. When you get to the end of the Walmart building, turn right and keep going. From there, it's the proverbial "you can't miss it." You'll drive into a kind of industrial oasis with the Drake's production brewery and

Beers brewed: Year-round: 1500 Pale Ale, Drake's IPA, Drake's Amber, Drake's Blonde Ale (Kolsch style), Drake's Hefe, Denogginizer Imperial IPA, and Drakonic Imperial Stout. Seasonals: Hopocalypse Double IPA (February–April), Hopocalypse Black Label Triple IPA (February–March brewery-only release), Alpha Session NorCal Bitter- (May–July), Aroma Coma IPA (July–September), Aroma Prieta New Zealand hopped IPA (July–September), Exxpedition Imperial Red Ale (September–November), and Jolly Rodger American Barleywine (November–January). In addition, regular one-offs, barrel-aged beers, and draft-only seasonals are available in the Bay Area and at the taproom, some of which are exclusive.

its adjacent Barrel House taproom. The recently opened taproom is a wonderful space, an open warehouse with a cold-box bar, simple tables and benches, and an outdoor patio. Giant posters hang on the warehouse walls, and on warm days the roll-up doors are thrown open. There are usually around two dozen Drake's beers on tap, including hard-to-find and one-of-a-kind offerings.

The Pick: Although it's available only in the summer, the Aroma Coma is worth waiting for. The aptly named beer could put you into a hops coma from just the nose, which is insanely strong and rife with grapefruit, pineapple, and spicy and zesty aromas. The flavor is an enormous hops bomb, with big citrus hops character and complex herbal notes, all held up by an equally big malt backbone.

With a name like the Barrel House, you shouldn't be surprised to see countless wooden barrels lining the taproom. This is Drake's barrel program, begun in 2007. The taproom always has a couple of barrel-aged beers to taste, and any others you find at bars and restaurant around the Bay Area were born here too. Maybe you tasted one of these beers a year later, miles from where it was made. You can also fill your growler and buy any of Drake's bottled beers in the retail store portion of the taproom.

The Barrel House taproom makes visiting Drake's a delight, but if you can choose when to go, pick one of the first Friday events. You'll really get a chance to see the brewery at its best.

Drake's Brewing

Opened: September 4, 1989.

Type: Production brewery, with taproom.

Owners: John Martin and Roy Kirkorian.

Brewers: John Gillooly (production manager) and Alexandra Nowell (lead brewer).

Guild membership: BA, CCBA.

System: 20-barrel JV Northwest, 20,000 barrels annual capacity.

Annual production: 11,000 barrels (2012), 20,000 barrels (2013 estimate).

Packages available: 12-ounce bottles in six-packs, 22-ounce bottles, growlers, and 5-, 7.75-, and 15.5-gallon kegs.

Tours: Tours available Fridays at 1:30 and 5:30 p.m., except for the first Friday of each month.

Hours: Wednesday and Thursday, 3 to 9 p.m.; Friday and Saturday, noon to 9 p.m.; Sunday, noon to 7 p.m. Closed Monday and Tuesday.

Food: A selection of snacks, including mixed nuts, goldfish crackers, pretzels, and beef jerky. Food trucks park at the brewery on a rotating schedule, available on the website.

Extras: The taproom has a collection of board games and several outdoor picnic tables. The inside space is heated during the winter, but no minors are permitted.

Gift shop: T-shirts, bottle openers, hoodies, and hats sold at the taproom and online.

Dying Vines

95 Linden Street, Suite 7/8, Oakland, CA 94607
510-205-1684 • www.dyingvines.com

Kel Alcala was an enthusiastic homebrewer and spent six years working at the Oak Barrel homebrew supply store in Berkeley. One evening in April 2010, his local homebrew club, the Bay Area Mashers, was having a meeting at Linden Street Brewing (see page 208) when owner Adam Lamoreaux issued a challenge: he encouraged members to open their own breweries and told them if they got their state licenses, he'd let them use his brewery. Alcala decided right then and there to open Dying Vines, and by December he was brewing and selling authentic English-style beers.

While many American brewers, especially on the hop-centric West Coast, are brewing big alcohol hops monsters, Dying Vines is carving a niche for itself by doing just the opposite. Kel's beers are low in alcohol, big on flavor, and well balanced. He has hoppy beers, but nothing extreme. Hop Candi has everything you want in a West Coast IPA, with nice citrus hops notes and a touch of rye that makes it unique. His Queen Bess IPA is closer to what you'd find across the pond, spicy and floral with a dry finish. The beer is named for Bessie Coleman, the first African American to get her pilot's license, who often flew into Oakland during her career. He also brews Old Brick Bitter, a special bitter; a Kolsch for Benchmark Pizza; and No Town Brown, which was exclusively for another restaurant. Dying Vines beers can be found in bars and restaurants throughout Alameda, San Francisco, and Marin Counties.

Dying Vines

Opened: December 5, 2010.

Type: Contract brewery.

Owner and brewer: Kel Alcala.

Guild membership: BA.

System: See Linden Street Brewing Company on page 208 for brewery information.

Annual production: 500 barrels (2012 estimate).

Packages available: Kegs only.

Beers brewed: Year-round: Dee'z English Mild, Old Brick Bitter, Hop Candi, and Queen Bess IPA. Seasonals: Kolsch and No Town Brown.

The Pick: I really love the Dee'z English Mild. This version has slightly more herbal hops, but works well and is very easy drinking and tasty, with lightly roasted malt character.

E. J. Phair Brewing Company

Brewery: 300 Cumberland Street, Pittsburg, CA 94565
Liberty Alehouse: 200 East Third Street, Pittsburg, CA 94565
Concord Alehouse: 2151 Salvio Street, Suite L, Concord, CA 94520
925-427-7204 / (brewery) 925-252-9895 (Liberty) / 925-691-4253 (Concord) • www. ejphair.com
Twitter @EJPhair • Facebook.com/EJPhairbrewing / Facebook.com/Concord.Pittsburg (alehouses)

E. J. Phair consists of a brewery and two separate alehouse restaurants, with one directly across the street from the new brewery. The original brewery was in Concord but was moved to Pittsburg next to the Liberty Hotel, which was opened as the second alehouse.

Founder J. J. Phair began homebrewing in 1990 and ten years later turned pro. He named the brewery in honor of his grandfather E. J. (Ewart John) Phair, an amateur winemaker and beer lover. Since opening the Pittsburg production brewery, Craig Cauwels was hired to be the brewmaster for E. J. Phair. Cauwels is also the brewer at Schooner's (see page 218).

The new brewery is located in a beautiful old brick building that's all wood inside, with separate private areas that resemble small wooden huts in an English village, holding foosball tables, darts, and other pleasures. The ceilings are very high, and a large open area dominates the space, with a stage in one corner shaped like a half-moon. Sofas, chairs, and tables are scattered throughout. There's a large L-shaped bar toward the back, with several big-screen televisions. Behind the bar on one side, you can see some of the serving tanks and fermenters behind glass windows. The brewhouse and cellar are hidden from sight, and there's a warren of cold storage and other rooms below the ground used for various aspects of the operations. It's a deceptively large facility, and the acoustics are ideal for music.

The former Liberty Hotel across the street holds the Liberty Alehouse, the brewery's newest

Beers brewed: Year-round: Bellywasher Scottish Ale, Steeltown Stout, Plankwalker Pale Ale, Ditzy Blonde, Shorty's Revenge English Strong Ale, Face Puncher IPA, Double Crossed Eye 'PA, Cumbre del Diablo India Pale Ale, 729 Anniversary Ale, Gooten Tog Vienna Lager, Phat Quail Amber, Duck Face Pilsner, Shorty's Vendetta, American Style Wheat Ale, Bocktagon German Styled Bock, 364 IPA, Too Short Amber Ale, and O.T.P. Pale Ale.

restaurant. The historic building has a small bar and several large rooms with tables and chairs. It's a nice, light, open restaurant with a large menu, and the old beautiful building is a treat to see and enjoy a pint. The Concord Alehouse may not appear as historic on the outside, but inside is a different story—it looks like an old pub that's been serving beer and good food for decades, with nooks and crannies filled with curios.

The Pick: I'm particularly fond of Shorty's Revenge. This English strong ale has nutty, almond aromas, and sweet caramel malt notes, with some underlying fruitiness and light, tart spiciness. At 8 percent ABV, it's deceptively strong but doesn't taste it.

E. J. Phair's beers were good before, but with Cauwels at the helm, they can only get better, as J. J. Phair builds his own mini-empire of brewing in the East Bay. His grandfather would be proud.

E. J. Phair Brewing Company

Opened: 2000.

Type: Production brewery, with separate alehouses.

Owners: J. J. Phair and Becky Wynn.

Brewer: Craig Cauwels.

System: 30-barrel DME mash tun with a Quality Stainless kettle, 6,000 barrels annual capacity.

Annual production: 1,500 barrels (2011 estimate).

Packages available: 22-ounce bottles, growlers, and kegs.

Tours: Brewery tours available on Friday and Saturday, but call for reservations.

Hours: Liberty Alehouse: Sunday through Wednesday, 11 a.m. to 9 p.m.; Thursday through Saturday, 11 a.m. to 10 p.m. Concord Alehouse: Monday through Friday, 11 a.m. to 11 p.m.; Saturday and Sunday, 10 a.m. to 11 p.m. Brewery: Monday through Saturday, 5 p.m. to close; closed Sunday.

Food: Menus are a little different at each alehouse, but both feature American and German cuisine, daily specials, an extensive list of appetizers and food for sharing, and plenty of salads, soups, burgers, sandwiches, and satisfying entrées.

Extras: The brewery has an extensive game room and hosts open mic nights, Brew-ha-ha comedy nights, and the concert series Live on Tap, with prominent local and nationally known musical acts. The Liberty Alehouse features all-day happy hour with $3 house beers on Tuesday, a Tricky Trivia contest every other Tuesday night, and a fish and chips meal with a beer for only $14 on Friday. The Concord Alehouse features beer and a burger for only $10 on Monday, all-day happy hour with $3 house beers on Tuesday, and a discount on your growler fill if you buy a burger on Wednesday. Concord also has live music on Thursday and Saturday, and serves breakfast on the weekends, complete with Mimosa specials. Both alehouses carry guest taps from other local breweries.

Gift shop: Brewery merchandise is available at the brewery and both alehouses.

Elevation 66 Brewing Company

10082 San Pablo Avenue, El Cerrito, CA 94611
510-525-4800 • www.elevation66.com
Facebook.com/pages/Elevation-66-Brewing-
Company/161621110523403

Though it changes with the shifting tides, Elevation 66 is exactly what it says: 66 feet above sea level. Co-owners Brian Kelly and David Goodstal met while working at the Pyramid Brewery in nearby Berkeley. Kelly is the talkative one, which makes sense, since he started out as a bartender at Pyramid and became enamored of craft beer, eventually giving tours of the brewery.

Goodstal is the brewer and prefers to stay behind the scenes making the beer, though given that the brewery is right behind the bar, he can't go too far. He graduated from UC Davis in 2003 and has brewed at Sudwerk, the now-defunct Beerman's Beerwerks, Trumer, and most recently Pyramid, before finally opening his own brewery. Because this is a startup, David often has to work the bar too, which has had unintended benefits. He's gotten to know a lot of the regulars, which are numerous, and the brewpub has the feel and all the benefits of a cozy, neighborhood bar.

The menu is nicely eclectic, with a good mix of the pub fare you'd expect—fish and chips, sausage, and mac and cheese—but made with great flourish, along with unique dishes such as Kahlua pork tacos, pan-seared scallops, and Grilled Cheese Spontanée. Everything on the menu is made from local ingredients, which are organic whenever possible.

The brewery almost always has six of its beers available, along with another half dozen guest beers. Perhaps the best thing about Elevation 66 is the neighborhood feel that pervades the place when you walk in. It may sound clichéd, but it seems like one of those places where, indeed,

Beers brewed: Year-round: East Bay IPA, Ramble Tamble Red Ale, Esthers Vanilla Stout (very smooth with terrific chocolate notes), Contra Costa Kolsch, Golden Age Golden Ale, and Big Bens British Style IPA. Seasonals: Old 66 Imperial Stout (December–February), White Rabbit Double IPA, Two Beagles Brown Ale, Cabertosser Scotch Ale, Laurel Leaf Pale Ale, Bourbon Barrel Aged Chocolate Stout, Rye Barrel Aged Red Ale, Choconut Stout, Accidental Ale, and August West Amber Ale.

The Pick: The East Bay IPA is a great, well-balanced West Coast IPA with big citrus—mostly orange—aromas, with some pine and nice Cascade notes. There are some bready and sweet caramel notes that come out nicely in the flavor, though the hops still shine brightly throughout. It's an easy-drinking IPA that's smooth and tasty, with great bittering and a dry finish.

everybody does know your name. Add to that some well-made, fresh beer and great food, both reasonably priced, and it's hard to beat Elevation 66.

Elevation 66 Brewing Company

Opened: September 1, 2011.

Type: Brewpub.

Owners: Brian Kelly, David and Esther Goodstal.

Brewer: David Goodstal.

Guild membership: BA, CCBA.

System: 7-barrel Premier Stainless, 440 barrels annual capacity.

Annual production: 400 barrels (2012 estimate).

Packages available: Draft only at the brewpub.

Tours: No formal tours are available, although you can watch the brewery from the bar, because it's situated directly behind it.

Hours: Sunday, 11:30 a.m. to 11 p.m.; Monday through Wednesday, 3 to 11 p.m.; Thursday, 11:30 a.m. to 11 p.m.; Friday and Saturday, 11:30 a.m. to midnight.

Food: The brewpub serves a full menu of well-chosen eclectic dishes, including salads, small plates, sandwiches, main dishes, desserts, and even some light snacks like housemade chips and pickles. The food is described as upscale pub food, and that's an apt description. All of the ingredients that chef Cindy Deetz uses are seasonal, local, sustainable, and often organic cuisine. She also uses the brewery's beers in some of the menu items, such as the beer batter for the fish and chips.

Extras: The brewpub has a private event room with a pool table and dartboards. Watch the Facebook page for details about the numerous beer-pairing dinners put on throughout the year.

Faction Brewing

2501 Monarch Street, Alameda, CA 94501
510-654-2605 • www.factionbrewing.com
Twitter @factionbrewing

Rodger Davis is a veteran of the Bay Area beer scene and a longtime beer fan. Once the brewing bug bit, Davis attended the Siebel Institute in Chicago to learn to be a professional brewer and moved to Northern California in 1997, where he's been brewing ever since. After recent stints brewing for Drake's and Triple Rock, Rodger and his wife, Claudia Pamparana, (who worked at 21st Amendment Restaurant and Brewery) decided to open their own brewery. Davis has long been known for his big, hoppy beers; the IPA he designed for Drake's won the gold medal in that category in 2002. He was also an early proponent of barrel-aged beers.

Faction will be the only brewery on the island of Alameda, just off the coast next to Oakland. It will be located in Hangar 22, right beside a craft distillery, St. George Spirits, on Alameda Point, once part of the Alameda Naval Station. Like the distillery, Faction Brewery will be located in a former 32,000-square-foot airplane hanger. Faction's brewhouse used to belong to Captain Lawrence Brewing in upstate New York; Davis obtained it when Captain Lawrence expanded. Davis has earned a reputation as a great brewer, and Faction Brewing should become one of the destination breweries in the East Bay.

Faction Brewing

Opened: Late summer 2013.

Type: Production brewery, with tasting room.

Owners: Rodger Davis and Claudia Pamparana.

Brewer: Rodger Davis.

System: 20-barrel brewhouse, 8,000 barrels annual capacity.

Packages available: 22-ounce, 375- and 750-milliliter bottles, and 5- and 15.5-gallon kegs.

Tours: Tours will be available; check the website for details.

Hours: Wednesday through Saturday, noon to 6 p.m.

Food: Food trucks will be parked outside during select events.

Extras: Outdoor seating with amazing views of San Francisco across the bay.

Gift shop: Merchandise will be available at the tasting room.

Beers brewed: Year-round: Pale Ale, Pilsner, Red Ale, Stout, Belgian-style beers, and IPA. Seasonals: Imperial IPA (spring), Pilsner (summer), Imperial Stout (winter).

Golden Gate Brewing Company

1017 22nd Avenue, Suite 300, Oakland, CA 94606
415-341-6326 • www.goldengatebrewingco.com
Twitter @GGbrewingco
Facebook.com/GoldenGateBrewingCompany

Despite its name, Golden Gate Brewing Company is currently located in the Grand Lake District of Oakland. The owners, the husband-and-wife team of Chris Wike and Alexandra Feinstein, are contracting their beer while they're in the process of creating a brewery and taproom to serve it.

Chris and Alexandra moved to the Bay Area from Fort Collins, Colorado, more than a dozen years ago. A six-pack of years later, Chris began homebrewing, and shortly thereafter, the couple decided to open their own brewery. The beers are already here, and the brewery is next.

In the meantime, Chris is also brewing on weekends on the brewery's pilot system, and you can go and sample the beers now at Golden Gate's temporary location, which is at the address listed above. Your best bet is to check the Facebook page for details on when the brewery is open. Chris's beers can also be found at various beer festivals in the area.

Golden Gate Brewing Company

Opened: 2013.

Type: Contract brewery.

Owners: Christopher Wike and Alexandra Feinstein.

Brewer: Christopher Wike.

System: 15-barrel with direct fire, with 30-barrel fermenters, 2,000 barrel annual capacity.

Annual production: 2,000 barrels (2012 estimate).

Packages available: Growlers and kegs.

Tours: Tours will be available, but please call for reservations.

Hours: Please call the taproom for hours.

Extras: There will be a beer garden approach in front of the brewery, as well as seating inside. In addition to its own beers, the brewery will also serve guest beers. For some special events, they will have music and food trucks.

Gift shop: Merchandise is available for purchase online and at events where they're pouring.

Beers brewed: Year-round: Red Rivet Ale, Twin Cable Pale Ale, 5 Ton Hook California Pils, and Black Friday Stout. Seasonals: Whistle at the Blonde, 10 Ton Hook Double Pils, Strauss ESB, XPA, and Dopplebock.

The Golden Gate Pick: The Red Rivet Ale is a delightfully traditional Scottish ale with good malt character, and American hops to give it a welcome West Coast twist.

High Water Brewing

1933 Davis Street, Suite 291, San Leandro, CA 94577
866-306-0482 • www.highwaterbrewing.com
Twitter @HighWaterBrewer • Facebook.com/pages/
High-Water-Brewing/154613544589148

High Water founder Steve Altimari, whose name means essentially "high seas" or "high water," began his brewing career by attending the American Brewers Guild. As a part of the curriculum, he apprenticed at the Eldorado Brewing Company in Stockton. He ended up staying and bought the brewery in 1996, but he changed the name to Valley Brewing Company to avoid confusion with another brewery of the same name.

A little over two years later, the owner of the Stockton building offered to buy the business, and Altimari became a salaried employee but continued to brew at Valley until he left in 2010. During that time, Altimari built a solid reputation with both hoppy beers like his Uberhoppy and maltier beers like the English mild London Tavern. After Valley put in a production brewery (now gone) and began bottling its beer, sales soared and the brewery hired a dedicated salesperson, John Anthony, whose experience included owning his own beer distributor.

When the owners of Valley wanted to sell the brewery, Altimari and Anthony got together, found investors, and made an offer. But negotiations broke down and they walked away. At this point, with investors and a plan already hatched, they shifted gears and decided instead to launch a new enterprise, and High Water Brewing was born.

High Water initially partnered with Drake's Brewing Company (see page 195), brewing High Water beers at Drake's brewhouse in San Leandro, with fermentation tanks owned by High Water on-site. Offices and storage are maintained near

Beers brewed: Year-round: Hop Riot IPA, Retribütion Imperial IPA, Aphotic Baltic Porter and Campfire Stout. Seasonals: Old & in the Way Barley Wine (February), No Boundary (February, May, and July), Anniversary Dopplesticke (March), Berliner Reisse (June), Le Petit Diablotin Sour Ale (July), Rio d'Oro Belgian Golden Strong Ale (September), and Blind Spot Winter Warmer (November). One-offs: Pom Cherry Bomb, Upper Decker, Bourbon Barrel-Aged Baltic Porter, and Brandy Barrel-Aged Baltic Porter.

The Pick: I really love Steve's Imperial IPA, Retribütion, which is a huge hops monster with a juicy fruit and fruit jam nose. It's creamy, surprisingly smooth, and redolent of citrus, peaches, and bready flavors, with a warming kick and a tongue-scraping finish.

Drake's, in the same San Leandro office complex. As initial sales have exceeded expectations, High Water has added production by also partnering with Devil's Canyon Brewing Company in Belmont and Hermitage Brewing in San Jose (see pages 132 and 150). High Water is currently searching for a location to build its own brewery and possibly a tasting room in Stockton. Nothing firm has been decided yet, but we will likely see a new High Water Brewery sometime in the near future. Given how good High Water's beers are, it will be great to see Altimari back behind the wheel of his own brewery.

High Water Brewing

Opened: March 8, 2011.

Type: Contract brewery, but soon to be production brewery.

Owners: John Anthony, Lanc Anthony, Kevin Sweeney, Davin Abrahamian, and Steve Altimari.

Brewer: Steve Altimari.

Guild membership: BA, CCBA, NCBG.

System: See Drake's Brewing on page 195 and Devil's Canyon Brewing on page 132 for brewery details; 30-barrel brewhouse to be purchased for production brewery.

Annual production: 1,200 barrels (2012), planned to expand to 6,000 barrels in 2013.

Packages available: 22-ounce bottles and 5- and 15.5-gallon kegs.

Tours: Brewery tours of Drake's are available every Friday at 1:30 and 5:30 p.m., except for the first Friday of each month. Once the new brewery is open, tours will be offered.

Extras: Once the production brewery is open, live music will be performed at the brewery.

Jack's Brewing Company

39176 Argonaut Way, Fremont, CA 94538
2410 San Ramon Valley Boulevard, San Ramon, CA 94538
510-796-2036 (Fremont) / 925-362-1059 (San Ramon)
www.jacksbrewingcompany.com
Facebook.com/JacksBrewing / Facebook.com/pages/Jacks-Brewing-
San-Ramon/148087038992

Jack's Brewing Company operates two brewpubs located about 25 miles apart in the East Bay. The original is in Fremont, and the newer one is in San Ramon. All of the brewing is done in Fremont, but some of the beer is transported to the San Ramon location, the only other place you can find it. The beer is solid, brewed by American Brewers Guild graduate Will Erickson. He grew up in Marin County and brewed for several locations before taking over at Jack's four years ago. He's worked at Moylan's, Great Divide Brewing, and Mammoth Brewing.

Both brewpubs are great sports bars, with hearty pub food and their own housemade beer. They have big crowds on weekends, especially for major sports events.

Jack's Brewing Company

Opened: Fremont: January 2000; San Ramon: August 2009.

Type: Brewpub.

Owners: Kurt Steadman and Krissy Wallace.

Brewer: Will Erickson.

System: 10-barrel Bohemian brewhouse system, 1,000 barrels annual capacity.

Annual production: 800 barrels (2012).

Packages available: 5- and 15.5-gallon kegs.

Tours: Brewery tours are available with reservations.

Hours: Sunday, 11 a.m. to 9:30 p.m.; Monday through Thursday, 11 a.m. to 10 p.m.; Friday and Saturday, 11 a.m. to 11 p.m.

Food: Hearty pub fare includes tasty-looking appetizers, salads, burgers, and grilled chicken sandwiches. Other favorites include beef barley soup and Black Jack Chili.

Extras: Multiple big-screen HDTVs, special events surrounding major sporting events, and beer dinners on occasion.

Gift shop: Merchandise is available at both brewpubs.

Beers brewed: Year-round: Boys of Summer Wheat, Hardwood Pale Ale, Grid Iron Amber Ale, Penalty Shot Porter, and India Pale Ale (IPA). Seasonals: Apricot Mango, Double Black Diamond ESB, Hefeweizen, and many others.

The Pick: The Hardwood Pale Ale is a solid pale with citrus aromas and a touch of floral, grassy hops character. The flavor is similarly hops restrained but shows the floral, fruity character well, balanced perfectly with a honey and caramel malt sweetness. The mouthfeel is satisfyingly full and chewy, with a clean finish.

Linden Street Brewery

95 Linden Street, Oakland, CA 94607
510-251-8898 • www.lindenbeer.com
Twitter @LindenStBrew
Facebook.com/pages/Linden-Street-Brewery/85713982704

In 2005, the Linden Street Brewery was the first production brewery to open in Oakland in nearly fifty years, making historic beers like California Common and the Pre-Prohibition lager The Town.

Founder Adam Lamoreaux's first taste of craft beer was during the first Gulf War. He was headed home from his first tour of duty with the U.S. Navy when his ship stopped in Perth, Australia, for a little R&R. Naturally, that meant tasting some of the local beers, including a chocolaty lager called Dogbolter. It was love at first sip—and launched his future career path. When Adam got back to his home in the Bay Area, he immediately began homebrewing, in part because he was just nineteen, and even though he was a war veteran, he could not yet legally drink beer, although he could learn to make it. He got his first beer industry job as an assistant brewer for the old Fisherman's Wharf Steelhead brewpub, and then later was a cellarman at Anderson Valley Brewing. Wanting to get back to the Bay Area, he became a beer and wine buyer for Whole Foods. All of these jobs taught him different aspects of the beer business.

Armed with that experience, he looked for a place in Oakland where he could set up a brewery. The building he eventually found was constructed in 1890 and originally belonged to Standard Underground Cable. Westinghouse used the building as its base of operations in the West as America made the transition from gas to electricity. The building still has the original pine floors, and inside you can see the old water tower supports in what is now the beer garden. In just a few years, Linden Street built a solid reputation and a huge following, causing it to expand twice, add a tasting room, then expand again.

This latest expansion is scheduled to open August 1 and splits the brewery into three sec-

Beers brewed: Year-round: Urban People's Common Lager, Burning Oak Black Lager, Deep Roots Red Lager, and The 'Town Lager. Seasonals: Stairway to Hopland.

The Pick: The Burning Oak Black Lager is light-bodied, refreshing, and only slightly sweet, balanced nicely with a toasty roastiness with just a hint of smoke. There are also some biscuity malt flavors and chocolate notes around the edges, with some subtle licorice and a smooth, sweet finish.

tions. In one corner is a comfortable lounge where visitors can relax with a beer or a glass of wine. The old tasting room will be a beer garden, with roll-up windows that allow the entire walls to be open on days when the weather cooperates.

Most impressive of all, the brewery's middle section is becoming a full restaurant featuring world-class chef James Syhabout, whose Commis is the city's only Michelin-starred restaurant. He also owns Hawker Fare and will be creating a menu of American gastropub fare for Linden Street, using only high-end ingredients, many of which will come from Campovida, an organic winery and farm in Hopland. Linden Street also grows its own hops at Campovida. Each night, the Campovida farm will tell Syhabout what produce will be available the next day, and he'll base each menu on what he has to cook with, concentrating on communal dishes meant to be shared. Naturally, the lounge will also stock Campovida's organic wines.

Adam's golden Urban Peoples' Common Lager (similar in style to Anchor Steam Beer) has turned heads since its introduction and is his most popular beer. On the other end of the spectrum is his Burning Oak Black Lager, a dark beer made with roasted malt that gives it a hint of smoke and malty sweet toasty character. Linden Street makes an exclusive beer for the well-known restaurant Hawker Fare, which is called Supafly and is made using a Chinese black rice known as forbidden rice, along with lemongrass and shiso, a Japanese mint.

Linden Street has quickly become an Oakland institution and continues to grow by leaps and bounds. As this newest phase is completed, only time will tell what they'll do next. For now, it's sounds like things will be hopping at what should become the coolest place in town.

Linden Street Brewery

Opened: June 10, 2009.
Type: Production brewery, with taproom.
Owner and brewer: Adam Lamoreaux.
Guild membership: CCBA.
System: 10-barrel Santa Rosa Stainless, Liquid Assets, 6,000 barrels annual capacity.
Annual production: 3,000 barrels (2012).
Packages available: Growlers and 5-, 7.75-, and 15.5-gallon kegs, along with 50-liter.
Tours: Brewery tours are available by appointment only.
Hours: Check the website or Facebook page for updated hours and times.
Food: The brewery is adding a restaurant, which will offer a full menu and Sunday brunch.
Extras: There's a newly built outdoor beer garden at the brewery.
Gift shop: T-shirts and pint glasses are available at the brewery.

Oakland Brewing Company

1010 22nd Avenue, Oakland CA 94606
510-394-HOPS (4677) • www.oaklandbrewing.com /
  oakland-brewing.com
Twitter @OaklandBrewing
Facebook.com/pages/Oakland-Brewing-Company/
  199183450110913

On a wing and a prayer, Oakland Brewing Company signed a lease, obtained a license, and began brewing in early 2011. Unfortunately, it's still contract brewing while the owners work to open the brewery's physical location. Brewers James Costa and Steve McDaniel continue to hold other brewing jobs in addition to making Oakland Brewing's beer, while "the Beer Chef," Bruce Paton, is plying his culinary trade around the Bay Area until he has his own kitchen at the brewery. All three are veterans of the local beer community. Costa has brewed for Moylan's, E. J. Phair, Santa Cruz Aleworks, and currently Half Moon Bay Brewing, while McDaniel was with 21st Amendment for years. Paton is famous for putting on epic beer dinners since the 1990s.

In the meantime, Oakland Brewing's beers can be found at better beer bars and stores in the Bay Area. The flagship IPA, Sticky Zipper, also enjoys wide distribution in 22-ounce bottles. Progress has been slow, but the partners are hopeful that 2013 will be the year.

Oakland Brewing Company

Opened: February 2011.

Type: Contract brewing; production brewery in the works.

Owners: James Costa, Steve McDaniel, and Bruce Paton.

Brewers: James Costa and Steve McDaniel.

Guild membership: BA.

System: 20-barrel U.S. made brewhouse, 4,000 barrels annual capacity.

Annual production: 480 barrels (2011 estimate).

Packages available: 22-ounce bottles and 5-, 13.2-, and 15.5-gallon kegs.

Tours: Once the brewery is open, tours will be available.

Gift shop: Merchandise is available at festivals and will be sold at the brewery.

Beers brewed: Year-round: Sticky Zipper and Huge Action. Seasonals and occasional releases: Total Slacker IPA, Needs More Dog Pale Lager, Mad Adder Session IPA, Five-and-Dime IPA, and 840 Double Up XXX IPA.

The Pick: The Sticky Zipper is one big IPA, with dank, spicy, and citrus hops character, and big grapefruit and pine aromas. It's balanced nicely with biscuity malt and a dry finish.

Pacific Coast Brewing Company

906 Washington Street, Oakland, CA 94607
510-836-2739 • www.pacificcoastbrewing.com
Twitter @PCBOAKLAND
Facebook.com/pcboaktown

Pacific Coast founders Steve Wolff and Don Gortemiller were fraternity brothers at UC Berkeley in the early 1970s when, on a whim, Wolff gave his friend Gortemiller a homebrewing kit for Christmas in 1975. The first beer he made was a stout, which Don remembers fondly, and when the next few batches were just as good, he was hooked.

After college, Gortemiller worked as a chemist for Chevron, while Wolff was a shop foreman for a company that repaired industrial generators and alternators. In the meantime, Don continued to homebrew, and the two friends watched as the earliest brewpubs opened around them— New Albion, Mendocino, Triple Rock—and thought it looked like fun. After Gulf bought Chevron and ended up with double the staff needed, Gortemiller took the company's buyout, and the two friends started shopping for a building.

The one they found, less than a block from the Oakland Convention Center, was originally constructed in 1876 as part of an intended major renovation of the city area known as Old Oakland. They meticulously restored the building and even got an elaborate stained-glass window from the Oakland Museum for the front of the brewpub. The window, the bar, and a beer cooler were once part of the historic Cox Saloon, which in its heyday wasn't far from where Pacific Coast Brewing is today. The brewery has dark hardwood floors, brick walls, and other antiques to give it the look of a Victorian pub. The inside is warm and inviting, and filled with regulars and locals on any given day. Despite its size, the restaurant has secluded areas that allow it to feel intimate, even when it's crowded. There's also a heated beer garden outside.

The brewery is tucked away in the basement, and has its own history. It was built in England

Beers brewed: Year-round: Gray Whale Ale, Blue Whale Ale, Elephant Seal Bitter, Emerald Ale, Code Blue Barleywine, Columbus IPA, Triple Whale Ale, Killer Whale Stout, Leslie's XPA, Old Oakland Ale, Megalodon Imperial IPA, Leviathan Imperial Stout, Luck o' the Irish Stout, and Yellow Jacket Ale. Seasonals and specialty releases: Anniversary Ale (various vintages), Holiday Abbey Style Ale, Abbey Ale, Acorn Ale, Amethyst Ale, Barbary Coast Beer, Belgian Bee, Bill Brand Memorial Porter, Comet Tail Ale, Deviator Dopplebock, El Diablo Abbey Style Ale, Gold Nugget Ale, Heart Throb Ale, Holiday Imperial Elephant Seal Bitter, Holiday Scottish Intense Ale, Humpback Alt, Leviathan Imperial Stout, New Oakland Ale, Orca Porter, Pearl Ale, Traditional IPA, and Paul's Leg Warmer.

and was the first turnkey brewery imported to the U.S. to be used by a microbrewery. It was originally used by Palo Alto Brewing Company and was also used to brew the first batch of Pete's Wicked Ale. It's also unique in that it's an extract brewery. Gortemiller started each batch of beer with malt extract, more common in homebrewing, adding hops and specialty malts for additional color and flavors; he sometimes dry-hops or uses oak chips too. It's one of the few commercial extract breweries in the entire nation.

Between the beautiful vintage pub, very tasty food, and even better beers, Pacific Coast Brewing has maintained its place among the best brewpubs in the Bay Area for twenty-five years, and shows no signs of slowing down.

Pacific Coast Brewing Company

Opened: October 16, 1988.

Type: Brewpub.

Owners: Steve Wolff and Don Gortemiller.

Brewer: Don Gortemiller.

Guild membership: BA, CCBA.

System: 7-barrel British Innbrewing brewhouse, with modified grundy tanks, 800 barrels annual capacity.

Annual production: 300 barrels (2012).

Packages available: Draft only at the brewpub and limited 5- and 15.5-gallon kegs.

Tours: Brewery tours are available during daytime hours if the brewer is available.

Hours: Sunday, 11:30 a.m. to midnight; Monday through Saturday, 11:30 a.m. to 1 a.m.

Food: The lunch menu features appetizers, soups, salads, burgers and sandwiches, and entrées such as New York steak, carbonnade à la flamande, and my favorite, shepherd's pie. The dinner menu has twice as many appetizers but fewer burgers and sandwiches, along with the lunchtime entrées and a selection of personal-size 10-inch pizzas.

Extras: The bar holds twenty-four taps; up to ten are beers made on the premises. Tuesday Pint Night features $1 off all pints from 8 to 11 p.m. The brewpub has free Wi-Fi, big-screen televisions, occasional live music, and special events such as Sunday brunch while showing NFL games. For more than twenty years, Pacific Coast has hosted a holiday beer and food extravaganza in mid-December. The brewpub is shut down for most of the day, and guests are treated to tastings of numerous rare and interesting beers, with various courses of food served.

Gift shop: Merchandise is available at the brewpub; a price list is on the website.

Pleasanton Main Street Brewery

830 Main Street, Pleasanton, CA 94566
925-462-8218 • http://www.mainstbrewery.com
Facebook.com/mainstreetbrewery

As you'd expect, this brewpub is located right on Main Street in the East Bay suburban town of Pleasanton. It feels likes a sleepy little town, but like many Bay Area towns, it's larger than you might think, with more than seventy thousand residents. If you blink, you might miss the brewpub while coming into town, as it's one of the first buildings on your left as you drive into the downtown area. It's also partially hidden by some trees and a low-hanging roof.

Under that roof is a spacious outdoor patio, with patio furniture and iron bars to separate your seating from the sidewalk. Banners and neon signs advertising many of the popular big brands of beer, of the sort you might see at a sports bar, hang on the bars and from the roof. Inside, the brewpub is likewise covered with banners, signs, neon, mirrors, and other breweriana, along with the logos for its own beers. It looks like a neighborhood bar because—well, because it is one. It just happens to have a brewery tucked away in a corner, next to the bar.

Pleasanton Main Street Brewery is something of a chameleon, being many different things: a brewpub, a neighborhood bar, a sports bar, a restaurant, and even a nightclub on the weekends. It seems to succeed in being all of these things at once. In short, it's obvious why this is one of the most popular spots in town. It really does have something for everyone. It just depends what you're looking for. If you want privacy, there are plenty of nooks and crannies to hide out in. If you want to be social, there's a large open area in the middle, a U-shaped open bar, and even an area that on weekends becomes a dance floor. If you want unique, original beers, there are always plenty of good ones on tap, but if you want something more familiar, there are some guest taps as well, and having a full bar means you can pretty much drink whatever you fancy. The menu also includes a lot of variety, so you won't go hungry no matter what you're in the mood for.

Beers brewed: Year-round: Pleasanton Pale Ale, Strawberry Blonde Hefeweizen, Trainwreck IPA, and Pyrat Porter. Seasonals: Bikini Bottom Golden Lager, Red Leaf Strong Ale (available in winter as a winter ale and in July as a summer release), Attaboy IPA (September), Caterwaulin Black Lager, War Pig Amber, DedHed Red, Olde Cogitator Imperial Porter, Zone 7 Porter, Double Mocha Porter, and 12-21 India Pale Lagers (a series of five strong lagers referencing the Mayan calendar).

Pleasanton Main Street Brewery

Opened: February 2, 1996.

Type: Brewpub.

Owners: Matt and Sharon Billings.

Brewer: Matt Billings, with a big assist from Mike Peasley.

System: 7-barrel old-time Schluter, 350 barrels annual capacity.

Annual production: 300 barrels (estimated).

Packages available: Growlers (stainless with swing-tops) and kegs, but kegs are sold only to business customers.

Tours: No tours are available, but you can view the tiny brewery from the brewpub. It's just to the left of the bar.

Hours: Monday, 4 to 10 p.m.; Tuesday through Thursday, 11:30 a.m. to 10 p.m.; Friday and Saturday, 11:30 a.m. to midnight; Sunday, 11:30 a.m. to 8:30 p.m.

Food: The menu has a large number of appetizers, including an entire section of beer-battered ones, as well as a dozen burgers, such as the Guinness Gouda Burger and ones with bourbon or garlic, deep fried pickles called Dilly Boppers, fish and chips, Brew City Fries—a personal favorite—hot and cold sandwiches, generous salads, vegetarian choices, and "south of the border" specialties, such as burritos, quesadillas, and tacos. There are daily specials and a separate kids' menu.

Extras: The brewpub has six large flat-screen televisions, along with a full bar and a rotating selection of local guest taps. Covered outdoor seating is available all year round. Most of the time the brewpub is a family restaurant, but on weekends it transforms into a nightclub featuring live music every Friday and Saturday from 9 p.m. to midnight, including some of the best rock and roll and blues bands in the Bay Area. There's even a dance floor should you feel the urge to move your hips. The brewpub also hosts frequent special events and holiday parties throughout the year.

Gift shop: T-shirts, tank tops, sweatshirts, and hats can be purchased at the bar.

The Pick: Though the hoppy beers and the porter are quite good, I really like the Red Leaf Strong Ale, which is a seasonal made twice a year, in both summer and winter. And that's a good thing, as far as I'm concerned, because the big malty beer, brewed with six different malts, is spicy and bittersweet, with great hops balance, making it a good beer no matter what time of the year it is. Weighing in at a healthy 8.6 percent ABV, it's a nice all-purpose beer, good with a variety of foods or just to sip on while sitting comfortably.

Pyramid Alehouse, Brewery & Restaurant

901 Gilman Street, Berkeley, CA 94710
510-528-9880
www.pyramidbrew.com/alehouses/berkeley
Twitter @PyramidBerkeley / @PyramidBrew
Facebook.com/PyramidAlehouseBerkeley /
Facebook.com/PyramidBrew

The original Pyramid Brewery was founded in 1984 in Kalama, Washington, but was known then as Hart Brewing. Its first line of beers was known as Pyramid Ales. The brewery experienced early success and bought Thomas Kemper Brewing in 1992, a Bainbridge Island (and later Poulsbo) brewery that also created a line of artisan soft drinks. By 1994, it was the fourth largest microbrewery in the U.S. In 1996, the first Alehouse location opened in Seattle, right across the street from what's now called Safeco Field, where the Seattle Mariners play, and just one block from Qwest Field, home of the Seattle Seahawks football team. In 1997, the company ventured out of Washington and opened the Pyramid Alehouse & Brewery in Berkeley, in a two-story warehouse with a covered parking lot. During the summer, films are projected onto a giant screen mounted on the side of the building. An outdoor beer garden seats around fifty, with tall palm trees surrounding tables, chairs, and shade umbrellas.

The inside of the brewpub has been completely renovated. It's gorgeous and huge, with tall ceilings giving it a very open feel. A curved copper bar is toward the back, on the other side of a big dining area. The brewery can be seen through large glass windows that line a far wall. Pyramid scene murals are scattered throughout.

There's also the Hefeweizen Room for smaller private events, and a dedicated gift shop. A mezzanine upstairs overlooks the central hall of the restaurant and has seating for another eighty or for private events. A second separate room upstairs, the Snow Cap Room, is similar in size to the Hefeweizen Room but even more private.

Brewmaster Simon Pesch has been there since it opened and is a UC Davis graduate, having

Beers brewed: Year-round: Hefeweien, Apricot Ale, Thunderhead IPA, Outburst, Wheaten IPA, and Weiss Cream Spiced Wheat Ale. Seasonals: Discord Dark IPA, Curve Ball Blonde Ale, Oktoberfest Snow Cap Winter Warmer, Wheat Lager, Wheat Passion, Weizenbock, Chai Wheat, Irish Red Ale, Honey Bock, Wit Beer, Imperial Pilsner, Red Eye, Brown Porter, Dunkel Dark Wheat Ale, and Oatmeal Stout. Brewpub exclusives: Single Hop Imperial IPA, Redwood Pale, Oak Smoked Wheat IPA, and Belgian Ale. Ignition Series: Super Snow Cap.

worked as both a winemaker and brewer. Before coming to Pyramid, for two years he ran the old BrewMakers BOP, which used to be located in Mountain View, and there he learned how to brew just about every style of beer.

Pyramid operates a second Alehouse in the East Bay but does not brew there. However, it offers all of Pyramid's beers and has virtually the same menu. It's located in Walnut Creek, at 1410 Locust Street (915-946-1520).

Both locations serve a great mix of good food and beer in a comfortable setting. Most of the brewery's regular beers have been around for so long that we tend to take them for granted, but there's a reason their popularity has endured—they taste good. But even so, brewmaster Pesch has started playing around with new beers in recent years, giving you even more reasons to stop by Pyramid to see what he's been up to lately. The brewpub has a number of exclusive beers and several new series on its seasonal lists, so there's always a plethora of interesting choices.

The Pick: The Snow Cap has long been a favorite holiday beer of mine. A British-style winter warmer that's only moderately strong, it boasts a thick, rich mouthfeel with mostly malt flavors balanced with spicy tartness and a warming essence running throughout.

Pyramid Alehouse, Brewery & Restaurant

Opened: 1984; the Berkeley Alehouse opened 1997.

Type: Brewpub.

Owner: North American Breweries.

Brewer: Simon Pesch.

Guild membership: BA, CCBA.

System: 125-barrel Steinecker, 150,000 barrels.

Annual production: 120,000 barrels.

Packages available: 12-ounce bottles in six-packs and 12-packs, 22-ounce bottles, growlers, and kegs.

Tours: Brewery tours are conducted every day at 4 p.m. and last about 45 minutes.

Hours: Sunday through Thursday, 11:30 a.m. to 10 p.m.; Friday and Saturday, 11:30 a.m. to 11 p.m.

Food: A selection of appetizers, soups and salads, burgers and sandwiches, pizza, and entrées. Don't miss the bacon potato pancakes.

Extras: Happy hour takes place Monday through Friday, 3:30 to 6:30 p.m., and Monday through Thursday, 9 to 10 p.m. The brewpub hosts a monthly brewer's dinner and has various daily specials and banquet space for up to 250 people.

Gift shop: A separate gift shop has a wide range of merchandise and bottled beer. Select merchandise is also available online.

The Rare Barrel

940 Parker Street, Berkeley, CA 94710
www.therarebarrel.com
Twitter @therarebarrel
Facebook.com/therarebarrel

The Rare Barrel is a unique brewery, one of the most unusual yet conceived, especially if you're a fan of sour beers. The concept was designed by college friends Jay Goodwin and Alex Wallash. While seniors at UC Santa Barbara, Wallash began homebrewing in their shared apartment, and Goodwin pitched in too. After graduation, Jay became a production assistant at the Bruery in Orange County. He spent four years there and became a brewer, then head of sensory analysis, and finally was named head of barrel aging.

After college, Wallash worked in biotech sales, specifically to learn more about managing a business, and also continued to hone his home-brewing skills. The pair decided to start an all-sour beer company for two main reasons: this is their favorite style of beer, and in their opinion, there aren't enough sour beers available.

Their plan is to contract brew their wort at a commercial brewery, and then transport it to their barrel house facility in Berkeley, where they will manage the fermentation process, barrel aging, blending, and finally the packaging of the finished product. In February 2013, they brewed their first batch of wort, started fermentation, and put it into oak barrels for aging. Their first sour beers are expected to be released at the end of 2013.

They currently have about two hundred oak barrels that in a previous life were used to make red wine. The barrel house has enough space to hold about fifteen hundred oak barrels, though, so there's plenty of room for expansion. The partners' long-range plans are to conduct experiments with different yeast and bacteria strains, fruit additions, spices, and barrel types. They conceive the Rare Barrel as a decades-long experiment in sour beer.

They also plan to have a tasting room inside the barrel house that is slated to open in late 2013. They describe the experience they hope to provide to customers at the facility: "Visitors can gaze out among a field of barrels as they contemplate

Beers brewed: Year-round: The Rare Barrel is an all-sour beer company and will be making a variety of sour beers.

the flavors they are experiencing in our sour beers." However, they still have to successfully navigate a public hearing for a use permit for the tasting room, so depending on the outcome, their plans may change. Check the website or Facebook page for details. With luck, they'll be successful, because that sounds like a perfect way to enjoy a sour beer.

The Rare Barrel

Opened: February 2013.

Type: Contract brewery for the wort; the brewing process is completed in-house.

Owners: Jay Goodwin and Alex Wallash.

Brewer: Jay Goodwin.

System: Wort will be brewed on a contract basis at outside breweries, then transported to the Berkeley location for fermentation, barrel aging, and packaging.

Annual production: 100 barrels (2013 estimate).

Packages available: 750-milliliter bottles and 5-gallon kegs.

Tours: Barrel house tours are available; call for details.

Hours: Check the website or Facebook page for current hours.

Food: Light snacks are expected to be served in the tasting room, which is scheduled to open in late 2013.

Gift shop: Merchandise is available at the brewery and online.

Schooner's Grille and Brewery

4250 Lone Tree Way, Antioch, CA 94531
925-776-1800 • www.schoonersbrewery.com
Facebook.com/pages/Schooners-Grille-and-
Brewery/153056991381191

Schooner's is a comfortable suburban restaurant that, for more than ten years, has been making some great beers to go along with its extensive menu. Most of the space is taken up by booths, tables, and chairs, although there is a small bar. You can watch the brewery in operation through a large picture window behind the bar.

Schooner's beer is made by Craig Cauwels, who has won numerous awards and built a solid reputation for the brewpub. He's also brewing at E. J. Phair (see page 198), splitting his time between the two breweries. Before becoming a brewer, he was running the core lab facility at the Dana Farber Cancer Institute at Harvard University. A molecular biologist by trade, he'd also been homebrewing as a hobby for many years. When Schooner's first brewer left in early 2003, the owner asked Cauwels, who was an old friend, and he leaped at the opportunity, moving here from Boston. Cauwels was also one credit away from having an engineering minor in college, and the combination has proven ideal for his new career as a brewer. Brewing is equal parts biology and engineering, so he unintentionally learned the perfect skill set for a brewer.

You'll be satisfied by the range and quality of the food served at Schooner's, and the portions are generous too. The appetizers are particularly good for sharing, making it a great place to go for a beer with friends.

Beers brewed: Year-round: Pine Tree Pale Ale, Irish Red Ale, Lone Tree India Pale Ale, American Cream Ale, and Irish Oatmeal Stout. Seasonals: Antioch Amber Ale, Delta Breeze Wheat Ale, Raspberry Wheat Ale, Black Devil Black IPA, and other one-off beers throughout the year.

The Pick: Most of the beers at Schooner's are solid, well made, and food-friendly. I especially like the Oatmeal Stout, which is soft, rich, and complex. With spicy notes, roast coffee and mocha, vanilla and sweet toffee, it's very smooth and drinkable.

Schooner's Grille and Brewery

Opened: March 2001.
Type: Brewpub.
Owner: Frank Jiminez.
Brewer: Craig Cauwels.

System: 15-barrel Pub Brewing System, 1,800 barrels annual capacity.

Annual production: 300 barrels (2011 estimate).

Packages available: 12-ounce bottles in singles and six-packs, 22-ounce bottles, growlers, and 3-, 5-, 7.75-, and 15.5-gallon kegs.

Tours: Brewery tours are available, but please call for reservations.

Hours: Monday through Thursday, 11 a.m. to 10 p.m.; Friday and Saturday, 11 a.m. to 12: 30 a.m.; Sunday, 10 a.m. to 10 p.m.

Food: The menu has a large number of dishes available, from an entire page of appetizers to full dinner entrées. The choices include chili, soup, dinner salads, wood-fired pizza, pub favorites, pasta, sandwiches, wraps, burgers, steaks, and more. There are also separate dessert, Sunday brunch, "hoppy hour," and kids' menus.

Extras: If you're sitting at the bar, you can enjoy a special menu of beers and appetizers during "hoppy hour," weekdays from 3 to 7:05 p.m. and weekends from 2 to 6:05 p.m. You can order off the same menu during the late-night Power Hour, Sunday through Thursday, 9 to 10:33 p.m., and Friday and Saturday, 9 to 11:33 p.m. On Wednesday, kids eat free with any adult meal order. There are also monthly and seasonal specials, breakfast specials, and daily drink specials. In addition to the tables inside, there's also outdoor seating. If you're going to be a regular, ask about joining the mug club.

Gift shop: Merchandise and bottles of beer are available at the restaurant.

Schubros Brewery

12893 Alcosta Boulevard, Suite N, San Ramon, CA 94583
925-327-0700 • www.schubrosbrewery.com
Twitter @SchubrosBrewery
Facebook.com/SchubrosBrewery

Schubros is a San Ramon brewery, which is where it sells most of its beer, although for now some of the beer is made at Hermitage Brewing in San Jose and the rest is made in Santa Cruz, where Schubros has an alternating proprietorship with Uncommon Brewers.

The separate San Ramon taproom recently opened for business, and there you can find all of the Schubros beers and merchandise. The small bar and stools are silver metal, and the bar has a thick butcher block wooden top. As many as ten Schubros beers will be on tap there, and there's a big-screen television. In addition to the taproom, the space is currently the brewery's distribution warehouse and an R&D brewery, but the long-range plan is to build a 7-barrel brewery there as well.

Schubros is shorthand for Schuster brothers, though for now Ian Schuster is flying solo until his brother finishes another year in the military. Schuster is a former naval officer and got his MBA at the London Business School. His path to beer appreciation is a familiar one for servicemen. He discovered that beer isn't just mass-produced light lagers while visiting Japan in the navy and then going to school in London, both of which afforded him eye-opening experiences that eventually led to his passion for good beer.

Mike Johannsen, a veteran of Firestone Walker and other brewing gigs, is the brewmaster, and he studied both fermentation and business at Cal Poly. While in the food sciences department, he built his own homebrew system from scratch.

The first two beers Schubros released were the Nico American Wheat, a refreshing filtered wheat beer made with rye, and 680 IPA, a hoppy beer

Beers brewed: Year-round: Nico American Wheat, Diablo Dark, and 680 IPA. Seasonals: Festbier and Diablo Sunrise. Passport Series: Alcosta Chocolate Orange Imperial Stout, with additional beers in the series to be released on a regular basis.

The Pick: The 680 IPA is my current favorite. It's a solid IPA, with floral and fruity, citrus aromas and a touch of vanilla. The flavors also include big hops character, but there's also an equally large malt backbone with sweet caramel notes and some toffee too, making it nicely hoppy but not bitter. This is a truly well-balanced IPA.

with caramel malts for darker color and malty balance. Johannsen has since added more brews, and now that the taproom is open, he'll be experimenting with new beers all the time, so expect to see a rotating selection there. All the beers are now organic too.

Schubros beers are available at more than a hundred locations in the local community and also in bottles throughout the Bay Area. And in a nod to the local community, 1 percent of the sales from every regular Schubros beer sold is donated to a rotating selection of charities benefiting local schools, parks, and other community-based organizations.

Schubros Brewery

Opened: June 14, 2012; taproom opened January 19, 2013.

Type: Alternating proprietorship and contract brewery, with separate taproom.

Owners: Ian Schuster and Mike Johanssen.

Brewer: Mike Johanssen.

Guild membership: BA, CCBA.

System: See Hermitage Brewing on page 150 and Uncommon Brewers on page 176 for brewery details.

Packages available: 22-ounce bottles, growlers, and kegs.

Hours: Thursday and Friday, 5 to 9 p.m.; Saturday, noon to 6 p.m. Closed Sunday through Wednesday.

Food: Pretzels and peanuts at the taproom.

Extras: You can challenge brewer Mike Johanssen to a game of cornhole at the taproom. But be warned, I'm told he's a ringer.

Gift shop: T-shirts, sweatshirts, and glassware are available at the taproom and online.

Triple Rock Brewery & Alehouse

1920 Shattuck Avenue, Berkeley, CA 94704
510-843-2739 • www.triplerock.com
Twitter @TripleRockBeer • Facebook.com/TripleRockBrewing

Triple Rock has the distinction of being the third brewpub to open in California, the fifth in America, and the only one still owned by the same family that started it. When brothers and homebrewers John and Reid Martin tried to start a brewpub in Berkeley, it was 1984 and they were in their mid-twenties. Most people thought they were crazy, especially the many city officials they needed to persuade to allow them to open a downtown brewery. Most of the bureaucrats they encountered simply had no idea what a brewpub even was, as the law allowing them in California had just been passed the previous year. Eventually the brothers managed to get the city's permission and began building the brewery in 1985. They brewed their very first batch on Christmas Day, with the second batch on New Year's Day. That March, Roaring Rock Brewery opened for business.

Unfortunately, the well-known Pennsylvania beer company Rolling Rock got wind of the new brewpub and thought the name was too close to its own. The courts agreed, and the Martins had to change it. At the time, the three beers they were making all referred to some kind of "rock" in their names—Pinnacle Pale Ale, Red Rock Ale, and Black Rock Porter—so they chose Triple Rock Brewery, adding "& Alehouse" since so few people knew what a brewpub was at the time, while an alehouse was more familiar.

The sheer number of well-known brewers who have worked the kettles at Triple Rock is truly amazing, and many have gone on to open their own breweries. Nowadays the head brewer is Jeff Kimpe, who is originally from Detroit. In the mid-1990s, he relocated to Southern California, where he began homebrewing and interned at a few brewpubs. In the early 2000s, he landed a job brewing at Pyramid in Berkeley, where he worked for seven years before moving to Drake's, also co-

Beers brewed: Year-round: Pinnacle Pale Ale, Red Rock American Red, Black Rock Porter, IPAX American IPA, Bug Juice Hoppy Pale Ale, Stonehenge Stout, Ballyhoo Belgian Dark Strong, and Titanium Strong Pale Ale, and Monkey Head Arboreal Ale every Thursday. Seasonals: Dragon's Milk American Brown Ale, Tree Frog Scotch Ale, Reindeer Imperial Red, Festivus MiracALE IPA, 7-Fity Dry-Hopped Pale Ale, Dimmer Switch Chocolate Milk Stout, and the Single Hop Experience, a series of rotating single-hopped pale ales. In addition, up to twenty-five one-offs and other seasonals rotate yearly.

owned by John Martin. The Martins used to own the now legendary Twenty Tank Brewery in San Francisco, which closed during the dot-com boom in 2000. Between them, they still own part of Big Time Brewery in Seattle, Drakes Brewing Company in San Leandro (see Drake's on page 195), and Jupiter in Berkeley.

(see Drake's on page 195)

The Pick: Triple Rock's IPAX is a West Coast monster of an IPA, dry hopped with Cascade hops. The nose is floral and pine, with citrus notes, grapefruit, and a light caramel sweetness. It's surprisingly drinkable, rich and chewy, with a spicy, bitter finish.

The Triple Rock Brewery resembles a neighborhood bar, with lots of dark wood and paneling. Behind glass windows, you can get a good look at the brewery. A wooden bar is on a raised platform in one corner, with booths and tables filling the rest of space. There's an upstairs balcony that's outside and mostly uncovered. The walls are filled with breweriana from throughout the twentieth century. It's a comfortable pub, though it can feel crowded at times, a consequence of its success. Happily, the brothers are in the process of expanding, with a larger brewery space, a new kitchen, and more seating planned to be completed in 2014. Triple Rock just keeps getting better and better.

Triple Rock Brewery & Alehouse

Opened: March 14, 1986.

Type: Brewpub.

Owners: John and Reid Martin.

Brewer: Jeff Kimpe.

Guild membership: BA, CCBA.

System: 7-barrel JV Northwest, 1,200 barrels annual capacity.

Annual production: 1,120 barrels (2012).

Packages available: Growlers and draft only at the pub; 1-liter bottles of Monkey Head Arboreal Ale can be purchased on Thursdays only.

Tours: Brewery tours are available by appointment only; please call for details.

Hours: Monday through Wednesday, 11:30 a.m. to 1 a.m.; Thursday through Saturday, 11:30 a.m. to 2 a.m.; Sunday, 11:30 a.m. to midnight.

Food: A wide range of food suits your every mood or hunger level, from a selection of light snacks at the bar to the Avalanche Double-Burger Mega Platter. Those are the extremes; there are also appetizers, soups, chili, salads, T-Rock nachos, baked potatoes, burgers, and a big list of hot and cold sandwiches, including several vegetarian options. The fries, available four ways, are exquisite.

Extras: Music always plays on the jukebox, and there are three large-screen televisions. On Friday, cask-conditioned ales are featured. Triple Rock hosts several yearly premiere beer events in the Bay Area, including Sour Sunday and the annual Firkin Fest.

Gift shop: T-shirts, hoodies, bottle openers, posters, and beanies sold at the brewpub.

Trumer Brauerei

SALZBURG
SEIT 1601

BERKELEY
EST 2004

TRUMER PILS™

1404 Fourth Street, Berkeley, CA 94710
510-526-1160 • www.trumerusa.com
Twitter @TrumerPilsUSA
Facebook.com/TrumerPilsUSA

The original Trumer Brauerei is located just outside of Salzburg, Austria, and has been brewing beer there since 1601. Fast-forward four centuries to 2003, when Carlos Alvarez of the Gambrinus Company of San Antonio, Texas—the group that owns Shiner Bock's Spoetzl Brewery, Pete's Wicked Ale, and Bridgeport Brewing Company—decided to buy the Golden Pacific Brewery on the outskirts of Berkeley. He approached Joseph Sigl VII, the owner of Trumer in Austria, and the two agreed to collaborate on bringing its German-style pilsner to the United States and transforming the Bay Area brewery into a German-style brauerei.

Lars Larson, who had been brewing at another Gambrinus Company brewery, BridgePort Brewing in Portland, Oregon, was brought in to spearhead what was then called the the Trumer Project. Larson was the perfect person for the job, having cut his teeth brewing in Germany, earning his brewmaster's degree there, and even having had to pass an intense final oral examination in German. He then worked at an Argentine brewery for four years, and later at the Longview, Texas, Stroh's Brewery, before joining the Gambrinus team.

Larson collaborated with the Salzburg brewers to re-create the Trumer Pils nearly six thousand miles away. One of the reasons Alvarez chose Berkeley was because its water, which comes from the Sierras, is similar to the soft Alpine waters of Salzburg, making the brewing of Trumer Pils that much easier. The brewers also worked out supply chains for the exact ingredients and figured out how to use the equipment in Berkeley to make the end result one of the best pilsners U.S. beer drinkers could find.

Beers brewed: Year-round: Trumer Pils.

The Pick: This would be an easy pick, even if Trumer Pils weren't the only beer brewed. If you make only one beer, it had better be good, and this is hands down one of the best pilsners made in the United States—and in fact anywhere, for that matter. Trumer is a beautiful example of a German-style pilsner, with a noble hops nose and graham cracker aromas. The beer is crisp and clean, a brilliant bright gold color, and hits all the right notes. The finish is especially lovely, soft with a subtle bitterness that leaves you wanting more.

In 2006, Larson's Trumer Pils won a gold medal in the prestigious World Beer Cup, besting pilsners from fifty-six countries, including Austria and Germany. It's just one of many impressive international awards the brewery has picked up, including gold medals in both the European Beer Star Awards and the Australian International Beer Awards.

The brewery tour is a fun one, a bit unlike many other tours. Even though it's not a very large brewery, it operates just like a big European brewery, in all the best ways. But it's a working brewery, with no frills, just pumping out some mighty fine pilsner.

Trumer Brauerei

Opened: January 1, 2004.

Type: Production brewery.

Owner: Carlos Alvarez.

Brewer: Lars Larson.

Guild membership: CCBA, NCBG.

System: 50-barrel RMDG (Briggs) system, 40,000 barrels annual capacity.

Annual production: 25,000 barrels (2012 estimate).

Packages available: 12-ounce bottles in six-packs and 12-packs, along with 7.75- and 15.5-gallon kegs.

Tours: Brewery tours are available on weekdays at 3:15 p.m., but reservations are recommended.

Hours: Monday through Friday, 8 a.m. to 4:30 p.m. Closed weekends.

Food: No food is served at the brewery. Also, no beer may be consumed on the brewery premises, though a beer taster is included with the tour. Beer to go may be purchased here, including kegs.

Gift shop: Merchandise is available at the brewery and online.

Working Man Brewing Company

5542 Brisa Street, Suite F, Livermore, CA 94550
925-269-9622 • www.workingmanbrewing.com
Twitter @workingmanbeer
Facebook.com/pages/WorkingManBrewingCompany/
    166602070035888

Founder Joel Pelote grew up in Redding, where he began homebrewing more than twenty years ago.

He and his wife and brewery cofounder, Corinne, moved to Livermore a dozen years back, but they only recently realized that their hobby had taken up so much of their lives that turning pro was the only sensible thing to do. So Pelote continued his day job as a working man, a software manager in the computer industry, while he and his wife came up with a business plan for their Working Man Brewery.

After a few delays, the Pelotes' small production brewery opened in early 2013 and is distributing its beer around the Livermore area and the East Bay. They also plan to open a tasting room, where you can stop by and sample all of the beers.

Working Man Brewing Company

Opened: Summer 2013.

Type: Production brewery, with tasting room.

Owners: Corinne and Joel Pelote.

Brewer: Joel Pelote.

Guild membership: BA, CCBA.

System: 15-barrel Global stainless steel gas-fired brewhouse system, 1,500 barrels annual capacity.

Annual production: 800 barrels (2013 estimate).

Packages available: Growlers and 5- and 15.5-gallon kegs.

Tours: Brewery tours are available by appointment only.

Hours: Friday, 4 to 7 p.m.; Saturday and Sunday, noon to 4 p.m. Check the website for current hours.

Gift shop: T-shirts, sweatshirts, and hats are sold at the brewery and online.

Beers brewed: Year-round: Part Time Wit Belgian Ale, Wage Slave Pale Ale, IPA, Double IPA, Bottom Line Rye IPA, and Swing Shift Porter. Seasonals: Holiday Bonus Strong Ale (winter) and Spring Fever Imperial IPA.

Brewing Beer

Brewing beer is both easy and very complex. Of course, it's not necessary to know a thing about it in order to enjoy the beer in your glass. You may be content with simply knowing you like beer and have no interest whatsoever in how it's made. You may equate it with sausage making, where many believe the less known, the better. If that sounds like your philosophy, I won't try to change your mind, even if I disagree with it. It's a part of my nature that I want to take apart anything I'm interested in and learn everything about it that I can. I'm not content to simply take someone else's word for why I should like something. I want to figure it out for myself and not just enjoy it, but also know why I like it. But it is a personal choice. If you want my oversimplified overview of how beer is made, read on, Macduff. If not, drink up.

Why I do think it's important to know something about brewing beer is that it's easier to appreciate anything the more you know about it. Understanding the process—what steps the brewer took, what ingredients were used, and how he or she put it all together—may not make it taste any better, but it will make you value it more accurately.

Beer is made from just a few ingredients, as little as three, though in truth almost always four: malt, hops, water, and yeast. More can be added, and sometimes are, but you can make a wide variety of beers using the four main ingredients, which have been more or less fixed for over half a millennium.

The process itself has only a few steps, though commercial brewers can employ endless variations in the way they set up their brewery, the equipment they choose, and more. While nearly every brewery has its own way of doing things, they all follow seven basic steps—malting, milling, mashing, boiling, fermenting, finishing, and packaging—in going from grain to glass.

Malting. To make beer, you first need a cereal grain. Barley is by and large the most common one used. Others include wheat and rye. After the grain is harvested from the field, it goes through the malting process, often at a malthouse, to turn it into malted barley. There are three main steps in malting.

The first step is called steeping, soaking the barley in water for nearly two days, usually around forty hours. Next is germination, which involves spreading the wet barley in a thin layer on a large floor and allowing it to sprout. This process take three to five days, during which time the starch inside the barley kernels becomes soft, but the enzymes in the seeds have not yet started breaking them down into sugars. When the seedling shoots reach a certain height, their growth is abruptly stopped. At this point the grain is called green malt. Finally, the barley is dried in a process known as kilning. The grain is put on metal racks and subjected to slowly increasing heat until it's completely dry. The rootlets are removed, often used for cattle feed, and the dried grain, now called malt, is stored in grain silos or packaged. Some grain goes through additional heating, or roasting, which makes it darker in color and adds flavor to the beer.

Milling. When the barley, wheat, or rye malt arrives at the brewery, usually in large sacks, the first step it goes through is milling. The kernels are fed into the hopper of a mill, where they're ground and crushed into grist to make it easier to extract the sugars in the next step. The grist is not a fine powder, like flour; the process only cracks open the barley kernels, at least enough to expose the cotyledon, which is where most of the carbohydrates and sugars are located.

Mashing. The milled malt is put into a mash tun, usually a metal vessel, and hot water is added. This mixture is then kept moving continuously for several hours by mechanical rakes or paddles; in older times, this was done by hand. The makeup of the water is often adjusted during this phase, changing its acidity or alkalinity as needed. This is the simplest form of mashing, but depending on the type of beer, the process might involve decoction mashing or infusion mashing. At the end of the mash, what's created is a sweet, sugar-rich liquid called wort (pronounced "whert").

The journey of the wort at this point is determined by the brewery's specific equipment, along with the kind of beer that's being made. In some cases, the water is drained through the bottom of the mash tun, leaving the wort behind. In other cases, often when brewing a lager, the wort is transferred to a separate vessel, called a lauter tun, where it is sparged, or sprayed with hot water to release more sugars.

Boiling. Eventually the wort is put into a brewkettle, or copper, where it is boiled for at least an hour, sometimes longer. It's usually a vigorous boil, and you'll often hear brewers talk about a rolling boil.

The boil stops the enzymes, sterilizes the mixture, precipitates proteins, and concentrates the wort.

This is also the stage where hops, as well as other herbs or spices, are added. Often the hop additions take place at specific times throughout the boil, which are timed to create certain effects in the finished beer. Early in the boil, adding hops produces bittering; later in the boil, it adds flavor; and very late, it adds hop aromas.

Depending on the brewery, the wort may then be moved to a whirlpool, where solid particles left in the liquid settle out and are removed, clarifying the young beer. In some cases, more hops are added during this step to intensify the aromas. Some brewers use a hopback at this stage, which runs the still-hot wort through a sealed tank that has been packed with hops, maximizing the hops aromas in the beer.

Next, the wort must be cooled so that yeast can be added to quickly stop any bacterial growth. A wort chiller, or heat exchanger, using either cold water or a coolant, similar to the radiator in your car, takes the near-boiling wort down to below 70 degrees Fahrenheit, somewhere around 65 ideally.

Fermenting. Once the wort is cool enough, it is put into a fermenter, a special anaerobic vessel where the yeast is pitched so it can begin its work on turning the wort into beer. Essentially, the yeast feeds on the sugars and creates alcohol and carbon dioxide in a process known as fermentation. Within the first twenty-four hours, fermentation is going gangbusters. To finish, it usually takes about seven to ten days, but can take a little more or less time depending on the type of beer being made.

There are several different kinds of yeast. The two main types used in brewing are ale yeast and lager yeast. Ale yeast is top-fermenting or, more correctly, top-cropping, meaning it does all its work on the top, creating a large layer of foam sitting on the top of the beer. Lager yeast, by contrast, is bottom-fermenting, or bottom-cropping, and does its feeding at the bottom of the tank of beer. Other types of yeasts and bacteria are sometimes used in beermaking, though less commonly, including wild or spontaneous yeast, *Brettanomyces*, *Lactobacillus*, and *Pediococcus*.

Finishing. After fermentation is finished—and the product now can finally be called beer—it can go through a few more steps to finish it and get it ready for whatever packaging it ultimately ends up in. Unlike the earlier steps, which are more or less required, the finishing steps are far more likely to reflect the individuality of each brewery. Some breweries will do some or all of them, whereas others may decide to do none.

There are three main types of finishing steps: maturation, conditioning, and filtering. Maturation, also known as racking, is fairly common, especially for bigger breweries. In this step, the new beer is transferred to yet another vessel, called a conditioning tank, bright tank, or, often in brewpubs, a serving tank. In this tank, it is aged to allow the flavors to ripen. The yeast is also allowed to settle to clarify the beer, making it clearer and brighter. In some cases, fresh yeast is added to start what's called a secondary fermentation. (Occasionally this is also done in the bottle or a cask, which I'll cover in the section on packaging.)

Other types of conditioning include kraeusening, where new wort is added to the newly finished beer. This helps enliven the beer, smooths it out, and also may remove many off flavors. Another is lagering, which, as you'd expect, is usually reserved for lager beers. The German word *lagern* means "to store," and essentially, lagering is aging the beer by storing it at a cold temperature for a period of time.

The other common finishing step is filtering the beer. There are several methods of filtering, but they all do essentially the same thing. Filtering strips out any remaining solid particles—mostly yeast, hops, and grain—from the beer and leaves it clearer and brighter in appearance. The downside is that although the beer may look prettier, filtering often strips out flavors as well.

Filters can be rough, fine, or sterile. The most common methods of filtering beer use sheet filters, which are pads that only let through particles of a certain size. This allows brewers to decide how much particulate matter they want to filter out and how much they want to keep. Another type of filter is the kieselguhr, which uses a powder of diatomaceous earth (DME) or perlite to clarify the beer. You sometimes hear the term cold filtering, but in reality all filtering is done at a cool temperature. Brewers use the term to differentiate how they condition the beer from heat pasteurization.

Packaging. The final step in making beer is getting the finished product ready for sale. This is actually more important than it might sound at first. It's not as simple as just putting it in a box, as with many manufactured products. Beer comes in several types of packages, and each requires careful preparation, filling, and sealing so that the beer is as fresh as possible when it finally reaches your glass.

Bottles, cans, and kegs (really, just giant cans) are all filled under pressure, and brewers do their best to make sure as little oxygen as possible gets into the package with the beer. Otherwise the beer will not stay fresh as long, because the oxygen will start to make the beer stale. This is known as oxidation, and it can give the beer a papery or wet cardboard flavor. This will happen to almost any beer if you wait long enough to open it, but it should not be apparent in a beer before it has passed its sell-by date.

In order to keep the beer fresher-tasting longer, some breweries, notably the bigger ones, often pasteurize it. This involves heating the beer, which isn't always all good for it. On the positive side, pasteurization kills any bacteria, yeast, or other organic material that might hasten the beer's demise. On the downside, it also kills some of the beer's flavors. Pasteurized beer lasts longer on the shelf: from four months to as long as thirteen months. Most kegs are not pasteurized.

There are two primary ways to pasteurize beer: tunnel pasteurization and flash pasteurization. In the tunnel method, hot water is sprayed on the bottles or cans for as long as an hour. The flash variety is just what it sounds like: superhot water or steam is flashed on the beer, but only for a few minutes at most.

Some bottles, and even casks (wooden kegs), are spiked with a small amount of yeast when they're bottled. These beers are known as bottle-conditioned or cask-conditioned. The beers continue to ferment, or referment, in their packages. As a result, they produce natural carbonation and tend to stay fresher, or at least drinkable, for a longer period of time. Beers conditioned this way are never filtered or pasteurized.

So that's a necessarily brief overview of the brewing process. Believe it or not, I tried to keep it as simple as I could while at the same time giving as complete a picture as possible. Beer is easy to make, although it's hard to make well or consistently, which is the most important goal for professional brewers. Since the industrial revolution and the technological advances it brought, beer moved from the home estate to a factory setting and has become increasingly inscrutable to most people ever since. But what has remained true, as brewing became a more scientific pursuit, is that at its best, it is still as much an art as a science. The science is merely the tools, the paint and brushes that the artistic brewer uses to create, and the brewery is his or her studio. And now you know your way around it.

The North Coast

The North Coast is the region located in the northwest corner of California, lying along the Pacific Ocean, or near enough to it. For the purposes of this book, the North Coast region includes the counties of Del Norte, Humboldt, Lake, and Mendocino. The four coastal counties are roughly the size of Massachusetts, with the population of St. Louis.

You can approach this area from either the picturesque Route 1 or the more inland Highway 101. While Route 1 is a beautiful drive, the narrow two-lane highway hugs the Pacific Ocean, so if you suffer from vertigo or are afraid of heights, I would recommend sticking to 101.

In fact, this whole region's relative inaccessibility has given it one of its most colorful nicknames: the Redwood Curtain. The Redwood Curtain symbolizes the area's rugged and weird individualism, its unique culture and proud provincialism.

As you'd expect, you'll find beach destinations all along the way up and down the coast, but there are also many inland rivers and forests, ten state parks, and a couple of national forests and parks. This is where you can find the giant coast redwoods, some as tall as 350 feet. The whole area is a big logging region. Humboldt County alone represents 20 percent of California's entire logging production, though much of the old-growth redwood forests are now protected.

The forests in the northernmost part of the region, Del Norte County, are famous for the most well-known Bigfoot sighting, when in 1967 Roger Patterson filmed an unidentified creature that he claimed was Bigfoot on the Klamath River near the town of Orleans. Some of the forest scenes from *Star Wars Episode VI: Return of the Jedi* were also filmed in this region.

The largest lake in the state, Clear Lake, is also in this area. You might think that Tahoe is a bigger lake, and you'd be right, but half of Lake Tahoe is in Nevada. Inland, and throughout the less forested area, a lot of wine is produced, primarily in Lake and Mendocino Counties.

Fort Bragg and Eureka each have a world-class brewery and are both great coastal tourist towns with many attractions to keep you occupied for an extended stay. Both are throwback towns with Old West architecture and oodles of charm. Either would make a great place to decompress for a while.

Fort Bragg is also home to the "Skunk Train," a heritage railroad known officially as the California Western Railroad. The train runs regularly between Fort Bragg and the inland town of Willits, forty miles away. Once a year, the Lagunitas Brewing Company sponsors a weekend run of the train, renamed the beer train, with a beer festival on board. The train makes its run to Willits, where the group camps for the evening and enjoys more festing and entertainment, before heading back to Fort Bragg the following day.

Anderson Valley Brewing Company

17700 Highway 253, Boonville, CA 95415
707-895-2337 • www.avbc.com
Twitter @avbc
Facebook.com/AndersonValleyBrewingCompany

The Buckhorn Saloon in downtown Boonville housed the original Anderson Valley brewery, down in its basement, when founder Ken Allen opened the brewpub in late 1987. After a few years, the brewery started to outgrow the space, and in 1996, Allen built a larger 30-barrel brewhouse a mile out of town, at the present-day 28-acre location at the intersection of State Routes 128 and 253. Two years later, he decided to add a 100-barrel copper brewhouse and began building a three-story Bavarian-style building to house it. It took two years, but the new brewhouse went online in August 2000.

After selling the Buckhorn Saloon, Allen built a taproom and visitors center on the brewery grounds that includes a small bar with tasting room, a gift shop, and special beers only available there. That's also where you pay your $5 greens fee to play the eighteen-hole Frisbee golf course. He also installed a photovoltaic solar array that provides almost half of the brewery's electrical needs and implemented a recycling program to reuse various materials and all of its organic waste. The brewery also has its own wastewater treatment plant onsite.

After twenty-three years, Ken Allen decided to retire and sold the business to Trey White, a veteran of the beverage industry with many years at United States Beverage and other beer, wine, and spirits companies. One of White's first actions as the new owner was to bring back longtime brewmaster Fal Allen, who'd left to open a brewery in Singapore. He expanded its line of barrel-aged and sour offerings and introduced a new line of big beers, the Bahl Hornin' Series.

Many of the beers use words from the local dialect called Boontling, which originated in the isolated Anderson Valley, primarily a farming and logging area, in the late 1800s. Locals began creat-

Beers brewed: Boont Amber, Poleeko Pale Ale, Barney Flats Oatmeal Stout, Hop Ottin' IPA, Boont Extra Special Beer (ESB), Heelch O'Hops Double IPA, El Steinber, Brother David's Double, and Brother David's Triple. Seasonals: Summer Solstice, Winter Solstice, Horn of the Beer Barley Wine, Drunken Horn Bourbon Barrel-Aged Barleywine, Wee Geech Session IPA, and Anderson Valley Wild Turkey Bourbon Barrel Stout. Bahl Hornin' Mendonesia Series: Imperial Boont, Boont Black IPA, Boony Hoppy Red Ale, and Mowkeef Saison.

ing unique words and phrases that eventually developed into a rudimentary language with more than a thousand different terms. "Bahl Hornin,'" which appears on Anderson Valley beer labels and is also the name of its experimental line of beers, means "good drinking." The labels also include "Barkley," or the "Legendary Boonville Beer," the fictional Anderson Valley native animal that's part bear and part deer (bear + deer = beer).

The brewery hosts one of the best beer festivals in Northern California, the Boonville Beer Festival. The festival takes place each year in early May at the Mendocino County Fairgrounds in downtown Boonville, with camping available right next to the fairgrounds. Since it's a healthy drive from San Francisco, the campground is always filled. The festival has grown bigger every year in the nearly two decades since it started and has added more breweries and entertainment. If you're planning a trip to the Anderson Valley, festival time may be the best weekend to go.

Anderson Valley Brewing Company

Opened: December 26, 1987.

Type: Production brewery, with taproom.

Owner: Trey White.

Brewers: Fal Allen (brewmaster) and David Gatlin (director of brewing operations).

Guild membership: BA, CCBA.

System: 3-vessel 100-barrel Huppmann copper brewhouse (originally manufactured in 1958) and an 8-barrel Czech/American hybrid brewing system, 150,000 barrels annual capacity.

Annual production: 45,000 barrels (2012 estimate).

Packages available: 12-ounce six-pack bottles, 22-ounce bottles, 12-ounce and 16-ounce cans, 2-liter growlers, firkins, and 5.17-, 13.2, and 15.5-gallon kegs.

Tours: Available at 1 and 3 p.m. daily; stop by the taproom to arrange a tour.

Hours: Seven days a week, 11 a.m. to 6 p.m. Call during the winter to confirm hours, as the brewery is usually closed Tuesday and Wednesday in January through March.

Extras: There's a disc golf course, along with horseshoes, a visitors' center, pub, beer garden, and retail shop. The brewery also sponsors the annual Boonville Beer Festival. The 28-acre grounds are dog- and goat-friendly and include a small hopfield, though no dogs are permitted during the Boonville Beer Festival. Outdoor cigar smoking is also okay.

Gift shop: Extensive brewery merchandise is available at the tasting room and online.

Eel River Brewing Company

Brewery: 600 K Bridge Street, Scotia, CA 95565

Taproom and grill: 1777 Alamar Way, Fortuna, CA 95540

707-764-1772 (brewery) 707-725-BREW (taproom)

www.eelriverbrewing.com

Twitter @EelRiverBrewing

Facebook.com/EelRiverBrewing

In the 1990s, Ted Vivatson and Margaret Frigon were serious home-brewers who decided they wanted to turn pro. In 1995, they found the ideal location in the former Clay Brown Redwood Lumber Mill in Fortuna. Like most places in this part of Humboldt County, Fortuna was originally a lumber town. In the 1950s, there were at least thirty mills in the town and the surrounding area.

Not surprisingly, there are still signs of the old mill throughout the brewpub, especially in the outdoor beer garden and the many old photographs that adorn the walls inside. Most of the beers were named for local features. For example, the award-winning California common was called Climax California Classic after a local steam locomotive, the Climax Engine, which once pulled giant redwood logs out of the forests surrounding Fortuna. While that particular beer is no longer made, it did give birth to one of the brewery's most memorable slogans: "Have you had your Climax today?"

One fateful day in the early years, a customer asked for a "naked beer," by which he meant free of pesticides and other harmful chemicals. That question led to the first organic beer the brewery made, Organic Amber Ale, which debuted in the spring of 1999. At that time, there were very few organic beers on the market, and the owners quickly realized the potential. Shortly thereafter, they had the entire brewery certified organic, making it the first such brewery not only in California, but in the entire country. That decision also led directly to the brewery's current colorful slogan: "Be Natural, Drink Naked."

By the mid-2000s, Eel River Brewing was outgrowing the Fortuna space and built a new, larger brewery just a few miles away in another lumber town. Nearby Scotia was a company town, wholly owned by the Pacific Lumber Company, which

Beers brewed: Year-round: Acai Berry Wheat Ale, Amber Ale, California Blonde Ale, IPA, Porter, Raven's Eye Imperial Stout, and Triple Exultation. Seasonals: Earth Thirst Double IPA and Climax California Classic.

built Mill A in 1887 and operated it for 120 years before declaring bankruptcy in 2007. That same year, Eel River Brewing put its production brewery in the old Scotia redwood mill. Mill A was so large that the brewery has 200,000 square feet and also shares the mill with several other tenants.

Eel River also became the first brewery in the U.S. to be powered by biomass, thanks to the town's biomass power plant. As a result, in addition to brewing all-organic beers, the brewery's power comes entirely from renewable, sustainable energy.

In addition to serving all of the regular Eel River beers, the taproom has a pilot brewery that brews special beers available only at the restaurant. The taproom naturally has lots of wood, with a long wooden bar and tables and chairs. The inside is quite comfortable, and I love the various international flags hung from the ceiling. But if it's a beautiful day, you'll want to sit and enjoy your beer in the beer garden out back.

The Pick: It's hard to beat the Triple Exultation, a very complex old ale. The nose is malty rich and sweet and hot, with vinous and sherry-like aromas too. The flavors include caramel, chocolate, and lightly roasted coffee, with the occasional hint of cinnamon or molasses or peaches. What really makes this beer for me is that it's different with every sip. The beer is always changing as it warms, and it's never exactly the same.

Eel River Brewing Company

Opened: December 1995.

Type: Production brewery and separate brewpub.

Owners: Ted Vivatson and Margaret Frigon.

Brewer: Mike Smith.

Guild membership: BA, CCBA, NCBG.

System: 40-barrel Pacific Brewing Systems, 20,000 barrels annual capacity.

Annual production: 9,000 barrels (2012).

Packages available: 12-ounce bottles in six-packs, growlers, and 5- and 15.5-gallon kegs.

Tours: Tours are available at the Scotia production facility during normal business hours, but call to make a reservation. No beer is served at the production brewery; the taproom is a short drive away, less than 10 miles (under fifteen minutes).

Hours: Seven days a week, 11 a.m. to 11 p.m.

Food: A full menu with soups and salads, an extensive list of "munchies," smoked meat dishes, grilled sandwiches, beef and chicken entrées, and Mexican fare.

Extras: Happy hour is Monday through Friday from 3 to 6:30 p.m. Theme nights include Show the Logo Night on Monday, when you get your first pint for a deep discount if you're wearing Eel River Brewing logo merchandise. Each week a different Eel River six-pack is on sale. A first Friday event each month features crafts from local artists.

Gift shop: Brewery merchandise is available at the taproom and grill and online.

Humboldt Regeneration Community Supported Brewery & Farm

2320 Central Avenue, Unit F, McKinleyville, CA 95519
707-738-8225 • www.HumboldtRegeneration.com
Facebook.com/humboldtregeneration.csbfarm

If nothing else, the Humboldt Regeneration Community Supported Brewery & Farm, with its mouthful of a name, is one of the most innovative brewery ideas I've ever come across. If it works—and I sincerely hope it does—it may revolutionize how small breweries function, especially in remote areas. Under this scheme, the brewery will not just be local, but community supported.

It will work like those farms that deliver produce to your house every week, known generally as community supported agriculture (CSA). In a CSA setup, you sign up as a member or subscriber, and at regular intervals, you get a box or basket of vegetables, fruit, or other farm products. The advantage works both ways: you get incredibly fresh food directly from the source, and the farmer already knows who his customers are and where much of his cash flow is coming from ahead of time. That's a win-win for everybody.

So what Jacob Pressey is attempting with his new brewery is similar to a CSA. His CSB, or community supported brewery, is selling shares that allow members to get his beer on a regular basis, with growler refills at regular intervals. As he plans to change the beer available regularly throughout the year, members will get a range of beers that are seasonally appropriate, with as many as thirty different brews in any given year.

He's also planning on an educational component that will include in-house floor malting, an informational area about the Humboldt Regeneration Beer Farm and other sustainable agriculture topics, advanced home-brewing classes taught through the local university, and a small tasting area located right in the brewhouse, where patrons can see the brewing process firsthand and talk to the brewer. The long-term plan has already begun, with both barley and hops having been planted locally, and eventually the brewery should be able to rely on these local crops. The hop yard includes Cascade, Centennial, Zeus, Mt. Hood,

Magnum, and Nugget hops. The crops are being grown with a no-till soil management regimen, cover crop rotation, and dry farming, along with seed stewardship and organic practices.

The small brewery is tucked away along the main road, but blink and you'll miss it. You have to watch the road carefully. It's tucked well back behind an industrial park, right on the back corner. During open hours, there's a bright "Beer To Go" sign that should help show the way. On the plus side, it's only hard to find it the first time.

Humboldt Regeneration Community Supported Brewery & Farm

Opened: August 2012.

Type: Community supported brewery.

Owner: Jacob Pressey.

Brewer: Jacob Pressey.

Guild membership: CCBA.

System: 1-barrel brewhouse custom designed and built with the help of a local stainless steel welder; 3-vessel system with a combo whirlpool–kettle, hard-lined pump-manifold, and a combo hopback–wort chiller. The conical fermenters and brite tank, all 1-barrel, are by Stout Tanks and Kettles of Portland, Oregon, 52 barrels annual capacity.

Annual production: 40 barrels (2012 estimate).

Packages available: Growlers and 6-ounce sample tastes in mini-Belgian glasses at the brewery.

Tours: Yes, during open hours.

Hours: Sunday through Tuesday, 10 a.m. to 6 p.m.

Food: Locally made snacks, such as crackers and chips.

Gift shop: A small gift shop carries locally made items, such as sandblasted growlers and taster glasses, handblown beer steins and goblets, and snacks, as well as educational books on brewing and sustainable agriculture.

Extras: Handicapped access.

Beers brewed: Year-round: Under the label Blasphemy Brew, a different beer will be available each week and will rotate through many different styles, mostly American, but with Belgian yeast. Some traditional Belgian styles like tripels, American-style lambics, and other sours will also be offered. Seasonals: Using a nonhouse yeast, some special beers will be made throughout the year, such as a hefeweizen in the summer. Roughly every six months, different sour barrel-aged beers will be released, such as fruit lambics, gueuze in chardonnay barrels, and a Flemish brown aged in wine barrels. Beers that Pressey has already brewed up include I Can't Put My Finger on It Golden Belgian Ale, a dark golden beer; Blasphemy Red Jay, a hoppy red ale with Belgian aromatics; Triple B (Blasphemy Breakfast Brew), a chocolaty porter; Bananas N Brew–Weinstephanweisen, a traditional-style Hefeweizen; and Blasphemy Zeus IPA, an India pale ale made with Zeus hops.

Kelsey Creek Brewing

3945 Main Street, Kelseyville, CA 95451
707-279-2311 • www.kelseycreekbrewing.com
Facebook.com/kelsey.creek.brewing.company

For most of his adult working life, Kelsey Creek Brewing founder Ron Chips was on the road, working on numerous Hollywood films. Late in life, he took up homebrewing and, like many homebrewers who ended up turning pro, was immediately hooked. Looking for a change after retiring from Hollywood, he quickly formulated a plan to open his own brewery, with the help of his wife, Cheryn, whose business card reads "beer wench."

The couple retired to Kelseyville, a small Lake County town just a few miles from Clear Lake. It's home to only a little over thirty-three hundred people and is known mostly for its annual Pear Festival. The brewery is behind a light, airy storefront along the town's old-fashioned-looking main street. The place is comfortable and cozy inside, and you'll feel as if you've stepped into someone's home, one that's been converted to a bar. There's an L-shaped bar, along with tables and chairs. Peanuts line the floor, because not only are customers encouraged to throw the shells on the floor, but it's downright mandatory.

Through the back, past the restrooms, is the backyard, which has been converted into an oasis of a beer garden. It's covered and has a concrete floor, but potted plants give it the right amount of greenery it needs to feel outdoorsy. You have all the benefits of being outside, without the possibility of getting wet.

Apart from snacks, no food is served, but people are encouraged to bring in their own, and in fact the brewery has worked with local restaurants to facilitate that, going so far as to even do the dishes afterward. For example, across the street from the brewery is a great sandwich shop, Studebakers Coffee Shop, which will make a sandwich to suit your tastes.

Beers brewed: Year-round: Kelsey Creek Pale Ale, No'-Na'Me Irish Red Ale, Clan McPherson Scottish 80 Shilling, and Night of the New Moon Stout. Seasonals: Wet Willie (available at harvest time) and a Holiday Spiced Ale.

The Pick: The malty, sweet No'Na'Me Irish Red Ale is a great, all-purpose session beer that's easy drinking and smooth. If you like spicy winter ales, see if the Holiday Spiced Ale is in season. It's a really nice mix of Christmas spices—a liquid cookie, in the best sense.

Ron is brewing four regular beers, a nice variety, along with the occasional seasonal offering. If you have any reason to be near Kelseyville, it's worth traveling downtown—and back in time, to some extent—for a visit to the Kelsey Creek Brewing Company. The creek, by the way, is behind brewery. And be sure to take a look at the painting of the Kelsey Creek logo behind the bar. It was painted by a local artist with Ron's stout, along with a drop of beet juice.

Kelsey Creek Brewing

Opened: July 14, 2012.

Type: Nanobrewery and tasting room.

Owners: Ron and Cheryn Chips.

Brewer: Ron Chips.

Guild membership: BA.

System: 3-barrel Premier Stainless, 1,400 barrels annual capacity.

Packages available: Growlers and 5-gallon kegs.

Tours: Tours are available without reservations whenever the brewer is there, which is almost anytime the brewery is open.

Hours: Monday through Saturday, 1 to 8 p.m. Closed Sunday. Open late during the Kelseyville Pear Festival in late September and during downtown street dances.

Food: Peanuts and popcorn are available in the tasting room, along with hot dogs during football season and the World Series. Kelsey Creek is working with local restaurants to bring in takeout food.

Extras: The tasting room features a big-screen television, an iPod full of blues music, and live music on Wednesday, beginning at 6 p.m. Children are welcome and can get soda and snacks. Well-behaved dogs are also permitted. A cigar club meets the first Tuesday of each month in the beer garden out back. The brewery offers Beer 101 appreciation classes from time to time; check the Facebook page for details. The brewery also encourages customers to throw the empty peanut shells on the floor; seriously, don't try to be neat—toss them down on the floor.

Gift shop: T-shirts, hoodies, hats, and glassware are available in the tasting room.

Lost Coast Brewery & Café

Brewery: 123 W. Third Street, Eureka, CA 95501
Café: 617 Fourth Street, Eureka, CA 95501
707-445-4484 (brewery) 707-445-4480 (café)
www.lostcoast.com
Twitter @lostcoastbrewer
Facebook.com/pages/Lost-Coast-Brewery/
18938996622

Homebrewers Barbara Groom and Wendy Pound began dreaming about opening their own brewery in the mid-1980s. Groom was a pharmacist and Pound was a family counselor, but experimenting with making new beers and touring breweries abroad made them the happiest. So they spent several years planning and learning all they could, and by the end of the decade were ready to take the plunge.

In 1989, they purchased the historic Pythian Castle in downtown Eureka, the Humboldt County seat, which had been constructed in 1892 for the local chapter of the Fraternal Order of the Knights of Pythias. They spent the rest of that year and half of the next renovating the wood frame building and transformed it into the Lost Coast Brewery & Café, which opened in July 1990.

By 2005, they'd outgrown the brewpub and moved production down the street to a separate production brewery space just a few blocks away. There, in an industrial setting, all of Lost Coast's beer is brewed and bottled. Currently, the beer is available in twenty-one states, Puerto Rico, and Canada.

Head brewer Kerry Embertson has been brewing professionally for the past five years. After graduating from nearby Humboldt State, she moved to San Diego to become a brewer with Karl Strauss Brewing Company. In 2011, she became the quality control manager for Lost Coast and was promoted to head brewer last year.

Last year, the Eureka Planning Commission

Beers brewed: Year-round: Tangerine Wheat Beer, Downtown Brown, Alleycat Amber Ale, Great White Beer, Pale Ale, Indica IPA, Raspberry Brown, and 8-Ball Stout. Seasonals: Winterbraun, Humboldt Nation Stout, Apricot Wheat, Harvest Wheat, Wheatbock, Double Trouble IPA, Barley Wine, and Barrel of Monkeys. The brewery also makes numerous one-offs and exclusive beers for the café.

The Pick: Lost Coast's 8-Ball Stout is one of the best stouts around, smooth and delicious, with a creamy mouthfeel. The nose is thick with chocolate and coffee notes. The complex flavor profile includes rich chocolate, bittersweet coffee, hints of vanilla, and brown sugar.

unanimously approved Lost Coast's next plans, to develop a 9.3-acre lot on Broadway at the intersection with Sunset Road. The owners are planning on building a new brewery that ultimately would allow them to increase their production to as much as 200,000 barrels annually.

But it's the café space that you'll want to visit. The old historic building may not hold the brewery any longer, but it's where all the beer is. Painted yellow with green trim and a large brewery logo high on the side, the wood building is immediately recognizable.

There's also lots of wood inside, with a long angled wooden bar, tables, and chairs. Tons of breweriana and colorful art adorn the walls and even hang from the ceiling. You'll find more seating upstairs in a wraparound balcony that overlooks the front of the restaurant below. There's history everywhere you look. An old hand-colored photograph on the wall behind the bar is a particular favorite of mine.

The range of beer is great, from the first beer Lost Coast made—the Downtown Brown—to the Great White and the Indica IPA, plus the many exclusive and special releases available only in the café. But the food is also plentiful and uniformly tasty, making it one of the best places to stop along U.S. Route 101. Eureka's a fun town to stay in for the weekend, with plenty to do, from the boardwalk to the many shops and restaurants in walking distance of the Lost Coast Brewery.

Lost Coast Brewery & Café

Opened: July 13, 1990.

Type: Production brewery, with the former brewpub now a separate café.

Owners: Barbara Groom and Wendy Pound.

Brewer: Kerry Embertson.

Guild membership: CCBA, NCBG.

System: 35-barrel custom-built Canadian brewhouse, 70,000 barrels annual capacity; installing a new 120-barrel Rolec brewery.

Annual production: 60,000 barrels (2011).

Packages available: 12-ounce bottles in six-packs, 22-ounce bottles, and 5- and 15.5-gallon kegs.

Tours: Brewery tours are not currently available.

Hours: Sunday through Thursday, 11 a.m. to 10 p.m.; Friday and Saturday, 11 a.m. to 11 p.m.

Food: A full menu includes appetizers, soups and salads, burgers and sandwiches, pasta, pizza, and several entrées, such as Eight Ball Stout Beef Stew and "Chicken Lips."

Extras: Happy hour is Monday through Friday, 4 to 6 p.m. The café also has free Wi-Fi, a pool table, and a few video games.

Gift shop: Merchandise is available at the café and online.

Mad River Brewing Company

101 Taylor Way, Blue Lake, CA 95525
707-668-4151
www.madriverbrewing.com
Facebook.com/madriverbrewing

Bob Smith, one of the founding members of the Humbrewers Guild, Humboldt County's homebrewers club, used to visit Ken Grossman in Chico to shop at the homebrew supply store Grossman operated there before he started Sierra Nevada Brewing Company. Grossman shared his plans to open a brewery, and Smith loved the idea so much that he decided he would do the same in Humboldt.

By the time Smith's vision became closer to reality in the spring of 1989, Sierra Nevada Brewing had outgrown the original brewhouse that Grossman had hand-built, and he offered to sell it to Smith for Mad River Brewing Company. Sierra Nevada's original brewhouse has been Mad River's brewery now for more than two decades.

The brewery is located in the tiny town of Blue Lake, with a population of just over twelve hundred residents. Blue Lake is in the Mad River Valley, though the town's namesake body of water has been reduced to a seasonal pond thanks to a levee built to control seasonal flooding. Like most towns in Humboldt County, it's an old logging town, as remote as they come. Even so, the brewery is located outside of the small downtown. The production brewery takes up most of a long industrial building, and the tasting room is in a separate building just around the corner. The small tasting room looks almost brand new, with a beautiful wooden bar built by neighbors, who are world renowned for their wood-carved bars. You can try all of Mad River's beers there, and some that aren't readily available, brewed on the specialty pilot brewery. There are bar stools, tables, and chairs, and a covered outdoor beer garden.

Mad River had been brewing somewhat under the radar, although it had lots of fans, both local and throughout California, but that changed in 2010, when it was named Small Brewery of the Year and head brewer Dylan Schatz was named Small Brewing Company Brewer of the Year at the Great American Beer Festival. A native of Blue

Beers brewed: Year-round: Steelhead Extra Pale Ale, Steelhead Double IPA, Steelhead Porter, Steelhead Extra Stout, Jamaica Red Ale, and Jamaica Sunset IPA. Seasonals: Serious Madness Black Ale (January–March), Double Dread Imperial Red Ale (April–June), Mad Summers Dream Wheat IPA (July–September), and John Barleycorn Barleywine (October–December). Specials and one-offs: Bohemian Pilsner, Flor de Jamaica, or the Mad Belgian are often found exclusively in the tasting room.

Lake, Schatz started in 1999 in the brewery's packaging department and immediately fell in love with the beer industry. He took classes at UC Davis and became a brewer, and in 2005 he was named Mad River's head brewer. Since then, Dylan has built up a solid reputation for Mad River's beers, introduced the Madness Series, and cultivated one of the most impressive beards in brewing.

Mad River beer is now available in twenty-eight states and Japan, but you should really have the beer at the source among the redwoods of Humboldt County in the Mad River Valley. It's worth the trip.

Mad River Brewing Company

Opened: 1989 (first beer sold December 4, 1990).

Type: Production brewery, with tasting room.

Owners: Small group of local shareholders.

Brewer: Dylan Schatz.

Guild membership: BA, CCBA, NCBG.

System: 17-barrel brewhouse, Sierra Nevada's original system built by Ken Grossman, 16,700 barrels annual capacity.

Annual production: 14,900 barrels (2011).

Packages available: 12-ounce bottles in six-packs and four-packs, growlers, 5- and 10-gallon casks, and 5-, 13.2-, and 15.5-gallon kegs.

Tours: Available Monday through Friday, by advance appointment only.

Hours: Production brewery: Monday through Friday, 8 a.m. to 5 p.m. Tasting room: usually Monday through Friday, 1 to 9 p.m.; Saturday, noon to 9 p.m.; Sunday, noon to 7 p.m. Call to make sure, because the hours change from time to time.

Food: Limited snacks, including prepackaged sandwiches, are available in the tasting room. On certain days, special food is available, such as the Wandering Weenie Wagon on Wednesday evening and Taqueria La Barca on Friday.

Extras: Specials include "Purl and Pour" day, when knitting is paired with Mad River beer. "Hoppy hour," featuring discounted pints, is from 4 to 6 p.m. throughout the week. There's outdoor seating in the beer garden, which is dog-friendly, and live entertainment, usually music in a variety of genres from bluegrass to jazz, but occasionally comedy. Mad River also participates in the Pints for Non-Profits Program, a local Humboldt County charity.

Gift shop: Hats, T-shirts, hoodies, bottle openers, disc golf discs, reusable shopping bags, aprons, tin tackers, and growlers are available in the tasting room or shown online (call to order).

Mendocino Brewing Company

Brewery: 1601 Airport Road, Ukiah, CA 95482
Alehouse: 1252 Airport Park Blvd, Ukiah, CA 95482
707-463-2627 (brewery) / 707-467-2337
(alehouse) • www.mendobrew.com
Twitter @MendoBrew
Facebook.com/mendocinobrewing /
Facebook.com/mendobrewalehouse

The original Mendocino Brewery was the first brewpub to open in California, and the second in the nation. It rose out of the ashes of the New Albion Brewery, when Michael Laybourn, Norman Franks, and John Scahill, with the help of Don Barkley, purchased the brewing equipment after New Albion closed (see "A Word About . . . New Albion, America's First Modern Microbrewery" on page 120) and installed it in Hopland to create Mendocino Brewery. Barkley and Michael Lovett were the original brewers, and even Jack McAuliffe helped out in the early days with the transition of the brewery to Hopland.

Mendocino's success led to the need for a larger brewery in the mid-1990s, and its owners bought a parcel of land on the outskirts of Ukiah and began building a bigger brewery from scratch. They chose the mission style of architecture for the cavernous building. Inside, it's a large-scale working brewery with few amenities. Although tours can be arranged, it's not set up as a tourist destination, and you'll see the inner workings of a brewery with no frills.

In 1997, an Indian businessman, Dr. Vijay Mallya, bought Mendocino Brewing Company and also established the Olde Saratoga Brewery in New York State the same year. Olde Saratoga brews Mendocino beers for the eastern half of the United States, along with its own beers under the Saratoga brand name. This allowed the brewery to increase distribution to forty-four states. Dr. Mallya also established the United Breweries (UB) Group, which owns the Indian brand Kingfisher, and Mendocino brews these beers under license for the American market. The brewery also acquired the beer brands Butte Creek, formerly of Chico, and Carmel Brewing, originally located in Carmel, both

Beers brewed: Year-round: Red Tail Ale, Blue Heron Pale Ale, Peregrine Czech Style Pilsner, Eye of the Hawk Select Ale, White Hawk IPA, Black Hawk Stout, Black-Eye Ale, Talon Extra Select Double IPA, Imperial IPA, Imperial Barley Wine Ale, Imperial Stout, Butte Creek Organic Pale Ale, Butte Creek Organic Pilsner, Butte Creek Organic IPA, Butte Creek Organic Porter, Caramel Wheat Beer, Honey Amber Rose, and Kingfisher (licensed brand). Seasonals: Blond Ale (summer), Oatmeal Stout (fall–winter), and Bock Beer (spring).

of which Mendocino continues to make and market from its Ukiah brewery. In recent years, the brewery has added more lines of Mendocino beer, such as the Imperial collection, to its list of long-standing regular beers.

The original Hopland Brewery was closed in 2010, when the landlord wouldn't extend the lease, and the taproom was moved closer to the Ukiah brewery. It's now only a quarter mile from the production brewery and is known as the Mendocino Brewing Ale House. This is the public spot to try all of the beers and get a bite to eat. It's open every day, and in addition to all of Mendocino Brewing's regular lineup, it also serves special beers that aren't available elsewhere. It's essentially a brewery tasting room, just detached from the brewery. It's a comfortable spot that feels more like a neighborhood sports bar.

The original Hopland building may be gone now, but the legacy of Mendocino Brewing is in every bottle or glass of its beer and the beautiful brewery in Ukiah.

Mendocino Brewing Company

Opened: August 14, 1983.

Type: Production brewery.

Owners: The UB Group, led by Chairman of the Board Dr. Vijay Mallya and President and CEO of Mendocino Brewing Company Yashpal Singh.

Brewer: Don Tubbs.

Guild membership: CCBA, NCBG.

System: 100-barrel Enerfab, 60,000 barrels annual capacity.

Annual production: 60,000 barrels (2012 estimate).

Packages available: 12-ounce bottles in four-packs, six-packs, twelve-packs, and twenty-four-packs; 22-ounce bottles; and 5- and 15.5-gallon kegs.

Tours: Brewery tours are available by appointment only.

Hours: Brewery: Monday through Friday, 8 a.m. to 5 p.m. Alehouse: Monday through Thursday, noon to 9 p.m.; Friday and Saturday, noon to 10 p.m.; Sunday, 1 to 8 p.m.

Food: A selection of appetizers, hot dogs, sausages, burgers, and burritos.

Extras: The alehouse has a pool table, dartboards, two big-screen TVs, free Wi-Fi, and occasional live music and open mic nights. Happy hour is Monday through Friday, 4 to 6 p.m. Wear any Mendocino logo items on a MendoGear Day Sunday and save $1 off your pint.

Gift shop: T-shirts, hats, glassware, and more available at the alehouse.

North Coast Brewing Company

Brewery: 455 N. Main Street, Fort Bragg, CA 95437
Taproom and grill: 444 N. Main Street, Fort Bragg,
   CA 95437
707-964-2739 (brewery) / 707-964-3400 (taproom)
www.northcoastbrewing.com
Twitter @NoCoastBrewCo
Facebook.com/northcoastbrewingcompany /
   Facebook.com/acmebrewing /
   Facebook.com/pages/No-Coast-Brewing-Company-
      Taproom-Grill/186796614675170 (taproom)

North Coast Brewing's founder, Mark Ruedrich, originally grew up on the East Coast, but thanks to John Steinbeck and a tiny English brewery, he made Northern California the home for his brewery. As a zoology student at North Carolina State, he read *Between Pacific Tides*, a book about California's tide pools. One of its coauthors, Ed Ricketts, was a friend of the novelist Steinbeck, and the book prompted Ruedrich to visit California, where he spent some time living in San Francisco.

In 1977, an opportunity to live in England took Ruedrich and his wife, Merle, to Devon, where he discovered English ales. They drank pints of Blackawton Bitter at their local pub, the Maltser's Arms, and Ruedrich was impressed by the fact that Blackawton was a one-man operation, with the ale made in a tiny brewery in the building behind the brewer's home. Ruedrich also started homebrewing while in England.

After two years, the Ruedrichs returned to the States and decided to settle in Fort Bragg, in part because of the coastline, tide pools, and the intertidal zone. Over the next ten years, Ruedrich continued to homebrew, and kept thinking about that little brewery.

When the Triple Rock brewpub opened in 1986 (see page 222), it showed the Ruedrichs that it was possible to have a successful small brewery in America, and they began seriously planning to open their own brewery. Along with two partners from the restaurant side, they opened the North Coast Brewpub in the summer of 1988 with just three beers: a stout (now known as Old No. 38), Scrimshaw Pilsner, and the brewery's flagship, Red Seal Ale.

They persevered through tough times early on, and by 1994 built a new, larger production brewery across the street from the brewpub. That's also the same year the brewery debuted one of its most famous beers, Old Rasputin Imperial Stout, one of the first imperial stouts brewed in America. Actually, it was most likely the second, after Bert Grant's Imperial Stout, which would mean it's the oldest one still being made.

When the brewery first opened, North Coast was already making a stout, what is now the Old No. 38, but Ruedrich decided he wanted to do something different and noticed that almost nobody was making an imperial stout. By that time, even in England few breweries were making it. Grant's version included honey, which is not a traditional ingredient for the style, so Ruedrich set to work brewing an authentic version. It was an immediate hit and remains one of the brewery's most popular beers today.

On the label of Old Rasputin is a quote written in the Cyrillic Russian alphabet. It's a traditional Russian saying or proverb translated as "A sincere friend is not born instantly." The brewery has since started making an even bigger version that is aged in bourbon barrels. The most current one is Old Rasputin XV, but that will be replaced in a year's time with the next vintage.

In 1996, Ruedrich discovered by accident that the Acme Brewing Company, once located in San Francisco and started in the 1860s, was no longer a registered trademark. So he registered the iconic brand, and North Coast began brewing several beers under the historic Acme name.

In addition to its regular beers, North Coast began a line known as the Ultra Series, which, in addition to Old Rasputin, includes Old Stock and the Belgian-style Pranqster. The brewery also launched two beers in 750-milliliter bottles, sealed with a cork and cage, under the Artisan line: Le Merle, a saison named for Mark Ruedrich's wife, Merle, and the Brother Thelonious Abbey Style Belgian Ale.

With the introduction of the Brother Thelonious beer in 2006, North Coast has been donating a portion of the proceeds realized from sales of that beer to the Thelonious Monk Institute of Jazz and has also become a sponsor of several jazz festivals, including the Monterey Jazz Festival, SFJazz, the Mendocino Music Festival, and the Oregon Jazz Party. It has also donated to the American Jazz Museum, Cleveland Jazz Orchestra, Mendocino Coast Jazz Society, and Redwood Jazz

Beers brewed: Year-round: Scrimshaw Pilsner Style Beer, Ruedrich's Red Seal Ale, Old No. 38 Stout, Blue Star Wheat Beer, Acme Pale Ale, Acme IPA, the Old Rasputin Russian Imperial Stout, PranQster, Brother Thelonious, Le Merle, Old Stock Ale, and Grand Cru. Occasional releases: Old Stock Cellar Reserve and Barrel-Aged Old Rasputin.

The Pick: The world-class Old Rasputin Imperial Stout is my go-to beer. It has a definite wow factor from the very first sip, with gorgeous milk chocolate and roasted coffee notes, as well as warming sweet flavors from its 9 percent ABV. It's as bold as they come and infinitely complex, an everlasting gob-stopper of a beer. It also enjoys near perfect balance. It's a sipping beer that changes as it warms in your glass. You'll want a snifter to get the full aromas of the beer.

Alliance, to name a few, and the taproom and grill regularly features local jazz musicians performing live.

North Coast's beers are now available in just about every state and are also sent to Europe and Asia. Even though Fort Bragg is quite remote and hard to get to, you should definitely make your way up the coast for a visit. While the town is populated by only a little over seven thousand people, it offers plenty to do, and there are few better places to spend a long weekend. You'll find parks and beaches, rustic walks, and shopping districts. Right behind the brewery is the Skunk Train, an old logging steam engine that makes daily 40-mile scenic trips to Willits and back.

Across the street from the original brewpub restaurant, which is now operated solely as a fine-dining restaurant, is one of the most amazing breweries you'll ever see. Perhaps the most remarkable thing about it is how successful it has been in the remote wilds of the North Coast. But North Coast Brewing makes a great range of different beers, each one as terrific as the next, and there's nothing quite like enjoying them in the ocean breeze of Northern California. When you taste these beers at the source, you'll understand why North Coast consistently wins awards and is so often named as one of the country's best breweries.

North Coast Brewing Company

Opened: August 17, 1988.

Type: Regional production brewery, with taproom.

Owners: Mark Ruedrich.

Brewers: Pat Broderick and Chuck Martins.

Guild membership: BA, CCBA.

System: 50-barrel brewhouse, with 50-, 100-, 250-, and 500-barrel fermenters, 55,000 barrels annual capacity.

Annual production: 54,000 barrels (2012 estimate).

Packages available: 12-ounce bottles in six-packs and twelve-packs, 375- and 750-milliliter bottles, and 5.16- and 15.5-gallon kegs.

Tours: Available by advance appointment; call for a reservation.

Hours: Brewery: call for hours. Taproom and grill: Wednesday and Thursday, 4 to 9:30 p.m.; Friday and Saturday, 4 to 10 p.m.; Sunday, 4 to 9:30 p.m.

Food: A full dinner menu, with steak and seafood entrées, burger and sandwiches, soups and salads, and an extensive list of appetizers. Dishes include authentic Carolina barbecue, oysters, pasta, and other beer-friendly food.

Extras: A private dining room, the Sequoia Room, is available for meetings and events.

Gift shop: Merchandise is available at a gift shop across the street and online.

Redwood Curtain Brewing Company

550 South G Street #6, Arcata, CA 95521
707-826-7222 • www.redwoodcurtainbrewing.com
Twitter @RedwoodCurtain
Facebook.com/pages/Redwood-Curtain-Brewing-
    Company/129771337093357

The Redwood Curtain was originally the brain-child of two friends that met at the University of Oregon, which is why green and gold signs saying, "Go Ducks," can be seen inside the Arcata brewery, although these days Drake Mollberg is the sole owner and brewer.

Originally a native of the Bay Area, Mollberg found Humboldt County to be closer to what he loved about Eugene, Oregon, from his college days. So he decided it was the perfect compromise—close to home but with the sensibilities of a college town. In fact, the relative inaccessibility of the state's whole North Coast region has inspired one of its most colorful nicknames: the Redwood Curtain. The Redwood Curtain symbolizes the area's rugged and weird individualism, its unique culture and proud provincialism. And it makes a great name for a brewery too.

The brewery is smack dab in the middle of a small industrial park, the Bayview Industrial Center. It's just one door along a row of similar-looking brown doors against alternating yellow and brown corrugated tin walls. But inside, it's a completely different world. The no-frills tasting room is right in the thick of things, and you can watch the brewers at work from the small bar, the stools and barrels that surround the brewing area, or the makeshift outdoor patio that's set up during warmer weather in the back. There's also a shelf of books and games to make your extended stay in the tasting room that much more enjoyable.

Although the brewery has been open only a few years, the brewhouse is impressive and

Beers brewed: Year-round: Imperial Golden Ale (IGA), Belgian Style Pale Ale (BPA), Belgian Style Porter, and India Pale Ale (IPA). Seasonals: Dubbel, Tripel. English Barley Wine, Belgian Style Dark Strong, Black Forest Imperial Stout, Belgian Red, Dusseldorf Altbier, Tripel du Chene, Dutch-Bier 5.0, Bohemian Pilsner, Oktoberfest (aka Marzen), Centennial Ale (aka Batch 100), Irish Dry Stout, and Flaming Sombrero (aka Rauchbier). Funky Notion Series: Peche Rustique, Sommer Sauer Weizen, Mure Reveche, Cerise Coup, and Aigre Carbonise. Double IPA Series: Double India Pale Ale (DIPA), Batch 69, Space Oddity, Mongrel Double IPA, and Bicentennial Double IPA (a.k.a. Batch 200). The brewery is also planning a third series of beers, to be called the ISO Series, which will feature beers made with isomerized hops.

appears to have been there for many more years than it actually has. It looks well used and well loved, and given how many different beers the tiny brewery is producing, I've no doubt that's true. In just a short time, Redwood Curtain has found a solid following, and it's already expanding the brewing space and taking over the space next door. The new tasting room might be slightly grander but will continue the spartan ethos that has been working so well for Redwood Curtain.

Currently, Redwood Curtain's beer is available only locally, at locations throughout Humboldt County, but that's likely to change in the coming years, as it will no doubt pierce the curtain and word will leak out beyond the trees. Until then, check out the brewery while it's still behind the veil, a hidden gem behind the Redwood Curtain.

The Pick: Given that the brewery makes a bewildering number of big beers, picking one is decidedly difficult. But I'd go with the IPA; it's a solid hops monster, thick and redolent of big citrus aromas. Despite its heft, it's very well balanced, with no astringency and a dry finish. It's also worth mentioning the Belgian Porter, which is unlike anything I've ever tasted and nicely mixes a traditional porter, loaded with chocolate notes, with Belgian yeast for a complex taste profile.

Redwood Curtain Brewing Company

Opened: April 2010.

Type: Production brewery, with tasting room.

Owner: Drake Mollberg.

Brewer: Drake Mollberg.

Guild membership: CCBA.

System: 8.5-barrel Specific Mechanical, 1,400 barrels annual capacity.

Annual production: 1,000 barrels (2012).

Packages available: Growlers and kegs.

Tours: Tours are available by advance reservation only.

Hours: Monday through Friday, 3 to 9 p.m.; Saturday and Sunday, noon to 9 p.m.

Food: The tasting room currently offers complimentary snacks; additional food options are planned for the future.

Extras: Board games are available to play and live music can be heard in the family-friendly tasting room two or three times a week. There are seasonal tasting room events, including the Fall Fever Bierfest, a spring anniversary party, and the summer Alpha Acid Test. Check the Facebook page for upcoming events.

Gift shop: Hoodies, T-shirts, "girly" wear, hats, beanies, logo glassware, posters, stickers, growlers, and growlitos are available at the tasting room and online.

Six Rivers Brewery

1300 Central Avenue, McKinleyville, CA 95519
707-839-7580 (restaurant) 707-839-7588 (brewery)
www.sixriversbrewery.com
Twitter @SixRiversBrew • Facebook.com/sixriversbrewery

In 2004, Talia Nachshon and Meredith Maier Ripley purchased Six Rivers Brewery, which had opened eight years earlier, and created a must-stop destination in Humboldt County. The brewpub is an oasis on the hill, with amazing views of the North Coast and the Pacific Ocean.

Nachshon had put herself through Humboldt State by bartending and discovered she had a passion for making customers happy, while Ripley, a communications graduate of the University of Massachusetts, was a natural for doing the marketing. The partnership worked beautifully, and with veteran brewmaster Carlos Sanchez making the beer, they've really turned Six Rivers into something special.

Sanchez has been brewing for more than two decades. He had been homebrewing for three years when he interned at the now defunct Humboldt Brewing Company, becoming assistant brewer there in 1990. He also worked with nearby Mad River Brewing and attended Chicago's Siebel Institute of Brewing Technology in 1992, studying microbiology and microscopy, before returning to Arcata. At Humboldt, he worked with head brewer Steve Parkes, who today owns and runs the American Brewers Guild brewing school, in creating the brewery's flagship beer, Red Nectar.

In 1996, the opportunity to brew at a local start-up tempted Sanchez to become Six Rivers' first brewmaster. He has also been its only brewmaster—for seventeen years as of this writing. In this time, he's created an impressive stable of beers, including many sound interpretations of classic styles, along with others that are utterly unique.

The brewery is in several rooms in the back of the brewpub and is somewhat hidden from view, though the brewhouse can be seen through a window behind the bar. The brewery is tucked into a wedge-shaped room, and a separate room is dedi-

Beers brewed: Year-round: IPA, Bluff Creek Pale Ale, Tru-la Pilsner, Los Kolsch, Moonstone Porter, Paradise Moon Coffee Porter, Raspberry-Lambic Style Ale, Weatherman Wheat, and Chili Pepper Ale. Seasonals: Rosie's Strawberry Wheat Ale (summer), Pigskin Pumpkin Ale (October), Sasquatch Ale (winter), and Blarney Stout (March). Rotating: Eshan Nut Brown, Red Diamond, Mimi's Macadamia Nut Porter, and barrel-aged and sour beers.

cated to bottling. Outside, the large blue building blends with the sky above, and the entrance is a golden orange, like a sun, beckoning you to come inside. Wooden floors, tables, and chairs focus your attention on the breweriana from the early days of craft beer that covers the walls. You'll see bottles, labels, and logos from breweries no longer with us. There's a centrally located U-shaped wooden bar, with the main dining area to your right and the pool room and additional seating to the left.

The bustling restaurant is usually full, but the service is quick and friendly, and the menu has a lot of choices. Big portions ensure that you won't leave hungry, and the tasty offerings of beer made by "Los" Sanchez guarantee you won't leave thirsty either.

Six Rivers Brewery

Opened: Originally 1996; under current ownership, March 17, 2004.

Type: Brewpub.

Owners: Meredith Maier Ripley and Talia Nachshon.

Brewer: Carlos Sanchez.

Guild membership: BA, CCBA.

System: 7-barrel brewhouse, 2,000 barrels annual capacity.

Annual production: 1,547 barrels (2011).

Packages available: 12-ounce bottles in six-packs, 22-ounce bottles, and kegs.

Tours: Yes, but reservations are preferred.

Hours: Monday, 4 to 11:30 p.m.; Tuesday and Wednesday, 11:30 a.m. to 11:30 p.m.; Thursday through Saturday, 11:30 a.m. to 12:30 a.m.; and Sunday, 11:30 a.m. to 11:30 p.m. The kitchen is open nightly until 10 p.m.

Food: An impressively vast menu uses fresh and organic ingredients when possible. There are a dozen tasty appetizers; I'm a sucker for the bar fries. The "6R" wings come in eight different varieties along the "Hot Wing Richter Scale," with the Death Wings at the spiciest end of the spectrum. There's also a long list of soups, salads, burgers, and sandwiches, plus stone-baled pizzas and several dinner entrées after 5 p.m. Six Rivers is locally known for its great dinner specials, including sushi on Monday and Smoked Out BBQ night on Wednesday.

Extras: A dozen house beers on draft, a full bar, and a separate pool room and a game cabinet stocked with board games. The brewpub features live music every evening. And this may be my favorite special: whenever it rains, it's happy hour. All ages are welcome until 10 p.m.

Gift shop: Hats, T-shirts, hoodies, and pint glasses available at the brewpub and online.

Ukiah Brewing Company & Restaurant

102 South State Street, Ukiah, CA 95482
707-468-5898 • www.ukiahbrewingco.com
or www.ubcr.com
Twitter @UkiahBrewingCo
Facebook.com/pages/Ukiah-Brewing-
Company-Restaurant/128434743851877

Ukiah Brewing Company was one of the country's first certified organic breweries and only the second restaurant to go through the certification process successfully. It was founded by Allen and Els Cooperrider, both biologists with an interest in environmental issues, and their sons Bret and Sid. Bret Cooperrider worked for years as a brewer in Fort Collins, Colorado, for New Belgium, Odell, and others before returning to Mendocino County to help his parents open the brewpub.

The family made an early commitment to buying as much of the meat, produce, cheese, and other foods for the restaurant locally as they possibly could, and they got their organic certification in June 2001. All of their beer is organic, and so is the wine they serve. They recently added a full liquor license, and cocktails are now included on the menu.

The area used to be a major hops growing area in the nineteenth century. Another first enjoyed by the brewery is that its Pilsner Ukiah was the first craft beer in California offered in cans, and it was also the first organic beer to be canned.

The brewpub is located in the beautiful historic 1899 Marks Building, situated on a corner in downtown Ukiah, the Mendocino County seat. There's plenty of space inside, with a gorgeous old wooden bar along one of the brick walls, lots of booths and tables, great old light fixtures, a balcony area, and a secluded room. You can see the brewhouse from the side room, and you could

Beers brewed: Year-round: Pilsner Ukiah, Orr Springs IPA, Comptche Logger, Potter Valley Pale, Big River ESB, Willits Wit, 10 Guilder, Old Mill Belgian, Black Bart Belgian, Palace Porter, Coops Stout, the Liberator, and the Emancipator. Seasonals: Sunhouse Amber, Yokayo Gold, Point Arena Pale, Full Moon Ale, O'Bohannans XXX Irish Ale, and Navarro Yarrow.

The Pick: The Pilsner Ukiah is a great hot-weather refresher, and it's particularly good when you realize it's organic too. The hops character is nicely crisp, with bready malt flavors and that clean bite you want on a hot day. Very clean, with nice fruit— mostly grapefruit and apple—notes and a touch of sweetness that finishes with a tart bite.

stand there and watch the brewer going about his business, should you be so inclined. I really like the feel of the place inside; it's clean but well worn and reminds me a bit of what I imagine a turn-of-the-century western tavern must have looked like.

Ukiah Brewing Company & Restaurant

Opened: 2000.

Type: Brewpub.

Owner: Bret Cooperrider.

Brewers: Bret Cooperrider and Scott Jones.

Guild membership: CCBA.

System: 7-barrel copper-clad brewhouse.

Annual production: 400 barrels (2012 estimate).

Packages available: 12-ounce cans, growlers, and kegs.

Tours: Brewery tours are given when the brewer is there, but please ask if he's available.

Hours: Restaurant: Sunday through Thursday, 11 a.m. to 9 p.m.; Friday and Saturday, 11 a.m. to 10 p.m.; dinner specials are available beginning at 5 p.m. Bar: Monday through Thursday, 11 a.m. to 11 p.m. (or later if there is live music); Friday and Saturday, 11 a.m. to 1 a.m.

Food: The pub-style menu features a number of vegetarian choices, as well as more salads than you usually see in a brewpub setting. There's also a good list of appetizers, along with organic pizza, sandwiches, burgers, and entrées like fish and chips and falafel. There are separate kids' and dessert menus, as well as daily specials. Check the website or Facebook page for information.

Extras: There's a small stage where local music is performed Thursday, Friday, and Saturday evenings. The schedule is on the Facebook page, along with announcements of special events at the brewpub. From time to time there are karaoke evenings too.

Gift shop: T-shirts, sweatshirts, and glassware are available at the brewpub.

Steam Beer

The story of steam beer is firmly entrenched in the history of Northern California. Steam beer is one of the few original American styles of beer, especially before the modern era of craft beer. While no one is absolutely certain of its origins or exactly how it was brewed, we do know that it was born of necessity.

When early brewers set up shop in San Francisco after the gold rush, hoping for some of the dollars that prospectors were bringing down from the hills up north, they encountered a big problem. The most popular beers at the time were the pilsners and lagers of Germany and central Europe, and these beers are traditionally brewed at colder temperatures, because the bottom-fermenting yeast they're brewed with works best when chilled. But the cold temperatures they needed were hard to find in California's vaunted sunshine, especially during the summer. Refrigeration had not yet been invented, and even once it was, it was prohibitively expensive, at least for several years after its introduction in 1876. In other places, ice was brought in from far-flung frozen tundras, but this, too, was prohibitively expensive in San Francisco.

So San Francisco brewers came up with a resourceful solution, and in the process they created one of America's few original beer styles. Since the tall, closed fermenters usually used for lager making wouldn't work, they instead used coolships, which are big, shallow, open fermenters. Coolships also have the advantage of being able to compensate for not having ice or refrigeration to a certain extent. And although California can be brutally hot, San Francisco is an oasis of sorts, as locals know, and is generally cooler than the surrounding area, a fact that the early brewers exploited.

In addition, they found or developed a lager strain of yeast that worked well at a slightly warmer temperature, cool rather than cold, to further work in the unique conditions of San Francisco. By selecting yeasts that, over time, showed a propensity to work well in warmer environs, brewers found they could make a beer people would drink, despite the challenges of the local weather conditions. It was most likely America's first hybrid yeast culled to suit the unique climate of Northern California. That yeast today is known as California lager yeast.

The San Francisco brewers brewed what was truly a local beer, most likely using six-row barley from the Central California Valley, which runs through the middle of the state. And the hops—probably the strain known as Cluster hops—likely was grown in the Russian River basin, where it can still be found growing wild today.

The beer made in this way was called *steam beer*. As the story goes, brewing the beer at warmer temperatures produced excessive carbonation, which caused a newly tapped keg to spray foam, simulating what steam escaping would have looked and sounded like. Whether that tale is true or mythic, the name stuck, at least until Prohibition.

After Prohibition was repealed, Anchor Brewery was the only former steam beer brewery to reopen. It struggled to stay open for several decades until Fritz Maytag bought the brewery in 1965 and eventually transformed American brewing (see "A word about . . . Anchor Brewing, America's Original Craft Brewer," on page 57). Many records had been lost during Prohibition, so Maytag had to figure out the actual recipe and process of making steam beer from what documents could be found. After much research and experimentation, Anchor became the first brewer to make steam beer since Prohibition when it debuted its flagship Steam Beer in 1971.

You might think that only one brewery still makes this historic style of beer, since the only place you see the term "steam beer" is on bottles of Anchor's beer. But that's not the case; there's another reason for that. In 1971, when Anchor brought back steam beer, no one else made anything close, so the brewery wisely trademarked the name. When others in the brewing world finally caught up and wanted to make steam beer too, they had to come up with a new generic name so as not to infringe on Anchor's trademark. So today steam beer made by other breweries is known as California common beer.

The Northern Cascade and Shasta Mountains

What I inelegantly call the Northern Cascade and Shasta Mountains is the inland region located in the northeast corner of California. The area reaches the borders of Oregon to the north and Nevada to the east and encompasses the mountainous areas of Northern California. For the purposes of this book, the Northern Cascade and Shasta Mountains region includes the counties of Butte, Glenn, Lassen, Modoc, Plumas, Shasta, Siskiyou, Tehama, and Trinity. This is the largest region within California—in fact, it's roughly the size of South Carolina and just slightly larger than the entire Czech Republic—but with only as many people living there as in Washington, D.C.

Some parts of this region are very remote, with three of the nine counties having just one incorporated city apiece. Another, Trinity County, boasts no incorporated cities whatsoever, along with not a single traffic light, parking meter, or freeway. Sadly, it has no breweries either.

In these more remote areas are several national forests and wildlife refuges. Lumber was a big part of the economy in these parts, and remnants and reminders of the mills and lumber business are on display at every turn, though in some cases it's not that remote. In Susanville, the seat of Lassen County, the last lumbermill closed as recently as 2007.

Lassen Volcanic National Park is also nearby, and there you can see Lassen Peak, the world's largest plug dome volcano.

Several of the counties, notably Siskiyou and Shasta, include areas that are popular tourist destinations. Many come to visit Mount Shasta and enjoy the numerous outdoor activities in the area, some created by the Shasta Dam, the tallest concrete dam in the United States. The man-made Shasta Lake is now the third-largest body of water in the state and has become a popular spot for boating, water-skiing, houseboats, and fishing, along with camping in the vicinity.

In the 1940s, this area engaged in a serious—some say semiserious—effort to create a new state, combining Northern California and parts of southern Oregon to form the State of Jefferson. Several years ago there was a Jefferson State Brewery, but like its namesake, it didn't last very long, closing in 2000.

Parts of the other counties are more built up. Butte County includes the city of Chico, home to one of the state's largest breweries, Sierra Nevada. It is also home to one of the biggest universities in the area, the Chico campus of California State University, as well as several museums, theaters, and parks, including the downtown Bidwell Park, one of the nation's largest municipal parks.

The Brewing Lair

67007 Highway 70, Blairsden-Graeagle, CA 96103
530-394-0940 • www.thebrewinglair.com
Twitter @TheBrewingLair
Facebook.com/TheBrewingLair

The full name of this remote brewery is the Brewing Lair of the Lost Sierra, evoking the idea of a new Indiana Jones adventure or an old Humphrey Bogart movie. The name is meant to convey the secluded nature of the brewery along with the idea of hiking in the Lost Sierra, a nickname for the off-the-beaten-path mountains that surround the brewery.

The name is new and had to be changed from UnderCover Ale Works after a legal dispute with another brewery, so if you've seen that brewery name, the two are one and the same. There aren't two breweries in Blairsden-Graeagle, a pair of small towns that together boasted a total of 776 residents in the 2010 census. The brewery owners, Rich DeLano and Susan Duniphin, live in nearby Quincy, a bustling metropolis in comparison, with a little over 1,700 citizens. The Brewing Lair is, in fact, the only brewery in the entire county of Plumas. What Plumas County does have in abundance is trees, wildlife, and solitude. It's a great place to get away from it all. But no matter how far into the wilderness you go, it's good to know that fresh beer is nearby.

Duniphin was an assistant brewer with Stone Brewing, while DeLano is a homebrewer with a degree in water conservation and ecology, though he's originally from Duluth, Minnesota. The couple love the Plumas County area for its spectacular hiking and vistas, skiing on the tall mountains, and swimming in granite basin lakes. The only thing they found wanting was a source for local beer. So they decided to pool their collective experience in brewing, construction, and the restaurant busi-

Beers brewed: Year-round: Goldie Glocks Gold, Incognito Saison, Ambush IPA, Espionage Red IPA, Uncle Elliot's IPA, Stake Out Coffee Porter, Coco Caliente Habanero Chocolate Stout, and Deep Cover Dark IPA. Seasonals: Odd Job Ale (fall–winter).

The Pick: Because of its remoteness, I have not had an opportunity to try all of the beers brewed by the Brewing Lair, but the Ambush IPA is an easy pick nonetheless. There are many hoppy beers in the Lair, but this one has a pleasant pine and citrus nose, with aromas of herbs and mountain flowers (the power of suggestion, perhaps?). It's slightly sweet up front, but a big hops wallop of grapefruit and a dry finish give you just what you're looking for.

ness and open their own brewery. They built the brewery and tasting room by hand, doing all the work themselves. The only items in the brewery that aren't new are the hand-cut square nails that DeLano hammered into the Douglas fir upstairs floor. Those were originally used on an old stagecoach stop in the late 1800s.

In case you didn't know, according to the brewery, a lair, which rhymes with bear, is "a wild animal's resting place, esp. one that is well hidden or a secret or private place in which a person seeks conceal-ment or seclusion." That definition perfectly describes the brewery, which is isolated, even in its remote area. Though it's small, there's plenty of space outdoors to walk in the woods, play disc golf, or sit at the patio and enjoy a beer in the fresh mountain air. The brewery resembles a mountain cabin, and there's wooden seating, picnic bench-es, and circles of chairs surrounding it. As the sun goes down, the glow of the brewery is the only light for miles around, and it paints an ethere-al picture in your mind. The only problem I can see at the Brewing Lair is that once you're comfortably settled in, you may not want to leave.

The Brewing Lair

Opened: March 1, 2012.
Type: Production brewery.
Owners: Rich DeLano and Susan Duniphin.
Brewer: Rich DeLano.
Guild membership: BA, CCBA.
System: 15-barrel brewhouse with three 15-barrel fermenters, 620 barrels annual capacity.
Annual production: 330 barrels (estimated).
Packages available: Growlers, 50-liter kegs, and pints at the brewery.
Tours: Tours are available; no reservations are necessary.
Hours: Seven days a week, 10 a.m. to around 8 p.m. (call to see if the brewery might stay open longer any given evening).
Food: No food is available at the brewery, but you're welcome to bring your own. It's the perfect place to bring a picnic basket.
Extras: Disc golf, bocci, horseshoes, and a real out-in-the-woods-in-the-middle-of-nowhere feeling. The brewery also has free Wi-Fi, is family- and pet-friendly, and allows cigar smoking.
Gift shop: T-shirts and pint glasses are available.

Dunsmuir Brewery Works

5701 Dunsmuir Avenue, Dunsmuir, CA 96025
530-235-1900 • www.dunsmuirbreweryworks.com
Facebook.com/dunsmuirbreweryworks

Dunsmuir cofounder and brewer Aaron Greener started homebrewing when he was just seventeen, and he knew even then that someday he'd own his own brewery. He later became a professional brewer and earned his degree at the American Brewers Guild, having been part of the last class before it began its correspondence program. Greener apprenticed with Denise Jones when she was still the brewmaster at Third Street Aleworks. He also worked for a time at Great Basin in Nevada, at the now defunct Sacramento Brewing Company, and for six months at Mt. Shasta Brewing in Weed.

He later took some time off from brewing and worked as a ski instructor in the winter and a fly fishing guide in the summer. It was during this time that he fell in love with the town of Dunsmuir and the surrounding area, and a plan began to take shape in his mind.

Greener mentioned his idea to open a brewery to his good friend and supervisor at the ski park, David Clarno, who had experience bartending and confessed that he had just told his wife he wanted to open his own place. It also turned out that the water in Dunsmuir was perfect for brewing beer. So the pair became partners and together opened the Dunsmuir Brewery Works in late 2009.

They found the perfect building downtown on the corner of Dunsmuir Avenue and Spruce Street, just off I-5 via the Dunsmuir exit. It was originally a gas station constructed in 1923, but additions had been built in the 1960s. Once you know that, the outside of the building makes more sense. They bought a brewhouse that had been used in a brewery in Ontario, shipping it down from north of the Great Lakes.

What was once the covered entrance to the gas station is now the private door to the brewery. The public way in is through the outdoor patio, a

Beers brewed: Year-round: OsoLicious Porter, West Coast ESB, Blood Sweat & Tears IPA, Rusty Spike Imperial Red Ale, Double Hop Bomb IPA, and Down Canyon Stout. Seasonals: Oktoberfest and Winter Spiced Ale.

The Pick: Not all of the beers were on tap when I visited Dunsmuir, but of the ones I tried, I very much enjoyed the OsoLicious Porter. The nose is pitted fruit and milk chocolate, which carries into the flavors too. There's also a touch of roasted malt character and cola nut, with a dry finish.

fenced-in area to your left with several tables and chairs shaded by umbrellas and some surrounding trees. A sign hangs by the opening, announcing that this is a microbrewery, restaurant, and pub.

Inside, it feels like a cozy home, with a handmade bar to your right and tables and chairs in an open space. Above the bar, brewery T-shirts and hats are displayed on a clothesline. The open kitchen is along another wall, perpendicular to the bar, with a second bar where you can sit and eat or drink. A hallway leads to the back, where there are restrooms and another way to get to the brewery. The brewery is located out of sight, although it can be seen through the double doors next to the bar. But if you're outside, around the side, the old roll-up garage door is usually open when the weather's nice, revealing the brewhouse.

The food is tasty, and although you might expect simple diner food, it's much better than that. The same is true of the beer, making the Dunsmuir Brewery Works something of a hidden gem, just out of sight along California's main interstate, which runs parallel to the Pacific Ocean from Mexico to Washington. If you're smart, you'll duck off the exit for a beer here.

Dunsmuir Brewery Works

Opened: December 18, 2009.

Type: Brewpub.

Owners: Aaron Greener and David Clarno.

Brewer: Aaron Greener.

System: 10-hectoliter Pacific Brewing, 240 barrels annual capacity, though planned upgrades in the near future should increase that to around 1,400 barrels.

Annual production: 190 barrels (2012).

Packages available: Growlers, bombers, and kegs.

Tours: Brewery tours are available if the brewer is around, although often one of the bartenders can also give a tour, so your best bet is to ask.

Hours: Tuesday through Sunday, 11 a.m. to 9 p.m. Closed Monday.

Food: The brewpub has a small but well-chosen menu of American cuisine. With starters like Brewery Beer-Cheese Bread, salads in full or half sizes, vegetarian offerings, and entrées such as half-pound burgers, tacos, Memphis-style pulled pork, and smoked bratwurst, you'll easily be able to find something to satisfy any craving.

Extras: Live music performances take place at the brewpub from time to time. Check the Facebook page for details on these and other special events. The brewery also brews its own root beer and stocks several guest beers on draft.

Gift shop: Hats, T-shirts, sweaters, and tie-died shirts (a former business and hobby of Aaron Greener) are available at the brewpub.

Etna Brewing Company

131 Callahan Street, Etna, CA 96027
530-467-5277 • www.etnabrew.net
Facebook.com/pages/Etna-Brewing-Company/
176111962468609

Founded by German native Charles Kappler, the original Etna Brewery opened in 1872 and thrived for a number of years before Prohibition forced its closure in 1919. After Prohibition was repealed, the brewery did not reopen, like many of the breweries shuttered by the Eighteenth Amendment.

More than fifty years after the Twenty-First Amendment ended Prohibition, in 1987, the stepson of one of Kappler's descendants, local rancher Andrew Hurlimann, bought the property and built a new brewery, reopening it as a microbrewery in 1990. Hurlimann even based his new labels on the 1915 label for the award-winning Export Lager, which is the same year the brewery won a gold medal at the Pan Pacific International Exposition in San Francisco.

In May 2001, local farmer and mechanical engineer Dave Krell and his wife, Marilyn, a former bank administrator, bought the brewery from Hurlimann. They opened the current pub two months later. Shortly thereafter, they hired Bill Behm as head brewer, and he's been making some terrific beers there ever since.

The brewery is down a short hill near the beginning of the downtown area. Kappler's original brewery from the nineteenth century is across the street from the present site, and a modern house now occupies the space where the brewing used to be done. The present brewery is located where the original bottling works were in the 1870s.

The restaurant serves a full menu of really good and filling food, with lots of choices. In addition to the four beers the brewery bottles, there

Beers brewed: Year-round: Classic Gold Ale, Phoenix Red, Blackberry Blonde, Old Grind Porter, Mossback IPA, Kappler Imperial Stout, and Grubstake Stout. Seasonals: Clubfoot Ale, Deadwood Dunkel, Double Barrel Bock, Dredger Dry, Export Lager, Holy Hefe, Marble Mountain Marzen, Pig Alley Pilsner, Ridge Runner Ruby, and Sno-Wooki Stout.

The Pick: The Old Grind Porter, made with nine different malts, is a really terrific dark ale that's sweet with nutty, caramel notes. It's thin-bodied, full-flavored, and nice and refreshing. If you're in the mood for something fruity, the Blackberry Blonde uses an uncommon brewing fruit to great advantage. Should you be craving something hoppy, the Mossback IPA is quite tasty.

are a number of brewpub-only, seasonal, and one-off beers. On warm days, you can sit outside on the small patio. Inside, the small brewpub has a long bar and several tables. The walls are covered with historic photos of the town and the brewery. One window overlooks the brewery down below.

The tiny town of Etna, population 737 in the 2010 census, has to be one of the most remote towns with a brewery in all of Northern California. It's not along any well-traveled route, nor is it near any of the usual tourist destinations. But don't let that deter you; it is worth the trouble to get there. Visiting the town is like stepping back in time, and there's a modest downtown shopping area lined with several shops and places to eat. If you're looking for the best time to visit, the town hosts the Scotts Valley Bluegrass Festival in mid-July. It may take you some time to get to Etna, but you'll be glad you came.

Etna Brewing Company

Opened: The original brewery opened in 1872; the microbrewery reopened in May 1990; the current brewpub opened July 2001.

Type: Brewpub.

Owners: Dave and Marilyn Krell.

Brewer: Bill Behm.

Guild membership: BA, CCBA.

Annual production: 500 barrels (2011 estimate).

Packages available: 22-ounce bottles and kegs.

Tours: Formal tours are not available, but ask to take a peek at the brewery, which is downstairs from the pub. As long as the brewer's not too busy that day, he'll do his best to accommodate you.

Hours: Tuesday, 11:30 a.m. to 4 p.m.; Wednesday and Thursday, 11:30 a.m. to 8 p.m.; Friday and Saturday, 11:30 a.m. to 9 p.m.; Sunday, 11:30 a.m. to 4 p.m. Closed Monday.

Food: The pub menu has a surprisingly large number of tasty items, from sandwiches, wraps, and burgers to salads, soups, and chili, as well as a selection of vegetarian dishes. On Friday and Saturday, you can get "smokehouse dinners" of beef or pork tri-tip or chicken breast. There's also a separate kids' menu.

Extras: On select evenings, often Saturdays and holidays, the pub features live music; check the Facebook page for details on upcoming events.

Gift shop: Merchandise and bottles of four of the brewery's beers are available at the brewpub.

Feather Falls Casino Brewing Company

FEATHER FALLS CASINO

3 Alverda Drive, Oroville, CA 95966
530-533-3885
www.featherfallscasino.com/brewing-co
Twitter @FeatherFalls
Facebook.com/pages/Feather-Falls-
Brewing-Company/120371337986093

The Feather Falls Casino was opened in the town of Oroville in June 1996 by the Mooretown Rancheria of Maidu Indians of California, a federally recognized tribe of Concow and Maidu people in Butte County. The Concow (sometimes spelled Konkow) people are the northwestern branch of the Maidu, whose language is traditionally Concow. The tribe owns and operates the Feather Falls Casino, the Feather Falls Casino Brewing Company, the Lodge at Feather Falls Casino, a KOA Kampground, Feather Falls Mini Mart, and the Feather Falls Smoke Shop.

The casino has slot machines, table and poker games, four restaurants, and a hotel. The gaming areas are open twenty-four hours a day, though the brewpub is not. The whole facility is over 118,000 square feet, of which the brewpub occupies nearly 25,000, including the brewery, restaurant, lounge, and showroom. It's an impressively grand space that underwent an extensive remodeling in 2010, with a brand new gleaming stainless steel brewhouse, outdoor patio dining, and a lounge area.

The brewpub is larger than most, with a huge curved bar. As you'd expect, there are slot machines and video poker games at most of the bar seats and other seating throughout. From one side of the bar, you can see into the brewery behind a plate-glass window that runs the length of the wall behind the bar. There's a stage for live performances and lots and lots of comfortable seating.

After a consultant built the brewery, Roland Allen was hired as brewmaster, and he's been brewing there since the very beginning. Allen

Beers brewed: Year-round: Soaring Eagle Pilsner, Dancing Trees Hefeweizen, Coyote Spirit Amber Ale, Feather Falls Thunder Apricot Wheat Ale, Mooretown Pale Ale, Naughty Native IPA, and Blackjack Brew Sweet Stout. Seasonals: Obsidian Blackberry Porter, Roland's Ed, Slam Dunkel German Style Dark Lager, Oktoberfest Marzen, I'll Be Bock, Seasons Cranberry Ale, Sticky Bee Honey Wheat Ale, Snake Eyes Double IPA, Squirrel Tail Brown Ale, Golden Feather Extra Pale Ale, and Wild Bill Winter Bock.

The Pick: All of the beers are solid, but I quite like the Mooretown Pale Ale, a really tasty pale with good hops character, restrained but ever present. It's chewy and sticky in the best possible way, a satisfying beer.

worked at Sierra Nevada Brewing for nearly a decade, beginning in 1986. He left to start his own brewery, Butte Creek Brewing, in 1995, but took some time off from brewing in the mid-2000s. His longtime experience shows, as he's making a nice range of beers, from standard ales and lagers to more extreme big beers and seasonals. If you have an itch to play some cards or pull on some slot machines, you may as well have some good beer while you're at it. Oroville may be a little off the beaten path, but with inexpensive rooms right there at the brewpub, a weekend trip is a great idea.

Feather Falls Casino Brewing Company

Opened: December 10, 2010.

Type: Brewpub.

Owners: The Mooretown Rancheria of Maidu Indians of California.

Brewer: Roland Allen.

Guild membership: BA.

System: 15-barrel Specific Mechanical Systems direct fire brewhouse, 900 barrels annual capacity.

Annual production: 900 barrels (2012).

Packages available: Growlers and draft at the brewpub.

Tours: No tours, but you can see the brewery behind large glass windows behind the bar.

Restaurant hours: Monday through Wednesday, 11 a.m. to 10 p.m.; Thursday through Saturday, 11 a.m. to 1 a.m.; Sunday, 11 a.m. to 10 p.m. Bar: Sunday through Tuesday, 9 a.m. to midnight; Wednesday through Saturday, 9 a.m. to 1:30 a.m.

Food: The brewpub menu is an impressive book, with a full page each devoted to appetizers, soups and salads, enticing entrées, pizza and pastas, burgers and sandwiches, sushi, and tempting desserts. With big portions, reasonable prices, pairing suggestions, and tasty choices, it's hard to go wrong no matter what you order.

Extras: On Tightwad Tuesday, the brewpub features a "Two for Twenty" special: for $20, two people receive one appetizer, two entrées, and a dessert to share. Every Friday and Saturday, live music is performed in the bar; there's a $5 cover charge, which includes one drink. The brewpub also hosts beer dinners and events for the release of new beers. Check the website for details.

Gift shop: T-shirts are available at the casino brewpub.

Feather River Brewing Company

14665 Forest Ridge Road, Magalia, CA 95954
530-873-0734 • www.featherriverbrewing.com

Roger Preecs had been homebrewing for a quarter century before he decided to open Feather River Brewing Company. On his rural property in Magalia, he built all the equipment to his exact specifications, using the skills he'd acquired in previous jobs as a metal fabricator, in building construction, and in a ceramic works.

The Feather River, the brewery's namesake, is the principal tributary for the Sacramento River, and the brewery is near the river's western branch. It's about a thirty-minute drive from Chico, nestled in the foothills of the Sierra Nevada. To get to the brewery, you'll need an accurate GPS, as the road weaves through a wooded area and the last few miles are dirt and gravel. Road signs are nailed to trees. Expect to make a few wrong turns. Despite the listed open hours, it's best to call or email ahead if you're going to visit the brewery.

The brewery is in a separate building behind the main house where owner and brewer Roger Preecs makes his home. The grounds around the home also include a circular area designed for outdoor events as well as a makeshift outdoor movie screen, although few events take place there now. It's tempting to think of the brewery as a garage, but it's bigger than that, although it has a roll-up door. Because all of the equipment was built by Preecs, it doesn't look like any other brewery you'll ever visit. But of course, it's perfectly suited to the way he wants to make his beer.

Even in that, Preecs is an individual, as he told me he believes most microbreweries are wrong to use as much hops as they do. Most beer sold in the United States, he reminds me, is sweet and very low in hops. It's no wonder small breweries account for only 5 percent of the total, he muses. So Feather River's goal is to make high-quality, unfiltered, small-batch beer that competes with the big brewers, favoring sweet and smooth over harsh and bitter.

Beers brewed: Year-round: Honey Ale and Raging Rapids Ale. Seasonal: Dark Canyon Ale (winter).

The Pick: The Honey Ale is as sweet as its name, though it's nicely restrained, so it has just a touch of honey, with fruity, jamlike notes and a dry finish. It's a nice alternative for a hot day or if you want something refreshing.

None of his three beers is very hoppy in the least, as you'd expect, but judging from some of his accolades, they are popular with beer drinkers. For example, at the California Festival of Beers in San Luis Obispo, Feather River won the People's Choice Award in both 2002 and 2003. You can find Feather River beer on tap in and around the Magalia area, as well as in 22-ounce bottles at local retailers.

Feather River Brewing Company

Opened: 2000.

Type: Production brewery.

Owner: Roger Preecs.

Brewer: Roger Preecs.

System: 14-barrel custom-built brewhouse, 300 barrels annual capacity.

Annual production: 300 barrels.

Packages available: 22-ounce bottles and 5- and 15.5-gallon kegs.

Tours: Yes, but reservations are required.

Hours: Monday through Friday, 8 a.m. to 5 p.m., but it's best to call or email before making the drive to this rather remote location.

Extras: Kids are permitted, as is cigar smoking.

Gift shop: T-shirts and sweatshirts are available online.

Great Sex Brewing Company

12763 Encanto Way, Redding, CA 96003
530-275-2705 (Jeff Talbot) /
970-949-1107 (Doug Talbot)
www.greatSEXbrewing.com
Facebook.com/pages/Great-Sex-Brewing-Company/
91043003068

The Great Sex Brewing Company is the brainchild of two brothers, Jeff and Doug Talbot. The initial plan was for Doug to open a brewery in a historic building in his hometown of Vail, Colorado. Things fell apart with that plan, however, and Jeff joined his brother in opening the company in Redding instead.

As they're fond of saying, Great Sex has been around since the turn of the century, as they incorporated in January 2000. The original brewing was done at Beermann's Beerworks, which is now closed, so they've since changed their contract brewer and are currently looking for their own space.

They produce just one beer, Adam & Eve Ale, essentially similar to an amber or pale ale, which is available in six-packs. Using provocative packaging and clever tongue-in-cheek language, Great Sex is a playful beer aimed at a mainstream customer.

Great Sex Brewing Company

Opened: January 26, 2000.

Type: Contract brewery.

Owners: Jeff and Doug Talbot.

Guild membership: BA.

Packages available: 12-ounce bottles in six-packs and 15.5-gallon kegs.

Gift shop: T-shirts, hoodies, and hats are available online.

Beers brewed: Adam & Eve Ale.

The Pick: The Adam & Eve is a sweet, malt-forward beer with restrained hops character. There are fruit aromas, possibly apples—or is that the power of suggestion?—and some subtle spicing with caramel malt flavors and a dry, sweet finish with a touch of sourness.

Lassen Ale Works at the Pioneer Saloon

724 Main Street, Susanville, CA 96130
530-257-7666 • www.lassenaleworks.com
Twitter @LassenAleWorks • Facebook.com/pages/Lassen-
 Ale-Works-at-the-Pioneer-Saloon/282520181780671

Susanville is a historic town in, quite frankly, the middle of nowhere. Well, maybe not exactly the middle of nowhere, but I swear you can see it from there. The town got its present name in 1857, but it existed long before that as a logging and mining town. With around eighteen thousand residents, Susanville is the Lassen County seat and has the county's largest population by a country mile; fully half the county lives there, along the Susan River. The next largest town has about 10 percent of Susanville's population. But it's no easy task to get there. The biggest roads in and out of town are two-lane blacktops, State Routes 36 and 139, and none of them are what you'd call straight or flat. Downtown is a good five-hour drive from San Francisco.

But once you're there, you may not want to leave, especially if you prefer to get away from the hustle and bustle of modern civilization. Downtown Susanville—or more specifically, the historic Uptown neighborhood—looks almost unchanged from the late 1800s, when it must have been as wild a western town as any.

The Pioneer Saloon first opened in 1862 as the Humboldt Exchange but changed its name to the Pioneer the following year. In the 150 years since it first opened, it has also been home to a barbershop, bank, tobacconist shop and liquor store, snooker and pool hall, card room, dart league, outdoor beer garden, and dance hall. Last year it became home to Lassen County's only brewery, Lassen Ale Works.

Outside, a big neon marquee sign shines brightly at night, announcing it as the Pioneer Café. "Home of Lassen Ale Works" is on the front windows, revealing what else you'll find. The entire inside was modernized and cleaned up, although

Beers brewed: Year-round: Bizz Johnson Blonde Ale, Almanor Amber Ale, Rooptown Red Ale, Eagle Lake IPA, Uptown Brown Ale, and Pioneer Porter. Seasonals: Off-the-Scale Barleywine, Devil's Corral Imperial Stout, Oktoberfest Lager, and Dry Hopped Eagle Lake IPA.

The Pick: I like the Rooptown Red best. It's a nice, easy-drinking beer with a bready malt nose and good hops aromas. It's creamy, mild, and refreshing, showing great balance, with clean malt flavors and just the right touch of spicy hops character, especially in the tangy finish.

the brewery retained the best of the original features. One of the coolest is the wall above the bar, which is directly to your right when you enter the saloon and is covered in hand-painted ranch brands from all over the area. The wall also includes the brand of Bing Crosby's ranch, which was in Elko, Nevada, but the actor and crooner apparently "bribed" the bartender to put his brand on the wall too. The bar itself, at 36 feet, is one of the longest I've ever seen.

The backroom is a large, open dining room, and there are pool tables and shuffleboard back there too. A large mural showing scenes from local history runs the entire length of the top half of the wall on the back and right. On the left wall, a series of large windows reveals the brewery behind them. When brewer Erik Jefferts is there, you can watch him going about his business.

Jefferts is a veteran brewer, having started out brewing in his hometown of Seattle at the Big Time Brewery. He was later a partner and brewer at Phantom Canyon Brewing in Colorado, a project that included now governor John Hickenlooper, who also cofounded the Wynkoop brewpub, where Jefferts did some brewery consulting.

At Lassen Ale Works, Jefferts has six well-chosen regular beers, along with a rotating series of seasonal offerings that he's just beginning to develop. I really like the mix of a shiny, gleaming new brewhouse in such an old, historic setting. It really is the best of both worlds.

Lassen Ale Works at the Pioneer Saloon

Opened: May 25, 2012.

Type: Brewpub.

Owners: Margaret Liddiard, Erik Jefferts, Julie Howard, and Mark Pfenning.

Brewer: Erik Jefferts.

Guild membership: BA, CCBA.

System: 10-barrel MetalCraft Fabricators brewhouse, 500 barrels annual capacity.

Annual production: 400 barrels (first-year estimate).

Packages available: Growlers and 5- and 15.5-gallon kegs.

Tours: Brewery tours are available any time the brewer is around.

Hours: Sunday through Thursday, 11 a.m. to 10 p.m.; Friday and Saturday, 11 a.m. to 11 p.m.

Food: The small but well-appointed menu includes tasty appetizers, soups and salads, burgers and sandwiches, and entrées such as Basque lamb stew and Pioneer Porter Bratwurst.

Extras: Pool tables and shuffleboard, and the barbershop is still there, should you need a haircut while you're waiting for your food.

Gift shop: Merchandise is available at the brewpub.

Mt. Shasta Brewing Company

360 College Avenue, Weed, CA 96094
530-938-2394 / 800-WEED-ALE (9333-253)
www.weedales.com
Twitter @mtshastabrewing
Facebook.com/weedales

Owner and founder Vaune Dillmann has beer in his blood. The son of German and Polish immigrants whose ancestors had been in the brewing business, he grew up in Milwaukee in the shadow of Pabst, Blatz, Schlitz, Hamm's, and the Miller Brewing Company. After college, he moved to California and became a decorated police officer with the city of Oakland. Dillmann's wife, Barbara Mazzini, on the other hand, grew up in Weed, and her ancestors were Siskiyou County pioneers. After they married, she persuaded Vaune to give up police work, and the couple moved to Weed, in the shadow of Mount Shasta.

Dillmann's next projects were remodeling Weed's notorious Black Butte Saloon, their ranch house, and many other area homes and businesses. In 1988, he completed rebuilding the famous Weed Arch (a structure that stretches across the street at the entrance to town), a project that took seven years to finish. During this time, Dillmann became enamored with microbrewing and started visiting breweries around the country and the world, which led to a new passion.

In 1992, he purchased the ailing Medo-Bel Creamery, which had been built forty years earlier. He set to work remodeling it into a brewery, a task that dragged on for a dozen years, but by 2002, Mt. Shasta was ready to start brewing. Dillmann approached the Zwanziger family, who were descendants of the man who founded the town, Abner Weed, and obtained permission to use the name in the brewery's first beer, Weed Golden Ale. It paid homage to him with its second beer, Abner

Beers brewed: Year-round: Weed Golden Ale, Mountain High IPA, Shastafarian Porter, Lemurian Lager, Abner Weed Amber Ale, and Jalapeno Weed Ale. Seasonals: Hempeweizen, 530 Belgian Pale Ale, Extraterrestrial Weed, Brewers Cherry Kriek, Stout of Jefferson Imperial Stout, Brewers Creek Trappist Ale, Burnt Roach, and Skip and Go Naked Strawberry Ginger Beer.

The Pick: The Shastafarian Porter is a really smooth porter, with aromas of sweet vanilla and especially chocolate, along with some espresso coffee notes. With mild coffee flavors, the bittersweet chocolate really shines, and the mouthfeel is chewier and more full-bodied than with the average porter.

Weed Amber Ale. The brewery finally opened in 2004 and began bottling its beer the next year.

In 2008, with things going well with the business, Mt. Shasta Brewing ran into another roadblock when the Alcohol and Tobacco Tax and Trade Bureau (TTB) refused to approve one of its beers because the crown had "Try Legal Weed" printed on it and demanded that the phrase be removed. The brewery's appeal was initially denied, and the government refused to change its decision. It became a national story, and the brewery received support from a broad range of people and organizations, including local politicians in Washington, D.C., who sent letters asking the TTB to reexamine the application. After considering that Weed was the name of the town and the town's founder, and that asking people to drink the beer was the opposite of encouraging drug use, the TTB lifted the ban and allowed "Try Legal Weed" to be printed on all of the brewery's bottle caps.

The building that houses the brewpub is quite large and includes the brewery, office space, meeting and event spaces, and a number of other rooms. Upstairs, there's a large space for events with a balcony overlooking part of the town, a dance floor, old-style booths, and a pool table. Downstairs, there's the bottling room, both breweries, a ballroom, and other rooms. The brewpub space has an old bar along the far wall and is open to the outside on warm days, when the roll-up is thrown open. Everywhere you look, you'll see knick-knacks, curios, and unique pieces of history and art, many rescued or created by Vaune Dillmann. The whole building has the feel of a museum, but with the only theme being fun—it essentially includes anything that Dillmann thought was interesting.

The town of Weed is in one of the northernmost counties in California, bordering Oregon, and it's fairly small, with fewer than three thousand residents. But if you're in this part of the state, you should definitely make it a point to visit Weed and the Mt. Shasta Brewing Company. As the label on every bottle of Mt. Shasta beer promises, "A friend in Weed is a friend indeed."

Mt. Shasta Brewing Company

Opened: 2004 (first batch of beer brewed in 2002).
Type: Production brewery and brewpub.
Owner: Vaune Dillmann.
Brewer: Marco Noriega.
Guild membership: NCBG.

System: 15-barrel Pub Brewing system, 1,400 barrels annual capacity; production brewery: 30-barrel copper brewhouse originally from Ulm, Germany.

Annual production: 800 barrels (2012 estimate).

Packages available: 12-ounce bottles in six-packs, 22-ounce bottles, growlers, and kegs.

Tours: No tours, but you can get a peek at the brewery from the entrance next to the bar.

Hours: Alehouse: Seven days a week, noon to closing time, which is often 11 p.m., but call first, as this changes seasonally and also depends on how busy the place is. Brewery: Monday through Friday, 9 a.m. to 1 p.m.

Food: The bistro has a small but well-chosen collection of appetizers, grilled wraps, flatbread pizza, soups, chili, panini, burgers, and sandwiches. Regardless of how long the brewpub stays open, the kitchen closes at 7 p.m.

Extras: On BrewGrass Thursday, live bluegrass music is performed by local musicians at the brewpub beginning at 7 p.m. Tuesday is trivia night beginning at 4 p.m. In addition, there are other special events and musical performances from time to time. Check the website or Facebook page for more information.

Gift shop: An extensive selection of merchandise is available at the brewpub and online.

Sierra Nevada Brewing Company

1075 East 20th Street, Chico, CA 95928
530-893-3520 • www.sierranevada.com
Twitter @sierranevada
Facebook.com/SierraNevadaBeer /
   Facebook.com/SierraNevadaTaproom

Sierra Nevada Brewing Company is California's largest craft brewery and also one of its oldest. Ken Grossman grew up in Southern California, and he and his brother Steve became homebrewers at a tender age. They learned brewing from Ken's best friend's father, in part so they'd stop drinking his homebrew. Grossman made his first batch of homebrew in 1969 or 1970 and used Blue Ribbon malt extract. He also tried his hand at winemaking, though the recipe called for Welch's grape juice and apparently didn't taste terribly good.

A lifelong cycling enthusiast, Grossman took a camping trip by bike down the coast of Northern California, detouring inland at one point to visit Chico to visit some friends at the university, and fell in the love with the area. After moving to Chico, he got a degree from the university in chemistry and physics, all the while continuing to homebrew. After college, he opened a homebrew supply store.

He and a homebrewing friend, Paul Camusi, were both becoming more and more obsessive about brewing and decided to open their own small brewery. The pair had visited both Anchor Brewing and Jack McAuliffe's New Albion, which convinced them that it could be done. After seeing McAuliffe's handmade brewhouse, Grossman enrolled at the local community college and took welding, refrigeration, electrical wiring, and other classes to learn how to build his own brewery, a 10-barrel brewhouse that he constructed from discarded dairy equipment and other scraps. The name came from Ken's favorite place to take a hike in the area, the nearby Sierra Nevada range.

By 1980, the brewery was up and running. The first test batch brewed on the new custom-made system was Sierra Nevada Stout, a beer the brewery still makes using essentially the same recipe. The second beer was the now famous Pale Ale. Grossman wanted a hops-forward beer and wanted it to taste a certain way. He dumped the first ten batches until he found just the right flavors he was looking for. It would be tempting to say it was an immediate hit, but while it sold reasonably well, the brewery had just gotten started in a brave new world where flavorful beers with big hops character was not yet the norm.

The following year, Sierra Nevada introduced its holiday ale, Celebration Ale, using fresh hops. Two years later, in 1983, it made the first batch of Bigfoot Barleywine Style Ale, one of the modern brewing world's first extreme beers, at almost 10 percent ABV and calculated IBUs of 100. Things at the brewery were starting to click, and Grossman knew he'd soon have to expand. That same year, homebrewer Steve Dresler was hired, and he's now the brewmaster, a position he's held for many years. He's also a big reason for Sierra Nevada's success and continues to direct the day-to-day business of brewing all of the beer.

Hearing about a used copper brewhouse for sale in Germany, Grossman traveled there, bought the 120-barrel brewhouse, and dismantled it to be shipped back to Chico. It would be five years before he had a place to put it back together. In 1987, Sierra Nevada bought the land on 20th Street where the brewery is located today and began construction on a new building. It took two more years, but in 1989, the bigger brewery went online and the taproom restaurant opened. Sierra Nevada also brewed its first lager that same year.

The brewery's second decade was marked by a number of milestones and firsts. In 1993, brewmaster Steve Dresler made the first fresh hops beer, using hops freshly picked from the fields, unkilned, to brew his Harvest Ale. Today Sierra Nevada makes this ale in two versions—one from the Northern Hemisphere, using hops grown by the brewery in Chico, and another from the Southern Hemisphere, using hops freshly picked in New Zealand and airlifted back to Chico.

That same year, production hit 100,000 barrels a year, meaning expansion would again be necessary to keep up with demand. So Sierra Nevada installed a brand new 200-barrel Huppmann brewhouse in 1997 and expanded the cellar to accommodate considerably more fermenters. Grossman

Beers brewed: Year-round: Pale Ale, Torpedo Extra IPA, Kellerweis, Porter, and Stout. Seasonals: Ruthless Rye IPA (January–March), Summerfest Summer Lager (April–June), Tumbler Autumn Brown Ale (July–September), Celebration Ale (October–December), Bigfoot Barleywine Style Ale (January–April), Hoptimum Imperial Whole-Cone IPA (May–August), Northern Hemisphere Harvest Ale (September), Southern Hemisphere Harvest Ale (May), and Estate Homegrown Ale (August). Other seasonal or specialty releases: Narwhal Imperial Stout, Old Chico Crystal Wheat, Barrel Aged Bigfoot, Wood Aged Celebration, Bourbon Barrel Aged Imperial Smoked Porter, Whiskey Barrel Aged Celebration, Schwarzbier, Bourbon Barrel Aged Brewer's Reserve Grand Cru, and many more. Ovila Abbey Ales Series: Golden, Saison, Dubbel, Quad, and Quad with Sugar Plums. Other specialty series: The Beer Camp Variety Pack and the 30th Anniversary Series (no longer being brewed but aging nicely if you can find one). Collaborations: Life & Limb (with Dogfish Head) and BRUX Domesticated Wild Ale (with Russian River).

also persuaded the coppersmiths who'd built the brewhouse he had earlier shipped from Germany to come out of retirement to match the new kettles by building the copper shell for the brewery.

The new century brought yet more changes to Sierra Nevada, as growth continued and the brewery worked hard to keep up. In 2000, a 350-seat concert venue called the Big Room opened, and it quickly became a hot spot for local music performances and special events. In 2004, the brewery installed 250-kilowatt cogeneration hydrogen fuel cells and hired a dedicated employee to work on keeping the brewery environmentally sound and sustainable.

The following year, a third brewhouse was constructed, but this one was decidedly smaller, a pilot system for R&D, experimentation, and small-batch limited releases. Sierra Nevada also opened a state-of-the-art lab with several components to focus on the science of brewing and quality control. At this time, the brewery began adding solar panels, which eventually led to its creating the largest private solar array in the United States.

Sierra Nevada Beer Camp was launched in 2008, providing a one-of-a-kind experience for lucky attendees. Over two days, beer campers design and brew their own small batch of beer. So far, more than a hundred beer camps have been held, with campers creating countless new beers, some of which have gone on to be made commercially. Some of the best ones are included in a Beer Camp Variety Pack that's for sale at the brewery and select retailers.

Celebrating its thirtieth anniversary in 2010, the brewery collaborated with four brewing legends, Fritz Maytag, Jack McAuliffe, Charlie Papazian, and Fred Eckhardt, to create a big beer with each one. Sierra Nevada also began using a device called the Hop Torpedo, created to infuse the beers with intense hops aromas. The brewery followed that by debuting its beer in cans. It also recently partnered with a nearby monastery, the

The Pick: Sierra Nevada continues to brew an amazing number of world-class beers, and choosing just one is a fool's errand. The brewery made its reputation on the strength of the Pale Ale, which essentially created the American Pale Ale, distancing it and other, similar beers from their English counterparts. It's quite surprising how fresh Sierra Nevada's Pale Ale still tastes, more than thirty years later. It's still my go-to beer in many bars that don't stock better beer. But for a hops monster, you can't beat the more recent Hoptimum, an insanely hoppy beer that was originally brewed during one of the brewery's famous Beer Camps. As great a beer as it is for hopheads, it's the malt balance that makes it such a great example of an imperial IPA. The hops are intense, with complex aromas of all manner of descriptors—everything from soup to nuts, flowers to grapefruit, onions to tropical fruit, and on and on. The flavors are equally commanding, with a chewy, thick mouthfeel and near perfect balance. Other beers not to be missed include the annual seasonal Bigfoot and the Christmastime Celebration, both of which are mandatory in their respective seasons.

Abbey of New Clairvaux in Vina, to create the Ovila Abbey Ales, a series of Belgian-inspired beers.

Sierra Nevada is currently building a second brewery near Asheville, North Carolina, which is expected to open in the fall of 2014. The new facility is on a 190-acre tract of land on the French Broad River. Sierra Nevada plans to keep most of the surrounding land intact and wild, with a trail system that will include access to the river.

Perhaps the best analogy for visiting the Sierra Nevada Brewery in Chico is that it's like Disneyland for beer lovers. No matter how many breweries you've visited, large or small, near or far, you can't visit there and walk away without having been changed by the experience. It's such an impressive place, and Sierra Nevada has managed to do virtually everything right. It's beautiful to look at, with artistic tiles, glass, and copper. It's also incredibly functional, with every detail meticulously thought out, although Sierra Nevada is continuously trying to improve.

The brewery tour focuses not only on the massively efficient brewing equipment, but also on all the steps the brewery has taken to be increasingly sustainable and lower its footprint. It's one of the greenest breweries you'll ever see. It also grows its own hops, some of which can be seen in a small field adjacent to the taproom, on the other side of the parking lot, and has planted some of its own barley too, though this is some distance from the brewery.

The taproom is a terrific spot, and at any other destination, this would be quite enough to recommend it. As it is, it's just one more part of the Sierra Nevada Beerland experience. Behind the great wooden bar, you'll find a number of experimental, beer camp, and other exclusive beers that can be found only right there at the brewery. All of the food is very well done, a cut above what's served in the average brewpub, and although the menu changes frequently, there are some core items you can always find on it. Executive chef Michael Iles has been in charge of the food for many years and has kept it as consistent and high quality as Sierra Nevada's beer. Most nights, the taproom is a crowded with a mix of locals and beer tourists.

Sierra Nevada Brewing is without question one of the jewels in the Northern California brewery crown. It has set the standard for quality, which has been emulated by breweries around the country. And it helped spark an interest for better beer, which led to the current explosion in craft breweries that shows no signs of slowing. But more than simply being an inspiration or a pioneer, Sierra Nevada has not rested on its laurels but continues to lead and innovate in the beer industry; both in brewing technology and in the beers it creates.

Sierra Nevada Brewing Company

Opened: November 15, 1980.

Type: Production brewery, with restaurant taproom.

Owners: Ken Grossman.

Brewer: Steve Dresler.

Guild membership: BA, BI, CCBA, NCBG.

System: 100-barrel Huppmann steam direct-fired system; 200-barrel Huppmann Calandria system; 10-barrel Huppmann pilot system; Mueller, Huppmann, and Zieman tanks and controls; 1,000,000 barrels annual capacity.

Annual production: 925,000 barrels (2012 estimate).

Packages available: 12-ounce bottles in six-, twelve-, and twenty-four-packs; 24-ounce bottles; 12- and 16-ounce cans; 375- and 750-milliliter bottles; growlers (at the taproom); casks (firkins and pins); and 5- and 15.5-gallon kegs.

Tours: Monday through Thursday, noon, 1, 2, and 4 p.m.; Friday and Saturday, hourly from noon to 5 p.m.; Sunday, hourly from noon to 4 p.m. Call or email tours@sierra nevada.com for special beer geek and sustainability tours. Reservations are not necessary but strongly suggested.

Hours: Taproom and restaurant: Sunday through Thursday, 11 a.m. to 9 p.m.; Friday and Saturday, 11 a.m. to 10 p.m.

Food: The cuisine at the restaurant is new American beer-centered food. The menu changes monthly, and in the summer it features a lot of produce directly from the organic estate gardens on-site at the brewery. There's a good selection of starters, soups and salads, burgers and sandwiches, wood-fired pizza, and large platters such as pork schnitzel, Thai seafood curry, and free-range chicken pot pie. There's also a separate kids' menu and a selection of desserts, like deconstructed banana split.

Extras: Sierra Nevada hosts several on-site festivals each year, as well as two or three musical acts each month in the performance theater, the Big Room, which is upstairs above the gift shop. The schedule of upcoming shows can be found on the website.

Gift shop: A large, separate gift shop is located at the brewery, a few doors down from the entrance to the restaurant taproom. In addition to packaged beer, it carries an extensive array of glassware, gifts, clothing, hats, neon signs, and much more. There's also an online store.

Western Pacific Brewing & Dining

2191 High Street, Oroville, CA 95965
530-534-9101 • westernpacificbrewing.blogspot.com
Twitter @westernpacific
Facebook.com/WesternPacificBrewing

In Spanish, "oro" means gold, and the Butte County seat of Oroville, the "City of Gold," is part of one of the original areas where gold was discovered. Nearby Bidwell Bar was one of the first settlements where gold was found, and Oroville's proximity to the Feather River ensured its place in gold rush history. The Western Pacific Railroad built the Feather Canyon route in the early twentieth century, and the Oroville station became an important stop for the famous California Zephyr train.

The brewery and dining establishment is located, as you'd expect given its name, in an old Western Pacific train depot, appropriately called the Old Depot or sometimes the Old Western Pacific Depot. After the station closed in 1970, the building lay unused until 1977, when David Deakins and his father, along with local winemaker Gary Quilici, refurbished the building and opened it as a steak restaurant, known simply as the Depot. Around the back, by the parking lot, there's a red caboose.

In 2008, when Deakins's father passed away and Quilici was looking to spend more time in his vineyards, Deakins became sole owner and made some significant changes to the restaurant, the biggest of which was adding a brewery and renaming it Western Pacific Brewing and Dining. The Old Depot and the brewery were operating separately until mid-2012, when the steakhouse closed and the brewery began serving its own food.

Inside the former train station, there are reminders everywhere of the building's history, with old photographs of trains gracing the walls; the railroad heritage is also reflected in the names of the beers. The center of the old station features a large, U-shaped wooden bar. The brewery is in a backroom but is visible through a window at the

Beers brewed: Year-round: Belden Golden Ale, "DD" Blonde, Keddie Red Ale, Chilcoot IPA, Pulga Pale Ale, and 844 Oatmeal Stout. Seasonals: Scottish Ale, Harvest Ale, and Anniversary Double IPA.

The Pick: The Chilcoot IPA is a nice, middle-of-the-road West Coast IPA that's not overly hoppy but has good hops character, with citrus, pine, and floral notes that predominate though never hit you over the head, balanced pleasantly with some caramel sweetness.

end of the bar. Behind the bar are plenty of tables and chairs, and a side lounge holds pool tables and an electronic dartboard. On the opposite end is a large ballroom where evening and weekend dancing or karaoke takes place.

Even though the old station's been closed for more than forty years and trains don't stop here anymore, they still pass by. And when they do, there's something classic about hearing and feeling the rumble of the iron and steel on the rails. If you're lucky, you'll have a beer in your hand to toast their passing.

Western Pacific Brewing & Dining

Opened: The Old Depot restaurant opened September 13, 1977; the brewery was added in February 2009.

Type: Brewpub.

Owner: David Deakins.

Brewer: Andy Klein.

Guild membership: BA.

System: 10-barrel Pub System.

Packages available: Kegs only at the brewpub and area bars and restaurants.

Tours: You don't need a reservation, but your best bet is to ask when the brewer is in the house.

Hours: Monday through Saturday, 11 a.m. to 8 p.m. Closed Sunday.

Food: The brewpub offers a modest menu, with starters, sandwiches on gourmet pretzel rolls, wraps, and dinner salads. The hand-cut fries are particularly tasty and come in a basket.

Extras: Musical entertainment includes karaoke from 6 to 10 p.m. on Monday and Wednesday, Acoustic Jam Night on Thursday, and DJ Rene on Saturday. A separate banquet hall is available for private events, and there's free Wi-Fi.

Gift shop: Brewery hats and shorts are available behind the bar.

Wildcard Brewing Company

REDDING, CA

WILDCARD

Brewing CO

9565 Crossroads Drive, Redding, CA 96003
530-722-9239 • www.wildcardbrewingco.com
Twitter @WildcardBrewCo
Facebook.com/WildcardBrewingCompany

The story of Wildcard Brewing is a romantic one that began a few weeks before the wedding of the founders of the Redding brewery, Jeff and Jenny Hansen. The couple had attended Cal Poly in the central California town of San Luis Obispo, and as a wedding favor for their guests, they brewed both a blonde and brown ale at the local BYOB, Central Coast Brewing. The experience proved so enjoyable that they immediately set about putting their favorite wedding gift, a homebrewing kit, to good use.

While they both enjoyed homebrewing, Jeff began talking about wanting to change his life plans in the direction of becoming a professional brewer. At Jenny's urging, he spent a year as an intern working for Marc Rosenblum at the Santa Cruz Aleworks to get some practical experience of what a professional brewer does on a daily basis. Jeff found it really was his passion and was accepted to Rosenblum's alma mater, the Brewlab brewing school in Sunderland, England.

Back in the States, Hansen took his first professional brewing job as the head brewer of the Iron Horse Brewery in Ellensberg, Washington. Over his two years there, the brewery increased its production from 1,000 barrels to more than 5,000 per year. In order to be closer to home, and in the place where the couple wanted to eventually open a brewery, Jeff started brewing with Peter Burrell at Dempsey's in Petaluma.

After a year there, and with a baby on the way, the Hansens decided it was time to realize their ambitions and open their own place. Jenny was from Santa Cruz, but Jeff grew up in Redding, and they discovered it was essentially an open market there, with no local brewery for miles. While Jeff

Beers brewed: Year-round: Suicide Jack California Cream Ale, Liar's Dice IPA, Double Down Red Imperial Red Ale, and Shot in the Dark Oatmeal Porter. Seasonals: Double IPA (winter), India Spring Ale (spring), Wheat (summer), and Maple Brown Ale (fall).

The Pick: I really enjoyed the Double Down, a big beer but nicely balanced. It has great hopping, with herbal, pine, and tea leaf aromas, and sweet caramel notes, making it perfect for hopheads and malt advocates alike.

continued honing his brewing skills, Jenny did all the research, wrote a business plan, filled out endless paperwork, and worked on securing loans. They moved back to Redding in July 2012, signed a lease in August, and opened in early November.

In the process, they worried their families to no end, taking risks and not settling for the easy path, especially considering that this was during the economic downturn. It was this wild, radical direction their lives took that led them to choose Wildcard for their brewery's name, seeing themselves as the wild card.

The brewery is set in an industrial park in Redding. At night, it's one of the few bright lights in the neighborhood. Inside, it's clean and new, with several small rooms off the main tasting room, where the bar sits. They currently brew on a small pilot system and also contract some of their brewing, but a new, larger brewery is being installed behind the tasting room, and when it's completed, the Hansens plan to continue to use the pilot brewery for experimentation and interesting one-offs.

Wildcard Brewing Company

Opened: November 8, 2012.

Type: Production brewery, with tasting room.

Owners: Jeff and Jenny Hansen.

Brewer: Jeff Hansen.

Guild membership: BA, CCBA.

System: 30-barrel brewhouse and 20-gallon pilot brewery.

Annual production: 850 barrels (first-year estimate).

Packages available: Growlers and 5- and 13.2-gallon kegs; 22-ounce bottles should be added in the future.

Tours: No tours are currently available.

Hours: Wednesday and Thursday, 2 to 8 p.m.; Friday, noon to 9 p.m.; Sunday, noon to 5 p.m. Closed Monday and Tuesday.

Food: The tasting room has peanuts and pretzels to snack on. Different local vendors make food available on Friday evenings. You are also welcome to bring your own food.

Extras: Inside the tasting room, there's a separate lounge area with a dartboard, and you can also play liar's dice at the tables. Kids are allowed, but there are no televisions. On Wednesday, growler fills are discounted. The first Monday of each month, brewer Jeff Hansen gives a brewing demonstration on the pilot brewery. And the first Tuesday of each month, known as Beer for Bettys, is an evening for women to learn beer appreciation; the event is catered with dishes to pair with each beer. Either event requires an advance reservation.

Gift shop: Shirts, sweatshirts, hats, glassware, posters, and tap handles are available at the tasting room.

Contract Brewing

People often have strong reactions to contract brewing, especially many hard-core beer geeks with specific ideas or rules as to what constitutes good beer. Few issues can divide beer lovers as quickly as bringing up the subject of contract brewing, so I figure it's best to just get it out in the open.

Regardless of how or where it's brewed, I chose to list every beer brand that's located in, or has some affiliation with, Northern California in this book for the perfectly reasonable view—at least reasonable to me—that such beers would be available to anyone visiting or living in the area, and thus they should be included in any book purporting to cover the entire region.

As far as I'm concerned, only one criterion should be used to judge a beer, be it a contract-brewed or any other beer: how does it taste? We can endlessly debate whether contract brewing is fair to brewery owners who spent the money to build their own places, or whether it's possible to make good beer under contract—it is; get over it—or even if contract brewers are somehow being deceptive (most are not).

It seems obvious to me that as many poorly made beers are brewed by companies that own their own facilities as by contract breweries. There are also many good, even great, contract-brewed beers. Quality does not seem to be the issue. What I feel it comes down to is perception. I honestly think it's a shame that some people absolutely refuse to entertain any beer that's been contract-brewed. They're really missing out. If you handed them a contract-brewed beer in a glass and asked them what they thought about it, would whether it was contracted be in any way part of the evaluation? Of course not, but in the end it's their choice.

Today a number of different types of contract brewing are being done, with varying degrees of involvement on the part of both sets of brewers. In an effort to demystify contract brewing, here are the most common types.

Contract brewery. In its most basic form, contract brewing involves a company hiring a brewery to make its beer for the company. The brewery usually only makes the beer based on recipes provided by the contractor, and all other aspects of the business, such as storage, sales, and marketing, are handled by the company that contracts to have the beer made. This is a way for a company that lacks the resources to build its own brewery, which is expensive, to start a beer business. It was a common strategy in the early days of craft brewing, but it declined beginning in the late 1990s. However, it has been enjoying a resurgence in recent years.

Gypsy brewer. This situation is similar to a contract brewery but differs in one respect. A contract brewery usually makes all of its beer at one location (occasionally more if it's a big brand) consistently over a period of time, often years. On the other hand, a gypsy, as the name implies, tends to move from place to place, brewing at many different breweries, and even brewing different beers at different places, even though they all may be marketed under one brand name.

Tenant brewery. In this case, instead of the host brewery making the beer according to the contract brewer's specifications, the brewery is turned over temporarily to a tenant brewer, who brews the beer him- or herself on the host's brewing equipment. Essentially, a beer company rents and uses the brewery to produce its own product, and the company's personnel do all of the work themselves.

Shared brewing. I made this one up, because as far as I know, there is no agreed-upon name for it, but this situation is somewhat of a mix between tenant brewing and an alternating proprietorship. Both High Water Brewing and Dying Vines have this type of arrangement with other breweries—High Water with Drake's and Dying Vines with Linden Street. They each purchased their own fermenters, which were installed at their respective contract breweries. After completing the brewing, the beer is put into each company's own tanks, and from fermentation through packaging, it is already under their control, using the host brewery for only a portion of the brewing.

Alternating proprietorship. This is a legal arrangement as stipulated by the federal agency that oversees alcohol, the Alcohol and Tobacco Tax and Trade Bureau (TTB). The TTB defines an alternating proprietorship as "an arrangement in which two or more people take turns using the physical premises of a brewery" and describes it as follows: "Generally, the proprietor of an existing brewery, the 'host brewery,' agrees to rent space and equipment to a new 'tenant brewer.' Alternating brewery proprietorships allow existing breweries to use excess capacity and give new entrants to the beer business an opportunity to begin on a small scale, without investing in premises and equipment."

The Central Valley North

The Central Valley North is the region located in the central interior of California. This book covers the northern portion of California's Central Valley, which is generally considered to extend farther south than is included here. For the purposes of this book, the Central Valley North region includes the counties of Colusa, Merced, Sacramento, San Joaquin, Solano, Stanislaus, and Yolo. These seven counties encompass a fairly large amount of land, which combined is slightly larger than all of New Jersey, but with the population of Connecticut or only about 40 percent of the Garden State's. Most of the Central Valley is fairly easy to traverse, thanks to its being more heavily populated and relatively flat compared with the surrounding regions.

The area is dominated by Sacramento, which is the state's sixth-largest city and its capital. San Jose was actually California's first state capital in 1850, but it was moved to Sacramento in 1854, which became the western end of both the Pony Express and the Transcontinental Railroad. Rapid growth and home building in the surrounding areas have made it a metropolis of 2.5 million people, the second-largest populated area in Northern California. Sacramento is also very hot. In fact, it's been declared "the sunniest location on the planet" from June through September, when it's also very dry.

Besides numerous state government buildings, agencies, and the like, Sacramento also has a number of attractions. If you like trains, don't miss the California State Railroad Museum, where I've taken my son, Porter, who's obsessed with trains, a few dozen times over the years. It's one of his favorite places to visit. There's also the California Automobile Museum, and if you love art, check out the Crocker Art Museum, the oldest public art museum west of the Mississippi.

Davis is also located in this region, and it is home to the University of California's Davis campus, which has a fermentation studies program that is part of the Department of Food Sciences and Technology. Professor of brewing science Charlie Bamforth and, before him, Michael Lewis have trained countless professional brewers, many of whom have continued to brew in Northern California breweries. Bamforth is also the author of a dozen books, some highly technical but others more accessible, like his two recent volumes, *Grape vs. Grain* and *Beer Is Proof God Loves Us*. In both books, Bamforth writes persuasively about the positive aspects of beer.

It's no accident that Northern California's only megabrewer, Anheuser-Busch InBev's Fairfield brewery, is just down the road from Davis. ABI has also endowed the university with both a professor and the August A. Busch III Brewing and Food Science Laboratory, built in 2006.

American River Brewing Company

11151 Trade Center Drive, Suite 104, Rancho Cordova, CA 95670

916-635-2537 • www.americanriverbrewingcompany.com
Facebook.com/pages/American-River-Brewing-Company/283484455027486

The two main parties in the new American River Brewing Company have thirty-four years of beer industry experience between them, so while their Rancho Cordova brewery is new, they bring their combined knowledge to the enterprise. And quite frankly, it shows. This is one of the most polished new breweries I've ever visited. It's well thought out from the smallest detail to the large, comfortable space with plenty of room to grow.

Founder David Mathis brewed for both Pyramid Breweries and the BJ's restaurant and brewpub chain for almost two decades. Brewmaster Andy Armstrong brewed in Oregon and California, including for a now defunct Sacramento brewery called Beermann's and also BJ's, where the pair first met.

Their state-of-the-art brewery is situated in a large warehouse space in Rancho Cordova, about twenty minutes due east from Sacramento. It's a short distance from its namesake river, which meets the Sacramento River nearby on its way from the Sierra Nevada southwest to Sacramento and on to the San Francisco Bay.

While it's primarily a production brewery, it has a spacious, comfortable tasting room, called the Riverbank, that's open for happy hour three days a week. One or both of the principals are there most nights, happy to answer questions or lead a tour. You might not even need the tour, though, because the brewery is on display through large windows in the tasting room, and part of the warehouse space in the brewery area is cordoned off and features picnic tables where you can enjoy your beer right in the brewery, in the shadow of the fermenters and the brewhouse.

Beers brewed: Year-round: AU Golden, Fire Break Red Ale, SSB IPA, and Coloma Brown. Seasonals: Sunrise English IPA (spring), Pumpkin Ale (fall), Insinerator Ale (fall–winter), and Honey Britches Ale (spring–summer).

The Pick: The Coloma Brown is a rich, malt-forward beer, with aromas of roasted coffee and sweet caramel. The flavor profile is similarly a nice mix of sweet caramel and toffee and lightly roasted coffee, with the competing sweet and bitter components working together in harmony, fully integrated into a very enjoyable brown ale.

Although no food is prepared on-site, most nights there's a food truck or two or three offering gourmet food to go with your pints. A chalkboard lists all of the places you can find the beer in the area, for the days when the Riverbank is not open. The brewery also started bottling its beer at the beginning of 2013 and little by little will be increasing the variety of beers that are bottled.

All of the beers are well made and are a nice mix of styles. They should please even the fussiest beer lover, from the hot and spicy Insinerator to the refreshing AU Golden. American River has even begun experimenting with aging its IPA in wine barrels. I expect big things from this brewery. Mathis and Armstrong have the experience, the skill, and the business savvy—oh, and they're making some damn fine beer too.

American River Brewing Company

Opened: January 13, 2012.

Type: Production brewery, with tasting room.

Owner: David Mathis.

Brewer: Andy Armstrong.

Guild membership: BA, CCBA, NCBG.

System: 15-barrel Specific Mechanical direct flame brewhouse, 1,000 barrels annual capacity.

Annual production: 500 barrels (2012 estimate).

Packages available: 22-ounce bottles, growlers. and 5- and 15.5-gallon kegs.

Tours: Brewery tours are available on request.

Hours: Wednesday through Friday, 4 to 8 p.m.

Food: There is no food at the brewery, but gourmet mobile food trucks are parked outside the tasting room most nights that it's open to the public.

Gift shop: Shirts and glassware are available in the tasting room.

Anheuser-Busch Fairfield Brewery

Anheuser-Busch

3101 Busch Drive, Fairfield, CA 94534
Local brewery: 707-429-2000; A-B hotline:
   800-DIAL-BUD • www.anheuser-busch.com
Facebook.com/Anheuser-Busch

The Fairfield brewery of Anheuser-Busch InBev (ABI) is the company's only plant in California and is the second smallest of its dozen breweries. It's also unique in that ABI only produces cans and kegs and does not bottle there. It's an amazing place to visit, especially if you've never visited a large, modern brewery.

Many craft beer lovers may not care for some of the products Budweiser makes, but that's not because they're not extremely well made. They are. ABI's breweries are technological marvels, and they've taken the science of brewing to new heights. You can argue about the results in the can or in your glass, but you can't take issue with the processes or the care with which the beers are brewed.

I've had the pleasure of knowing quite a few A-B brewers over the years, and they are terrific and talented people. Fairfield's brewmaster, Scott Ungermann, is no exception. Like many of his fellow brewers, Ungermann is a graduate of nearby UC Davis's brewing sciences program.

The tour at the Fairfield brewery is something to behold. It's like being in a giant city devoted to beer. The facility is on 170 acres, though most of it is concentrated in one very large building in the center of the grounds. You'll need to sign in to get to the tour area and the extensive gift shop. After the tour, there's a tasting room where you can sample products made in the building you just toured.

Fairfield also offers Beer School, which is described as "a fun, interactive, and informative experience that explains the steps for beer appreciation." For $10 per person—twenty-one or older, of

Beers brewed: Year-round: Budweiser, Bud Light, Bud Ice, Shock Top, Busch, Busch Light, Busch Ice, Natural Light, Natural Ice, King Cobra, Hurricane HG, and Rolling Rock.

The Pick: Despite all of ABI's technical knowhow, I'm not a fan of many of the products. It's not that there's anything wrong with them; they're simply not suited to my taste preferences. If I were pressed to choose one, the original Budweiser is closest to what I look for in a beer. It's clean and, of course, well made. I once had an unfiltered version of that beer, produced just for test purposes, and it had a strong banana component in the nose, a product of the house yeast character. And it was much more full-flavored than the filtered version, which strips the beer of much of that character. I wish they bottled or canned that one.

course—you spend forty-five minutes learning about styles of beer, ingredients, the art of pouring, and beer-food pairings. Class size is limited to ten, so call to check when school is in, as dates and times vary. The school is aimed more at beginners with little knowledge about brewing, so if you're a homebrewer or have visited a number of smaller breweries, it may not be for you, but it's perfect as an introduction to big beer.

Whichever of the available tours is best suited to your level of experience and interest, you should make a point of taking it whenever you're in the neighborhood. It's educational on so many levels and can help you appreciate the different ways that beer can be made, from the smallest nanobrewery to a scale that's hard to even imagine. Luckily, you don't have to just imagine it. You can see it firsthand in Fairfield.

Anheuser-Busch Fairfield Brewery

Opened: 1976.

Type: Production brewery.

Owners: Anheuser-Busch InBev.

Brewers: Scott Ungermann (brewmaster) and Kevin Finger (general manager).

Guild membership: BI.

System: Custom built 700-barrel brewhouse, Huppmann Lauter tub, 4.5 million barrels annual capacity.

Annual production: 4.5 million barrels.

Packages available: 12-, 16-, and 24-ounce cans in six-, twelve-, eighteen-, twenty-four-, thirty-, and thirty-six-packs, plus 7.75- and 15.5-gallon kegs.

Tours: Complimentary tours are offered from 10 a.m. to 4 p.m., Tuesday through Saturday September through May, and Monday through Saturday June through August; no reservations are required. BeerMaster Tours are offered at 10 a.m. and 2 p.m., Tuesday through Saturday September through May, and Monday through Saturday June through August; reservations are required for the BeerMaster Tours. For more information or to make reservations, call 707-429-7595 or visit the tour website at www.budweisertours.com. All ages are welcome on the complimentary tours, but for the BeerMaster Tours, guests must be at least thirteen years old.

Hours: Apart from tour times, the brewery is not open to the public.

Food: There is no food in the tour center, but there is a Subway sandwich shop on-site.

Extras: The tour center hosts an event showcasing local bands on the first Friday of each month from October through May. There is also an annual classic car show in September at the brewery. From time to time, the Budweiser Clydesdales visit and put on an exhibition in the parking lot.

Gift shop: The gift shop has a variety of branded merchandise, such as clothing, glassware, and assorted novelty items. Merchandise is also available at www.budshop.com.

Berryessa Brewing Company

27260 Highway 128, Winters, CA 95697
530-795-3526 • www.BerryessaBrewingCo.com
Twitter @twitter
Facebook.com/BerryessaBrewingCo

Chris Miller grew up in the city of Seattle and worked briefly for the short-lived Pacific Rim Brewery there. But he made a name for himself in Sunnyside, Washington, at Snipes Mountain Brewing, especially with his Zombie Killer Fresh Hop IPA.

Looking to open his own brewery, he moved to Northern California to found Berryessa Brewing Company with some local investors. Winters is part of the Sacramento metropolitan area, though it's nearly 30 miles from the state capital and is as close to the Yolo County border as you can get without leaving. Frankly, associating it with a metropolitan area is a bit of a stretch, because Winters seems fairly remote and desolate, with less than seven thousand residents, all living near Lake Berryessa.

The lake, which is technically the biggest lake in Napa County, provided the brewery with its name. Winters is located just over the border in the next county and is the closest town to the recreational hot spot. The outline of the lake is that odd-looking shape on the brewery's logo.

The brewery and its taproom share a building with the Berryessa Gap Winery, which operates a tasting room next door. From the outside, it more resembles a roadhouse, and it feels pretty remote, along a desolate road with no other buildings in sight from the bend in the road until Valley Oak Park at the outskirts of the town of Winters.

But inside the rustic roadhouse brewery, there are plain tan walls and a simple bar made from corrugated tin with a shiny metal top. A chalkboard hangs on the wall behind the bar, listing the available beers. Tap handles are made out of chain links, with a solid circle on the top that has the Berryessa logo on one side and the name of the beer on the other. It's spartan, but it works. There's also outdoor seating, and games are available.

Beers brewed: Year-round: Baltic Porter, Freshie, Common Sense, Roadhouse Amber, The House IPA, and Double Tap IPA. Seasonals: Trendy Imperial IPA, Disorderly Strong Ale, Saisonic, Winters, Belgo, Pumpkin Death Stout, Third Wheel Session IPA, Propaganda Pils, Cease & Desist, Whippersnapper, and Nightshade.

The brewery is out of sight behind the large, spacious taproom. The brewhouse sits along one wall, with a few fermenters next to it and more on the opposite wall. A roll-up door leads to the parking lot in the back. Racks of beer aging in wooden bourbon and wine barrels dot the room. Miller also creates some of his beers on cask and usually has six different varieties on tap.

Despite the seemingly desolate remoteness of the location, the joint is jumping, and it's packed every single night it's open. But once you taste Chris Miller's beer, you'll understand why. Miller seems much more comfortable in the back, talking about his beer, rather than being in front of the house with the crowds. But that's why people come, because it's easy to get caught up in the passion that he puts into each beer. Every beer tastes like it was made by someone who really cared about it every step of the way. So he's reluctantly there at the last stage too, when people come to enjoy it, seeing it through from beginning to end. The brewery recently began canning its beer in 16-ounce bombers, meaning you'll be able to find Berryessa beer in many more places.

The Pick: Miller is known for his big, hoppy beers, and his best is the Double Tap IPA. With sticky hops aromas of oranges and lemons, mangoes and papayas, it's a tropical fruit bonanza with some garlic notes. The mouthfeel is thick and chewy, and the hops character hits you like a sledgehammer, until its malt brothers rescue the beer from being nothing more. The balance ultimately is wonderful and lets the hops shine as they should. The finish is tart and slightly dry, but surprisingly not very bitter, just warming hops character. If you're looking for something that's not too hoppy, you can't go wrong with the Common Sense, a 4.5 percent session beer with light aromas that's more malt-forward with delicate flavors. Or try the Saisonic, Miller's take on a farmhouse ale, with Belgian yeast aromas, citrus fruit flavors, and good spicing.

Berryessa Brewing Company

Opened: October 1, 2011.

Type: Production brewery, with taproom.

Owners: Chris Miller and other investors.

Brewer: Chris Miller.

Guild membership: BA, CCBA, NCBG.

System: 20-barrel Premier Stainless, 2,500 barrels annual capacity.

Annual production: 1,000 barrels (2012 estimate).

Packages available: Growlers, 16-ounce cans in four-packs, and 5- and 15.5-gallon kegs. Pints, half pints, and a sample tray can also be ordered in the taproom.

Tours: Brewery tours are available, but reservations are recommended, as it tends to get very crowded during open hours.

Hours: Friday, 3 to 8 p.m.; Saturday and Sunday, noon to 6 p.m.

Food: No food is available at the brewery, although food trucks park there most days.

Extras: Live music is performed most days the taproom is open.

Gift shop: T-shirts, hats, hoodies, and other brewery swag are available in the taproom.

Black Dragon Brewery

175 West Main Street, Suite B, Woodland, CA 95695
530-666-KEGS (5347) • www.blackdragonbrew.com

Black Dragon is a homebrewing hobby gone awry. After opening the Woodland Homebrew Supply store, Jason and Heather Breatt decided that wasn't quite enough. They wanted to serve their own beer too, and Jason was a graduate of the American Brewers Guild who had worked professionally at numerous Bay Area breweries over the past decade, so they opened the Black Dragon Brewery right next door.

Brewmaster Jason Breatt continues to teach classes through the homebrew shop, which gives students a chance to see and work on actual commercial brewing equipment. Classes are typically held the first Saturday of each month, but it's probably best to check the website for details. They alternate between extract and all-grain brewing and last five to six hours.

Things are just getting going at the brewery, and they currently have four beers on draft in the taproom, with plans to serve at least sixteen original beers. They will eventually feature live music on the weekends and festivals on the lawn area. The space is amazingly clean, with corrugated tin on the bar and walls, giving it a modern industrial feel. The brewery is open and sits to one side of the bar. Patrons can sit at the numerous tables and chairs and watch the brewing process from almost any vantage point in the space.

Beers brewed: Year-round: Gypsy Blonde Ale, Black Dragon Blueberry Blonde Ale, Black Dragon Fairy Fart, Black Dragon Blackberry Blonde Ale, Impaled Ale, Black Dragon Honey Pale, Fog California Common, Red Scale, Firestorm Irish Red, Broad Sword Brown, Darkness Robust Brown, Expedition Amber, Araya IPA, Natas Hoppas IPA, Hopslayer Imperial IPA, Dragon's Eye Porter, Hibernation Winter Warmer Ale, and Unspoken Stout. Seasonals: Abyss Barleywine.

The Pick: Since this is such a new brewery, I've not yet had the opportunity to try all of its offerings, but the Dragon's Eye Porter is a good place to start. It's a smooth porter with nice chocolate notes, treacly sweetness, and only a touch of roastiness.

Black Dragon Brewery

Opened: September 6, 2012.
Type: Production brewery and brewpub.
Owners: Jason and Heather Breatt.
Brewer: Jason Breatt.

System: 15-barrel brewing system, 60,000 barrels annual capacity.

Packages available: Growlers and kegs, with bottling in the future.

Tours: Tours are available during business hours, with no reservations necessary.

Hours: Tuesday through Thursday, 11 a.m. to 7 p.m.; Friday, 11 a.m. to 9 p.m.; Saturday, 10:30 a.m. to 9 p.m.; Sunday 10: a.m. to 5 p.m. Closed Monday.

Food: The brewery serves a daily changing menu of appetizers and sliders, such as spicy chicken bacon ranch, BBQ roast beef, chicken pesto, and chicken teriyaki. The signature dish, called Dragon Scales, consists of Kettle chips layered with bacon, blue cheese, balsamic glaze, and green onions.

Gift shop: If you feel like trying your hand at brewing your own beer, the Woodland Homebrew Supply is conveniently attached to the brewery and is right next door. It's under the same management. There, in addition to brewing supplies, you can also find Black Dragon T-shirts, pint glasses, koozies, gift certificates, and other logo items.

Blue Frog Grog and Grill

1740 Travis Boulevard, Fairfield, CA 94533
707-429-2337 • www.bigbluefrog.com
Twitter @bluefrogbrew • Facebook.com/pages/
Blue-Frog-Grog-Grill/59597358465

The story goes that when brewpub founder Dennis Landis and his wife were a young couple, the Peter, Paul, and Mary song "I'm in Love with a Big Blue Frog" was one of their favorites, so when it came time to choose a name for their business, this was what leaped to mind. And in fact, the first thing you see when you walk into the restaurant is a very large statue of a frog wearing a crown.

The brewpub is located just off the main road through town, I-80, and it's a short hop from the Anheuser-Busch InBev brewery. It sits in a corner of a shopping complex that includes a large mall, hotels, and several chain restaurants. Outside, a tall unused fermenter is easy to spot and leaves little confusion what's being made inside.

Inside, the brewpub is much larger than it first appears, with separate rooms and hideaways. Behind the signature frog structure is a central bar area, with smaller tables, separated by a short wall that surrounds it. To the right, the kitchen is open for all to see, and you could watch them cook your meal if you really wanted to. The brewery is tightly packed behind the bar but completely visible through large paned windows that line the wall. It's actually two stories, with the mill and storage upstairs. There's a red spiral staircase between the floors and not much room to move around, but somehow the brewer manages it.

There's also an outdoor patio area that's fully covered, the best of both worlds, where you're both inside and out at the same time. That space is also ideal for private functions. The main dining area features high wooden ceilings and a giant fireplace at one end, and there's booth seating and tables both large and small.

After enjoying a great meal, you can buy beer in 22-ounce bottles at the brewpub to take with you when you leave. Bottles of Blue Frog beer are also available throughout Northern California.

Blue Frog Grog and Grill

Opened: 1999.

Type: Brewpub.

Owners: Dennis Landis.

Brewer: Scott Macky.

Guild membership: NCBG.

System: 10-barrel DME, 1,000 barrels annual capacity.

Annual production: 850 barrels (2011).

Packages available: 22-ounce bottles and 5- and 15.5-gallon kegs.

Tours: Brewery tours are available, subject to the brewer's schedule; no tours are available on bottling days.

Hours: Monday through Thursday, 11:30 a.m. to 10 p.m.; Friday and Saturday, 11:30 a.m. to 11 p.m.; Sunday, 11:30 a.m. to 9 p.m.

Food: The menu has a good selection of pub fare, including appetizers, wood-fired pizzas, soups and salads, sandwiches and burgers, pasta, seafood, and specialties such as rotisserie chicken, pan-seared lamb chops, prime rib, and cowboy steak. There's also a kids' menu, "for our tadpoles," as well as an extensive menu of small, inexpensive bites the brewpub calls "Recession Busters!" These include such items as deviled eggs, fish tacos, sliders, and spaghetti and a meatball.

Extras: "Hoppy hour" takes place daily from 3 to 6 p.m. and features special prices for pints, $1 off wine, and $2 off appetizers and large pizzas. Wear red socks during "hoppy hour" for extra savings, but under no circumstances should you wear socks that are either striped or argyle. Don't say you haven't been warned. There's a separate banquet room for private functions, and Blue Frog does outside catering as well. The brewery also makes its own root beer and cream soda.

Gift shop: At the front of the brewpub, there's a case with T-shirts, hats, and other merchandise. There's also a cooler with 22-ounce beer bottles you can buy to take some home with you.

Beers brewed: Year-round: Hefeweizen, Blond Ale, India Pale Ale, and Red Ale. Seasonals: The Big DIPA, Froggy Bottom Pils, Frogenbock, Frog in the Rye, Porter, Imperial Red, and Walkin' the Dog Brown.

The Pick: While it's not available all the time, the imperial IPA known simply as The Big DIPA is another beer created out of a happy accident, when a double helping of hops was accidentally added to the beer. It's a very complex hops monster with loads of different—and changing—taste sensations, a warming heat, and a very long, lingering finish. Since the DIPA is available at only certain times of the year, the rest of the year you can count on the Red Ale to satisfy your thirst. It's malt-forward, but with just the right amount of hops character, a solid strong amber ale. The flavors are caramel and subtle spices, with a lingering grapefruit, bitter finish.

Bradley's Brewing Company

8942 Greenback Lane, Suite E, Orangevale, CA 95662
916-988-2723 • www.bradleysbrewing.com

Bradley Martin grew up in South Lake Tahoe and became a metal fabricator, opening his own shop in Orangevale, near Sacramento. He specialized in precision stainless fabrication, which led to a passion for baking and the culinary arts. That, in turn, brought him to brewing in the early 1990s. He attended UC Davis and the American Brewers Guild to learn the craft, and then, using his fabricating skills, he built a state-of-the-art 15-barrel brewhouse.

His metalworking skills also led him to build movable stages for some impressive rock-and-roll acts, who started asking him about catering too. To help with that, he built custom mobile food and party vehicles, which could easily move elaborate kitchens, tapping equipment, and other party essentials from place to place. In order to provide his own beer, he built a brewhouse back at his shop and produces kegs of beer for his clients' parties and events. It's an impressively immaculate brewery that's tucked into a spacious area next to his fabricating shop, and there's also a private bar in the shop.

But the shop is not open to the public, and you can't stop by to try his beer. He only brews in anticipation of a catering job or for himself. He can set up everything you need for an impressive outdoor event, leaving none of the comforts of home behind. His custom-built vans and trucks can transform on-site to accommodate parties both large and small. You can find his events from Lake Tahoe to Sacramento, but only if you're invited to one of them. That's the only way to drink Bradley's beer. Or you could hire him to cater your event.

Bradley's Brewing Company

Opened: 1999.
Type: Production brewery.
Owner: Bradley Martin.
Brewer: Bradley Martin.
System: 15-barrel custom-built brewhouse.
Packages available: Kegs.
Tours: No tours are available.

Beers brewed: Year-round: American Missy Blond, German Barley Pop Kolsch, Pro Street Pale Ale, and Rippin Red. Seasonals: Bushido Super Dry, White Water Hefe (summer), Hale Scotch Ale (fall), and Blackout Stout (winter).

Chau Tien and BeerGuy of America, Inc.

CON RỒNG

CHÁU TIÊN

Est 1985

P.O. Box 2441, Fairfield, CA 94533
P.O. Box 221185, Carmel, CA 93923
707-280-8044 • www.beerguy.com /
www.paleale.com
Facebook.com/pages/Beer-Guy-of-America/
117611828269049 /
Facebook.com/pages/Chau-Tien-Beer-Co-USA/
118873908138821

Tuan Chau Tien was born in Vietnam at the height of the conflict there. His father was a diplomat, and he lived in Washington, D.C., in the late 1960s and early 1970s, before returning to Vietnam to attend Jesuit school. When the war ended in 1975, he went through some very tough times. At fourteen, he was old enough to be drafted and was imprisoned when he was caught trying to leave Vietnam. Eventually released, he was shuttled around among numerous refugee camps in the Pacific, before a U.S. Marine officer brought the youth back with him to Laguna Beach.

Tuan was eventually reunited with his family and graduated from high school in Hawaii. He then attended City College in San Francisco, where he discovered a love of good beer. When he told his mother he was leaving college to make beer, she didn't say one word. But she did pick up a shoe and throw it at him.

Chau Tien beer was first brewed at Sierra Nevada Brewing, but it was not a contract brew. The beer was originally a joint venture partnership, with Tuan licensing the brand, an arrangement he also had for a time with Anderson Valley Brewing. As far as he knows, it was the first American-made Asian beer. He's since moved on to contract brew the line, as well as his BeerGuy brand of beers. That logo debuted in 1988 and was created by the same designer who made Starbucks' iconic logo.

Tuan operates both brands as separate companies and makes a number of regular beers and sea-

Beers brewed: Year-round: BeerGuy Over the Top IPA, BeerGuy Groovy Ale, BeerGuy Stoutier Stout, BeerGuy At the Top Lager, BeerGuy Howlin' Ale, BeerGuy Black Ale, BeerGuy Sweet Mama Honey Wheat, BeerGuy Very Very American Lager, HomeBoy Homie's Reserve Malt Liquor, Chau Tien Pale Ale, Chau Tien Prolific Porter, Chau Tien Emperor Ale, Chau Tien Chiconese Pale Ale, Chau Tien Mandarin Stout, Chau Tien Dragon IPA, and Chau Tien Luna Angel Wheat. Seasonals: McCloud Stout, McCloud Pale Ale, Tuanee Boon Extra Special Brown, Brother Tuan Double Belgian, Tiki Tuan Lager, Chilo Machino Gold, Doc Allen Prenuptial Bitter, and DoucheBag White Ale.

sonals under each banner. Eventually he would like to open a chain of BeerGuy breweries with taprooms, and he is in the process of raising capital to open the first one. Look for both brands in restaurants and retail stores throughout the Bay Area.

The Pick: The Over the Top IPA is a refreshing beer with grassy, pine, and grapefruit aromas. It has a chewy mouthfeel and good malt balance, with a bitter finish.

Chau Tien and BeerGuy of America, Inc.

Opened: January 1, 1988.

Type: Contract brewery.

Owner: Tuan Chau Tien.

Brewer: Tuan Chau Tien.

System: 30-barrel brewhouse, 15,000 barrels annual capacity.

Annual production: 2,000 barrels (2012 estimate).

Packages available: 12-ounce bottles sixpacks, 22-ounce bottles, and 5- and 15.5-gallon kegs.

Gift shop: Merchandise for both the Chau Tien and BeerGuy brands is available at the websites.

Dust Bowl Brewing Company

Brewery: 3100 Spengler Way, Turlock, CA 95380
Tap room: 200 West Main Street, Turlock, CA 95380
209-250-2042 (taproom) 209-250-2044 (office)
www.dustbowlbrewing.com
Twitter @dustbowlbrew
Facebook.com/Dustbowlbrewing

Dust Bowl founder Brett Tate's grandfather, a hobo who rode the rails during the Depression in order to feed his family, lived a life worthy of a John Steinbeck novel. In the 1930s, Grandpa Tate loaded up their Model A and relocated his family from the Dust Bowl of Oklahoma to Turlock, California. The family history left a deep impression on Tate, a retired high school teacher and coach, and when he needed a name for his new brewery, he drew on his grandfather's experience for inspiration.

But he also needed a brewer. Enter another local Turlocker: Don Oliver. Oliver was a longtime homebrewer, having learned to brew from his father. Homebrewing became a passion even as he embarked on a career as a helicopter mechanic with the U.S. Marine Corps. One day during a tour of duty in Japan, he had an epiphany and decided he wanted to become a professional brewer. A few years later, while in business school, Oliver won the 2006 Samuel Adams Longshot Homebrew Competition for his Old Ale homebrew recipe, one of only three winners. His ale was produced commercially by the Boston Beer Company and sold in a six-pack. The story made its way into the local newspaper, where Brett Tate read about the local award-winning homebrewer.

Tate clipped out the article, and a year later, he got in touch with Oliver and the pair met in person. After a three-hour meeting, the two concluded that they both wanted the same thing—to build a new brewery in Turlock. Oliver then enrolled at UC Davis to take the Master Brewers Program and graduated with top honors in 2008.

The following year, the pair, along with business

Beers brewed: Year-round: Hops of Wrath IPA, Lager, Buckwheat Ale, Hobo Crystal Wheat, Fruit Wheat, Rye Extra Pale, Galaxy Pale Ale, Schweet, Belgian Blonde, Vienna Lager, Belgian Pale, Stout, Scottish Ale, Scorpio Pale Ale, ESB, and Red IPA. Seasonals: Christmas Bonus Smoked Bock, Winter Ale, Whiskey Barrel-Aged, Soul Crusher, Coffee Porter, Marzen, Russian Imperial Stout, Stock Ale, Therapist Triple IPA, Doppelbock, Scotch Ale, Belgian Style Dark Ale, Double IPA, Barleywine, Baltic Porter, Tripel, Super Tramp, XR4Ti, and Galactic Wrath Anniversary IPA.

partner Brett Honoré, founded the production brewery. Two years after that, miles from the brewery in the heart of downtown Turlock, the Dust Bowl opened a taproom in a corner building with an enclosed outdoor patio. Inside, it's light and airy, rustic modern, with plenty of room, a long bar, and comfortable seating. The food is particularly good and satisfying, with generous portions. The number of different beers on tap at any given time is also impressive, and the beers rotate frequently, so there's always something new and different to drink. Turlock feels like a remote town, with little around it but farms and space. But with Dust Bowl Brewing there now, it's definitely a destination.

Dust Bowl Brewing Company

Opened: Taproom opened August 1, 2011; brewery established May 2009.

Type: Production brewery, with taproom.

Owners: Brett Tate and Brett Honoré.

Brewer: Don Oliver.

Guild membership: CCBA.

System: 10-barrel Premier Stainless brewhouse, 1,700 barrels annual capacity.

Annual production: 1,680 barrels (2012)

Packages available: 12-ounce bottle six-packs, 22-ounce bottles, 64-ounce growlers, and 5- and 15.5-gallon kegs.

Tours: The production brewery is not open to the public.

Hours: Tuesday through Thursday, 11 a.m. to 10 p.m.; Friday and Saturday, 11 a.m. to 11 p.m.; Sunday, 11 a.m. to 8 p.m. Closed Monday.

Food: The taproom serves a wide range of food, from traditional burgers and sandwiches to the unique and utterly wonderful Fried Squeakers, which are local cheese curds. There are daily soup specials, and special entrées are featured on Friday. There are separate lunch and dinner menus, a kids' menu, and a dessert menu with housemade treats like peanut butter cup cheesecake and rustic apple tart.

Extras: You can dine on the outdoor patio, which has a clear surround curtain and heaters for when the temperature is cooler. The restaurant and patio have flat-screen TVs, but muted with subtitles, so you can watch while you listen to the music on the playlist. Want to hear a different song? Customers can download an app to their smart phones to access the taproom's playlist and choose the next selection. Tuesday through Thursday, "hoppy hour" features $1 off the brewery's beers, and the same deal applies all day on Sunday. On Wednesday, you also get $2 off when filling your growler.

Gift shop: T-shirts, hats, pint glasses, and openers are sold at the taproom.

Heretic Brewing Company

1052 Horizon Drive, Suite B, Fairfield, CA 94533
925-526-6364 • www.hereticbrewing.com
Twitter @hereticbrew • Facebook.com/hereticbrew

Jamil Zainasheff was a legend in local and national homebrewing circles for many years before he decided to open his own brewery. Zainasheff is the coauthor of two books on brewing, *Yeast: The Practical Guide to Beer Fermentation*, published in 2010 along with White Labs founder Chris White, and *Brewing Classic Styles: 80 Winning Recipes Anyone Can Brew*, written in 2007 with homebrew writer John Palmer. He's also written countless articles for homebrewing magazines and has his own show on the Brewing Network, *The Jamil Show*.

Jamil was originally a software engineer, but when his wife bought him a homebrewing kit for Christmas in 1999, that got him started on the path to becoming a professional brewer. From early on, he began taking awards at homebrew competitions, both local and national, winning the Ninkasi Award in both 2004 and 2007. He also became a certified Beer Judge Certification Program (BJCP) judge and learned everything he could about beer and brewing. He eventually became the assistant IT director of the BJCP and was named its representative of the West Region, which encompasses California and Hawaii, in 2008.

He had some trouble coming up with the perfect name for the brewery, as most of the ideas he came up with that he felt represented his goals with the beer he wanted to make were already taken. Zainasheff tells the story about how he finally hit upon "heretic," which, he says, is "a person who practices heresy, and heresy is when you hold an opinion at odds with what is generally accepted. Galileo was considered a heretic for supporting the theory that the earth revolves around the sun. In a world where over 90% of beer drinkers believe mass market light lagers constitute the universe of beer, craft beer lovers are all heretics. Some folks may think a heretic has to have some sort of traditional religious meaning, but that is not true even though great beer is a religion for many craft beer lovers."

Originally, Heretic brewed its beer at the E. J. Phair brewery in Pittsburg as part of an alternat-

Beers brewed: Year-round: Evil Twin, Evil Cousin, Shallow Grave, and Gramarye. Special releases: Worry, Tartuffe, One Nut in the Grave, Tafelbully, Torment, Miscreant, and Dead Weight Barleywine.

ing proprietorship. But in late 2012, Jamil took over his own space in Fairfield, in a large industrial park at the end of Horizon Road, just past the Fairfield Animal Hospital, on a road parallel to Air Base Parkway. There he built his own brewery, with enough space to take him all the way to 100,000 barrels a year of production. He is currently considering adding cans to the range of packages the brewery offers.

As a brewer, Jamil Zainasheff is a perfectionist and doesn't suffer fools gladly. He'd much rather you tell him what you don't like about his beer, in specific, so he can fix it. He doesn't want you to just be polite. And that drive to always improve his beers shows in the range of beers that Heretic is offering. With Jamil's own dedicated brewery, I expect Heretic's beer to only get better, and that's from a pretty high starting point. With more space, the brewery will also be able to do more seasonal and special releases, along with some barrel-aged beers too.

The Pick: It's hard to pick just one, because Jamil makes some spectacular beers. I particularly love his Gramarye, a rye session pale ale. It may be low-alcohol, at 4.4 percent ABV, but it's loaded with flavor. The rye adds a touch of magic to the beer, and given that the name is taken from the word *grimoire*, referring to a book of magic, this makes perfect sense. The ale has grapefruit and other citrus aromas, and the rye malt gives a breadlike taste and character to the flavor profile, which is well conditioned and hits all the right notes. I also can't say enough about the Shallow Grave porter, which is a bittersweet chocolate monster with notes of molasses, chili, and coffee that finishes sweet.

Heretic Brewing Company

Opened: May 20, 2011.

Type: Production brewery.

Owner: Jamil Zainasheff.

Brewers: Brewmaster: Jamil Zainasheff.

Head Brewer: Chris Kennedy.

Guild membership: BA, CCBA, NCBG.

System: 30-barrel brewhouse built by AAA of Oregon, 45,000 barrels annual capacity.

Annual production: 1,700 barrels (2012), 6,000 barrels (estimated for 2013).

Packages available: 22-ounce bottles, 375-milliliter cork-and-cage bottles, 50- and 20-liter kegs, and cask beer, but kegs and cask are only sold wholesale through authorized distributors.

Tours: Wednesday and Thursday, 2 to 5 p.m. For reservations, email tours@heretic brewing.com.

Hours: Monday through Friday, 9 a.m. to 5 p.m., though plans are to add a new tasting room with extended hours.

Gift shop: Merchandise is sold online and will also be available at the new location.

Hoppy Brewing Company

6300 Folsom Boulevard, Sacramento, CA 95819
916-451-4677 (restaurant/reservations) /
916-451-6328 (office) • www.hoppy.com
Twitter @HoppyBrewing
Facebook.com/HoppyBrewingCompany

I first encountered Hoppy when it was a San Jose startup and contracted its beer while looking for a location to build a brewery. Initially, clever graphics and some great beer names brought Hoppy success, but the fact that it made good beer kept people coming back.

After years of searching, the owners finally found the spot they were looking for and moved the brewery to east Sacramento in 1999. When you visit, you can understand why they moved the brewery several hours north. It's a vast and spacious place, with a long bar, separate dining areas, and plenty of room in the back for the brewery and for storing kegs and other beer. There's ambience for whatever mood you're in, with open areas and secluded spots to rendezvous, as well as plentiful outdoor seating at the front entrance, where on many days you can enjoy the Sacramento sunshine.

Hoppy offers a wide array of beers, a number of which are available all the time, along with regular seasonals and around two special new releases each month. That's twenty-four new beers a year in addition to the usual suspects. There's always something new to try, which makes going to Hoppy always a treat. The food is a cut above what you find at the average brewpub, and your choices are vast, with a staggering number of dishes on the menu.

It may sound clichéd, but you really can find something here to please everybody. Good beer and good food, and lots of it. What else could you want? Don't worry, be Hoppy.

Beers brewed: Year-round: Golden Nugget Cream Ale, Liquid Sunshine Blonde Ale, Heff-a-Weizen, Hoppy Face Amber Ale, Burnt Sienna Ale, Stoney Face Red Ale, and Total Eclipse Black Ale. Seasonals: Hoppy Claus Holiday Ale, plus two brewer's specials each month, such as Super Hoppy, an imperial IPA, and Pacific J, a pale ale.

The Pick: Hoppy's black ale, Total Eclipse, is my favorite, with rich chocolate notes and a touch of coffee and hops bitterness. It's very easy drinking, light-bodied, with delicate sassafras and licorice notes. Though the Liquid Sunshine Blonde Ale may be best on really hot days, almost any other time I'll pick the Total Eclipse.

Hoppy Brewing Company

Opened: July 1, 1994; brewpub opened June 1, 1999.

Type: Brewpub.

Owners: Troy Paski and shareholders.

Brewer: Ed Kopta.

Guild membership: BA, CCBA.

System: 15-barrel Pub System, 1,800 barrels annual capacity.

Annual production: 1,200 barrels.

Packages available: 22-ounce bottles and 5- and 13.2-gallon kegs.

Tours: Tours are available, but reservations are required.

Hours: Monday through Wednesday, 11 a.m. to midnight; Thursday and Friday, 11 a.m. to 1 a.m.; Saturday, 10 a.m. to 1 a.m.; Sunday 10 a.m. to midnight.

Food: The brewpub serves more than just pub food and has quite an extensive menu—or actually, series of menus, with separate ones for brunch, lunch, dinner, kids, and dessert. The brunch menu is served only on weekends and Monday holidays beginning at 10 a.m. In addition to appetizers and many lunch items, it also includes a full breakfast menu from burritos to "hop" cakes, Hoppy's version of pancakes. Both the lunch and dinner menus have a full page of appetizers, along with lots of salads, pastas, warm sandwiches, burgers, and others items. The dinner menu has all that plus pizza and nearly a dozen entrées, such as Caribbean pork chops, bison rib eye, and blackened salmon.

Extras: The brewpub has outdoor seating and a stage and lounge area with a big-screen television. On the first Saturday of each month from 11 a.m. to 1 p.m., acoustic bluegrass musicians take the stage. "Hoppy hour" is all day Monday and 3 to 6 p.m. daily, plus late nights after 9:30 p.m. Other specials include a trivia contest Tuesday beginning at 10 p.m.; Beer Ambassador Day on Saturday, when you can purchase pints for $2.50 if you have on any Brewers Association logo wear; and a 22-ounce bottle of beer to take home with the purchase of an entrée on Sunday. The brewpub is family-friendly, with $1 kids' meals on Sunday and Monday. Cigar smoking is permitted.

Gift shop: Merchandise is available at the brewpub and online.

Lockdown Brewing Company

Folsom: 718 Sutter Street, Suite 200, Folsom, CA 95630

Rancho Cordova: 11327 Trade Center Drive #350, Rancho Cordova, CA 95742

916-358-9645 (Folsom)

www.lockdownbrewingcompany.com

Facebook.com/LockdownBrewingCo

Lockdown Brewing began with a different type of incarceration. A couple of friends locked into the college experience found salvation, as so many do, in a bottle of very tasty craft beer. While at Chico State, Myles Deniz and Robert Whistler discovered an appreciation for better beer, but they had not yet realized they could make their own.

After graduation, they moved to Folsom and received homebrew kits for Christmas, then found the Brewmeister homebrew shop in Old Town Folsom, turning their interest into a monthly event and a full-fledged passion. Then they upped the ante and switched to all-grain brewing. By chance, another friend's father was closing his manufacturing plant, leaving the space available. They hatched a plan to use that space over a few homebrews, and when they heard the lockdown bell ring out from the nearby Folsom Prison, their fate was sealed. Someone suggested Lockdown Brewing, and that was that, with the addition of the tagline "Home of the Folsom Prison Brews."

They now operate a production/tasting room in Rancho Cordova that's open for sales three nights a week, but it's really the Folsom tasting room that you should visit. It's a beautiful spot in the heart of Old Town Folsom, located upstairs along the main street of the town's historic district. From there, a long balcony looks down on the street. There are plentiful tables, made from old barrels, and chairs on the balcony, and on warm days, there's no better spot in town to enjoy a beer.

Inside, the bar is long and narrow, but also light from the balcony windows. A Lockdown mural is painted on the far wall. Through an arrangement with the adjacent Beach Hut Deli, you can order

Beers brewed: Year-round: Emma's Blonde Ale, Sutter St. Common, Powerhouse Pale Ale, Powerhouse India Pale Ale, Repressa Red Ale, Stony Bar Scotch Ale, Folsom Breakout Stout, and Hey Honey Porter.

The Pick: Emma's Blonde Ale, named for a notorious Folsom blonde who ran the town brothel in the early 1900s, is also tart, with a lightly sweet nose and subtle citrus hops aromas. It's a refreshing beer, easy-drinking, with mild flavors and a clean finish.

food while you're there. After a long day of sightseeing, shopping, and walking around Old Town Folsom, this is the spot to end your day.

Lockdown Brewing Company

Opened: October 2004; Folsom tasting room opened November 10, 2011.

Type: Contract brewery, with taproom.

Owners: Myles Deniz, Jonathan Knowles, Andrew Mering, and Robert Whistler.

Brewer: Robert Whistler.

Guild membership: NCBG.

Packages available: 12-ounce bottles in six-packs and 5- and 15.5-gallon kegs.

Hours: Folsom: Monday and Tuesday, 11 a.m. to 3 p.m.; Wednesday and Thursday, 11 a.m. to 10 p.m.; Friday and Saturday, 11 a.m. to midnight; Sunday, 11 a.m. to 6 p.m. Rancho Cordova: Wednesday through Friday, 4 to 8 p.m.

Food: The Folsom tasting room serves food from the Beach Hut Deli. You can also bring in your own food to enjoy on the balcony overlooking Sutter Street. No food is available in Rancho Cordova.

Extras: Folsom has happy hour from 4 to 6 p.m., Wednesday through Friday. Wednesday is open mic night, hosted by the Sutter Junkies, from 7 to 10 p.m., and Thursday from 7 to 9:30 p.m. is trivia night. On Friday and Saturday, there's live music from 8:30 to 11:30 p.m. There are also big-screen televisions, dartboards, and pool tables.

Gift shop: Merchandise is available in the taproom.

Lodi Beer Company

105 South School Street, Lodi, CA 95240
209-368-9931 • www.lodibeercompany.com
Facebook.com/lodibeercompany

Most people have probably heard of Lodi thanks to the Creedence Clearwater Revival song of the same name, but the town is also known as the "Zinfandel Capital of the World." And until 2004, it had always been a wine town, but Lodi Beer Company changed all that when it became the first brewery to open there.

Lodi Beer Company's founder and first brewer, Roger Rehmke, grew up on a dairy farm in nearby Galt, where he learned mechanical and food processing skills. He was working as a mechanic and auto-body repair technician when he was bitten by the homebrewing bug. After being kicked out of his kitchen, he took his brewing into the backyard. He started entering competitions and found himself becoming increasingly passionate as he racked up medal after medal, eventually deciding to open a brewpub.

He found a beautiful historic 1917 building in downtown Lodi that was originally a bank, though over the years it's been home to many other businesses. The building looks great on the outside, but on the inside it really shines. It has a tall stamped tin ceiling, with a brick wall on one side and another that features paintings of the brewpub's beer labels. On the left is a dark mahogany bar with an ornate brass tap tower that has the brewery's name on it in brass letters. The bar has an Old West look and feel, with a giant mirror hanging on the brick wall behind it.

The brewery is located dead center and is the focal point of the brewpub. It's a gorgeous copper 15-barrel Bohemian brewhouse that used to be in Southern California. But it perfectly suits the

Beers brewed: Year-round: Lodi Lite Lager, Umna Hefeweizen, Mo Kel Ko Red Ale, Gilt Edge Marzen, and Plowshear Porter. Seasonals: Tart Cherry Wheat, Summer Wheat, Western Pacific IPA, Southern English Brown, Framboise, White IPA, Doppelbock, Eisbock, and Christmas Ale.

The Pick: Given the climate in Lodi, it's not surprising that the Lite Lager is the brewery's most popular beer, though I think the Tart Cherry Wheat, brewed with local cherries, and the Umna Hefeweizen are more satisfying thirst quenchers. But my Pick is the Mo Kel Ko Red Ale, which is a nice malty amber with good hops character, just enough to gently bite at your taste buds yet still keep the focus on the sweeter caramel malt character and a smooth touch of chocolate that is more pronounced in the finish.

space and looks as if it's always been there. Surrounding the square brewery space are tables and a short walled fence, along with tall wooden columns. The brewery overlooks the entire dining area, and surrounding it are all of the booths, bar, kitchen, and tables and chairs on all four sides.

Several years ago, another homebrewer, Peter York, met Roger Rehmke at a homebrew club meeting that he had recently joined. The two became friends and started homebrewing together. York's father was a world-renowned food sciences professor at UC Davis, and Peter grew up with an appreciation for the fermentation process. He started homebrewing at an early age and worked for a time as the assistant brewer at the now defunct Sacramento Brewing Company. Eventually Rehmke persuaded York to become the head brewer at Lodi, where he's now been for more than five years. There are generally around ten Lodi beers on at any given time, split evenly between regular beers and an ever-changing lineup of seasonals and specialty releases.

Lodi Beer Company

Opened: November 2004.

Type: Brewpub.

Owner: Roger Rehmke.

Brewer: Peter York.

Guild membership: BA.

System: 15-barrel Bohemian Brewing Systems, 850 barrels annual capacity.

Annual production: 660 barrels (2012).

Packages available: Growlers and 5- and 15.5-gallon kegs.

Tours: No tours are available at this time because of a local fire ordinance.

Hours: Sunday through Thursday, 11 a.m. to 9 p.m.; Friday and Saturday, 11 a.m. to 10 p.m.

Food: The brewpub features a big menu with lots of choices, including a dozen starters, fresh salads, soup, sandwiches and burgers, pizza, steak and ribs, and brewery favorites like fish and chips, jambalaya, and Acapulco mahi mahi. There's also a dessert menu and housemade root beer. All menu items are available to go.

Extras: Ask your server for details about joining the Pint Club; for an annual fee, you can get a 22-ounce pour of regular Lodi beer every day of the year, along with other perks and discounts for members. Live music is featured on Friday and Saturday nights, and banquet space is available for private functions.

Gift shop: Shirts and glassware are available at the brewpub.

New Helvetia Brewing Company

1730 Broadway, Sacramento, CA 95818
916-469-9889 • www.newhelvetiabrew.com
Twitter @NewHelvetiaBrew
Facebook.com/pages/New-Helvetia-Brewing-Co/
150569735022356

John Sutter, the Swiss-born man who found gold and started the California gold rush, named his landholdings New Helvetia, for his home country. Helvetia is the female personification of Switzerland. So when local real estate developer Dave Gull opened his brewery, he looked to Sacramento's history for inspiration and chose the name New Helvetia. The brewery is re-creating the beers of one of Sacramento's most famous breweries, Buffalo Brewing Company, which was founded in 1890 and for a time was the largest brewery on the West Coast. Updating its old tagline, "Buffalo Beer Is Back . . . Again," Gull is reintroducing the historic lager. The brewery is in an old brick building completely remodeled to accommodate a brewery and tasting room.

River City brewer Brian Cofresi (see page 314) is moonlighting at New Helvetia as the brewmaster and has worked from historical data and experience to make the beers as near as possible to their roots.

New Helvetia Brewing Company

Opened: December 2012.

Type: Production brewery.

Owners: Dave and Amy Gull.

Brewer: Brian Cofresi

Guild membership: BA, CCBA, NCBG.

System: 10-hectoliter brewhouse; 1,200 barrels annual.

Annual production: 400 barrels (2013 estimate).

Packages available: Growlers, kegs, and pints.

Tours: By reservation only.

Hours: Wednesday and Thursday, 4 p.m. to 9 p.m.; Friday, 4 p.m. to 10 p.m.; Saturday, 1 p.m. to 10 p.m.; and Sunday, 1 p.m. to 6 p.m.

Extras: Live music, trivia nights, courtyard seating.

Gift shop: T-shirts, hats, sweatshirts, pint glasses.

Beers brewed: Year-round: Saison Solon, Colonial Pale Ale, Thunderbeast IPA, Rough and Ready Red IPA, Indomitable City Double IPA, Homeland Stout and Auroch American Wild Ale. Seasonals: The Alpha Lager, B.T. Bourbon Barrel Aged Imperial Stout, Edgar Allan Porter, and Buffalo Craft Lager.

The Pick: The Thunderbeast IPA is incredibly smooth and creamy, with solid but mild hop flavors. It's balanced nicely with sweet strength and finishes with a lingering bitterness, but no astringency.

River City Brewing Company

545 Downtown Plaza, Suite 1115, Sacramento, CA 95814
916-447-BREW (2739) • www.rivercitybrewing.net
Twitter @RiverCityBrew • Facebook.com/RiverCityBrewingCo

In the nearly twenty years that River City brewmaster Brian Cofresi has been brewing in Sacramento, he's seen a lot of changes—to the local beer scene, to craft beer more generally, and even to his own brewpub. Although Cofresi began brewing there as an intern in 1995, the brewpub originally opened in 1993, and by the turn of the century it had merged with another small brewpub chain. In 2007, it became independent once again when it was purchased by several River City employees.

Cofresi returned in 1999 and was hired as the head brewer, and he's been there brewing happily ever since. He brews at least twenty different beers each year—the usual six, some regular seasonals, and a wide selection of one-off beers throughout the year. So no matter when you go, there's always something new to discover or an old favorite to enjoy. Cofresi's beers are always well made, and I don't believe I've ever had one of his beers that wasn't worth drinking.

The brewpub is somewhat hidden from passersby, in the interior of a shopping mall. You almost have to know where it is to find it. It's on the west end of Sacramento's Downtown Plaza, a two-story mall anchored by a Macy's and Century Theater. The brewpub is tucked into the ground floor in a sunlit courtyard outside the theater, making it an ideal spot for drinks and a meal before or after taking in a movie. If you want to enjoy the sunshine, you can have your meal and beer on an outdoor patio just outside the restaurant. The tables have shade umbrellas and are surrounded by planter boxes.

Beers brewed: Year-round: K Street Kolsch, Hefeweizen, Vienna, Cap City IPA, Woodenhead Ale, and Black River Stout (N2). Seasonals: Maibock, Irish Red Rye Ale, and Belgian White, plus many other one-off beers throughout the year.

The Pick: I'm torn between two of Brian's beers, as both are styles that many breweries don't get quite right. But his K Street Kolsch and his Vienna lager are both great examples of these underserved styles. The Kolsch is nicely sessionable, at only 4.25 percent ABV, and boasts a crisp malt nose with clean, slightly fruit-forward flavors and a soft, delicate mouthfeel. The Vienna, an amber lager, is an elegant beer with sweet malt notes and a treacly maple finish.

Inside, the dark wood creates a cozy atmosphere despite the high ceilings and feels like an escape from the warm sunshine outside. The long wooden bar that greets you when you first walk in is also a great place to get a quick bite for lunch, especially if you're by yourself. The open dining room takes up the center of a large interior, and the brewery, fermenters, and serving tanks are all upstairs along a balcony overlooking the restaurant.

The food is quite tasty, and two of the chefs have been cooking for the brewpub since it first opened and are now part of the ownership team. They've created a nice menu of traditional favorites and inventive dishes that are reasonably priced and won't leave you hungry. But it's Cofresi's beers that are the star of the show, as far as I'm concerned, and you should save room for several pints.

River City Brewing Company

Opened: November 23, 1993.

Type: Brewpub.

Owners: Steve Cuneo, Beth Ayres, Chantalle Malneck, and Ignacio Sanchez.

Brewer: Brian Cofresi.

Guild membership: BA, CCBA, NCBG.

System: 15-barrel Century Manufacturing brewhouse, made in Alexandria, Ohio, in 1993, 1,400 barrels annual capacity.

Annual production: 509 barrels (2011).

Packages available: 1-gallon City's Block boxes, 5-liter keglets, and 5-, 7.75- and 15.5-gallon kegs.

Tours: Tours are generally available any time that the brewer is around, usually any weekday except Wednesday.

Hours: Monday through Thursday, 11:30 a.m. to 9:30 p.m.; Friday and Saturday, 11:30 a.m. to 10:30 p.m.; and Sunday, 11:30 a.m. to 8:30 p.m.

Food: The lunch menu has a small but well-chosen selection of appetizers, salads, wood-fired pizza, and "main attractions," which include a few choices each of pasta, fish, sandwiches, and burgers. The dinner menu includes most of the lunch items, along with some additional dishes, such as slow beer-braised pot roast, grilled German sausages, and marinated pork tenderloin.

Extras: Happy hours at the bar, 3 to 6 p.m. Monday through Friday, include $3.50 pints, and on Wednesday evenings from 6 p.m. to close, pints are just $2.50.

Gift shop: The restaurant has a display case with T-shirts, hats, and logo shot glasses.

Rubicon Brewing Company

Brewpub: 2004 Capitol Avenue, Sacramento, CA 95811
Production brewery: 885 Stillwater Road, Sacramento,
    CA 95605
916-448-7032 • www.rubiconbrewing.com
Twitter @rubiconman • Facebook.com/RubiconBrewing

The Rubicon was originally crossed—and opened—in late 1987 by Ed Brown, an old friend of the current owner, Glynn Phillips. The two first met in the 1970s through Brown's nephews, who all grew up together in the East Bay, around Moraga. Phillips worked for a number of years in the brewing industry, first at Great Basin in Nevada, and later, for much longer, at Marin Brewing. The two kept in touch, and when Brown was ready to retire, Phillips was the natural successor and bought the brewery in 2004. Over the last decade, he has put his own stamp on the place, increasing community involvement and charity work, and putting Rubicon beer in 22-ounce bottles.

Rubicon also boasts one of the most experienced brewers anywhere with Scott Cramlet, who's been brewing there for more than twenty years. Cramlet learned under Rubicon's original brewer, Phil Moeller, taking over the reigns from him in 1990.

When the categories for India pale ale were first split into English-style and American-style for Great American Beer Festival judging in 1990, Cramlet's IPA won the gold medal. He repeated his success again the next year, bringing home back-to-back gold medals, an impressive feat for the category that year after year has more entries than any other style.

The brewpub is nestled along a tree-lined street in downtown Sacramento, an unassuming spot. An iron fence turns part of the sidewalk into an outdoor patio space, with a few tables and chairs for outdoor dining or a spot to enjoy a pint during warm weather. Inside, there's a copper-top bar to your right, and tables and chairs everywhere else. It's a comfortable space, if a little cramped, but that shouldn't be a deterrent. It's just a small space that's grown more popular as the years pass. The brewery is tucked into the back, behind a wall running along one side of the

Beers brewed: Year-round: India Pale Ale, Monkey Knife Fight Pale Ale, Amber, Irish Red Ale, Irish Stout, Maggie Brown Ale, and American Stout. Seasonals: Rosebud Special Ale, Winter Wheatwine, Capricorn Black Ale and Hopsauce Double IPA.

building, though you can see parts of it though glass windows at strategic points. There's also a small bottling line that slowly puts select beers into bottles for the retail trade.

Perhaps most exciting of all, Rubicon is building a separate production brewery in West Sacramento, within sight of I-80. The building is 16,000 square feet and will hold a 15-barrel brewhouse to start with, but plans are to add a 30-barrel one in the future. The brewery will bottle its 22-ounce bottles there and also add 12-ounce bottles in six-packs. They'll keg their beer there too. Soon many more people will be able to cross the Rubicon and find Scott Cramlet's delicious beers.

Rubicon Brewing Company

Opened: November 1, 1987.

Type: Brewpub.

Owners: Glynn Phillips.

Brewer: Scott Cramlet.

Guild membership: BA, CCBA, NCBG.

System: 10-barrel Western Brewers Systems of Santa Rosa, designed by Dr. Michael Lewis of UC Davis, 2,400 barrels annual capacity. The new production brewery has a 15-barrel brewhouse with 30-barrel fermenters.

Annual production: 2,400 barrels (2012).

Packages available: 22-ounce bottles, growlers, casks, and 5- and 15.5-gallon kegs; 12-ounce bottles in six-packs will also be available with the addition of the production brewery.

Tours: Brewery tours are available; reservations are required on weekends.

Hours: Monday through Thursday, 11 a.m. to 11:30 p.m.; Friday and Saturday, 11 a.m. to 12:30 a.m.; Sunday, 11 a.m. to 10 p.m.

Food: The brewpub offers a full menu of pub fare that includes a large selection of appetizers, soups and salads, burgers and sandwiches, including vegetarian items. After 5 p.m., additional entrées are available, including several pasta dishes, fish and chips, tri-tip, and a tasty sausage platter. Don't miss the waffle fries.

Extras: Daily specials include Happy Hour Monday, special pricing for pints all day on Tuesday, all-you-can-eat fish and chips after 5 p.m. on Wednesday, a new cask beer tapped beginning at 5 p.m. on Thursday, and seafood specials for lunch and dinner on Friday. The brewpub also hosts various charity events. Details can be found on the website or Facebook page.

Gift shop: Merchandise is available at the brewpub and online.

Ruhstaller Beer

RUHSTALLER
SACRAMENTO'S BEER
SINCE 1881

630 K Street, Sacramento, CA 95814
916-919-5691 • www.ruhstallerbeer.com
Twitter @ruhstallerbeer
Facebook.com/RuhstallerBeer

A Ruhstaller brewery was originally founded in Sacramento in 1881 by Capt. Frank Ruhstaller, a Swiss-born soldier who came to California seeking his fortune. He was only thirty-five years old when he founded the brewery. It was the third brewery that he'd started (he'd also worked at Sacramento's other well-known historic brewery, Buffalo Brewing Company), and at the time, it was the largest one west of the Mississippi River. With access to local hops growers and barley farmers, it was an ideal spot for brewing. And the brewery flourished until Prohibition.

J. E. Paino learned this history while researching a project at UC Davis working on his MBA. He'd been an architecture major at Princeton but went into construction and real estate after college. It struck Paino that there was an opportunity to pay homage to Sacramento's rich brewing heritage and at the same time bring back hop growing to California. Before Prohibition, California had been the largest hop-growing state in the country, but afterward, hops moved to the Pacific Northwest, and wine grapes and other agriculture replaced it here. For his first beers, Paino found California barley grown by Ron and Ann McGill in the Klamath River Basin near the border of Oregon.

He next discovered the Kuchinski Hop Ranch in Lake County, about 100 miles from Sacramento, which was started by Marty and Claudia Kuchinski in 2007. It was the first commercial hops farm in California since the last one closed in 1985. The Kuchinskis farm 200 acres of hops, 15 percent of which are organic. But he also wanted some hops closer to home and persuaded farmer Sean McNa-

Beers brewed: Year-round: 1881 California Red Ale (Kuchinski Hop Ranch) and CAPT. California Black IPA. Seasonals: Gilt Edge, Hop Sac 2012 Late Harvest Wet Hop Ale (Blue Heron Hop Yard), The Kenyan, Exquisite Kolsch, Tripel Dipper, and Founders Blend.

The Pick: While not a historic beer style, the CAPT., named for Captain Ruhstaller, is a black IPA with a good hops aromas of citrus and pine, as well as roasted malt, coffee, and chocolate. They meld together seamlessly, the most important aspect of a hoppy black ale, and there's a subtle spicing that almost acts like the glue. The zesty spicing also gives the beer burnt toast flavors along with tangerine and marmalade notes.

mara to plant Chinook, Cascade, Nugget, and Centennial hops on his Sierra Orchards farm in Winters, near the Putah Creek.

Paino called on volunteers via Facebook to help with the first hops harvest last year, and he bottled Hop Sac—with each bottle packaged in a burlap sack like hops—in limited quantities. For the same reason, all Ruhstaller bottles have their necks wrapped in burlap too, making them unique looking on the average store shelf.

Although Paino is contracting the brewing, he is using local breweries, and plans are afoot to build his own production brewery. He believes that each beer he makes has at least 94 percent California ingredients, including barley, hops, and water, and some have more than that. Between that and his nod to the area's brewing history, it's a great story. What really makes it work is that the beer tastes great too. The story, the packaging, the local angle—all of these things might make you pick up a bottle and give it a try. But what's ultimately making Ruhstaller a success a second time is that the modern brewery is making some terrific beers.

Ruhstaller Beer

Opened: July 10, 2011.

Type: Contract brewery.

Owner: Jan-Erik (J. E.) Paino.

Guild membership: CCBA, NCBG.

Packages available: 22-ounce bottles, 16-ounce cans in four-packs, and kegs.

Gift shop: Merchandise is available online.

St. Stan's Brewing Company

821 L Street, Modesto, CA 95354
209-524-2337 • www.ststans.com
  (and heroesmodesto.com)
Twitter @ststansbrewing • Facebook.com/pages/St-
  Stans-Brewing-Co/52657497061

St. Stan's was one of the first successful production breweries in Northern California. At one time, it was nearly as popular as Sierra Nevada and other early microbrewery favorites. It was originally founded by Garith and Romy Helm, who developed a taste for German-style beers after a series of visits to Germany in the 1970s. Garith became an avid homebrewer and began trying to re-create his favorite German beer, a Dusseldorf alt, which would become St. Stan's flagship beer, its Amber Alt.

They decided to build a new brewery to turn their hobby into a full-scale business and hired a friend of the family, the current brewer Bill Coffey's father, to build the brewery, a project that was started in 1981 but took three years to complete. Their first beer was kegged in July 1984, and by 1987 they added a bottling line and were selling six-packs of their beer. But they ran into a problem: they couldn't brew enough beer to keep up with demand.

So they built a larger brewing facility in downtown Modesto, which opened in September 1990 and is still the location of the brewery today. When the original brewery was built, Bill Coffey was only fourteen years old, although he remembers being fascinated with the brewery and began working there even before he was able to drink beer. Over St. Stan's entire history, there were only three or four years when Coffey was not involved with the brewery, during which time he owned Parrotts Ferry Brewing Company in Columbia, consulted with the Chinese govern-

Beers brewed: Year-round: St. Stan's Amber, Blonde Lager, Red Sky Ale, Whistle Stop Ale, Graffiti Wheat, and St. Stan's Porter. Seasonals: Bill's Brown Bag Barley Wine, Very Hoppy Bitter, St Stan's Dark, and St. Stan's Fest.

The Pick: St. Stan's Amber Alt is billed as the first altbier made in the United States, and it was certainly the first one I had, back in the mid-1980s, when it was one of the most popular brands in Northern California. Its star power may have waned, but it still tastes as good as I remember it. With a crisp, bready, toffee malt focus, it's balanced nicely with a mix of American, English, and German noble hops. It's nicely bitter but easy drinking and clean, with a tart and slightly sweet finish.

ment on building breweries, and worked as head of quality control for Pyramid Breweries.

After a rollicking start, St. Stan's fell upon some hard times, beginning sometime in the mid-1990s, when craft beer's streak of big growth began to falter for a lot of breweries. The brewery went through a series of new owners, with mixed results, but they kept the doors open. St. Stan's also started using its excess capacity to do contract brewing for various clients. Attached to the brewery today is a bar and restaurant called Hero's Modesto, which is a separate business that is owned by brewmaster Bill Coffey.

What the future will hold for St. Stan's is anybody's guess, but as it was one of the unsung heroes of the "microbrewery revolution," it's nice to see it hanging on, and I sincerely hope it will continue to do so. Having the continuity of Bill Coffey's presence as brewmaster—and to some extent, historian—may well be the glue that keeps it together. The beer still tastes every bit as good as it always did; the brewery probably just needs to sell more of it. Perhaps now would be a good time to go visit the place and do your part.

St. Stan's Brewing Company

Opened: July 1984.

Type: Production brewery.

Owner: Greg Olson.

Brewer: Bill Coffey.

Guild membership: NCBG.

System: 30-barrel custom-built, with 30-, 60- and 120-barrel fermenters, 25,000 barrels annual capacity.

Annual production: 7,000 barrels (2012).

Packages available: 12-ounce bottles in six-packs, 22-ounce bottles, and 5- and 15.5-gallon kegs.

Tours: Brewery tours are available on Saturdays or by appointment during the week.

Hours: Brewery: Monday through Saturday, 8 a.m. to 5 p.m. Hero's: Monday through Thursday, 11 a.m. to 10 p.m.; Friday and Saturday, 11 a.m. to midnight; Sunday, 10 a.m. to 7 p.m.

Food: Hero's extensive menu incudes an array of appetizers, salads and soup, sandwiches and burgers, pizza and calzones.

Extras: Happy hour at Hero's is every weekday from 3 to 6 p.m. In addition to the ten St. Stan's beers on tap, Hero's has a dozen guest taps, mostly local craft beer. Hero's also features live music and has banquet facilities.

Gift shop: St. Stan's brewery merchandise is available at Hero's.

Sudwerk Privatbrauerei Hübsch

2001 Second Street, Davis, CA 95618
530-756-BREW (brewery) / 530-758-8700 (restaurant)
www.sudwerkbrew.com (brewery) /
www.sudwerk.com (restaurant)
Twitter @sudwerkbrew
Facebook.com/sudwerkbrew

Sudwerk was originally founded by Ron Broward and Dean Unger in 1989, but in 2006, the restaurant was sold to Tim McDonnell, who also owns the Spinnaker in Sausalito and Tarantino's in San Francisco on Fisherman's Wharf. Broward and Unger continue to operate the brewery independently, with an agreement for the two companies to share part of the space and provide beer for the brewpub.

Sudwerk was one of the first microbreweries to focus on lagers. The original copper-clad brewhouse can be seen in the middle of the brewpub, and it's still used for experimental and small batches. Behind a bank of windows, you can see open-top fermenters. And the old system worked fine, at least until 1993, when Sudwerk had become the largest brewpub in the U.S. by volume. The following year, it expanded, putting in a warehouse in the back, adding a new brewhouse four times the size of the original, and installing a bottling line. The new brewery was also one of the first to use a computerized process control.

Above the new brewery, there's a classroom used by UC Davis for its Master Brewers extension courses and other classes. Many California brewers have gone through the brewing program at UC Davis, including Sudwerk's brewmaster Jay Prahl, who worked there during his time in the program and for two years afterward, before opening and running new startup breweries in Mexico and Peru. He returned to take over Sudwerk's brewing in 2003 and has been at the helm for the last decade. In addition to the classroom, there's also an R&D lab for White Labs, a brewing yeast company headquartered in San Diego.

Beers brewed: Year-round: Pilsner, HefeWeizen, Marzen, and Lager. Seasonals: Oatmeal Stout, IPA, Extra Pale Ale, Doppel Bock, MaiBock, Fest Marzen, Aggie Lager, Berliner Weisse, and Dunkel Weizen. Signature Series: Imperial Pilsner and Dunkel Weiss Bock (currently retired).

The Pick: I'm particularly fond of the big seasonal bocks, but for everyday drinking give me the Pilsner, a German-style lager. It has nice biscuity malt and noble hops aromas with just a slight bite, as it should. It's a refreshing pilsner with great balance and a tart finish.

If you're planning a visit to try the beer, the best time to go, hands down, is during the Dock Store Brews events, which take place back in the brewery at the dock. During these events, the brewery serves different experimental beers that you can't find elsewhere. They are rotated frequently, but recent offerings included Bruised Banana (a fusion of a dunkel weizen and a hefeweizen), Dry Hopped Extra Pale Ale (dry hopped with Cascade hops), Monk Stand Up (a Belgian tripel), PLGRM (a blend of pilsner, helles lager, and märzen), and Three Best Friends (a vanilla dry stout).

Each June, Sudwerk puts on a local beer festival, the Davis Beerfest, benefitting Citizens Who Care. In Folsom, the brewery also operates Sudwerk Riverside (9900 Greenback Lane, sudwerkriverside.com), a restaurant that exclusively serves Sudwerk beers and has a similar menu.

The beer at Sudwerk pairs nicely with the food and is generally solid and well made. Although Sudwerk is just off the highway, it requires a little effort driving down some access roads to get there. Happily, it's worth making the effort.

Sudwerk Privatbrauerei Hübsch

Opened: April 1990 (first started brewing in 1989).

Type: Brewpub and small production brewery.

Owners: Ron Broward, Dean Unger, and Peggy Unger.

Brewer: Jay Prahl.

Guild membership: BA, NCBG.

System: 75-hectoliter Steinecker, with a 20-hectoliter Caspary pilot brewery, 17,000 barrels annual capacity.

Annual production: 5,200 barrels (2012).

Packages available: 12-ounce bottles in six-packs and twelve-packs, 22-ounce bottles, growlers, and 5-, 7.75-, and 15.5-gallon kegs.

Tours: Fridays beginning at 6 p.m. and Saturdays from 4 and 6 p.m. Email or call for other times or reservations.

Hours: Sunday through Tuesday, 11:30 a.m. to 9:30 p.m.; Wednesday and Thursday, 11:30 a.m. to 9 p.m.; Friday and Saturday, 11:30 a.m. to 10:30 p.m. Dock Store Brews: Thursday and Friday, 4 to 8 p.m.; Saturday, 3 to 8 p.m.

Food: Tasty appetizers, soups and salads, burgers and sandwiches, pasta, pizza, and entrées such as Parmesan-Romano crusted Chicken and Brewmaster Schnitzel. There are also vegetarian choices, housemade treats, and a kids' menu.

Extras: Live music Saturday nights from May to October and $1 Pint Night Wednesdays; banquet facilities available.

Gift shop: The brewpub has a glass case with merchandise for sale.

Track 7 Brewing Company

3747 West Pacific Avenue, Suite F, Sacramento, CA 95820
916-520-HOPS (4677) • www.track7brewing.com
Twitter @track7brewing
Facebook.com/Track7Brewing

One block west of Curtis Park in Sacramento, the mainline tracks of the old Western Pacific Railroad run past West Pacific Avenue, where one of Sacramento's newest breweries makes its home. That, and some coincidences with the number seven, led the brewery owners to call their enterprise Track 7 Brewing Company.

It must have been good luck, because the brewery's been slammed with business since the day its doors opened. Track 7 was founded by two couples—the Grahams and the Scotts—all of whom are involved in running the business. Ryan Graham is the full-time head brewer, and Geoff Scott also brews while holding down a desk job. Becca Scott manages the taproom, while Jeanna Graham coordinates all the events.

The tasting room is a great open space, with high ceilings, a small bar, and scattered picnic tables and chairs. To one side, there's a separate room with a sofa and chairs for small groups to have their own space. A large chalkboard colorfully lists the available beers and pricing. The roll-up door is up when the place is open, and when it's sunny, a portable canopy provides shade.

The brewery is in the back, behind the bar. That's where Ryan and Geoff brew up a tasty lineup of solid beers. Their beer has quickly and justifiably become popular, and the tasting room is full most days. They produce six year-round beers plus one seasonal at any given time. In addition, they've done special releases throughout their first year. In their second year, the brewery will double in size, increasing the footprint from 2,150

Beers brewed: Year-round: Alkali Wit, Daylight Amber, Bee Line Blonde, Soulman Stout, Panic IPA, and Big 4 Ale. Seasonals: Riot Act Rye Ale (April), Trien Wrak Belgium IPA (May), and Tracktoberfest (fall), with many more coming. Three special beers were created for the brewery's first anniversary: Chocolate Soul Stout, Belgian Dubbel, and Left Eye, Right Eye Double IPA.

The Pick: The Daylight Amber may be called an amber ale, but it drinks like an IPA, at 65 IBUs and 6.25 percent ABV. Given the proliferation of extreme IPAs, this one's a welcome departure. It's a more sessionable beer, with a floral, spicy hops nose and flavors, balanced nicely with toffee, caramel malt, and a tart finish.

to 4,400 square feet. You can also find Track 7 beer at nearly two dozen area bars and restaurants.

Track 7 Brewing Company

Opened: December 31, 2011.

Type: Production brewery.

Owners: Ryan and Jeanna Graham, Rebecca and Geoff Scott.

Brewers: Ryan Graham and Geoff Scott.

Guild membership: CCBA, NCBG.

System: 7-barrel Blackstone Ventures brewhouse, 3,000 barrels annual capacity.

Annual production: 500 barrels (2012).

Packages available: Growlers and 5- and 15.5-gallon kegs.

Tours: No formal tours are offered, although the entire brewery can be seen from the taproom. But if a brewer is there, feel free to ask to take a look around. If he can spare the time, he'll be happy to show you around the brewery.

Hours: Wednesday through Friday, 5 to 9 p.m.; Saturday, 2 to 9 p.m.; Sunday, 2 to 6 p.m.

Food: Snacks are sold at the brewery. Food trucks are on-site on Friday and Saturday evenings.

Extras: Family-friendly and dog-friendly.

Gift shop: T-shirts, tank tops, hats, and pint glasses are available.

Twelve Rounds Brewing

866 57th Street, Sacramento, CA 95819
916-500-1059 • www.twelveroundsbrewing.com
Twitter @12RoundsBrewing
Facebook.com/pages/Twelve-Rounds-Brewing-
  Company/500687546621772

Daniel Murphy is a twenty-year veteran of home-brewing, having won numerous awards, including two first-place awards at the 2011 California State Fair. Daniel's wife, Elle, also shares his passion for beer and cooking. The couple decided to take their love of DIY and turn it into a family business. Their Twelve Rounds brewpub will feature fresh, local food, and a menu that will change seasonally. Daniel's beer will likewise be fresh and seasonal. The brewery is planned to open in August. The restaurant will serve local guest beers on tap, then add Murphy's beer once the brewery operation is built.

The Murphys are striving to have their East Sacramento location be seen as "a neighborhood pub where community can naturally develop," and make all of their business decisions with that goal in mind.

Twelve Rounds Brewing

Opened: August 2013.

Type: Production brewery, with a restaurant.

Owners: Daniel and Elle Murphy.

Brewer: Daniel Murphy.

System: 15-barrel steam-fired brewhouse, 1,200 barrels annual capacity.

Annual production: 800 barrels (2103 estimate).

Packages available: 22-ounce bottles, growlers, and 5- and 15.5-gallon kegs.

Tours: Tours will be available.

Hours: Thursday and Friday, 4 to 11 p.m.; Saturday and Sunday, 11 a.m. to 11 p.m. Hours slated to increase in 2014.

Beers brewed: Year-round: Hefeweizen, Pale Ale, Chocolate Stout, IPA, Porter, and American Strong Ale. Seasonals: Marzen (spring), Scottish Ale (spring), Blueberry Blonde (summer), Oktoberfest (fall), Pumpkin Ale (fall), Imperial Stout (winter), and Mayan Chocolate Christmas Ale (winter). Featured: the Daniel Joseph Signature Series, a line of barrel-aged stouts, strong ales, and barleywine.

Food: The menu will specialize in charcuterie, with smoked and cured meats. The owners plan to make many of the menu items. My favorite, given the brewpub's name, is the Knuckle Sandwich.

Extras: There will be outdoor seating in the beer garden and darts.

Gift shop: The brewery sells T-shirts, glassware, growlers, and coasters.

Beer Weeks

Beer weeks are a relatively new trend, with a city or region hosting a variety of beer-themed events over a period of a week to ten days. The stated goals of most beer weeks are to showcase local beer scenes, increase tourism, and introduce beer in new and different ways to neophytes and seasoned beer lovers alike. They usually include not just traditional beer festivals, but also beer dinners; specific food and beer pairing events, such as beer with cheese, chocolate, or charcuterie; and many other innovative events that display beer in new ways.

With local beer scenes having their own unique personalities and dynamics, each beer week has the potential of being an organic celebration that takes on as many forms as there are places willing to host one. And that means we're moving away from the relative similarity of the beer festivals to more imaginative, inventive, and ultimately personal ways of presenting beer. The beer week concept, with a diversity of events that include virtually something for everyone, has a greater potential of introducing hordes of new people to craft beer—people who might otherwise not have attended a beer festival. The turnout to these events has shown that the interest is definitely there. Of course, I may be biased—in 2009, I helped found SF Beer Week, which was one of the first major beer weeks.

SF Beer Week (sfbeerweek.org). In 2003, I was the general manager of the *Celebrator Beer News*, the local beer magazine that I was running with publisher Tom Dalldorf. That year, we celebrated the publication's fifteenth anniversary and came up with what we called Beerapalooza. The *Celebrator* usually threw an anniversary party each February, and it was normally held the day after the Toronado Barleywine Festival began, since a number of out-of-town brewers and beer fans were already in town for that. The weekend before that was the Bistro's Double IPA Festival, which had started in 2001. Tom and I talked with the owners and staff of local breweries, restaurants, and bars and filled in the rest of the week between the two festivals with one beer event for each day. It worked pretty well, and Beerapalooza kept going for the next several years, with a few more events becoming annual institutions, such as Rogue's Thursday cheese tasting at the North Beach Public House and Bruce Paton's beer and chocolate dinner.

In 2008, Tom Dalldorf and I, along with many others from the Bay Area, attended the first Philly Beer Week, where they had managed to put together a series of hundreds of beer events throughout the week. We were inspired by their efforts and thought we should be doing something like that back home. People started talking.

After we returned to California, Magnolia owner Dave McLean, Shaun O'Sullivan from 21st Amendment, Beer Chef Bruce Paton, Tom Dalldorf, and I, along with Dave Keene from the Toronado, got together and held a meeting to discuss the possibility of our own beer week. It took a lot of hard work on all our parts, with very little money or support from outside the beer community, to get SF Beer Week off the ground in 2009. I think a lot of people thought we were crazy.

Beginning the second year, the San Francisco Brewers Guild became the main sponsor and managed the event, which helped it grow considerably. The first few years, I stayed heavily involved, but last year I backed away, preferring to continue in a more honorary and advisory way, though I hope they'll keep allowing me to do the opening toast, which I wrote for the first year and have given each year since.

In 2013, the fifth annual SF Beer Week hosted somewhere north of 450 beer events throughout the greater Bay Area. The opening gala celebration, now at larger quarters—the Concourse Exhibition Center on Eighth Street in San Francisco—has already proven to be the ideal space for years to come. If you're planning on coming to the Bay Area for a "beercation," you couldn't pick a better time than SF Beer Week.

Sacramento Beer Week (sacramentobeerweek.com). Our neighbors to the north in the state capital launched their own companion beer week the year after the first SF Beer Week, in 2010. Sacramento Beer Week has traditionally started two weeks after SF Beer Week ends, in late February, and hosts events throughout the Sacramento Valley and Gold Country.

Founded by Dan Scott, who also does political and public health work, Sacramento Beer Week will most likely be a nonprofit by 2013. So far, it's been a grassroots effort, put on by local beer enthusiasts, with Scott doing a lot of the heavy lifting. The 2012 beer week had 440 beer events, including two cornerstone events: the Capital Beerfest and the Sacramento Brewers Showcase, which spotlighted twenty local brewers.

Stockton Beer Week (stocktonbeerweek.com). Billed as an effort to "increase excitement in Stockton bars and restaurants and to support our craft beer industry," the first Stockton Beer Week, in 2012, was held over four days at a dozen local venues. It sounds as though it was a rousing success, and I hope it will continue in the years to come.

Silicon Valley Beer Week. The year 2013 will also mark the start of another Northern California beer week, this one planned to take place in the South Bay, in San Jose, from July 28 through August 3. It will be presented by the Naglee Park Garage and will culminate with the second annual Summer Kraftbrew Beer Fest on August 3. The goal of Silicon Valley Beer Week is to highlight beer restaurants, retailers, bars, and breweries in the Silicon Valley, which is Santa Clara County, throughout the week.

Since being involved in starting SF Beer Week, I've tried to keep tabs on all the other beer weeks taking place. So far, I'm aware of roughly a hundred beer weeks taking place on four continents, though the vast majority are in North America. Other countries that have held or scheduled beer weeks are Australia, Germany, Great Britain, Italy, and Japan.

Gold Country

The Gold Country region forms a long strip between the Central Valley to the west and the Sierra Nevada to the east. For the purposes of this book, the Gold Country region includes the counties of Amador, El Dorado, Nevada, Placer, Sierra, Sutter, and Yuba. These seven counties are about the same size as the island of Fiji, or roughly one-third as big as West Virginia.

This is the area where gold was discovered in 1849, kicking off the gold rush, California's path to statehood and its brewing industry. Sutter's Mill, where James W. Marshall first found gold nuggets on Sutter's property at the bank of the South Fork of the American River, was located in Coloma, in El Dorado County. This was the place to be in the latter half if the nineteenth century, when gold was seemingly everywhere. One county, El Dorado, was named for the fabled city of gold that Spanish conquistadores spent decades searching for in South America. Today the region has slightly fewer residents than the entire state of South Dakota, and there are a number of ghost towns, abandoned after the area was picked clean of gold.

Gold Country also includes numerous national forests, such as Eldorado, Plumas, Tahoe, and Toiyabe. There's a lot of open space. The roads are not as difficult as in some of the more mountainous regions, but they do tend to be smaller local roads, so travel is often somewhat slower as a result.

You'll find ample heritage and history on display in the countless small towns that dot the landscape. Many have morphed into tourist towns, resembling the old mining towns of yesteryear. A lot of these towns have a similar look and feel, with old wooden façades and main streets lined with antique shops and other quaint pleasures. You could whisk through these towns on your way to the next brewery, but you'd miss something special. They're lovely time capsules where it's easy to imagine a simpler time.

For modern diversions, there's South Lake Tahoe, a tourist destination in its own right. In the winter, Tahoe boasts at least a dozen major ski resorts, and in the summer, the lake provides sunnier activities. All year round, visitors enjoy hiking and mountain biking along endless trails. The massive lake is the center of life here. It's the largest alpine lake in North America, and only one other lake is deeper. It straddles the border with Nevada, and only part of the lake is on the California side. On this side there's golf and skiing, but the Nevada side also offers casinos.

Alibi Ale Works

Kings Beach, CA
530-308-1942 • www.alibialeworks.com
Twitter @AlibiAleWorks • Facebook.com/AlibiAleWorks

Founded by Tahoe locals Kevin Drake and Rich Romo, Alibi Ale Works is the first brewery ever to be located in Kings Beach, on the north shore of Lake Tahoe. Drake is an award-winning homebrewer who's been making beer for more than fifteen years, while Romo brings years of construction, plumbing, HVAC, and business experience to the enterprise. They built a small nanobrewery production brewery from scratch, with an adjacent tasting room, and distribute Alibi beer throughout the Tahoe area.

Alibi Ale Works

Opened: June 2013.

Type: Production brewery, with tasting room.

Owners: Kevin Drake and Rich Romo.

Brewers: Kevin Drake and Rich Romo.

Guild membership: CCBA.

System: 3-barrel direct-fire brewhouse.

Packages available: 22-ounce bottles, 750-milliliter bottles, growlers, and 5- and 15.5-gallon kegs.

Beers brewed: Sunrise Session Pale Ale, Moonrise Black RyePA, Smooth Criminal Black Ale, Lie Detector Peanut Butter Cup Stout, and Saison d' Funk, with many more to come.

Auburn Alehouse

A U B U R N

ALEHOUSE

289 Washington Street, Auburn, CA 95603
530-885-2537 • www.auburnalehouse.com
Twitter @auburn_alehouse
Facebook.com/pages/Auburn-Alehouse-Craft-Brewery-
　　Restaurant/100895326662371

Old Town Auburn is one of the most unspoiled downtowns in the West and is a great mix of old and new, resembling an Old West mining town but having all the modern conveniences. Most of the buildings were built in the mid-nineteenth century, although the imposing Placer County Courthouse, which looks down on Old Town, was erected in 1898. Just off I-80 by a giant statue of a man panning for gold, Auburn Alehouse is in the center of Old Town, and from there a day's worth of shopping, museums, and diversions are within walking distance. When you're exhausted and have built up a powerful thirst, you can end your day at the brewpub.

The brewery is housed in the American Block Building, which used to be the home of the Shanghai Bar & Restaurant, a former downtown institution that was there for nearly a hundred years before closing in 2005. It was also the spot where several scenes were filmed for the John Travolta film *Phenomenon* in 1995. The building was originally built in 1856, a year after a big fire destroyed much of the downtown area, and was nearly brought down by another fire in 1905.

Alehouse founder Brian Ford grew up near Auburn, in Weimar, and his parents owned a local bar there, so he was exposed to beer culture at an early age. His first career was as a contractor, but a chance encounter with an Australian beer, Redback Wheat, changed his perception of what beer could be, and he began homebrewing. Deciding it was for him, he enrolled at the American Brewers Guild brewing course and interned at Sacramento's Rubicon Brewing. His first paying gig was at the now gone Old Nevada Brewing

Beers brewed: Year-round: Gold Country Pilsner, Gold Digger IPA, Fool's Gold Ale, Auburn Export Lager, PU 240 Imperial IPA, American River Pale Ale, Old Town Brown Ale, and Shanghai Stout. Seasonals: Old Prospector Barleywine-Style Ale, McFord's Irish Red Ale, Miner's Wheat, Isotope Imperial IPA, Oktoberfest Marzen, Irish Dry Stout, and Rye Not? Brewer's Special Series: Route 40 Red, Alt, Grave Digger, Scarlot Harlot Red Ale, Sierra Gold Single Hop Varietal, "Lil" Digger Session IPA, Californium IPA, Northwest IPA, Placer Porter, Black Lassie Dark Ale, Independence Day Ale (IDA), and ZZ Hop Triple IPA.

Company, which also challenged his contracting skills, because he first had to design the brewhouse from scratch.

His next challenge came closer to home, when he helped build, open, and brew at two breweries for Beermann's Beerwerks, with a location in Lincoln and one in Roseville. Ford spent five years there and really put the breweries on the map, brewing some terrific beers, but it seems that the owners lacked passion for the beer, and he left before they ultimately closed down their operations.

Ford bought the old brewhouse that had been used at Fresno's Bull Dog Brewing Company and began the search for the perfect location for his own brewery. He and his wife, Lisa, finally found it in the old Shanghai, which had been gutted after it closed and was completely empty inside. The building had to be completely renovated from the ground floor up.

It obviously paid off, because the place is beautiful inside and out. The exterior look like it must have when it opened in the 1800s, but the interior blends the best of old and new. The brick walls and dark wood retain the feel of an old saloon, but modern flourishes abound as well. There's a long wooden bar to your left as you come in the front door. Tables and booths fill the restaurant, but some well-placed partitions keep privacy in a tight space, so that you never feel too crowded. The beer serving tanks can be seen through glass windows that look down from above the restaurant, while the brewery is also enclosed in glass at the back of the building and can be seen along a long corridor to one side. Outside, on one side of the building is a small, walled-in, two-story patio where you can drink and eat on nice days.

Brian Ford has been one of my favorite unsung brewers for many years, and he has managed to make a winning line of beers at his own place. He—and his beers—deserve to be better known. As success has made him busier, Ford has brought in Bill Wood as brewer. Wood was the brewer at the Elk Grove Brewery, which closed in 2008, and in fact, he was its only brewer the entire thirteen years it was open. I never had a beer from Elk Grove I didn't like, so the addition of Wood has made the Auburn Alehouse even better. It's a powerhouse brewing

The Pick: Ford's Gold Digger IPA is a stellar example of a West Coast hops monster, but one with great balance. It's bright golden with grassy, pine, and citrus hops aromas and a creamy mouthfeel. But it's in the flavors that the beer really shines, with a complex palate that includes grapefruit, onions, floral, and so many more descriptors. It's also very well-rounded, with good malt flavors and even a touch of sweetness permeating the beer, though it's pleasantly bitter in the long, dry finish. Auburn Alehouse's wonderful triple IPA, the ZZ Hop, is also worth mentioning, although it's not available all the time. If you do find some, don't pass it up. It's one of the best triple-hopped beers out there.

team the likes of which you don't often see in a small brewpub. But the end result is terrific beer, and coupled with an amazing setting and good food, it makes the Auburn Alehouse pretty hard to beat.

Auburn Alehouse

Opened: June 21, 2007.

Type: Brewpub.

Owners: Brian and Lisa Ford.

Brewer: Bill Wood.

Guild membership: BA, CCBA, NCBG.

System: 10-barrel Pub Brewing system, 3,120 barrels annual capacity.

Annual production: 1,300 barrels (2011).

Packages available: 22-ounce bottles, growlers, and 5- and 15.5-gallon kegs.

Tours: Brewery tours are available if the brewer's there and has free time, though reservations are recommended.

Hours: Monday, 11 a.m. to 10 p.m.; Tuesday, 4 to 10 p.m.; Wednesday and Thursday, 11 a.m. to 11 p.m.; Friday, 11 a.m. to midnight; Saturday, 9 a.m. to midnight; Sunday, 9 a.m. to 10 p.m. The kitchen generally closes an hour before the bar.

Food: The alehouse serves a full menu of tasty dishes, including a great selection of starts such as pub pickle chips, sweet potato fries, and a tasty cheese loaf, along with soups and salads, pizza, sandwiches and burgers, and entrées like pot roast, jambalaya, filet mignon, a pasta and fish of the day, and prime rib on Friday. Each day at 4 p.m., there's a food special at the bar, and on Thursday, Friday, and Saturday, there's a different menu special each night. There's also a separate kids' menu. Breakfast is served from 9 a.m. to noon on weekends.

Extras: Each Wednesday at 5 p.m., a new cask of beer is tapped. There's live music on Thursday from 7 to 10 p.m. The alehouse also has a mug club you can join; ask about it the next time you're there.

Gift shop: Merchandise is available at the brewpub. You can also see some of the brewery swag online, but you'll need to call to order.

The Brewery at Lake Tahoe

3542 Lake Tahoe Boulevard, South Lake Tahoe, CA 96150

530-544-2739 • www.brewerylaketahoe.com

Facebook.com/pages/The-Brewery-at-Lake-Tahoe/ 102755284877

The Brewery at Lake Tahoe was the area's first brewpub when it opened in 1992. Located right in the heart of downtown South Lake Tahoe, the red brick building was actually a house when it was built in the 1930s, which gives it an enchanting storybook look. It's like a roadhouse, but surrounded by tall trees. It's set back from the main road a bit, and in between is a large grassy area with picnic tables and a big colorful sign announcing the brewery. There are also a few tables and chairs on what's essentially the front porch, with concrete floors but still outdoors.

The brewery originally focused almost only on the beer, with a limited menu, but that's no longer the case, and the restaurant now offers a full menu with dozens of choices. In fact, if you enter through the front door, the house restaurant is what you'll see. The brewery portion of the space is to the side and is entered through the main part of the building or the separate entrance to the right. It's possible that the brewery area may have been the garage at one time, but now it's an A-frame with tall pointed ceilings and beams. Windows high up on the walls bring in lots of light, and there's a bar on one side and a shelf on the other with bar stools for additional seating in the narrow room.

Behind the bar, the brewing equipment lines the walls. From almost any vantage point in the bar, you can watch the brewing process unfold while enjoying the fruits of that process. Brew-

Beers brewed: Year-round: Washoe Wheat Ale, Needle Peak Ale, Palisades Pilsner, Indian Pale Ale, Bad Ass Ale, Alpine Amber Ale, and Paramount Porter. Seasonals: Belgian-style White Ale, Star Lake Stout, Killibrew Brown Ale, Dunkle Weiss, Pumpkin Ale, and Simcoe Ob-session Ale.

The Pick: The Bad Ass Ale is not only the brewery's best-selling beer—in a vacation town, how could it not be? —but it's also one of its best. It's not so much any particular style, just a strong, hoppy beer, with a beautiful copper red color and a rich malt nose with spicy hops aromas. It's a sweet beer, balanced nicely with spicy and grapefruit hops character, but it's the toffee sweetness that makes it work. At 9 percent ABV, which gives it a sweet bite, it's also a little tart and hot in the finish.

master Steve Canali was an avid homebrewer when he apprenticed at the brewery for about eight months with the previous brewer, who had learned brewing at UC Davis. When he left, Canali took over and has been brewing there for more than seven years, and it is he who developed all of the recipes that the brewpub is now pouring.

Canali keeps eight housemade beers on at all times: six regular offerings and two additional seasonals or one-offs. He also started a line of single-hops session beers, the first of which was Simcoe Ob-session Ale, brewed and dry hopped with only Simcoe hops. He's planning on introducing additional beers using a variety of different hops.

In 2008, the owners opened a second brewpub just over a mile away along the same thoroughfare and closer to the casinos, only about a block from the Nevada border (see Stateline Brewery on page 359).

The Brewery at Lake Tahoe

Opened: 1992.

Type: Brewpub.

Owners: Sheila O'Connell and Russell Penn.

Brewer: Steve Canali.

System: 7-barrel custom-built brewhouse, 1,500 barrels annual capacity.

Annual production: 1,100 barrels (2012).

Packages available: Growlers and draft only at the brewpub.

Tours: No tours are available, although you can see the brewery from the bar, and the brewer will be happy to talk to you about the brewery.

Hours: Sunday through Thursday, 11 a.m. to 9 p.m.; Friday and Saturday, 11 a.m. to 10 p.m.

Food: The full menu includes a dozen appetizers, fresh gourmet salads, burgers and sandwiches, wraps and paninis, pasta, pizza and calzones, seafood, and entrées such as BBQ St. Louis ribs, baked cheesy mac, and chicken pot pie.

Extras: Happy hour is every day from 3 to 5 p.m. with special discounts on pints of beer, wine, shots, and select food items. The brewery has a full bar that serves cocktails too.

Gift shop: A good selection of merchandise is available at the brewpub.

FiftyFifty Brewing Company

11197 Brockway Road #1, Truckee, CA 96161
530-587-BEER (2337) • www.fiftyfiftybrewing.com
Twitter @5050Brewing • Facebook.com/5050Brewing

After ten years in the corporate rat race, working for Hewlett-Packard, Andy and Alicia Barr were looking for a way out. Their family owned a vacation home in Truckee, and they spent many weekends there decompressing before it hit them that they should figure out a way to live in the Truckee area all year long. They were casual homebrewers and loved both beer and food, which led them to the decision to create FiftyFifty Brewing. All they needed was a brewer.

Brewmaster Todd Ashman is something of a legend in brewing. A native of Santa Rosa, he started homebrewing in the 1980s after tasting his first Sierra Nevada Pale Ale. In 1995, he attended the American Brewers Guild, in the last class taught by UC Davis professor emeritus Michael Lewis. After a short stint with a brewery in New Mexico, Ashman spent most of the next nine years at Flossmoor Station, a brewpub in Illinois. Flossmoor is a village in Cook County, better known for its largest city, Chicago, but in the world of beer, Ashman put the brewpub on the map. While brewing for Flossmoor Station, he racked up an impressive eleven GABF medals and five World Beer Cup awards. He also won the very first medal for a bourbon barrel-aged beer at GABF, and that beer became the basis for FiftyFifty's famous Eclipse Barrel-Aged Imperial Stout.

After a brief stint with Titletown Brewing in Green Bay, Wisconsin, Ashman retired from brewing to take a job with Brewers Supply Group, a company selling ingredients to the beer industry. But it didn't take long before he was itching to get back in the brewhouse. Around that same time, FiftyFifty's owners posted a notice on the Brewers Association's Brewers Forum looking for a brewer. The Barrs received more than thirty interested applicants, but they hired Ashman without a for-

Beers brewed: Year-round: Base Camp Golden Ale, Manifesto Pale Ale, Rockslide IPA, Trifecta Belgian Style Tripel, Donner Party Porter, and Roundabout Oatmeal Stout. Seasonals: Truckee Blonde Reserve, 4 Wheat, California Pale Ale, RyePA, Charlie Brown, Barrel Aged Really Tasty, Honey Rye (Roggen Schatz), Red Is the New Black IPA, Trifecta Aged in Bourbon Barrels, Blonde #X, Blonde Barleywine, Evil on Jack, Farmhouse Ale, Landslide Double IPA, Old Conundrum Barleywine Aged in Brand Barrels, Totality Imperial Stout, Concentrated Evil Belgian Dark Strong Ale, and Eclipse Barrel-Aged Imperial Stout.

mal interview, having Googled his name and discovered his stellar reputation.

Ashman is an amazing brewer, and FiftyFifty was a hit from the get-go. He's not just good at one particular kind of beer, but can make anything well, and his range of beers at FiftyFifty is staggeringly good. Whether it's a hoppy West Coast IPA, malty English-style porter, or Belgian tripel, Ashman makes a terrific example of one. He started aging one of his most popular beers, the Totality Imperial Stout, in different types of bourbon and other barrels, creating the Eclipse Barrel-Aged Imperial Stout line, with vintage years and different colors of wax on the neck and crown denoting what type of barrel it was aged In. FiftyFifty's website has a Style Guide key to decode the bottles. For example, a 2012 vintage Eclipse with a blue wax top was aged in Old Fitzgerald sour mash bourbon barrels.

FiftyFifty came up with a unique way to deal with sales of its increasingly rare beer, selling "futures" of the Eclipse. Since it tends to sell out quickly, it's a good way to ensure that you'll get some when the new vintage is released in December of each year. The brewpub is closed down for an annual Eclipse release party, and after that the remaining bottles are available for sale at retail stores.

The brewpub looks like it should be part of a ski resort, which is fitting, given that Truckee is a tourist town a dozen miles from Lake Tahoe with easy access not only to skiing, but to numerous other outdoor activities such as hiking, biking, fishing, horseback riding, and boating. Inside, the restaurant is clean and bright, with dark wood, high ceilings, and a disco ball hanging down in the middle of the room. The open dining area includes booth seating as well as tables and chairs, with smaller, tall round tables with bar stools adjacent to the U-shaped bar along the far wall as you walk in. Next to the bar, the brewery is visible through large glass cathedral windows. If you're in the Truckee area, especially in the winter, I can't think of a better place to escape the weather.

FiftyFifty is currently building a 30-barrel production brewery in a new building across the parking lot from the brewpub. In addition, about a mile or so from the brewpub, there is a separate storage facility where all of the beer in barrels is being aged.

The Pick: Honestly, everything at FiftyFifty is good, and I cannot recommend the Eclipse Barrel-Aged Imperial Stout too strongly, even though it is often hard to come by. Sample as many of the different versions as you can, compare and contrast, or just enjoy them. Of the more easily available beers, I love both Ashman's Rockslide IPA and the newer RyePA. Rockslide is all grapefruit and pine, with a big malt backbone balancing with sweet caramel notes. The finish is clean and drying. The RyePA is similar to the Rockslide, but with the zestiness of rye malt giving the beer added dimensions.

FiftyFifty Brewing Company

Opened: 2007.

Type: Brewpub.

Owners: Andy and Alicia Barr.

Brewer: Todd Ashman.

Guild membership: BA, CCBA, NCGB.

System: 10-barrel Newmans, 900 barrels annual capacity.

Annual production: 900 barrels (2012).

Packages available: 22-ounce bottles, growlers, and 5- and 15.5-gallon kegs.

Tours: Brewery tours are available with reservations.

Hours: Sunday through Thursday, 11 a.m. to 9 p.m.; Friday and Saturday, 11 a.m. to 9:30 p.m.

Food: The brewpub offers a full menu of starters, soups and salads, burgers and sandwiches, pizza and calzone, specialties such as huevos rancheros and fish and chips, and entrées including baby back ribs, skirt steak, and pan-seared salmon. There are several vegetarian items.

Extras: Happy hour is Monday through Friday, 3 to 5:30 p.m. Also on Monday through Friday, from 11 a.m. to 3 p.m., you can get a burger, fries, and a pint of beer for $10. Daily specials can be found on the Facebook page. Major sporting events are shown on a big projector screen, and from time to time there's live music.

Gift shop: T-shirts, hoodies, hats, and glassware are available at the brewpub and online.

Gold Hill Vineyard & Brewery

5660 Vineyard Lane, Placerville, CA 95667
530-626-6522 • www.goldhillvineyard.com
Facebook.com/goldhill.vineyard

Gold Hill was originally just a vineyard when, in 1980, Hank Battjes, an electrical engineer from Palo Alto whose hobby was home winemaking, bought 5 acres in the Coloma Valley near Placerville. The grounds are located just a mile from the historic gold-mining town of Coloma and Sutter's Mill, the spot where gold was first discovered in California. Battjes and his daughters worked the land for a number of years and turned it into a viable winery in 1985. The property eventually swelled to 80 acres. Battjes passed away in 2012, and his daughter Byrna, who'd become general manager of the brewery in 2010, took over the winery along with her husband, Ken Dacus.

Gold Hill Vineyard has eleven grape varietals planted and has made Bordeaux-style reds and chardonnay since 1985, more recently producing Italian and Rhone varietals. The barrel room holds twenty-five hundred cases of wines that Gold Hill produces each year. The Dacuses added a brewery in 1999 and by the following year were brewing four different beers.

The grounds are very impressive and include several large buildings surrounded by picturesque vineyards. There are trails all around the grounds, and private areas with picnic tables dot the landscape, including Cornelia's Meadow, by the lower pond. With such beautiful surroundings and built-in facilities to accommodate large groups, it's become a destination spot for weddings, and the grounds also include two outdoor stages for ceremonies. The dining and banquet room is raised and lined with windows, offering gorgeous views of the greenery and hills beyond. Even if you're not getting married, it's a beautiful spot for a picnic.

The brewery is located out of sight, downstairs, in a side room off the 4,000-square-foot barrel room. Matou' Horák, who's also an electrician and homebrewer, took over brewing duties last

Beers brewed: Year-round: 49'er Red Ale, Gold Trail Pale Ale, Hank's Honey Porter, and Old Miners Scotch. Seasonals: Gold Strike Light (summer) and Axe Pic n Stout (winter).

The Pick: The Gold Trail Pale Ale is my fave from the Gold Hill Brewery. It's bright golden with an ivory head and a light citrus hops nose. The mouthfeel is nicely creamy and effervescent, with mild bittering, fruit, and earthy flavors showing good balance, and a finish that's clean and dry.

year. A tasting room where you can sample both the wine and beer is upstairs next to the banquet facilities. Bring a picnic lunch and try both the wine and the beer, in one of the greenest idyllic settings you're ever likely to come across.

Gold Hill Vineyard & Brewery

Opened: 2000.

Type: Production brewery.

Owner: Byrna and Ken Dacus.

Brewer: Matou' Horák.

System: 7-barrel brewhouse, 1,000 barrels annual capacity.

Annual production: 60 barrels (2012 estimate).

Packages available: 22-ounce bottles and 15.5-gallon kegs.

Tours: Brewery tours are given if staff is available; reservations are recommended.

Hours: Thursday through Sunday, 11 a.m. to 5 p.m.

Food: Food is available only during events.

Extras: There is outdoor seating overlooking the vineyard and meadows with picturesque ponds. The grounds are a spacious eighty acres, and family picnicking is encouraged. During the summer, there's live music every other Friday; check the website for details. Children and dogs are both welcome.

Gift shop: Logo pint glasses and 22-ounce bottles are available in the tasting room.

Jack Russell Farm Brewery & Winery

2380 Larsen Drive, Camino, CA 95709
530-647-9704 • www.jackrussellbrewing.com
Facebook.com/jackrussellfarmbrewery

The first thing you notice while driving to the Jack Russell Farm Brewery is that it's out in the country and surrounded by quite a lot of farmland. The immediate area is known as Apple Hill. So when you finally reach the brewery, you can be forgiven for thinking you're at the wrong place. If you've visited your fair share of breweries, you've no doubt become accustomed to a certain industrial look and feel that's common to most of them. But this brewery lives up to its name and more resembles a farm at first glance. From the gravel parking lot, you're first greeted with a large grassy plot filled with potted Japanese maples and picnic tables, many of which have shade umbrellas. There's a plain, squat, one-story building beyond, and the Jack Russell logo above a pair of windows is your first clue you haven't made a wrong turn.

A sign on the building helpfully tells you what you'll find, depending on which direction you choose: to the left are the winery, cave, meadery, and hard cider; to your right is the brewery. At busy times and during events, you'll often find local crafts for sale, food vendors, and other interesting diversions.

Inside is a tasting room, with a wooden floor, bar, and stools. It's a cozy space, with a few tables, a wood stove, and a small gift store and cooler where you can purchase bottled beer to go. Behind the bar, a chalkboard lists not only what beers are currently flowing, but also each one's ABV and where it falls on a spectrum of light to dark and hoppy to malty.

The brewery is behind closed doors, mostly hidden from view, and is where the real work of brewing and bottling is done. Owner and brewer David Coody is a veteran of local brewing. Earlier, he founded Hangtown Brewing and also briefly ran a microcanning brewery, making beer for Dave's Ale Works. He bought the Jack Russell brewery in 2009, and by the following year had reopened it.

Beers brewed: Year-round: Whitewater Pale Ale, Captain Boomer's IPA, Jackweiser Ale, Strong Blonde, Irish Red Ale, London Porter, and Stout. Seasonals: Blackberry Abbey Ale, Farmhouse Ale, Scottish Ale, Oatmeal Stout, Belgifornia IPA, Vanilla Stout, Raspberry Red Ale, All-American Premium Ale, Blueberry Ale, Harvest Apple Ale, Olde Ale, Huntsman's Lager, and Pumpkin.

If you went to the left, instead of toward the brewery, you would walk through a cement patio with more tables, chairs, and shade umbrellas that go around the corner and continue in the back of the building. In addition to beer, Jack Russell makes wine, mead, apple cider, and cyser, a fermented honey and apple blend. And these can be found around the back too. A really cool faux cave tasting room is there, which you can enter from the back patio. Inside, it's dark and resembles a cave, with a hand-painted bar and colored lights hanging from the ceiling providing atmosphere.

To the side of the brewery and beyond the back patio is a large patch of land where several crops are being farmed, including hops. Jack Russell is modeled after an English farm brewery, but it's utterly unique in Northern California and offers a one-of-a-kind experience as an urban getaway. With the great beer, country air, and an amazing farm setting, you'll definitely want to stay all day and possibly into the night.

The Pick: Maybe it's the surrounding country farm setting, but my Pick is easily the Farmhouse Ale. Saisons are less of a style than a summer seasonal that originated in Wallonia, Belgium. They were meant to be refreshing beers, but had to be hardy enough to stay fresh throughout the warmer months after the traditional brewing season ended. Jack Russell's version does just that. It has a honey sweet nose with light spiciness. The flavors are creamy and complex, with lots going on— cloves and other spices; fruits like peaches, apricots, and pineapple; and just a touch of barnyard funkiness. It's well rounded and terrific on a breezy, warm day.

Jack Russell Farm Brewery & Winery

Opened: March 1996.

Type: Production brewery, with tasting room.

Owner: David Coody.

Brewer: David Coody.

System: 15-barrel Pacific Mechanical, 5,000 barrels annual capacity.

Annual production: 1,500 barrels (2012 estimate).

Packages available: Growlers, 12-ounce bottles in six-packs, 22-ounce bottles, and 5-, 7.75-, and 15.5-gallon kegs.

Tours: Brewery tours are not currently available.

Hours: Monday through Saturday, 11 a.m. to 6:30 p.m.; Sunday, 11 a.m. to 6 p.m.

Food: No food available, but you can bring your own for picnics.

Extras: Picnic tables are on the farm grounds. Special events take place throughout the year, such as Art in the Orchard, a cornhole tournament, barbecues, and a Guy Fawkes bonfire. There's also live music at the brewery from time to time. Check the Facebook page for details.

Gift shop: T-shirts, hoodies, polo shirts, hats, and pint glasses are available in the tasting room.

Knee Deep Brewing Company

645 Fifth Street, Lincoln, CA 95648
916-757-1861 • www.kneedeepbrewing.com
Twitter @KneeDeepBrewing
Facebook.com/kneedeepbrewco

Founder Jeremy Warren was attending college at the University of Nevada, Reno, but was already a passionate brewer and credits homebrewing with helping him make it successfully through his university experience. After graduation, he founded Knee Deep Brewing Company as a contract brewery and began selling kegs in Northern Nevada. At that time, Warren met Jerry Moore, who was convinced that Knee Deep could be a bigger, more successful enterprise, and the pair partnered together to make that happen.

The first thing the owners of the new Knee Deep did was to find a place for their own brewery and move operations across the state line to Lincoln, a suburb of Sacramento. In the space where Beermann's Beerwerks used to be, they leased the brewery space in the back, while the front of the building was reopened as a separate business, a pub and restaurant. While in the back, Knee Deep went about its business brewing and selling its beer, and the Beermann's pub became one of its first loyal customers. But it wasn't the only one, as Knee Deep quickly made a name for itself with big and very hoppy beers. In fact, its most popular beer, an IPA called The Hoptologist, is also Warren's nickname.

Knee Deep's portion of the old Beermann's brewery is a little less than 1,000 square feet and is completely separate from the pub in the front of the building, although there's a big window that looks into the front bar. It's primarily an L-shaped space, with the brewhouse and one row of fermenters down one side, and the mill and other equipment down the other, leading to the loading dock. Some of the beers are also aged in a separate off-site barrel facility.

In just a short time, Knee Deep is . . . well, knee deep in good press, critical acclaim, and awards. It

Beers brewed: Year-round: Citra Extra Pale Ale, Hoptologist DIPA, Knee Deep IPA, Tanilla, Imperial Tanilla, Bourbon Barrel Imperial Stout, McCarthy's Bane Imperial Red Ale, Simtra Triple IPA, and Hop Shortage Triple IPA. Seasonals and Monthly Experimental Pilot Series (MEPS): Marris Otter Pale Ale, Hopoholic Quadruple IPA, Bob's Bourbon Barrel Stout, Beautiful Blonde Ale, California Brown Ale, Belgo Hoptologist DIPA, Double Dry Hopped Double Wheat IPA, No Name IPA, and Midnight Hoppyness Double Black Rye IPA. Collaborations: Shakenbake Rye IPA and Belgian DIPA.

took first place at the Bistro Double IPA Festival in 2012, and the owners are making grand plans to expand the operation. With hoppy and extreme beers increasing in numbers at a dizzying pace, expect Knee Deep to keep up with the trend while it continues to satisfy the demand in grand, delicious fashion.

Knee Deep Brewing Company

Opened: July 1, 2010.

Type: Production brewery.

Owners: Jerry Moore and Jeremy Warren.

Brewer: Jeremy Warren.

Guild membership: BA, CCBA, NCBG.

System: 15-barrel Bohemian Breweries system, 2,500 barrels annual capacity.

Annual production: 2,500 barrels (2012).

Packages available: 22-ounce bottles, growlers (on Fridays only), and 5- and 15.5-gallon kegs.

Tours: Brewery tours are available; reservations are required.

Hours: Friday, 5 to 8 p.m.

Extras: Friday is the only day when the brewery is open to the public, and even then just at the dock for Loading Dock Friday Growler Sales. For an annual fee, you can join the growler club, which gets you a Knee Deep growler and a dozen refills, which you can redeem weekly, monthly, or whenever you like throughout the year.

Gift shop: Merchandise is available at the brewery when open and online.

The Pick: Warren's namesake, the Hoptologist DIPA, is understandably one of his most popular beers. It's a huge hops monster, with big hops aromas of pine, citrus, and tropical fruit, along with whiffs of caramel, bready sweetness, and some peppery spiciness. Despite its massive hops presence, an equally big malt backbone makes it work. An imperial IPA is by its nature a dance, and this one tangos elegantly.

Lazy Daze Brewery
(The Brewery at Mary's Pizza Shack)

711 Pleasant Grove Boulevard, Roseville/Rocklin, CA 95678

916-780-7600 • maryspizzashack.com/locations/rosevillerocklin

Twitter @MarysRoseville

Facebook.com/MarysRoseville

While a family pizza restaurant might seem like an unlikely place for a brewery, the peculiarities of alcohol law in Placer County convinced the family owners of Mary's Pizza Shack that it made perfect sense. Of course, pizza and beer are a near perfect combination. Until recently, Mary's Pizza Shack quietly operated the brewery along with the restaurant but made no particular push for the beer.

The Mary of the eponymous Pizza Shack, Mary Fazio, founded her first Italian restaurant in 1959 in Boyes Hot Springs, a tiny town in Sonoma County, and today there are nineteen of them, most still owned by the Fazio family. They all feature open kitchens, where you can watch your meal being cooked, and serve a full menu of Italian dishes in addition to their signature pizzas. They take pride in cooking every order from scratch.

Until recently, the Roseville location was part of the family, but last year it was purchased by long-time Mary's Pizza Shack employee and director of operations Ty Marestein and his wife, Carla. Their plans are to focus on the brewing side of the operations while continuing to offer the same great food. As a result, they'll be rebranding the brewery as the Lazy Daze Brewery.

Brewer Gary Juels, who's been brewing there since the beginning, will step up his efforts on the brewing side. He's a UC Davis graduate and interned at Trumer Brauerei, volunteered at Mt. Shasta Brewing, and worked with Peter Kruger, head brewer at Bear Republic, before coming to Lazy Daze.

In addition to the four regular beers the brewery offers, each one designed to complement the

Beers brewed: Year-round: Grano Hefeweizen, Testarosa Red Amber, Pazzo American Pale Ale, and I-80 IPA. Seasonals: Imperial Red Ale, Capodanno Winter Ale, Sonoma Pilsner, and Schultzy's Oktoberfest.

The Pick: The Pazzo Pale is my choice. It's a really nice pale ale with good balance, having citrus and floral hops aromas and a sweet caramel malt character. It pairs quite well with most of the dishes.

food, he's beginning to make more seasonal and special releases. With a great selection of food already, along with a larger number of good beers, the Lazy Daze Brewery at Mary's Pizza Shack should give you even more reasons to stop by.

Lazy Daze Brewery
(The Brewery at Mary's Pizza Shack)

Opened: May 31, 1959; Roseville brewery location opened November 2007.

Type: Brewpub.

Owners: Ty and Carla Marestein.

Brewer: Gary Juels.

System: 10-barrel direct-fire Canadian brewhouse, 1,200 barrels annual capacity.

Annual production: 1,000 barrels (2012 estimate).

Packages available: Draft only at the restaurant.

Tours: The brewery's a bit too cramped for tours, but you can see most of it through the windows behind the bar.

Hours: Sunday through Thursday, 11 a.m. to 10 p.m.; Friday and Saturday, 11 a.m. to 11 p.m.

Food: Mary's Pizza Shack is known for its Italian food and especially its pizza. And its reputation is justly deserved—the pizzas are really good, with homemade dough and all fresh ingredients. A number of specialty pizzas are offered, or you can build your own. The menu also includes appetizers, soup and salads, sandwiches, and a large number of pasta and other entrées. The calzones are particularly terrific.

Extras: Happy hour is weekdays from 3 to 6 p.m., and there's also late-night happy hour seven days a week from 8 p.m. to close.

Loomis Basin Brewing Company

3277 Swetzer Road, Loomis, CA 95650
916-259-2739 • www.loomisbasinbrewing.com
Facebook.com/pages/Loomis-Basin-Brewing-Co/
191379404238975

The Loomis Basin Brewery is a father-son business whose roots go back to when Jim Gowan was stationed in Bitburg, Germany, in the late 1970s. When he returned to California, he found he could no longer drink the popular light American lagers, instead preferring the flavorful beers of Germany.

After years of hearing him complain, his wife gave him a homebrewing kit for Christmas in 1990, and he was hooked. His hobby was relegated to the backyard after he made a mess of his wife's kitchen, and he and some friends designed and built an all-grain homebrewing system to make 55-gallon batches of homebrew. There was no turning back.

Before the decade was out, he'd completed the brewing program at the American Brewers Guild and began working at Sacramento Brewing, where he learned that he had a talent for working with brewing equipment while upgrading their brewhouse. Gowan went on to design and build brewing systems for several Northern California breweries, including Lockdown Brewing, Western Pacific Brewing, and Auburn Alehouse.

Eventually he decided it would be fun to build his own place and recruited his son Kenny, who had been working in the restaurant industry, having started restaurants in San Diego and the Sacramento area. The result was Loomis Basin Brewing Company, a production brewery with a tasting room.

Tucked away in an industrial park, the brewery is an oasis among the concrete buildings. Up front is the clean, cozy tasting room, where all of Loomis Basin's beers are served. A copper bar with stools is to the right as you walk inside, and tables and chairs are to the left. There are bigger tables and

Beers brewed: Year-round: Vindicator IPA, Sweeter Pale Ale, Red Robin Red Ale, and Alohawk Ale (Big Ale). Seasonals: Golden Eagle Mandarin Wheat (spring–fall), Avenger XXIP (available three times a year), Jacked Up Recession Ale (whiskey barrel aged; released December 1), English Brown, and Stout.

The Pick: The Vindicator IPA is a really nice hoppy beer, with a terrific nose of citrus, pine, and honey. It's well balanced and not overly hoppy, with a good malt backbone. It's not extreme at any point, just very pleasant and delicious, and the finish is clean and dry.

chairs for larger groups through the roll-up to the right of the entrance. Brewery merchandise is displayed on a wall and in an enclosed case. The labels look as though they were adapted from vintage fruit crate art, and they look great on both the 22-ounce bottles and T-shirts.

In the back are a beautiful new brewhouse and fermenters, all built from scratch by the Gowans. They are definitely worth seeing even if you've been on a hundred brewery tours, though you will need a reservation. But even if you stay in the front, you'll find a variety of great beers to drink. The brewery is comfortable and has a very good vibe, and it appears to be a wonderful new place to go for happy hour or on a weekend afternoon.

Loomis Basin Brewing Company

Opened: March 23, 2011.

Type: Production brewery, with tasting room.

Owners: Jim and Kenny Gowan.

Brewers: Jim and Kenny Gowan.

Guild membership: CCBA.

System: 15-barrel Premier Stainless Systems, 2,000 barrels annual capacity.

Annual production: 1,500 barrels (2012 estimate).

Packages available: 22-ounce bottles, growlers, and 5-, 7.75-, and 15.5-gallon kegs.

Tours: Brewery tours are available by reservation only.

Hours: Tuesday through Thursday, 3 to 7 p.m.; Friday and Saturday, 3 to 8 p.m. Closed Sunday and Monday.

Food: Food truck vendors park outside the brewery on Thursday, Friday, and Saturday.

Extras: Music is featured at the brewery once a month, with eighty seats outside, where you can also watch the brewing process. Cigar smoking is permitted. Children are not allowed at the brewery.

Old Hangtown Beer Works

117 Elm Avenue, Placerville, CA 95667
530-919-5166
Facebook.com/pages/Old-Hangtown-Beer-Works/
112091415508385

Billed as "Placerville's Only Nano-Brewery," Old Hangtown Beer Works is definitely one of the smallest breweries I've seen. Brewmaster Michael Frenn had been homebrewing for a decade when a change in jobs left him with more free time. He'd been considering starting a brewery, and when he learned about the concept of a nanobrewery, he decided that was the way to go.

He converted his garage into a place for cold storage, a mill, and ingredients, while the rest of brewery, including the brewhouse, is outside or in the backyard. There's a firepit in his small yard that's just off a back deck. The handmade brewing equipment is scattered about the yard but is mostly against a concrete wall on the side. With the woods behind the house, it may be the most pleasant place to brew some beer I've ever seen.

Frenn only sells kegs to local bars and restaurant, and it's the local and small aspects of his business that he believes have led to his success. Being both has gotten him tap handles in and around his hometown of Placerville.

Despite having a population of just over ten thousand people, Placerville is the seat of El Dorado County, which is nestled in the foothills of the Sierra Nevada near the Nevada border. It was originally a mining town but earned the nickname "Hangtown" because numerous hangings took place in the downtown area. In the mid-1850s, at the urgings of religious and temperance leaders, the name was changed to its gentler, less violent, current name. But it's the older version that the brewery takes its name from, and when you walk the historic downtown, you can even see the platform where the hangings took place.

Beers brewed: Year-round: Razzilicious, IPA, Attitude Amber, and Mine Shaft Stout. Seasonals: Imperial Porter, Sluice Boy Red, Mad Dog and Englishman Bitter, Mountain Meadow Honey Basil Pale, Lotus, Chili Bar Pepper Beer, Strumpkin, Nervous Sheep Scotch Ale, and Smoky Canyon Rauchbier.

The Pick: The Mine Shaft Stout is my favorite of the Old Hangtown beers I've tried. Its deep brown color and thick, tan head show great conditioning. It has aromas of milk chocolate, and the flavors are similarly chocolaty, with sweet, chalky, and dry notes and a subtly spicy finish.

Michael Frenn's best marketing device may be his car, which he has dubbed the "Ale Camino"—his Chevy El Camino with two tap handles that dispense Old Hangtown beer attached to the back. It's a great calling card, immediately recognizable to everyone who sees it. And best of all, it has great beer.

Old Hangtown Beer Works

Opened: June 1, 2010.
Type: Production brewery.
Owner: Michael Frenn.
Brewer: Michael Frenn.
Guild membership: BA, CCBA, NCBG.
System: 18-gallon custom-built brewhouse, 110 barrels annual capacity.
Annual production: 60 barrels (2012 estimate).
Packages available: 5- and 15.5-gallon kegs.
Tours: The brewery is not open to the public.

ol' Republic Brewery

124 Argall Way, Nevada City, CA 95959
530-264-7263 • www.olrepublicbrewery.com
Twitter @olrepublicbrew
Facebook.com/pages/Ol-Republic-Brewery/
189551881086056

While ol' Republic founder Jim Harte spent most of his adult life working in the wine industry, for such companies as Cosentino Signature Wineries and the Global Wine Group, his hobby was homebrewing. When he left the wine business behind, he and longtime homebrewing friend and former brother-in-law Simon Olney, a graphic designer from Great Britain, decided to open a brewery in Nevada City.

They found an ideal location in the Seven Hills neighborhood, below the well-known SPD Market, with the entrance essentially around the corner and behind the market. In front of the building is a small parking lot, and there's a fenced-in beer garden with benches along the front of the building and following the fence line around the garden, like a front porch.

Inside, the tasting room is clean and modern, with tile floors, small tables with bar stools and chairs, along with high-backed curved sofas. Tables are made out of wooden barrels cut in half. Because it's a basement space, the ceilings seem low and the room is narrow. An eclectic mix of art hangs on the walls, and a television is mounted on the wall on one side of the tasting room. Two long bars greet you as you walk inside. Each one has a tap tower where you can get one of six different beers.

It's cramped but still comfortable, with plenty of nooks and crannies for intimate conversation, as well as spaces for larger groups to congregate for the evening session. It's reminiscent of a modern English pub, although it looks nothing like one; it just has that same comfortable feel. When ol' Republic first opened, the brewery was to your

Beers brewed: Year-round: Dortmunder (a.k.a. Dead Canary), Helles (a.k.a. Hell Bier), Bavarian Black Lager Schwarzbier, California Common, Celtic Red, India Pale Ale, and Export Stout. Seasonals: Biere de Garde, ESB, Sierra Lighting, Nut Brown Ale, Porter, and Vienna. Project X Series: Cello Stout.

The Pick: I'm a big fan of ol' Republic's Bavarian Black Lager, a classic German schwarzbier with some unique flourishes. It pours a beautiful deep mahogany and boasts a delicate, lightly sweet nose with a subtle whiff of flowery hops. For a session beer—it's a mere 3.4 percent ABV—it packs in a lot of taste, with caramel and nutty flavors and some underlying coffee notes that, surprisingly, are never bitter.

left, open for all to see. But it took up a significant portion of the building, and with the brewery's early success, it needed more capacity to keep up with the demand for beer.

Shortly after its first anniversary, the brewery added 4,000 square feet, more than doubling its size. The brewhouse and most of the brewing equipment were moved a good 100 feet from the front door but are now more out of the way. The brewery also has added more fermenters and serving tanks. This will allow it to increase production as well as the variety of beers, and the owners expect to have more than a dozen different ones, adding more ales in both British and U.S. West Coast styles. Some of the beer will be aged in barrels, and plans are in motion to begin bottling ol' Republic beer as well.

Harte and Olney pay a great deal of attention to everything they do, from way the brewery looks to the design of the labels and logos, and most important, to how good the beers taste. Their goal is to make great beers, and they chose the name Republic for its Greek derivation, *res publica*, meaning "for the people," which also gave the brewery its apt motto: "Beer for the People!"

ol' Republic Brewery

Opened: February 2012.

Type: Production brewery, with taproom.

Owners: Jim Harte and Simon Olney.

Brewers: Jim Harte and Simon Olney.

Guild membership: CCBA, NCGB.

System: 7-barrel Newlands brewhouse, 2,000 barrels annual capacity.

Annual production: 500 barrels (2012).

Packages available: Growlers and kegs.

Tours: Brewery tours are available when one of the brewers is free; no reservations are necessary.

Hours: Sunday, noon to 7 p.m.; Monday through Thursday, noon to 9 p.m.; Friday and Saturday, noon to 11 p.m.

Food: The brewery is BYOF, meaning you're free to bring your own food when you visit ol' Republic. Several local restaurants also deliver meals to the brewery, and food is available as part of the specials on certain evenings; see "Extras" for details.

Extras: The brewery features discounted growler fills and catered food on Tuesday from 5 p.m., BBQ food from the Smiley Guys Smokehouse on Wednesday from 5 p.m., Pie Night at the Brewery on Thursday from 4 p.m., and Taco Friday starting at 5 p.m. There's local music on Saturday evening from 7 to 10 p.m.

Gift shop: Merchandise is available at the brewery.

Placerville Brewing Company

155 Placerville Drive, Placerville, CA 95667
530-295-9166 • www.placervillebrewing.com
Facebook.com/pages/Placerville-Brewing-
    Company/114138865283568

Placerville Brewing Company founder Steven Meylor began homebrewing in 1989, so by the time he started his brewery, he'd been brewing for more than twenty-five years, and only a few of those as a professional. Meylor grew up in a suburb of Sacramento, in the Citrus Heights area, but moved to Placerville around 1995, when he was working as a cameraman for ESPN.

Endlessly traveling around the country to cover sporting events eventually took its toll, and Meylor started looking for a new challenge. He'd been helping out with the brewing at the Hangtown Brewery, which had been founded in 1993, and eventually became a paid brewer there. Meylor worked as the assistant brewer for four years before Hangtown declared bankruptcy in 2004.

Seeing an opportunity, Meylor bought the brewery and some of the other assets of Hangtown from the bankruptcy court. He renovated the space and reopened it, rechristened Placerville Brewing Company, in 2005. Meylor is making an interesting mix of the beers you expect at a brewpub, plus some you wouldn't ordinarily see. His Strong Blonde ale, an 8 percent ABV American strong, is his best-selling beer, and the Vanilla Stout is a local favorite too. He's also making several beers with more unusual types of fruit, such as tangerine and boysenberry.

The brewpub building is an unassuming structure, tucked along a main thoroughfare that you get to via an access road. It's up a small hill, so it looks down on the road. Part of the brewery, including the brewhouse, is outside, partially hid-

Beers brewed: Year-round: Golden Ale, Tangerine Ale, Pale Ale, Boysenberry Ale, Strong Blonde, Stout, and Vanilla Stout. Seasonals: Black IPA, Cascade, Copper Ale, India Pale Ale, Belltower Brown Ale, Dry Diggins, Barley Wine, and Whiskey Barrel Aged Ale.

The Pick: It's hard to argue with Placerville Brewing's most popular beer, especially when it's an American strong ale. The Strong Blonde is just that—it's bright gold, with a malty sweet nose and a whiff of sugary sweet alcohol. The mouthfeel is thick and chewy, with the alcohol definitely in evidence, and there are sweet, earthy flavors and a tart, hot finish. This is a beer made for sipping.

den behind a fence. Most of the fermenters and serving tanks are inside, though, and you can see some of them as you walk in, behind a wall with windows cut into it, revealing one fermenter with Placerville Brewing's logo printed on it.

Inside, the restaurant is clean with light-colored wood. Just past the brewery, to your left, is a U-shaped bar with the kitchen behind it. Big-screen TVs are above the bar and in a few other strategic spots, so it's easy to see whatever's being shown. There are dining tables on both sides, and a good-size outdoor patio overlooks the road, with metal tables and chairs, and shade umbrellas at each table.

The food is plentiful and tasty, as are Meylor's beers. It may not be apparent from the vanilla exterior, but good things are happening inside. The place is usually busy, and it's definitely a local hangout. It's easy to understand why.

Placerville Brewing Company

Opened: 2005.

Type: Brewpub.

Owners: Steven Meylor, Allen Vickers, and Niki Norwood.

Brewer: Steven Meylor.

Guild membership: NCBG.

System: 15-barrel JV Northwest brewehouse, 550 barrels annual capacity.

Annual production: 465 barrels (2012).

Packages available: Growlers and 5- and 15.5-gallon kegs.

Tours: Brewery tours are available if the brewer is free; reservations are recommended.

Hours: Wednesday through Monday, 11 a.m. to 11 p.m. Closed Tuesday.

Food: The brewpub offers a full menu of pub fare, with a dozen appetizers, salads and soups, an exhaustive list of sandwiches and burgers, and specialties like fish and chips and fish tacos. If you're feeling hungrier, dinner plates like the BBQ tri-tip, chicken marsala, or BBQ baby back ribs should do the trick. There are dinner specials weekly, and on Friday and Saturday after 5 p.m., you can also get prime rib or the Captain's Platter, a big plate full of oysters, clam strips, and beer-battered cod. One of the restaurant partners is a meat specialist, and his grilled meats are pretty spectacular. There's also a separate kids' menu.

Extras: Every Wednesday is brewer's night, with special discounts on pints. Happy hour is each weekday from 3 to 5 p.m., with specials on both beer and food. Occasionally there's live music. You can find out more by checking the Facebook page or website.

Gift shop: Shirts and pint glasses are available at the brewpub.

Roseville Brewing Company

501 Derek Place, Roseville, CA 95678
916-783-BEER (2337)
www.rosevillebrewingcompany.com
Twitter @rosevillebrewco
Facebook.com/rosevillebrewingcompany

Roseville Brewing Company is tucked back in an industrial park, not too far from the railroad tracks that its logo, beer names, and imagery pay homage to. After weaving and wending to the right address, you'll see a small sign pointing you to the back of the building. You may consider giving up, but don't. You're almost there now. Just drive as far as you're able, and turn right. It's right there. There's a chance you'll almost run over a food truck, so watch out for that too. That's also a good sign not only that you're in the right place, but that it's open.

The Roseville brewery is the realization of a dream for a group of five friends living in the Northern Sacramento area. Brewer Brett Ratcliff is originally from New Orleans but now calls Roseville his home. His passion for beer came from traveling the world and sampling the local beers, which led him to start homebrewing several years ago. He'd been working as a teacher for the Roseville City School District and was even once named Roseville City Teacher of the Year.

Ratcliff's wife introduced him to Kelly Rue, who had been managing retail stores for more than a decade but was itching to open his own business. The pair hit it off and started planning the brewery. Then they partnered with Kevin Kemper, who owns the building where the brewery is located. With the addition of Phil Gottschalk and Scott "The Bear" Hemings, the team was complete, and they opened their brewery just in time for Sacramento Beer Week 2012. They chose a logo for their brewery that ties it into the local rail heritage, as do many of their beer names as well as their "Iron Triangle" branding, which is the term for a switching station in the railroad business.

Ratcliff and his partners are making some audacious beers and serving them to the local market, and they are currently available at more than two dozen places in the immediate area. While noth-

Beers brewed: Year-round: Apricot Wheat, Big Engine Blackberry Wheat, Armstrong Amber, Iron Mule IPA, Orange Chocolate Stout (a.k.a. Smokestack Chocolate Stout), and Heavy Rail Pale Ale. Seasonals: Randall Belgian Strong, Wild Brown, Railweizen West Coast Wheat, Strawberry Wheat, Steam Horse Stout, Cinnamon Coffee Stout, and Spike Driver Double IPA.

ing's been decided for sure, the owners are considering adding bottled product to the brewery's lineup in the future.

Inside the cozy tasting room, there's a small entrance room with a shelf of brewery swag, a cash register, and a table with information on local attractions. A short corridor leads into the tasting room proper, which has a small bar with four or five stools, along with a few tables and chairs. A chalkboard lists the beers currently available, which usually number half a dozen. On the walls are railroad paraphernalia and historic photographs, and old bottles and growlers are displayed on high shelves. A big-screen TV is hung in the corner but can be seen by just about everyone in the tasting room. Despite being somewhat out of the way, Roseville Brewing is quickly become a popular destination. With the range of beers being made and the comfortable vibe in the tasting room, the brewery will likely keep chugging along like a speeding freight train for the foreseeable future.

The Pick: I found the Orange Chocolate Stout to be a really nice take on a traditional stout. The orange flavors add an interesting dimension to the beer, giving it a tart, citrusy sweetness. The aromas are all chocolate and oranges, like those orange-shaped milk chocolate candies. The flavors also include chocolate, with some roasted coffee notes and nutty flavors, both common in a stout. But it's the zesty flavors from the orange that make this is a standout.

Roseville Brewing Company

Opened: February 24, 2012.

Type: Production brewery, with tasting room.

Owners: Kelly Rue, Phil Gottschalk, Scott Hemings, Kevin Kemper, and Brett Ratcliff.

Brewer: Brett Ratcliff.

Guild membership: CCBA, NCBG.

System: 7-barrel Chinese-built brewhouse, 2,000 barrels annual capacity.

Annual production: 350 barrels.

Packages available: Pints at the tasting room and 5-, 13.2-, and 15.5-gallon kegs.

Tours: Brewery tours are available without reservations.

Hours: Monday through Friday, 5 to 8 p.m.; Saturday, 2 to 6 p.m. Closed Sunday.

Food: No food is available at the brewery. You're welcome to bring your own, and food trucks park outside on Thursday, Friday, and sometimes Saturday.

Extras: Taproom trivia contests take place on Monday, beginning at 6:30 p.m. On Washout Wednesday, pints are discounted all night. Live music is featured on Friday evening.

Gift shop: Merchandise is available in the tasting room and online.

Stateline Brewery & Restaurant

4118 Lake Tahoe Boulevard, South Lake Tahoe,
  CA 96150
530-542-9000 • www.statelinebrewery.com
Facebook.com/pages/Stateline-Brewery/
  193256417355843

The land where the Stateline Brewery sits today is the new home of Cecil's Market, a local institution built in 1940 by Cecil Caple. The market was a quintessential general store with a delicatessen, and it even housed the post office. In 2000, Cecil's was demolished and a brand new building for the market was constructed just a few blocks from the original at the corner of Lake Tahoe Boulevard and Transit Way, one block from the Nevada border.

Cecil's Market today still sells a bit of everything, from food and drinks to clothing and souvenirs. It also stocks logo T-shirts, hats, and glassware for the Stateline Brewery, which is located one floor down, below Cecil's. It's part of Heavenly Village, adjacent to the Heavenly Gondola and a stone's throw from the Embassy Suites Lake Tahoe and Marriott's Timber Lodge.

Steps lead down to the brewery entrance on all sides, and once you're down there, you've stepped into another world, an escape from the hot sunshine or cold, depending on the time of year. Down below, it's a large, open space, though partitions give the diners a certain amount of privacy. Big-screen televisions are mounted on walls all around. A long bar runs the length of one side of the space, with the brewery at the far end, right out in the open, next to a row of tall, circular tables with bar stools. If the brewer is working, it's the ideal spot to have a pint and watch him make your next one.

Brewmaster Ryan Parker originally apprenticed at Rooster's, a brewpub in Ogden, Utah. He worked there as brewer for another two years before coming to Lake Tahoe more than four years ago. He keeps four house beers on all times—

Beers brewed: Year-round: White-Out Wit, Acclimator IPA, Avalanche Ale, and Darker Parker. Seasonals: Stateline Pilsner and Double Time Strong Ale.

The Pick: The Avalanche Ale is a decent pale ale, with light hops aromas and zesty effervescence. It has clean flavors, floral and citrus hops character, and caramel malt sweetness, and the bitter finish will leave you wanting another. Which is good, because you can drink more than a few of these.

three regular year-round offerings and a rotating handle that changes with the seasons.

The owners of Stateline also operate another brewpub in town, just over a mile away and also along Lake Tahoe Boulevard, but farther into the interior of California (see the Brewery at Lake Tahoe on page 336).

Stateline Brewery & Restaurant

Opened: July 2008.

Type: Brewpub.

Owners: Sheila O'Connell and Russell Penn.

Brewer: Ryan Parker.

System: 10-barrel custom-built brewhouse, with some equipment by Non Ferrous Fabrications of Dorset, England; 500 barrels annual capacity.

Annual production: 300 barrels (2012).

Packages available: Draft only.

Tours: No tours are available, although the brewery is out in the open at the end of the bar and you can easily walk right up to it.

Hours: Sunday through Thursday, 11 a.m. to 9 p.m.; Friday and Saturday, 11 a.m. to 10 p.m.

Food: The restaurant offers separate lunch and dinner menus, with lunch from 11 a.m. to 4 p.m. and dinner beginning at 4:30 p.m. The lunch menu includes appetizers, salads, burgers, sandwiches, pasta, and entrées such as beer-battered fish and chips and mahi mahi fish tacos. The dinner menu offers a slightly different selection from lunchtime, with the addition of heartier entrées like osso bucco (braised pork shank), filet medallions, seafood, and Drunken Dummies, chicken drumsticks glazed with tequila and blue agave nectar. In addition, there are separate menus for pizza and desserts, as well as a kids' menu.

Extras: Happy hour takes place each day from 3 to 5 p.m., with discounts on select drinks and menu items. There's a full bar, and of the twelve tap handles, eight are guest taps, mostly from West Coast craft breweries.

Gift shop: Cecil's Market, a souvenir shop that's on the ground floor above the brewpub, carries a wide selection of brewery merchandise.

Sutter Buttes Brewing

421 Center Street, Yuba City, CA 95991
530-790-7999 • www.sutterbuttesbrewing.com
Facebook.com/pages/Sutter-Buttes-Brewing/
170109181855

Mark Martin was a longtime homebrewer and truck driver when the idea of opening his own brewery became too irresistible to pass up. He attended UC Davis to learn his craft and consulted with former Sacramento Brewing Company brewer Peter Hoey to help with the launch of the brewpub and the beers. The brewpub is on a quiet street downtown. Inside, the fermenters and serving tanks line the wall behind the bar, with the copper brewhouse in the back. In addition to the bar stools, there is a small dining area, and the brewpub has a full menu. Tall windows across the front of the brewpub, with its high ceilings, keep it well lit with natural sunlight. This small, clean brewpub is a friendly spot to enjoy a few pints and get a bite to eat.

Sutter Buttes Brewing

Opened: 2010.

Type: Brewpub.

Owner and brewer: Mark Martin.

Guild membership: BA, CCBA, NCBG.

System: 8.5-barrel Pacific Brewing system, annual capacity 350 barrels.

Packages available: Growlers and 5- and 15.5-gallon kegs. Plans are afoot to add bottled product in the near future.

Tours: Hosted tours not available, but the majority of the brewing operations can be seen from the restaurant.

Hours: Monday, 11 a.m. to 4 p.m.; Tuesday through Thursday, 11 a.m. to 10 p.m.; Friday and Saturday, 11 a.m. to 11 p.m.

Food: A selection of appetizers and salads, sandwiches, burgers, and fish and chips. There are five varieties of french fries.

Extras: Happy hour is 5 to 7 p.m. Every Tuesday evening is open mic night. There are also several guest taps from local breweries, and a hard cider.

Gift shop: T-shirts, tank tops, pullovers, growlers, and pint glasses available at the brewery.

Beers brewed: Year-round: Addy's Ale, Franklin DIPA, Beale's Best Bitter, Riley's Red, Dry Stout, Annie Brown, Mocha Stout, Kolsch, Sutter Wheat, Extra Pale Ale, and Golden. Seasonals: Harvest Ale, Sutter Fest, Wee Heavy, and Oatmeal Imperial Stout.

The Pick: The Franklin DIPA is a surprisingly restrained imperial with big hops flavor that is not overly bitter. It has a huge malt backbone and a touch of honeyed sweetness, which provide essential balance. At 8 percent ABV, it's almost a session double IPA.

Tahoe Mountain Brewing Company

Brewpub: 475 North Lake Boulevard, Tahoe City, CA 96145

Production brewery: 10990 Industrial Way, Truckee, CA 96161

530-581-HOPS (4677) • www.tahoebrewing.com

Twitter @tahoebrewing

Facebook.com/pages/Tahoe-Mountain-Brewing-Company/381341471878031

Tahoe Mountain Brewing is, in a sense, two breweries. There's a production brewery in nearby Truckee that provides some of the beer to the picturesque brewpub in Tahoe City, situated right across the street from the lake. The grand vision of a brewing empire also includes a fully stocked homebrew supply store adjacent to the production brewery. It's the brainchild of Aaron Bigelow, a twenty-year veteran homebrewer as well as a local building contractor and real estate developer. At the Truckee production brewery, there's a copper-clad 10-barrel Pub Brewing system located in an industrial park. In the front of the building, Bigelow plans to have a homebrew supply store and eventually a tasting room for the brewery. Currently, Tahoe Mountain beer is available only on draft, but there are plans to offer it in bottles or cans, or possibly both.

Brewmaster Clay Brackley is a veteran brewer who began as a homebrewer in his hometown of Reno, Nevada, while studying forestry in college. His first brewing job was at the Reno BJ's Restaurant and Brewery. From there, he moved to Alaska to become head brewer at Sleeping Lady Brewing, followed by stints at Victory Brewing in Pennsylvania and Kane Brewing in New Jersey, before moving closer to home to brew for Tahoe Mountain.

The brewpub couldn't be in a more idyllic location, along North Lake Boulevard in the Cobblestone Center, a Bavarian-style village filled with tourist shops and other diversions for the visitor. Directly across the street is Lake Tahoe, and there are gorgeous views from the outdoor patio in front of the restaurant. The patio is covered by a retractable awning, so it's perfect in almost any weather.

Beers brewed: Year-round: Paddleboard Pale Ale, Hop Song IPA, Hopped Up Monk, Sugar Pine Porter, Wild Hair Wheat, Hop Dragon Double IPA, Ranch Dog Red, Local Lager, DAPA (Dry American Pale Ale), and Dolly Varden Golden Ale. Seasonals: Motley Grand Cru Belgian Strong Ale, Auld Bitch Barley Wine, Cremesickle Porter, Satan's Breath Sour, Saison Savourese, Saison d'Croquette, Ugly Duchess Tripel, White Rabbit, Rubicon Raspberry Lambic, The Rise and Shiner Imperial Breakfast Stout, and Pepe Pilsner.

Inside, the brewpub resembles a rustic mountain cabin, with an L-shaped bar as you enter. Behind the stone fireplace is an open dining room with booths and tables and chairs. The walls are mounted with big fish and seven big-screen televisions. The decorations are described as "classic boathouse chic meets luxury man cave."

Upstairs behind the kitchen is a 3-barrel pilot brewery, where Brackley brews and ages his sour beers. The warm location presents several challenges, but if the sour beers I tasted are any indication, they're not ones that can't be overcome. The food is well done, with lots of choices, and the beers are coming along nicely. Now that the production brewery is online, it should free up Brackley to engage in making more experimental sours, a relative rarity for brewpubs, but one that sets Tahoe Mountain Brewing apart from the others.

Tahoe Mountain Brewing Company

Opened: June 2, 2012.

Type: Brewpub and separate production brewery.

Owners: Aaron Bigelow and Tanya Thayer.

Brewer: Clay Brackley.

System: 3-barrel Portland Kettleworks at the brewpub, 10-barrel Pub Brewing brewhouse at the production brewery, with 20-barrel fermenters, 1,600 barrels annual capacity.

Annual production: 1,600 barrels (2012 estimate).

Packages available: Growlers and kegs. Bottles and cans are expected to be added to the brewery's portfolio.

Tours: The production brewery in Truckee is not currently open to the public, nor is the brewpub brewery, which is located upstairs behind the kitchen, where all of the sour beers are created.

Hours: Seven days a week, 11 a.m. to midnight.

Food: The extensive lunch and dinner menus feature gourmet pub fare, along with the brewpub's own innovative dishes, which include smokehouse items like St. Louis pork ribs, oak grilled chicken, pulled pork, and brisket. There are also wood-fired flatbread pizzas, panini sandwiches, salads, seafood, and pasta. Vegan and vegetarian options are available.

Extras: Directly across the street from the brewpub is Lake Tahoe, and the outdoor patio, which runs along the main thoroughfare, offers beautiful views. Special events and live music shows take place from time to time, so watch the website and Facebook page.

Gift shop: Hats, T-shirts, sweatshirts, and gift items are available at the brewpub or online.

Food and Beer

In addition to great beer, California is also blessed with a great food culture. Much of the nation's food is grown here, so fresh, locally grown produce is easier to find than in many other places, especially in the variety that California enjoys. "California cuisine" was an outgrowth of the ability to grow a wide variety of crops along with the state being a melting pot of cultures. Instead of sticking to the cuisine of just one culture, chefs in California were able to experiment with combining elements of many different cooking traditions.

One who epitomized this concept was Alice Waters, who in 1971 opened her now world-famous Chez Panisse restaurant in Berkeley. She also emphasized local ingredients, so it's no surprise that the concept of locavores—Oxford's 2007 "word of the year"—was coined here in the Bay Area, by a group of four women in San Francisco. The original idea was to restrict your diet to food grown or produced within a hundred-mile radius. The movement emphasizes that local ingredients are fresher, more nutritious, taste better, and ultimately better for the environment. Craft breweries have been trying to get across the same message with their beer since the very beginning.

Rather than just follow traditional cooking rules, California chefs, like brewers experimenting with new innovations or different ingredients, broke them with wild abandon. Also known as "California fusion," the idea was to combine flavors from various cultures to create something entirely new.

Several decades later, California cuisine is its own well-respected type of cooking tradition, albeit one with fewer rules. Most likely because of this innovative spirit, San Francisco and the rest of Northern California still boast a vibrant food scene that is world renowned, and many breweries and brewpubs serve food that's a cut above the usual pub fare. Some even rise to the level of "gastropub," an inelegant term that's become popular in Great Britain to describe a pub that also serves high-end food.

Beer and food pair together extraordinarily well, far better than most people often believe, due in part to years of beers that weren't particularly flavorful. Because of this, most restaurants still concentrate more heavily on their wine lists. But with the rise of craft beer, no self-respecting chef can afford to ignore the beers now available to him or her both as cooking ingredients and to pair with specific dishes.

But until most chefs get their acts together, your best bet is to attend a beer dinner. Many restaurants are finally getting in on this action, with the help of our many local brewers who do understand the connection of beer and food. Not just during beer week, but throughout the year, brewers are pairing up with local restaurants to put on a beer dinner, which is usually a multicourse dinner where each dish is paired with a specific beer, chosen to enhance the experience and work in concert with the flavors in the food.

The Bay Area also has at least two chefs who specialize in beer and food. The first, who's been putting on beer dinners since 1995, is Bruce Paton, also known as the Beer Chef. Until the hotel was torn down recently to make way for a hospital, Paton hosted regular beer dinners at San Francisco's Cathedral Hill Hotel, including a beer and chocolate dinner every February. But he's still doing the occasional beer dinner in the East Bay, where he currently resides. You can find out when and where the next of his beer dinners will be held at his website (see the Beer Blogs section at the back of the book).

Another local chef who specializes in beer is Sean Z. Paxton, the Homebrew Chef. I like to describe Paxton as a mad alchemist, because he tends to use multiple beers in each dish, and then pairs each with one, two, or even three beers. His dinners tend to be grand spectacles and often run to a dozen courses, where it's not uncommon to see nitrogen, dry ice, or as many as ten different—and all handmade—salts used in a single meal. Paxton doesn't have his own place, so he uses a mobile kitchen or whatever he can find to put on his dinners. You can find out where his latest dinner will take place at his website (see the Beer Blogs section).

The High Sierras

The High Sierras is the region located along the eastern edge of California, along the border of Nevada, and encompasses the tall, majestic Sierra Nevadas. For the purposes of this book, the High Sierras region includes the counties of Alpine, Calaveras, Mariposa, Mono, and Tuolumne. The whole area is roughly the same size as New Jersey but contains only four working breweries.

It's a remote area with more than its share of grandiose beauty. No matter which brewery you're heading to, it will be a long drive, made even longer by the perpetually winding roads. Regardless of where you are, the Sierra Nevadas look down at you, as the mountains run the length of this area from north to south, stretching four hundred miles through and beyond.

The five counties contain only three incorporated cities, so it's fairly rural area. It's also the area of Northern California with the fewest people. The five counties together have slightly less people than the entire town of Clarksville, Tennessee, made famous by the Monkees in their song about "the last train." You won't find many Starbucks or chain stores around each bend, so you may feel almost like you've been transported back in time, which can be a very satisfying feeling, especially if you're looking to get away from it all.

What you *will* find is nature writ large. In addition to the mountains, there's Yosemite National Park, one of the jewels in the National Park Service crown. The park spans over 760,000 acres, 95 percent of it wilderness. Most of Yosemite's 4 million annual visitors stay in the seven square miles known as Yosemite Valley. And there's plenty to see and do there. It's definitely worth a stop for at least the day, or longer if your travels allow.

Traveling east from Yosemite, through an even more remote stretch, you'll encounter even more stunning vistas. Mono Lake is worth a stop to see its otherworldly limestone tufa "tower" formations, which rise eerily from the saline soda lake and along its shorelines. The area around Mammoth Lakes has a lot to offer and is a great place for outdoor activities, such as hiking among the redwoods, skiing, or soaking in the natural hot springs. Another feature is the amazing Devils Postpile National Monument, a largely unheralded park built around a natural formation of hexagonal basalt columns.

The area was also part of the mining efforts that so occupied nineteenth-century California, and you'll find reminders of the mining heritage everywhere, including many caverns and old mines open to the public. Mark Twain spent a number of years in this area of California, and his famous 1865 short story, "The Celebrated Jumping Frog of Calaveras County," was set in the town of Angels Camp in that county.

Chappell Brewery

El Capitan

1818 Black Bear Mountain Court, Mariposa,
   CA 95338
209-966-3812
Facebook.com/pages/Chappell-Brewery/
   116053911754681

The Chappell Brewery may well be the smallest commercial brewery in the mountainous regions of Northern California. Its founder, owner, and brewer, Scott Chappell, grew up in Southern California and started homebrewing as a hobby that eventually got out of control. He relocated to Mariposa and turned pro. It's a one-man operation, and Chappell brews, markets, sells, and delivers his own beer.

For a time, he operated a tasting room on State Route 140, the main road through town, but he closed it down in late 2012 to concentrate on selling to retailers, bars, and restaurants. So although the tasting room may appear in an older book or on a website with information that's not up-to-date, be aware that it's no longer open.

Chappell built a small barn specifically for his brewery and sells bottles of his beer in area stores, so either make an appointment to visit the brewery or keep an eye out for his beer when you're in the Yosemite area.

Chappell Brewery

Opened: October 2009.
Type: Production brewery.
Owner: Scott Chappell.
Brewer: Scott Chappell.
Guild membership: BA.
System: 1-barrel nanobrewery, 48 barrels annual capacity.
Annual production: 7 barrels (2011).
Packages available: 12-ounce and 22-ounce bottles.
Tours: By appointment only.

Beers brewed: Year-round: Yosemite Red Ale, Dawn Patrol Belgium Blond Ale, El Capitan Porter, Miners Gold Pale Ale, Mariposa Mild Ale, Nut Brown Ale, and Raspberry Wheat.

The Pick: The High Sierra mountains pair perfectly with the Dawn Patrol, a creamy lemon citrus beer with Belgian character and sweet flavors. This is the beer I want in my snowed-in cabin on top of the mountain. It's like a tropical oasis.

Mammoth Brewing Company

94 Berner Street, Mammoth Lakes, CA 93546
760-934-7141 • www.mammothbrewingco.com
Facebook.com/MammothBrewing

Mammoth Brewing opened in 1995, but Sean and Joyce Turner took over the brewery only a few years ago, in 2007. In that short time, however, they've turned it into a most impressive enterprise. Sean Turner is a veteran beer man, having worked for numerous craft breweries in a variety of positions before putting that experience to good use running his own brewery.

Mammoth Lakes, where the brewery is located, is one of the most remote spots in California and is best known for its skiing and outdoor activities. At 8,000 feet above sea level, it has the highest elevation of any brewery on the West Coast. Because of that, the water is especially pure, but the altitude causes other problems, like water boiling at 198 degrees and 4-foot snowdrifts.

You have to want to go there. Mammoth Lakes is located on the eastern side of Yosemite National Park, along a remote stretch of Route 395, the only road for miles. From the Bay Area, you pretty much have to travel through Yosemite and along Mono Lake, and you'll pass by or near a number of less well-known spots of natural beauty, like Devils Postpile National Monument. If you're coming from Southern California, there's a slightly more direct route, but not by much. Make no mistake—it will take you a long time to get there.

The happy news is that despite the effort to get there, it is worth it. Besides the skiing, there are amazing vistas, hiking trails, and geological wonders nearby. It's an empty wilderness, and the town of Mammoth Lakes is a magnet for anyone spending time in the area. The resort town boasts plentiful restaurants, shopping, activities—and a brewery.

Because of its remoteness, perhaps the best time to go is during early August. That's when the Mammoth Festival of Beers & Bluesapalooza, a four-day series of blues concerts and a beer festival, takes place. It's held right among the trees of

Beers brewed: Year-round: Golden Trout Pilsner, Paranoids Pale Ale, Real McCoy Amber, Lake Tahoe Red Ale, Double Nut Brown, Floating Rock Hefeweizen, Epic IPA, and IPA 395. Seasonals: Devil's Post Pale Ale (summer), Owens Valley Wet Harvest (fall), Hair of the Bear (winter), Wild Sierra Farm House Ale (spring), Blondi Bock, and Charley Wine.

Sam's Wood Site, just a short walk from downtown and the brewery. The wooded grove fills up with lounge chairs and blankets as people come and spend the day listening to great music and drinking beer. The festival has been going strong since 1995, and it has been sponsored by the brewery since the beginning. It's one of most impressive music and beer festivals I've ever attended, and it should be on your bucket list.

The recently built tasting room is a great destination. You can try all of Mammoth Brewing's beers there, buy a sweatshirt to keep you warm, and pick up some take-out beer for your cabin or hotel. The brewery is located off-site, just off the main thoroughfare. It's in an unassuming nondescript building with a roll-up, but inside, you'll find a spacious bar and gift shop. There's limited seating, but you can belly up to the bar. Turner is actively searching for a new location where he can build a bigger brewery to keep up with rising demand.

Spend as much time as you can in Mammoth Lakes. It may be a while before you can make another trek into the California wilderness, so you should see as much as you can. Go skiing. Take a hike. Relax in one of the hot springs. Visit the Devils Postpile. No matter what you do, at the end of the day there's always more Mammoth beer.

The Pick: After a long drive to reach Mammoth Brewing along Route 395, the road's namesake beer, IPA 395, hits just the right notes. It's a big West Coast style hops monster, an imperial IPA that's brash and bold, with piney, citrusy, and pineapple hops character and massive malt balance. It's also brewed with sage and juniper berries, which give it a little something extra, an intangible spicing that makes it unlike any other double IPA you've had.

Mammoth Brewing Company

Opened: December 1995.

Type: Production brewery, with tasting room.

Owners: Sean and Joyce Turner.

Brewer: Jason Senior.

Guild membership: CCBA.

System: 15-barrel Liquid Assets system, 5,500 barrels annual capacity.

Annual production: 5,500 barrels.

Packages available: 12-ounce cans and bottles in six-packs, 22-ounce bottles, growlers, and 5.16-, 7.75-, and 13.2-gallon kegs.

Tours: Tours are not available.

Hours: Tasting room is open seven days a week, 10 a.m. to 6 p.m.

Food: Pretzels available in the tasting room.

Extras: Children are welcome in the tasting room, where they can get Mammoth Imperial Root Beer. The first Wednesday of every month is half-price growler fill day.

Gift shop: Retail store with T-shirts, hoodies, glassware, books, and signs.

Prospectors Brewing Company

Production Brewery: 5004 Fairgrounds Road, Mariposa, CA 95338
Tap room: 4966-A Seventh Street, Mariposa, CA 95338
Brewery: 209-742-6896 / taproom: 209-966-3966
prospectorsbrewing.com
Prospectorsbrew
Facebook.com/ProspectorsBrewingCompany

Mariposa is Spanish for butterfly, but the area is known more for its mountains and mining. In modern times, people visit the Mariposa area for its natural beauty. Like many old mining towns, today it's filled with shops, restaurants, and museums, and more than four million people pass through the remote town each year.

Outside of town, by the county fairgrounds, Prospectors Brewing Company built its production facility, where Justin Burnsed brews all of the brewery's beer. Burnsed originally worked in the world of high finance, but the economic downturn forced him to rethink his options. As an international relations major at Chico State, he had been inspired by Sierra Nevada Brewing to take up homebrewing, so now he shifted gears and enrolled in the Master Brewers Program at UC Davis. After stints brewing at Stone Brewing near San Diego and at BrewDog in Scotland, he found the opportunity to brew in the High Sierras was too good to pass up.

In downtown Mariposa, a stone's throw from the main thoroughfare—literally; you really could throw a stone and hit it—is the Prospectors Brewing Company taproom. An old house was converted into a great space where Prospectors can serve its beer and where people can bring their own food and listen to live music. The whole house was lovingly remodeled from scratch, and like the brewery, it's clean and comfortable. The bar was built out of reclaimed wood with a granite top. There's also a beer garden in what used to be the backyard.

Beers brewed: Year-round: Bootjack Blonde German American Ale, Long Tom IPA, Mariposa Midnight Smoked & Oaked Stout, and Pistol Whipped Wheat. Seasonals: Ragged Ass Rye Brown Ale, Gossner's Gold Extra Pale Ale, and The World's Still Here.

The Pick: When I visited the brewery, not all of the beers were finished, but I really liked the Bootjack Blonde Ale, which has a fresh citrus nose with spicy aromas. Essentially a hybrid of a German pilsner and an ale, it has tart hopping, rich malty sweetness, and an earthy, herbal flavor profile that really works despite its split personality.

Prospectors is off to a very good start. Burnsed's beers are unique, interesting, uniformly well made, and great tasting. If you find yourself in the vicinity of Yosemite National Park, stop by nearby Mariposa and have a beer at Prospectors.

Prospectors Brewing Company

Opened: August 11, 2012.

Type: Production brewery, with taproom.

Owner: Terry Evans, managing partner.

Brewer: Justin Burnsed.

Guild membership: BA.

System: 5-barrel Premiere Stainless System, 800 barrels annual capacity.

Annual production: 450 barrels (2012 estimate).

Packages available: Growlers and 5- and 15.5-gallon kegs.

Tours: By reservation only.

Hours: Monday through Friday, 3 to 10 p.m.; Saturday and Sunday, 11 a.m. to 10 p.m.

Food: Food from local restaurants can be ordered at the taproom.

Extras: Live music at the taproom.

Gift shop: Hats, shirts, and glassware are available at the taproom.

Snowshoe Brewing Company

2050 Highway 4, Arnold, CA 95223
209-795-2272 • www.snowshoebrewing.com
Facebook.com/pages/Snowshoe-Brewing-
   Company/108246532533638

Located along State Route 4, about 4 miles south of Calaveras Big Trees State Park and due west of the Stanislaus National Forest, the Snowshoe brewpub has been a High Sierras institution for nearly twenty years. It's fairly remote, along one of the few roads to cut through this sparsely populated area. It's roughly in between El Dorado National Forest to the north and Yosemite National Park to the south. It's also 111 miles from South Lake Tahoe, though since the route is a winding, mountainous one, it will take you three hours to drive there.

The brewpub is a family-style restaurant with an extensive menu. The plates are filled with good pub food at good prices, and the service is quick and friendly. A centrally located U-shaped bar is the hub of the brewpub, surrounded by tables and chairs. One wall is all windows, with smaller tables and high bar-stool chairs running the length of the restaurant. The windows look out over a grassy knoll.

The brewery is in a separate room adjacent to the restaurant, but you can see it through a couple of well-placed windows. Several regulars are brewed all year round, along with several seasonals that rotate during the year. The brewery bottles its three most popular beers: the Snoweizen Wheat Ale, Thompson Pale Ale, and Grizzly Brown Ale. The beers got their name from local history. For instance, the pale ale is named for Snowshoe Thompson, who traveled through the nearby mountains on snowshoes delivering the mail in the 1860s.

Overall, the brewpub is a great respite in the wilderness of Calaveras County and the Sierra Nevada. There isn't another brewery for miles and

Beers brewed: Year-round: Snoweizen Wheat Ale, Apricot Wheat Ale, Thompson Pale Ale, Lodgepole IPA, and Grizzly Brown Ale. Seasonals: Irish Red, Midnight Moon Oatmeal Stout, Wit, Cutthroat Strong Ale, Oktoberfest, Summerfest, Westridge Winter Ale, Double Mash Cutthroat, Scarlet Red, and Black Bart Porter.

The Pick: The Thompson Pale Ale is a solid beer, with a restrained nose of grapefruit and sweet, perfumy aromas. It's light-bodied and refreshing, with caramel and bread notes, and it has a clean finish with some lingering tartness.

miles, and you'll breathe a sigh of relief when you take your first sip of fresh beer in hours.

Snowshoe Brewing Company

Opened: 1995.

Type: Brewpub.

Owner: Jeff Yarnell.

Brewer: Tom Schuermann.

Guild membership: BA, CCBA.

System: 15-barrel Pub Brewing system.

Packages available: 12-ounce bottles in six-packs, growlers, and kegs.

Hours: Monday, 4 to 8:30 p.m.; Tuesday through Saturday, 11:30 a.m. to 8:30 p.m.; Sunday 11:30 a.m. to 8 p.m. Restaurant hours can change seasonally, so check the website.

Food: The menu includes a wide variety of appetizers (the beer-battered fries are particularly tasty), along with salads, sandwiches, burgers, pizza, Mexican dishes, and pasta. After 4 p.m., the lunch menu is extended to include choices from the Fireside Grill, like prime rib, pork loin, baby back ribs, steaks, and other entrées. There are also vegetarian and low-fat selections, as well as a separate kids' menu. The brewpub also has a full-service take-and-bake pizza parlor, with made-to-order pizzas that you can take home, or to your nearby rental, and bake in your oven.

Extras: Happy hour is Monday through Friday, 3:30 to 5:30 p.m.

Gift shop: Hats, T-shirts, pint glasses, and six-packs are available at the brewpub.

Coming Soon

I strove to make this book as complete and up-to-date as possible. But even so, in the months between its writing and its publication, it is impossible to predict what will happen to the Northern California brewing scene. Nearly fifty breweries were in the planning stages and may or may not have opened. Some of the brewers may have abandoned their efforts. Others are likely hard at work trying to realize their dream of a new craft brewery. Following is a list of the in-planning breweries not expected to be open by the spring of 2013.

Ale House Brewing (alehousebrewing.com), Colmery Court, San Jose.

Barrelhouse Brewing (barrelhousebrewing.com), Divisadero Street, San Francisco.

Bernal Heights Brewing, Cortland Avenue, San Francisco.

Bike Dog Brewing (bikedogbrewing.com), 2534 Industrial Boulevard, Suite 110, West Sacramento.

Boneshaker Brewery & Public House (boneshakerpub.com), Sunset Boulevard, Rocklin.

Bosworth Brewery (bosworthbrewery.com), Bosworth Street, San Francisco.

Brass Balls Beer Company (brassballsbeerco.com), Sacramento.

The Bread Agency, Summit Drive, Corte Madera.

B Squared Brewing, Lagoon Court, Rocklin.

California Brewing, (californiabrewingcompany.com), Anderson.

Carneros Brewing (carnerosbrewing.com), Fremont Drive, Sonoma.

Cedar Street Brewing, Santa Cruz.

Cleophus Quealy Beer Company (www.cleoph.us), Belmont.

Corralitos Brewing, (corralitosbrewingco.com), Watsonville.

Device Brewing, (devicebrewing.com), 8166 14th Avenue, Sacramento.

Diablo Brewing, a.k.a. BNE Brewing, Danville.

Diving Dog Brewhouse [a BYO], (facebook.com/DivingDogBrewhouse), 1802 Telegraph Avenue, Oakland.

Eckert Malting & Brewing Company, 2280 Ivy Street, Suite 130, Chico

8-Bit Brewing (8bitbrewing.blogspot.com), Sebastopol.

Eight Bridges Brewing Company, (8bridgesbrewing.com), Pleasanton.

El Dorado Brewing (eldobrew.com), Camino. Opened in 1998; currently closed but planning a relaunch under new ownership.

Elizabeth Street Brewing (elizabethstreetbrewery.com), Noe Valley, San Francisco.

Fall River Brewing, (facebook.com/FallRiverBrewingCompany), 24339 Highway 89 North, Burney.

510 Brewing (510brewing.com), Fremont.

47 Hills Brewing (47hillsbrewingcompany.com), San Francisco.

4th Way Brewing Company (4thwaybrewingco.com), East Bay.

Gold Country Brewing, Pinecroft Road, Colfax.

Headlands Brewing, (headlandsbrewing.com), San Francisco.

Heatherdowns Brewing, Hydesville.

Holy Craft Brewing Company, (holycraftbrewery.com), San Francisco.

Local Brewing Company (localbrewingco.com), San Francisco.

Mad Canyon Brewing, Summit Drive, Rocklin.

Midtown Brewing, Sacramento.

Mount St. Helena Brewing (sainthelenabrewery.com), Middletown. Opened in 1996; currently closed but rumored to be opening again in the future.

Mraz Brewing, (mrazbrewingcompany.com), 2222 Francisco Drive, Suite 510, El Dorado Hills.

Oak Park Brewing Company, (facebook.com/OakParkBrewingCompany), Sacramento.

Odonata Beer Company, (odonatabeer.com), Sacramento. Will likely be relauched in late 2013.

Old Glory Brewing, (oldglorybrewingcompany.com), 8251 Alpine Avenue, Sacramento.

Out of Bounds Brewing, (outofboundsbrewing.com), 4480 Yankee Hill Road, Suite 100, Rocklin.

Phantom Coast Gastropub and Brewery, 65 Taylor Street, San Francisco.

PNE Holding, 110 Minna Street, San Francisco.

Sandude Brewing (facebook.com/sandude.brewing), Freitas Park, Turlock.

San Jose Cooperative Brewery and Pub, (sjcoopbrewpub), San Jose.

Santa Clara Valley Brewing, (scvbrewing.com, facebook.com/SantaClaraValleyBrewingCo), 1805 Little Orchard Street #104, San Jose.

Shizmo Brewing (shizmobrewery.com), San Jose.

Sonnenbräu, (sonnenbrau.com), Genoa Place, San Francisco.

Spike Dog Brewing, Sacramento.

St. Clair Brown Winery & Brewery, Napa.

Three Monkeys Brewing, (3monkeysbrewing.com), Madera. May or may not still be brewing, numerous attempts to communicate with the brewery over several months have gone unanswered.

Trautmann's Brewing & Malting, a.k.a. MacArthur Garage Brewery (facebook.com/MacArthurGarageBrewery), Oakland.

Turning Gear Brewing (facebook.com/pages/Turning-Gear-Brewing-Co/221421961223032), Lodi.

Undertaker Brewing (undertakerbrewing.com), Alma Avenue, San Jose.

Union Brewery, (Roseville).

Unmasqued Brewing (unmasquedbeer.com), San Francisco.

Unnamed Berkeley Nanobrewery, 1763 Alcatraz Avenue, Berkeley.

Van Houten Brewing (vanhoutenbrewing.blogspot.com), Caletta Avenue, San Anselmo.

Walden Tide Brewing (waldentide.com), Pacific Avenue, Pacifica.

Woodfour Brewing, Calder Avenue, Sebastopol.

Beerwebs

The Internet can be a treasure trove of information about beer and breweries, with thousands of websites dedicated to beer. Not all of them are objective, accurate, or even worth your time. Caveat lector. Following are a few useful ones that focus on California or are otherwise broad enough in their scope to include the Golden State, as well as general beer knowledge, information, and news.

California Breweries

CalBreweries.com

This is a website that I set up specifically for this book, a place to add breweries as they open in Northern California, update information, correct any mistakes, or let you know if any of the breweries listed in this book have closed. As I learn of any changes, I'll post them there, so please check for any new or updated information. If you discover any errors or if any of the information in a listing has changed, please be so kind as to drop me a note and I'll update the information on the website. In that way, the most-up-to-date information will be available for the next visitor.

California Craft Brewers Association

CaliforniaCraftBeer.com

This is the official website of the California Craft Brewers Association (CCBA), a state trade association for California brewers. Executive director Tom McCormick keeps the website up-to-date with news that affects California breweries and also maintains a blog about what's happening in the California beer scene.

Brookston Beer Bulletin

BrookstonBeerBulletin.com

This is my own personal beer blog, the one that I'm not paid to write. As a result, it's a more unvarnished, opinionated look at the beer industry. I include news, reviews, event coverage, and the occasional rant.

The Brewing Network

thebrewingnetwork.com

Founded by Justin Crossley, the Brewing Network, a.k.a. the BN Army, is essential radio for beer lovers, especially homebrewers. BN Radio has a number of regular shows on different aspects of beer and brewing. The website offers a wealth of information too. National in focus, it nonetheless is based in the Bay Area and tends to cover Northern California more vigorously.

Beer Advocate

beeradvocate.com

One of the two eight-hundred-pound gorillas of beer websites, Beer Advocate was originally conceived by brothers Jason and Todd Alström as a ratings site. They've since added popular forums and all manner of great content and have branched out into the print world, publishing beer's only monthly, *Beer Advocate* magazine. They also put on several great beer festivals in the Boston area throughout the year.

Rate Beer

ratebeer.com

Rate Beer is the other great beer website. This one is located on the West Coast, where executive director Joe Tucker runs it from Sonoma. As a result, it arguably has more local California members and focus. It also has a wealth of information, as well as ratings of beer and active forums for any beer-related topic you can think of.

Beer Pulse

beerpulse.com

Beer Pulse does a good job of bringing together a lot of the beer news out there in the world and aggregating it in one place. Adam Nasan, who runs the website, posts press releases, news links, and upcoming beers from breweries as they file for label approval.

The Full Pint

thefullpint.com

Despite being based in Southern California, the Full Pint covers beer in all of California. It's written by Danny and Jonny Fullpint—not their real names—along with a team of additional bloggers.

Beervana

beervana.blogspot.com

Based in Portland, Jeff Alworth not only tackles local beer, but also waxes philosophically about larger issues that affect beer lovers everywhere.

Beer Institute

beerinstitute.org

The Beer Institute is a trade organization of brewers that was founded in 1986 as the successor to older beer associations that had struggled when the number of breweries in American seriously declined. Originally created for mostly large brewers, today its membership includes most of the regional and larger craft breweries, and many smaller ones too. It puts out great information on the beer industry as a whole and also runs the website Beer Serves America (beerservesamerica.com).

Brewers Association

brewersassociation.org

The Brewers Association (BA) is a trade group that represents and promotes the interests of small brewers. If you have questions about beer that are more technical, business-related, or legal in nature, the BA's website is a good place to find answers.

Craft Beer

craftbeer.com

The Brewers Association also recently launched this website, which features great information about beer that's aimed more at consumers and beer lovers. You can find all sorts of useful news and knowledge about craft beer here.

American Homebrewers Association

homebrewersassociation.org

The American Homebrewers Association (AHA) is the homebrewing arm of the Brewers Association. The AHA's website is a great place to start to find out everything you'd ever want to know about making your own beer at home.

Cicerone

cicerone.org

Essentially, a cicerone is the beer equivalent of a sommelier for wine. The Cicerone Certification Program offers certification at three levels. Details of the program can be found at this website.

Beer Blogs

Beer blogs are more personal online destinations, usually written by a single person or occasionally a small number of people. The word *blog* is a portmanteau for "web log." Blogs first appeared in the late 1990s, and today there are nearly two hundred million blogs worldwide. Of these, about fifteen hundred are considered beer blogs. In addition, many breweries, beer distributors, importers, and other beer companies maintain business blogs that are beer related. They are often a good source of local information, news, and interesting opinions, but by their very nature they are a mixed bag. Because they are personality driven, you will undoubtedly like some better than others. Shop around and find the ones that speak to you. There are beer blogs for everyone.

Bay Area Beer Bloggers

The Bay Area in California is particularly rich in beer bloggers, as well as breweries. I noticed this fact several years ago and brought many of them together when I founded the Bay Area Beer Bloggers (BABB) in 2008. BABB is a loose organization of beer bloggers. Members get together monthly at various beer destinations around the area, have bottle-sharing events, and talk shop. Below is a list of the current active members of the Bay Area Beer Bloggers.

allbrews (allbrews.blogspot.com), written by Chuck Lenatti.

All Over Beer (alloverbeer.com), written by Brian Stechschulte.

Beer-a-Day 365 (beeraday365.com), written by Dave McAvoy.

Beer by BART (beerbybart.com), written by Steve Shapiro and Gail Williams.

The Beer Chef (beer-chef.com), written by Bruce Paton.

Beer 47 (beer47.com), written by David Jensen.

The Beer Geek (thebeergeek.com), written by Chris Nelson and Merideth Canham-Nelson.

Beer Samizdat (beersamizdat.net), written by Jay Hinman.

The Beer Warrior (thebeerwarrior.com), written by Matt Knopf.

Berkeley Craft Beer Examiner (examiner.com/craft-beer-in-oakland/jen-muehlbauer), written by Jen Muehlbauer.

BetterBeerBlog (betterbeerblog.com), written by Peter Estaniel.

Brewed for Thought (brewedforthought.com), written by Mario Rubio.

Broken Spirits (brokenspiritsbeer.blogspot.com), written by Jon Campbell.

Drink with the Wench (drinkwiththewench.com), written by Ashley Routson.

Episuds (episuds.com), videotaped by Jesse Molina.

The Homebrew Chef (homebrewchef.com), written by Sean Z. Paxton.

. . . learning about beer (dk-beer.blogspot.com), written by dk.

NorCal Beer Blog (norcalbeerblog.blogspot.com), written by Mark Harvey.

Nor Cal Beer Guide (norcalbeerguide.com), written by John Heylin.

Overcarbed (overcarbed.com), written by Simon Ford.

Plastic Love Monkey (plasticlovemonkey.wordpress.com), written by Rail Arson.

Ramblings of a Beer Runner (beer-runner.blogspot.com), written by Derrick Peterman.

SF Weekly/SFoodie Blog (blogs.sfweekly.com/author.php?author_id=2427), written
    by Jason Henry.

Ünnecessary Ümlaut (unnecessaryumlaut.com), written by Fred Abercrombie.

Ken Weaver's blog (kenweaver.com), written by the eponymous Ken Weaver.

Wet Your Whistles (wetyourwhistles.com), written by Jen and Joey McDaniel.

Other Beer Blogs

Here are several additional beer blogs that focus on beer in areas outside California or are more national or international in their scope.
These are ones that I personally enjoy and believe to be worth your
time. I should confess that most of these are written by colleagues—
fellow beer writers—who are also my friends.

Appellation Beer (appellationbeer.com/blog), written by author Stan Hieronymus. Stan
has penned at least half a dozen beer books and also writes several other beer blogs.
But this is perhaps the most personal one, and it's certainly his most active and engag-
ing. Stan is always a thoughtful writer, and his musings should be on every beer lover's
must-read list.

Seen through a Glass (lewbryson.blogspot.com), written by Lew Bryson. Though Lew is
an East Coast beer writer, living just outside Philadelphia, his lively writing encompasses
topics well beyond his local market.

The World of Beer (worldofbeer.wordpress.com), written by Canadian drinks writer
Stephen Beaumont. Stephen is author of almost a dozen books, including his most
recent, *The World Atlas of Beer*, cowritten with Tim Webb. I've known Stephen longer
than I've been writing about beer. Several years ago, he started an overhaul of his old
worldofbeer.com website and temporarily moved his online writing to a WordPress blog.
That was four years ago. You'll still find his unvarnished, opinionated musings there.

Zythophile (zythophile.wordpress.com), written by Martyn Cornell. Martyn is hands down my favorite beer historian. If you want the truth, he's your man. If you want your cherished beer myths shattered to bits, he's also your man. Get over it. Truth may sometimes be stranger than fiction, but it's also more satisfying to be right, as he almost always is.

If I left off your favorite beer blogger or website, don't take that as a sign that I don't think it's good too. This is necessarily a very short list, another starting point from which to discover your own favorites. You can also find a useful list of just about every citizen beer blog, defined as ones "not designed to promote a brewery or other business," nearly fifteen hundred beer blogs worldwide, at beerbloggersconference.org/blogs/complete-list-of-beer-blogs/.

Festival Calendar

With so many breweries in Northern California, it is not surprising that the region also hosts a plethora of great beer festivals and other beer events. Once upon a time, beer festivals were summer affairs, but the combination of California weather and the rising number of craft beer aficionados has led to festivals being held all year round, with something for every season. Each year the dates change slightly, so check the event websites for current details and information.

January

Bay Area Brew Festival (bayareabrewfestival.com), San Francisco.

The Brewing Network Winter Brews Festival (thebrewingnetwork.com), Concord.

Winter KraftBrew Beer Fest (nagleeparkgarage.com/entertainment.html), San Jose.

February

Bistro Double IPA Festival (the-bistro.com), Hayward.

Celebrator Beer News Anniversary Party (celebrator.com), East Bay.

Sacramento Beer Week (sacramentobeerweek.com), Sacramento.

SF Beer Week (sfbeerweek.org), Bay Area.

Strong Beer Month (strongbeermonth.com), San Francisco.

Toronado Barleywine Festival (toronado.com), San Francisco.

Triple Rock Sour Sunday (triplerock.com), Berkeley.

March

Battle of the Brews (battleofthebrews.com), Santa Rosa.

Fairfax Brewfest (fairfaxbrewfest.com), Fairfax.

April

Bay Area Craft Beer Festival (bayareacraftbeerfestival.com), Martinez.

Bistro IPA Festival (the-bistro.com), Hayward.

Oroville Beer Fest (orovillechamber.net), Oroville.

Sacramento Turn Verein Bockbierfest (sacramentoturnverein.com), Sacramento.

San Francisco International Beer Festival (sfbeerfest.com), San Francisco.

May

Boonville Beer Festival (avbc.com), Boonville.

Brew at the Zoo (sequoiaparkzoo.net/Brew.html), Eureka.

Great Petaluma Chili Cook-Off, Salsa & Beer Tasting (cinnabartheater.org/chili/), Petaluma.

Lagunitas Beer Circus (lagunitas.com), Petaluma.

NorCal Session Fest (Facebook.com/events/372233709549990/), San Leandro.Raley Field Brewfest (raleyfield.com and northerncalbrewers.com), Sacramento.

West Coast Brew Fest (matsonian.com/wcbf/), Sacramento.

June

Beerfest (f2f.org and beerfestsonomacounty.wordpress.com), Santa Rosa.

Bell Tower Beerfest (Placerville-downtown.org/Events.html), Placerville.

Bidwell Rancho Soroptimist International Microbrew Festival (sibidwellrancho.org/?q=node/29), Chico.

Brewfest (southplacerrotary.org), Rocklin.

Cloverdale Beer Fest (facebook.com/cloverdalebeerfest), Cloverdale.

Davis Beerfest (davisbeerfest.org), Davis.

Firestone Walker Invitational Beer Fest (firestonebeerfest.com), Paso Robles.

O'Reilly's San Francisco Oysterfest (oreillysoysterfestival.com), San Francisco.

San Jose Beer Festival, a.k.a. Subzero Festival of Art and Culture (subzerofestival.com), San Jose.

Truckee Brew Fest (truckeeoptimist.com/truckbrewfest.htm), Truckee.

July

The BreastFest (thebreastfest.org), San Francisco.

California Beer Festival (californiabeerfestival.com), Santa Cruz.

Northstar Beerfest & Bluegrass Festival (northstarattahoe.com), Lake Tahoe.

Santa Cruz Hop N' Barley Festival (hopnbarley.org), Scotts Valley.

State of Jefferson Brewfest (jeffersonbrewfest.chirrpy.com), Mount Shasta.

Summer KraftBrew Beer Fest (nagleeparkgarage.com/entertainment.html), San Jose.

August

Blues, Brews & BBQ (donapa.com), Napa.

Brews, Jazz and Funk Fest (squaw.com), Olympic Valley.

Hops in Humboldt (hopsinhumboldt.com), Fortuna.

Mammoth Festival of Beers and Bluesapalooza (mammothbluesbrewsfest.com), Mammoth Lakes.

Russian River Beer Revival and BBQ Cookoff (stumptown.com/revival/), Guerneville.

Sierra Brewfest (musicinthemountains.org), Grass Valley.

September

Beer in the Plaza (sihealdsburg.org/beerintheplaza.html), Healdsburg.

Biketoberfest Marin (biketoberfestmarin.com), Fairfax.

Blues and Beer (haywardareahistory.org), Hayward.

Brews on the Bay (sfbrewersguild.org), San Francisco.

California Beer Festival (californiabeerfestival.com), Novato.

California Brewers Festival (calbrewfest.com), Sacramento.

Clayton Oktoberfest (claytonoktoberfest.com), Clayton.

Cruisin' Calistoga Beer & Wine Festival (win-rods.com), Calistoga.

Drake's Flocktoberfest (drinkdrakes.com), San Leandro.

Eat Real Festival (eatrealfest.com), Oakland.

NorCal Oktoberfest (norcaloktoberfest.com), Modesto.

Northern California Beer Festival (northerncaliforniabeerfestival.com), Oakland.

Northern California Homebrew Festival (nchfinfo.org), Dobbins.

Oktoberfest by the Bay (oktoberfestbythebay.com), San Francisco.

Placerville Oktoberfest (placerville-downtown.org), Placerville.

Sonoma County Country Music & Beer Fest (countrymusicbeerfest.com), Windsor.

Woodland Chili Throwdown & Brew-Off (woodlandchamber.org), Woodland.

October

Bistro Wet Hop Festival (the-bistro.com), Hayward.

California Beer & Wine Festival (californiabeerandwinefestival.com), Yuba City.

Oaktoberfest in the Diamond (oaktoberfest.org), Oakland.

Oktoberfest (spkids.org), Antioch.

Oktoberfest (campbellchamber.net/oktoberfest.html), Campbell.

Oktoberfest (oktoberfestcortemadera.org), Corte Madera.

Oktoberfest (modchamber.org), Modesto.

Oktoberfest (squaw.com), Olympic Valley.

Oktoberfest (twainhartecc.com), Twain Harte.

Oktobrewfest (changeofpace.com/oktobrewfest.html), Davis.

Peninsula Oktoberfest (peninsulaoktoberfest.com), Redwood City.

November

Bistro West Coast Barrel Aged Festival (the-bistro.com), Hayward.

StrangeBrew BeerFest (theeurekatheater.org), Eureka.

December

Pacific Coast Brewing Holiday Beer Tasting (pacificcoastbrewing.com), Oakland.

Trappist Kerstbier Fest (thetrappist.com), Oakland.

Beer Bars

If it weren't for the many bars, pubs, taverns, and nightclubs, a lot of craft breweries would be out of business. They need a place where people can find and buy their beer. Here is a short list of Northern California bars that specialize in beer.

The Abbot's Cellar (abbotscellar.com), 742 Valencia St., San Francisco, 415-626-8700.

Albatross Pub (albatrosspub.com), 1822 San Pablo Ave., Berkeley, 510-843-2473.

The Alehouse Pub (reddingalehouse.com), 2181 Hilltop Dr., Redding, 530-221-7990.

Alembic Bar (alembicbar.com), 1725 Haight St., San Francisco, 415-666-0822.

Amsterdam Café (amsterdamcafesf.com), 937 Geary St., San Francisco, 415-409-1111.

Anchor & Hope (anchorandhopesf.com), 83 Minna St., San Francisco, 415-501-9100.

Barclay's Pub (barclayspub.com), 5940 College Ave., Oakland, 510-654-1650.

Barley and Hops Tavern (barleynhops.com), 3688 Bohemian Hwy., Occidental, 707-874-9037.

Ben & Nick's Bar & Grill (benandnicks.com), 5612 College Ave., Oakland, 510-923-0327.

Billco's Billiards & Darts Parlor (billcos.com), 1234 Third St., Napa, 707-226-7506.

The Bistro (the-bistro.com), 1001 B St., Hayward, 510-886-8525.

Bobby G's Pizzeria (bobbygspizzeria.com), 2072 University Ave., Berkeley, 510-665-8866.

Boneshaker Public House (boneshakerpub.com), 2168 Sunset Blvd., St. 104, Rocklin, 916-259-2337.

Cato's Ale House (mrcato.com), 3891 Piedmont Ave., Oakland, 510-655-3349.

Church Key (@ChurchKeySF), 1402 Grant Ave., San Francisco, 415-963-1713.

CommonWealth Café & Public House (cmonoakland.com), 2882 Telegraph Ave., Oakland, 510-663-3001.

Creek Monkey Tap House (creekmonkey.com), 611 Escobar St., Martinez, 925-228-8787.

The Englander (englanderpub.com), 101 Parrott St., San Leandro, 510-357-3571.

Fox & Goose (foxandgoose.com), 1001 R St., Sacramento, 916-443-8825.

Harry's Hofbrau (harryshofbrau.com), 390 Saratoga Ave., Santa Clara, 408-243-0434.

Hero's (herosmodesto.com). 821 L St., Modesto, 209-524-2337.

Hopmonk (hopmonk.com), 230 Petaluma Ave., Sebastopol, 707-829-7300 (there are additional Hopmonk locations in Novato and Sonoma).

The Hopyard (hopyard.com), 3015-H Hopyard Rd., Pleasanton, 925-426-9600.

The Hopyard (hopyard.com), 470 Market Pl., San Ramon, 925-277-9600.

Jupiter (jupiterbeer.com), 2181 Shattauck Ave., Berkeley, 510-843-8277. Drake's Brewing (see page 195) brews exclusive house beers for Jupiter.

Lanesplitter Pub and Pizza (lanesplitterpizza.com), 2033 San Pablo Ave., Berkeley, 510-845-1652.

La Trappe Café & Trappist Lounge (latrappecafe.com), 800 Greenwich St., San Francisco, 415-440-8727.

Liquid Bread (liquidbreadcampbell). 379 E. Campbell Ave., Campbell, 408-370-3400.

Luka's Taproom (lukasoakland.com), 2221 Broadway, Oakland, 510-451-4677.

Manderes (manderes.com), 402 E. Bidwell St., Folsom, 916-986-9655.

Mission Pizza & Pub (missionpizza.com), 1572 Washington Blvd., Fremont, 510-651-6858.

Monk's Kettle (monkskettle), 3141 16th St., San Francisco, 415-865-9523.

The Olde Depot Public House (oldedepotpublichouse.com), 468 3rd St., Oakland.

Original Gravity Public House (originalgravitypub.com), 66 S. First St., San Jose, 408-915-2337.

Pangaea Two Brews Café (pangaeatwobrews.com), 2743 Franklin Blvd., Sacramento, 916-454-4942.

The Parish Publick House (theparishpublickhouse.com), 841 Almar Ave., Santa Cruz, 831-421-0507.

Pete's Brass Rail & Car Wash (petesbrassrail.com), 201 Hartz Ave., Danville, 925-820-8281.

Pi Bar (pibarsf.com), 1432 Valencia St., San Francisco, 415-970-9670.

Public House (publichousesf.com), 24 Willie Mays Plaza, San Francisco, 415-644-0240.

Pyramid Walnut Creek Alehouse (pyramidbrew.com/alehouses/walnut-creek). 1410 Locust St., Walnut Creek, 925-946-1520.

Rogue Ales Public House (rogue.com), 673 Union St., San Francisco, 415-362-7880.

Rosamunde Sausage Grill (rosamundesausagegrill.com), 2832 Mission St., San Francisco, 415-970-9015; 545 Haight St., San Francisco, 415-37-6851; and 911 Washington St., Oakland, 510-338-3108.

Rose & Crown (roseandcrownpa.com), 547 Emerson St., Palo Alto, 650-327-7673.

Samuel Horne's Tavern (samuelhornestavern.com), 719 Sutter St., Folsom, 916-293-8207.

Shotwell's Bar (shotwellsbar.com), 3349 20th St., San Francisco, 415-648-4104.

Suppenkuche (suppenkuche.com), 525 Laguna St., San Francisco, 415-252-9289.

Surfrider Café (surfridercafe.net), 429 Front St., Santa Cruz, 831-713-5258.

Taps (petalumataps.com), 205 Kentucky St., Petaluma, 707-763-6700.

Tap 25 (taptwentyfive.com), 25 S. Livermore Ave., Livermore, 925-294-8970.

Toad in the Hole Pub (thetoadpub), 116 Fifth St., Santa Rosa, 707-544-8623.

Toronado (toronado.com), 547 Haight St., San Francisco, 415-863-2276.

The Trappist (thetrappist.com), 460 Eighth St., Oakland, 510-238-8900.

Zeitgeist (zeitgeistsf.com), 199 Valencia St., San Francisco, 415-255-7505.

Chains

BJ's Brewhouse (bjsbrewhouse.com). This Southern California chain of brewpubs and restaurants operates sixty-one locations in California, of which a third are located in Northern California. They used to brew a lot of their beer at individual brewpub restaurants and distribute around to the other nearby restaurants, but now most of their beer is contract-brewed. But they do still serve all of their own unique beers at each location and also carry a good list of guest beers and bottled beers.

Yard House (yardhouse.com). The national Yard House chain of pub-style restaurants operates in thirteen states, with seventeen restaurants in California, including two in the northern part of the state: one in Roseville and the other in San Jose. Each Yard House offers a rotating list of both draft and bottled beers, including some that are created exclusively for the restaurant by prominent breweries.

Beer Stores

If you want to take some beer home with you, it's good to know that there are places that carry more variety than the average grocery store or corner liquor store, where you can find a good selection of local beers, as well as more interesting imports and out-of-state craft beers. Following are some of the Northern California outlets that specialize in beer.

Beercraft (beercraft.com), 5704 Commerce Blvd., Rohnert Park, 888-989-BEER or
    707-206-9440.

Beer Revolution (beer-revolution.com), 464 Third St., Oakland, 510-452 BEER.

Berkeley Bowl Market (berkeleybowl.com), 920 Heinz Ave., Berkeley, 510-898-9555.

Bobby's Liquors (bobbysliquors.com), 2327 El Camino Real, 408-984-1120.

Bottle Barn (bottlebarn.com), 3331 Industrial Dr., Santa Rosa, 707-528-1161.

City Beer Store (citybeerstore.com), 1168 Folsom St., San Francisco, 415-503-1033.

Corti Brothers (cortibros.biz), 5810 Folsom Blvd., Sacramento, 916-736-3802.

The Davis Beer Shoppe, 211 G St., Davis, 530-756-5212.

The Good Hop (thegoodhop.com), 2421 Telegraph Avenue, Oakland.

Healthy Spirits (Healthy-Spirits.blogspot.com), 2299 15th St., San Francisco,
    415-255-0610.

Jane's Beer Store (JanesBeerStore.com), 720 Villa St., Mountain View.

K&L Wine Merchants (klwines.com), 3005 El Camino Real, Redwood City, 650-364-8544.

Ledger's Liquors (ledgersliquors.com), 1399 University Ave., Berkeley, 510-540-9243.

Manor Market, 3100 W. Line St., Bishop, 760-873-4296.

Market Beer Store (Facebook.com/MarketBeerCo), 100 N. Almaden Ave., San Jose.

ØL Beercafe & Bottle Shop (beer-shop.org), 1541 Giammona Dr., Walnut Creek,
    925-210-1147.

Petaluma Market (petalumamarket.com), 210 Western Ave., Petaluma, 707-762-5464.

Perry's Liquors (perrysliquor.com), 1522 Railroad Ave., Livermore, 925-443-0550.

Chain Stores

Beverages & More (bevmo.com). Once upon a time, I was the chain beer buyer here, when the chain had only 25 stores. There are now over 125 BevMo stores in three states, including at least 100 in California. Every BevMo store has a different selection of beer, because they focus on local breweries whenever possible, but they all feature a diverse selection of beers.

Total Wine (totalwine.com). Despite the name, this national chain with stores in a dozen states also offers an excellent selection of beers. It currently has only two stores in Northern California, in Roseville and Sacramento.

Whole Foods (wholefoodsmarket.com). This national grocery chain of organic and high-end foods also carries a good selection of craft beer and better imports. It has over thirty stores in Northern California.

Glossary

ABC. The ABC is how brewers refer to the California Department of Alcoholic Beverage Control, the state agency that, like the TTB (see below) at the federal level, collects excises taxes and oversees breweries, ensuring that they are complying with all of their legal obligations.

ABV. Alcohol by volume (ABV) is the most common way alcoholic strength is expressed in the United States. You'll see something like "5% ABV" on a bottle of beer, and that means that 5 percent of the volume of beer inside is alcohol.

ABW. Alcohol by weight (ABW) is another method of expressing alcohol strength. It used to be more common, but in the United States ABV is used more often. ABW measures the alcohol in terms of the percentage weight per volume. Some states have what's called 3.2 (pronounced "three-two") beer. This beer is 3.2 percent alcohol by weight, which is the same as 3.2 grams of alcohol per 100 centiliters of beer. It's around 20 percent less than ABV, so beer that's 3.2 percent ABW is the same as beer that's 4 percent ABV.

Adjuncts. An adjunct is fermentable material that's used in place of barley or other traditional brewing grains, like wheat or rye. The most common adjuncts are corn and rice. These are often used by the big breweries in order to make their beer lighter in color, lighter-bodied, and less expensive to make. But it's not a new innovation, and using corn and rice in brewing was common long before Prohibition. A number of breweries, large and small, have experimented in recent years by making a beer they call a pre-Prohibition beer or lager. These almost always are made with adjuncts because the old recipes they use call for them. If you hear a beer referred to as all-malt, that generally means it's made without any adjuncts.

Ale. In simplest terms, an ale is one of the two most common types of beer, the other being lager. What makes ales distinctive is that they're brewed with top-fermenting yeast and are fermented at warmer temperatures than lagers. They're also usually served warmer, at cellar temperature. Common ales include pale ale, amber ale, India pale ale (IPA), brown ale, porter, and stout. (See also *lager.*)

Alternating proprietorship. A type of contract brewer or brewery, sort of. See "A word about . . . Contract Brewing" on page 286.

Barley. The most common grain used in brewing. Almost all beer has barley as its base malt. Barley is a cereal grain derived from the annual grass *Hordeum vulgare.*

Barleywine. One of the strongest traditional ale styles. It originated in England but became popular in the United States after Anchor Brewing made the first barleywine in America, Old Foghorn, which debuted in 1975. Its popularity was helped along, especially in the Bay Area, by the Toronado Barleywine Festival, which celebrated its twentieth year in February 2013.

Barrels. A barrel (bbl) is the standard measure of volume used in the United States to describe how much beer a brewery can make. A barrel is 31.5 gallons, though for federal tax purposes it is 31 gallons, which is why we call 15.5 gallons a half keg. If a brewing system is said to be 10-barrel, that means it can brew batches of 10 barrels, or 310 gallons. Some breweries instead use the metric unit hectoliters (hl), as often used in continental European countries, where many brewing equipment manufacturers are located (see *hectoliter*).

Beer. In simplest terms, beer is defined as a beverage containing alcohol that is produced by fermenting a grain. The modern definition generally includes four ingredients—water, yeast, malt, and hops—something along the lines of an alcoholic beverage created from yeast-fermented grain, flavored with hops. While that's generally how we think of beer today, all that's necessary for it to be a beer is the cereal grain; it doesn't have to be flavored with hops. Other items can be added for flavoring— during a hops shortage, Moonlight Brewing brewed a beer made with redwood tips instead of hops—or it can have nothing else added at all. Either way, it still fits the definition of beer.

Beer geek. Once a derogatory term, many beer geeks now embrace the title and happily consider themselves as such. In an article I wrote for *Beer Advocate* magazine, I defined the modern geek as "an obsessive enthusiast, often single-mindedly accomplished, yet with a lingering social awkwardness, at least outside the cocoon of their chosen form of geekdom." For the beer geek, I think that still fits. Essentially beer geeks are members of a loosely organized tribe of people who really, really love beer.

Beer styles. We humans love to categorize everything, and beer is no exception. Beer styles give us a way to group like beers together with other similar ones. This is important in beer competitions, where it's far easier to judge one beer against another if they're similar. So style guidelines have been created that determine the characteristics that define each particular style of beer. A beer that's considered to be a particular style will have to meet the guidelines for a number of key characteristics, such as its color (how light or dark it is), how strong it is, how much malt or hops character it shows, and a number of other factors. People endlessly debate beer styles, but outside of competitions, the only thing they're useful for is knowing generally what to expect when you order a beer. This can be helpful if you want certain flavors with what you're eating or are simply in the mood for a particular taste.

BOP. A "B-O-P," which means "Brew On Premises," is a type of brewery that's a hybrid of homebrewing and commercial brewing. A BOP provides, for a fee, all of the equipment, ingredients, recipes and technical know-how for people to come and brew their own batch of beer at the BOP location. They then return to bottle the beer once it's done fermenting, often creating their own labels. This type of brewery used to be more popular in the mid- to late-1990s, but the number of BOPs has dwindled in recent years. They generally offer a fun and relatively easy way to see if brewing is something you'd enjoy doing, and also offer a way to better appreciate what goes into making a beer.

Bottle-conditioned. This refers to beers that are spiked with a small amount of yeast during bottling and undergo a secondary fermentation in the bottle. Bottle conditioning produces natural carbonation, so the beers stay fresher, or at least drinkable, for a longer period of time.

Braggot. Also sometimes called a bracket, a braggot is essentially a mead made with malt. Mead is normally only made with honey and water, but braggots are essentially a hybrid or bridge between beer and mead. They are sometimes made with a beer base, but are different from a beer brewed with some honey, though they may be considered a malt mead or a honey beer. The difference is generally dependent upon what percentage of the finished product was grain and what was honey. Braggots may, or may not, be made with hops. During Chaucer's time, it is thought that they may also have been blended.

Brettanomyces. A type of wild yeast used for brewing particular kinds of beers, such as sour Belgian-style beers, *Brettanomyces* is a non-spore-forming genus in the Saccharomycetaceae family. The genus name is Greek for "British fungus." Three different strains are commonly used in brewing: *Brettanomyces bruxellensis*, *Brettanomyces lambicus*, and *Brettanomyces anomalus*. Often called simply brett, the yeast gives beer a distinctive farm or barnyard nose, referred to as "horse blanket." Brett can spoil and ruin wine, so winemakers do everything they can to keep it out of their wineries, but brewers use it carefully to craft sour styles of beer. Brett and the bacteria *Pediococcus* and *Lactobacillus*, also used in brewing beer, are sometimes collectively referred to humorously as "bugs" or "critters."

Breweriana. Some hobbyists collect beer labels, trays, cans, crowns, coasters, marketing materials, advertising, and signs created by a brewery. Collectively, these items are referred to as breweriana. Virtually anything with a brewery's name or logo on it is a collectible piece of breweriana.

Brewery types. All breweries use essentially the same kind of equipment to make beer. But while it's all the same, it's also different for every brewery. That's because although the basic process is the same, the individual variations and equipment that each brewery uses differ according to the type of beers being made, the brewer's individual preferences, the amount of money the brewery owners have or are willing to spend, and countless other factors. To the untrained eye, every brewery may look exactly the same, but if you look closer, subtle difference begin to emerge and stand out. The more breweries you visit, the more you'll begin to notice those differences.

But brewery type also has another meaning, one that has little to do with how the beer is made. In order to classify how the brewery business is organized and often how it's taxed, both state and federal agencies classify breweries according to how they do business, not how they make their beer. And that's also how trade organizations like the Brewers Association classify breweries too, in order to keep consistent data and statistics on their members. Here is how the BA classifies breweries:

Large brewery: Makes 6,000,000 or more barrels of beer per year.

Regional brewery: Makes between 15,000 and 6 million barrels per year.

Microbrewery: Makes less than 15,000 barrels per year and sells 75 percent of its beer off-site, away from the brewery through wholesalers or at retail stores.

Brewpub: A microbrewery that sells 25 percent or more of the beer it makes on-site, at the same place where it's brewed. Usually a brewpub also operates as a restaurant that serves its own beer. Most brewpubs are permitted by law to sell to-go beer, usually in growlers.

Contract brewery: In simplest terms, a contract brewery refers to a situation where a company hires, or contracts, a brewery to make its beer for it. There are several types of contract breweries, which are delineated and discussed more fully in "A word about . . . Contract Brewing" on page 286.

Two other types of breweries are not currently part of the BA's definitions. One of these terms has been gaining wider acceptance lately, and the other may or may not have a future, but they are both worth considering as more and more breweries open.

Nanobrewery: There's no standard definition for a nanobrewery, though it's commonly used to refer to a brewery that is extremely small. The first modern microbrewery, New Albion Brewing, had a 1-barrel brewing system, so it may properly be thought of as the first nanobrewery, even though it was decades ahead of that designation. An increasing number of new breweries are starting up as nanobreweries.

Picobrewery: A term for breweries that are even smaller than nanobreweries. This term is little used, although I continue to believe it could become useful in the future. Back in 2007, I wrote a piece suggesting that we divide microbreweries into three subdivisions: microbreweries, nanobreweries, and picobreweries, from largest to smallest. In computer or math parlance, *nano* is directly below *micro* in terms of size. Next below *nano* is *pico*, and that's where I got the idea, although I should hasten to point out that I was not the first to suggest this, and others have made similar suggestions, though they have never caught on.

Brewhouse. This term refers collectively to the equipment used to begin the process of brewing beer, commonly consisting of a mash tun and a kettle or brewkettle. Depending on the way a brewery is set up, and to brew what kind of beer, the brewhouse could also include a lauter tun or other equipment, too.

Brewpub. See *brewery types*.

Carbonation. This is what adds the bubbles in the beer. It's the process of creating carbon dioxide in the beer, which is typically done through fermentation, although in some cases it's accomplished by injecting the finished beer with carbon dioxide or by adding young wort to finished beer in order to renew fermentation, a process known as kraeusening.

Cask. Any closed container, usually barrel-shaped, used for holding beer. Most casks were originally made from wooden staves, held together with iron hoops, and were manufactured by skilled artisans known as coopers. Today they are more commonly made of stainless steel and aluminum.

Cicerone. Created by Ray Daniels, a Cicerone is the beer equivalent of a sommelier for wine. The word is pronounced "sis-uh-rohn,"

Contract brewery. See "A word about . . . Contract Brewing" on page 286.

Crown. This is the technical name for the metal beer cap that seals a bottle of beer.

Draft or draught. Beer not bottled or canned and instead drawn from a keg, cask, or serving tank. This is accomplished using pressure from an air pump (when hand pumped) or, more typically in the United States, using injected carbon dioxide that's put into the beer container, either natural or artificially, before it's sealed. Occasionally, beer in a growler is also considered to be draft beer.

Dry-hopping. Any hops added for aroma late in the brewing process, from the end of the boil, or in the phases involving the whirlpool or hopback during the primary or secondary fermentation. Dry-hopping typically does not increase bitterness, but instead makes the hop aromas more pronounced.

Esters. There are as many as sixty different possible esters in beer, but only half a dozen have much influence over the flavors. Esters produce aromas and flavors that resemble anise, artificial bananas, circus peanuts, general fruitiness, Juicy Fruit gum, nail polish, pineapple, red apples, and tropical fruit. Typically found more often in ales, they're organic compounds that result from the interaction of acids and alcohol.

Fermentation. The process in which yeast converts sugar to alcohol and carbon dioxide.

Flagship. Most breweries sell more of one beer than their others, usually by a wide margin. It's the one they're famous for. It's the one that pays the bills and makes it possible for them to make their other, less popular beers or to experiment with special releases or seasonals. Think Anchor Steam, Sierra Nevada Pale Ale, or Lagunitas IPA. Those are all flagship beers.

GABF. The Great American Beer Festival, held each fall in Denver, Colorado, and put on by the Brewers Association.

Gastropub. A British term coined as recently as 1991 to describe a pub (which is short for "public house") that serves high-quality food. The term is beginning migrate to the United States, so you're likely to hear it more often. Another way to think about it is that it's like a French brasserie or bistro, but with a beer rather than wine focus. A gastropub straddles the line between a traditional pub and a restaurant, being equal parts both. In the end, it's not just that the food must be different from traditional pub fare; what matters most is that it be made from scratch using fresh, ideally local, food. The food must simply be as real as the beer. The only satisfactory way to describe a gastropub is to say that you'll know one when you see it, taste it, and drink it in.

Growler. Though they're not legal in all states, growlers are a mainstay of California brewpubs and breweries. Historically, they were pails or jugs used to carry draft beer bought at a bar. Today growlers are usually made of glass, though a growing number of designers are making them out of metal, usually aluminum or stainless steel, like miniature kegs. You used to sometimes see ceramic growlers, but their use seems to be fading. They're sealed with either a screw top or a hinged porcelain gasket cap. Some brewers charge a deposit for their growlers, and many also offer a discount on refills, making them an economical way to buy fresh beer, especially if the brewery is near your home. Beer in growlers will usually stay fresh for only a few days, though I've found that if you seal the top with duct tape or other sealing tape, you can extend the beer's life considerably. Growlers typically hold as little as half a gallon but can be as large as 2 liters. Commons sizes are 64 ounces (half a gallon), 128 ounces (1 gallon), 1 liter, and 2 liters.

Guest beer or tap. A guest beer is one that a brewpub or brewery carries that was made by another brewery. A guest tap is the same idea, but on draft.

Guild. A guild is an organization or association of persons with a specific craft, skill, or occupation. Brewers guilds have been around since the Civil War, when the government first starting taxing breweries. They perform several functions in modern times, such as supporting the industry, lobbying for favorable treatment by lawmakers, and putting on events to promote their members. There are several national, state, and local guilds that a brewery in Northern California might join.

Brewers Association (BA), www.brewersassociation.com

California Craft Brewers Association (CCBA),
    www.californiacraftbeer.com

Northern California Brewers Guild (NCBG),
    www.northerncalbrewers.com

San Francisco Brewers Guild (SFBG), www.sfbrewersguild.org

Bay Brewers Guild (BBG), a newly forming guild for brewers in the
    South Bay

Gypsy brewer. A type of contract brewer or brewery. See "A word about . . . Contract Brewing" on page 286.

Hectoliters. A hectoliter (hl) is a unit of volume used in many countries, especially those that use the metric system. It is equivalent to 100 liters, and 1 liter is approximately 1.056 liquid quarts or 0.264 gallon. Some breweries use hectoliters to express the size of their brewing systems. A 10-hectoliter system can make a batch of beer that is 10 hectoliters, or roughly 264 gallons. However, most U.S. breweries instead use the British unit of barrels, and 10 hectoliters equals 8.4 barrels (see *barrels*).

Homebrewing. Homebrewing is just what the term implies: brewing beer in your home for personal consumption. In 1978, homebrewing was again legalized, and an adult is permitted to brew up to 100 gallons of homebrew each year, up to a household maximum of 200 gallons, so long as at least two adults are living there.

Hops. The scientific name for hops is *Humulus lupulus*, and they come in many varieties. Hops are the spice of beer, providing bittering and balance to the sweet malt, and it is thought they originally were added as a preservative. They're closely related to marijuana—known scientifically as hemp (*Cannabis*)—and in fact are part of the same family, Cannabaceae, which also includes hackberries (*Celtis*). Neither hops nor hackberries include tetrahydrocannabinol (THC), the stuff that gives pot smokers the munchies and makes it so popular with your good-for-nothing brother-in-law. There are a few other uses for hops—you can eat the shoots, which are similar to asparagus but more bitter, and they're sometimes used for tea or in pillows (it's said you'll have vivid, romantic dreams while sleeping on a hops pillow)—the vast majority, probably 99 percent, is put to a single purpose: making beer.

IBUs. International Bitterness Units (IBUs) are used to describe how hoppy a beer is. Humans can only begin to perceive bitterness at around 8 to 12 IBUs, and thereafter can perceive changes in increments of 5 or more. In other words, it's impossible to distinguish between a beer that has 20 IBUs and one with 22 IBUs. To perceive any difference, the second beer would have to have at least 25 IBUs, or 5 more than the first sample. IBUs are often simply calculated, not tested, so most beer labels that list the IBUs are essentially guessing. It's an intelligent guess in many cases, but a guess nonetheless. The higher the IBU number goes, the more difficult the calculation becomes.

Imperial. A modifier indicating that the beer is bigger or stronger than its unmodified version. The example most people think of first is imperial stout, though the use of the term imperial was around at least as early as the mid-1800s and often indicated it was the "biggest" beer a brewery offered, without regard to a specific style. That sense has been revived in recent years, the most famous example being imperial IPAs, denoting bigger, more intensely hopped India pale ales. In addition to IPAs, brewers have also made imperial pilsners, imperial Oktoberfests, and even the oxymoronic imperial mild.

IPA. India pale ale (IPA) has been the fastest-growing style of beer over the last few years. A fun fact is that in parts of South America and non-English-speaking Europe, people pronounce it as if it were a word: "eepa."

Keg. One of the most common ways that beer is served, especially at bars and other public spaces, is in a keg, which is just one method of dispensing draft beer. Kegs are typically made of steel or aluminum and contain beer that's stored under pressure. There are a number of common sizes of kegs. A half keg holds 15.5 gallons and is actually a full keg, because it's the largest size sold to the public. A quarter keg, a.k.a. pony keg, contains 7.75 gallons. A sixtel, so named because it's roughly one-sixth of a barrel, may have 5, 5.16, 5.23, or 5.25 gallons. Kegs imported from Europe often come in 50-, 30-, and 20-liter sizes. You'll sometimes hear a 50-liter keg referred to as 13.2 gallons.

Lager. Lagers are the other common type of beer, besides ales. What makes lagers distinctive is that they're brewed with bottom-fermenting yeast and are fermented at cooler temperatures than ales. They're also often served colder, at temperatures approaching freezing. Common beers that are lagers include bocks, helles, märzens, pilsners, and Vienna lager. (See also *ale*.)

Lambic. Lambics are some of the most distinctive beers in the world. Traditional lambics are made in just one place on earth, in a small valley known as Payottenland, where the Senne River passes through, part of the Flemish Brabant of Belgium. What makes this area unique is the microflora in the air, the wild yeasts and bacteria. Lambics are beers made with unmalted wheat and old hops that are spontaneously fermented. Most beers have a specific yeast that's pitched to start fermentation. Lambics, by contrast, are put in open fermenters, where the wild yeasts drift in on the wind from the surrounding country. There are several types of lambics, including Gueuze (a blend of new and old lambic), Faro (sweetened), Framboise (refermented with raspberries), and Kriek (refermented with cherries), to name just a few. Pure lambic is cloudy, uncarbonated, and very sour, and it is generally not sold until it's at least three years old. For many people, it is an acquired taste. But if you take the time and effort to learn to appreciate them, these beers are incredibly complex and rewarding to drink.

Malt. After brewing grains, such as barley or wheat, are allowed to germinate and then heated and dried to maximize their sugar content, they are known as malt, barley malt, or wheat malt, as appropriate. Malt is shipped to a brewery for milling, the first step in the brewing process.

Mash. One of the first steps in brewing, where the malt is put into a vessel known as a mash tun, along with water and hops, and boiled to create wort.

Microbrewery. See *Brewery Types*.

Nanobrewery. See *Brewery Types*.

Pasteurization. The process, developed by French microbiologist Louis Pasteur, that kills any bacteria, yeast, or other organic material that might cause beer, milk, or other beverages to go bad or to go bad faster. In the process, the beer is heated using one of two methods: tunnel pasteurization or flash pasteurization. In tunnel pasteurization, hot water is sprayed on the bottles or cans for as long as an hour; in flash pasteurization, superhot water or steam is sprayed on the beer, but only for a few minutes at most. Although pasteurization is effective, it alters the flavors of the beer, and often not for the better, so there is definitely a trade-off.

Picobrewery. See *Brewery Types*.

Pilsner. This is the most popular style of beer made throughout the world. It was first brewed in 1842 in the Bohemian town of Plze', or Pilsen, which is where the beer gets its name, and is today part of the Czech Republic. From there, this light-colored lager spread across the globe. Many popular beers made by global macrobrewers are based on pilsners but have been adapted over the years to be even lighter in both color and flavor.

Pitch, or pitching. This is what brewers call the step in brewing when they add yeast, saying it's time to "pitch the yeast."

Prohibition. Prohibition was a failed social experiment in which alcohol was made illegal and criminalized with the Eighteenth Amendment, beginning in 1920. Prohibition lasted for thirteen years and ended shortly after the passage of the Twenty-first Amendment on December 5, 1933. Many breweries did not survive this long period, and most were unable to reopen after Repeal.

Regional brewery. See *Brewery Types*.

Reinheitsgebot. In 1516, Bavarian brewers created one of the first quality control or food safety laws in history, known as the Reinheitsgebot, or beer purity law. It was created, at least in part, to protect wheat and rye for breadmaking. The Reinheitsgebot stipulated that only three ingredients could be used in brewing—barley, hops, and water—omitting the essential ingredient yeast, which had not yet been discovered.

Session beer. This is not a particular style of beer, but rather a concept. There is no agreed-upon definition or hard-and-fast rules for session beers. They are essentially low-alcohol beers—low simply relative to the alcohol content of beers of average strength—that are also full-flavored. They are beers that can withstand an evening of leisurely paced drinking without reducing one to belligerence, sloppiness, or incoherence. In other words, it's a beer that allows you to stay lucid and keep up your end of the conversation throughout a drinking session, however long (within reason, of course) as the evening waxes and wanes or the discussion meanders.

Session beers are not without their controversies. Originally a British notion, some insist that traditional English session beers were 4 percent ABV or below and therefore must ever remain so. Most Americans reject such inflexibility, and some even avoid any fixed number for inclusion. But reason suggests that a session beer at least be lower in alcohol than the prevailing average-strength beer; otherwise there is no distinction at all. Pennsylvania beer writer Lew Bryson launched his Session Beer Project six years ago to shed a light on these often under-appreciated beers. Bryson defines session beers as "4.5% alcohol by volume or less, flavorful enough to be interesting, balanced enough for multiple pints, conducive to conversation and reasonably priced." He also simplifies that definition to state that session beers are "low-alcohol, but not low-taste." While certain styles naturally lend themselves to being session beers, in reality almost any style could be produced at a lower strength while retaining the essence of its flavor profile. It really requires only that the brewer apply deft skill and a delicate hand in brewing the beer, because the one thing that lower-alcohol beers have in common is that defects are decidedly harder to hide. Any faults the beer might have become more apparent in their low-octane versions. So like any lighter beer, they are deceptively difficult to make well but are well worth the effort.

Shared brewery. A type of contract brewer or brewery. See "A word about . . . Contract Brewing" on page 286.

Sixtel. See *keg*.

Tenant brewery. A type of contract brewer or brewery. See "A word about . . . Contract Brewing" on page 286.

Three-tier system. After Prohibition ended, the government wanted to ensure that alcohol sales remained safe and regulated and came up with the three-tier system, though they left it to each individual state to decide how to regulate alcohol within the state. The three tiers are the manufacturer, in this case the brewery; the retailer; and the distributor, who acts as the middleman, buying the beer from the brewery and then selling it to the retailer. Retailers include bars, restaurants, grocery stores, and anyone licensed to sell alcoholic beverages to the public.

TTB. The TTB is shorthand for the Alcohol and Tobacco Tax and Trade Bureau, the federal agency that collects excise taxes and approves labels and other legal requirements for brewers. Several years ago, it was called the ATF, for Alcohol, Tobacco and Firearms. When the ATF was reorganized in 2003, it was renamed, but the shorter TTB is what everybody now calls it. The TTB is responsible for just one set of taxes and other legal hurdles that breweries must navigate. Each state has similar requirements and state excise taxes that the brewery must pay, whether it's located within that state or doing business in that state. For California, see *ABC*.

Wort. Pronounced "whert," this is sweet, sugar-rich liquid created during the first stages of brewing, when water, malt, and hops are vigorously boiled to convert the starches in the malt to sugar that can be fermented.

Yeast. Technically part of the kingdom of fungi, yeast is a single-celled eukaryotic microorganism. Yeast is a necessary part of the brewing process—some say the most important part, since fermentation cannot take place without it. There are some fifteen hundred known species of yeast, not all of which will make beer. Two are the most common in brewing: *Saccharomyces cerevisiae*, which is ale yeast, and *Saccharomyces pastorianus*, what today we call lager yeast. The latter used to be called *Saccharomyces carlsbergensis* because it was first isolated at the Carlsberg Brewery by Emil Christian Hansen. These two yeasts—each of which has thousands of different strains with unique properties—make the vast majority of beer brewed today, though there are also some wild yeasts (see *Brettanomyces*, for example). After malt, hops, and water are boiled for a period of time, making wort, it is cooled and placed in a fermenter, where the yeast is "pitched," or added to the mixture. The yeast essentially feeds on the sugars in the wort, creating alcohol and carbon dioxide, in the process known as fermentation. For most of the thousands of years that mankind has been making beer, the existence of yeast was unknown. Brewers knew something was taking place but had no idea what. It was often thought to be a kind of magic, or divine intervention, and honestly, tasting beer today, it still seems miraculous.

Index